CRITICAL RACE THEORY

IN EDUCATION

ALL GOD'S CHILDREN GOT A SONG

EDITED BY

ADRIENNE D. DIXSON AND CELIA K. ROUSSEAU

Routledge
Taylor & Francis Group
New York   London

Routledge is an imprint of the
Taylor & Francis Group, an informa business

The Foreword and Chapters 2, 4, 9, 10 and 14 are reprinted with permission of Routledge.
http://www.tandf.co.uk/journals/titles/13613324.asp

Routledge
Taylor & Francis Group
270 Madison Avenue
New York, NY 10016

Routledge
Taylor & Francis Group
2 Park Square
Milton Park, Abingdon
Oxon OX14 4RN

© 2006 by Taylor & Francis Group, LLC
Routledge is an imprint of Taylor & Francis Group, an Informa business

10 9 8 7 6 5 4 3 2 1

International Standard Book Number-10: 0-415-95292-1 (Softcover) 0-415-95291-3 (Hardcover)
International Standard Book Number-13: 978-0-415-95292-7 (Softcover) 978-0-415-95291-0 (Hardcover)

Library of Congress Cataloging-in-Publication Data

Dixson, Adrienne D.
   Critical race theory in education : all God's children got a song / Adrienne D. Dixson and Celia K. Rousseau.
      p. cm.
   Includes bibliographical references and index.
   ISBN 0-415-95291-3 (alk. paper) -- ISBN 0-415-95292-1 (pbk. : alk. paper)
   1. Critical pedagogy. 2. Racism in education. 3. Discrimination in education. I. Rousseau, Celia K. II. Title.

LC196.D59 2006
370.11'5--dc22   2005036818

Visit the Taylor & Francis Web site at
http://www.taylorandfrancis.com

and the Routledge Web site at
http://www.routledge-ny.com

Contents

Foreword

They're Trying to Wash Us Away: The Adolescence
of Critical Race Theory in Education

GLORIA LADSON-BILLINGS

Louisiana, Louisiana
They're trying to wash us away,
They're trying to wash us away

Randy Newman, songwriter (1974)

It has happened to all of us at least once. There is a song, an expression or an image that gets stuck in our brains. As a consequence, we cannot stop singing it, saying it, or seeing it. A few months ago on a transatlantic flight I saw the film "Walk the Line," a biographical film of country-western singer Johnny Cash. It seems like every time I walked out to the parking lot I start humming "we got married in a fever, hotter than a pepper spout." This is the first line to the song "Jackson" (Lieber and Edd-Wheeler, 1967), which Joaquin Phoenix and Reese Witherspoon sing in the film. I do not particularly like the song; I just cannot get it out of my mind.

Something else is stuck in my mind—Hurricane Katrina and the abandonment of the people of the Gulf Coast regions, particularly those in New Orleans. Some might say that it makes sense to still carry the images of the Katrina disaster. After all, it was the worst natural disaster to strike the United States. I watched coverage on the BBC (I was in London at the time the hurricane hit), CNN World and my local news (once I returned to the U.S.). I read newspaper and news magazine accounts. I listened to National Public Radio coverage of the disaster. But it is not merely the disaster that keeps me fixated on New Orleans, it is what the aftermath has come to symbolize. If my mind were drawn to disaster and horror I would carry images of the terrorist attacks on September 11, 2001 in New York and Washington, D.C. As with the Katrina disaster I watched, read and listened to available news outlets. But, September 11th has faded for me. I can go to New York and Washington, D.C. without fear or sadness. But thoughts of New Orleans provoke a range of emotions—anger, fear, sadness and confusion. New Orleans is emblematic of the Critical Race Theory (CRT) in education analysis I have been attempting to put forth for more than a decade.

Katrina reminds us that race still matters, property rights trump human rights and the intersection of race and property creates an analytic tool through which we can understand inequality (Ladson-Billings and Tate, 1995). Katrina showed the world that some people were worthy of rescue while some people were not. It also showed the world that even in the midst of suffering, people could be demonized. Dwyer and Drew (2005) reported that many of the horrific incidents—murder, rape, robbery and general chaos and disorder—never happened. That Americans could believe that about a largely poor and African American community reminds us that race still matters. That we are appalled that desperate people went into stores searching for water, food, diapers and other merchandise they might barter reminds us that property rights trump human rights. Katrina hit the U.S. at the same moment that CRT in education is approaching puberty and, like most teenagers, it is growing rapidly in unpredictable and surprising ways. It is awkward yet full of promise. It sometimes thinks before it acts. It is loud and "inappropriate." However, it never goes unnoticed and its growth signals the likelihood that we will have even more challenging scholarship with which to contend in the years to come.

The chapters in this volume arise from a symposium held at the annual meeting of the American Educational Research Association (AERA) in April 2004. The title of the session was "And We Are *Still* Not Saved." This title is a modification of two sources. One source is the CRT scholar Derrick Bell (1992), who used it in the title of his book on the "elusive quest for racial justice." The other is its original source—the Biblical passage from the prophet Jeremiah (Jer 8:20) who mourned for his peoples' lack of deliverance with the words, "The harvest is past, the summer is ended, and we are not saved." Bell used this scriptural passage because he felt it appropriately described the plight of people of color, particularly African American people in this present age.

The symposium organizers amended the title to say, "And We Are *Still* Not Saved" as an indicator of the limited (and in some cases retrograde) progress that we have made in educational equity since William Tate and I (Ladson-Billings & Tate, 1995) introduced the notion of CRT in education research more than 10 years ago at AERA and subsequently in the *Teachers College Record*. The present book is about taking stock and looking forward. It includes expanded versions of the original symposium papers and additional chapters that flesh out the contours of CRT at this critical junction.

Rousseau and Dixson set a frame for understanding the construction of this volume. They point out that they wanted to look at what education researchers were "doing" with (and in) CRT to determine its viability as a theoretical and conceptual tool that has the possibility of breaking open the frozen conversations and perspectives on race and racial analyses in education. The initial chapters address the storytelling aspect of CRT. This is often seen as problematic because it is regarded as "unscientific" and subjective, but

CRT never makes claims of objectivity or rationality. Rather, it sees itself as an approach to scholarship that integrates lived experience with racial realism. This work is reminiscent of the complex renderings of race apparent in the work of Howard Winant (2001). It articulates the race-making project in modernity and provides an important historical and international context in which to understand our present racial predicament. For example, in the U.S. we find ourselves stuck in a Black/White racial binary that does not consider the more complex iterations of race in a global context.

Even in the U.S. demographic literature (Lee, 1993) we can see that the question of racial identification has been in flux. In 1890 when question four ("what is your race?") was first included in the census, there were almost 16 racial categories ranging from White to Black. There were categories for degrees of Blackness such as "mulatto," "quadroon," and "octoroon." Over the more than 100-year history of the question on the census form the two stable categories have been Black and White and, while other groups may not have been able to take full advantage of the privilege of whiteness, there are historical instances where they have been categorized as such.

Asian Indians were phenotypically determined to be White. In the Lemon Grove School District Incident, Mexican American parents won their suit against having their children sent to a segregated school because they were categorized as White. For a short time, the Cherokee Indians were considered White as they attempted to assimilate into mainstream U.S. society. Thus, the real issue is not necessarily the Black/White binary as much as it is the way *everyone* regardless of his or her declared racial or ethnic identity is positioned in relation to whiteness. Scholars like Vijay Prashad (2001) challenge the hegemony of White racial discourses and help us reorganize our discourses from "us versus them" to look at both symbolic and structural barriers that are constructed as a result of White supremacist discourses.

The chapters in the next section of this volume attempt to expand CRT in education scholarship by pulling on interdisciplinary perspectives. This work is in keeping with the model that legal scholars of CRT offer in their work. This moving across disciplinary boundaries invokes the strategies proposed by scholars in the 1960s that offered "new studies" that came to be known as Black Studies, Chicano Studies, American Indian Studies, Asian American Studies and Women's Studies. In each of these new scholarly traditions the disciplinary boundaries were made permeable. History, literature, sociology and the arts were tapped as important knowledge sources for documenting and conveying the experiences of people. This new approach to scholarship insisted that no one discipline could fully reveal the complexities of human experience and thus amalgamations were deemed necessary.

In the case of legal scholarship, the use of other disciplinary traditions was considered heretical. The field was deeply entrenched in a tradition of precedent and case law and departures from these canons were rejected. However, when Bell (1992) published *And We Are Not Saved* he broke the rules and created a new kind of legal scholarship that incorporated critical sociological theory and narrative inquiry into an analysis of the law. In this volume, we see examples of disciplinary mergers that pull on the traditions of education, sociology, anthropology, music and art scholarship.

CRT scholars are waging a similar battle in education scholarship. For much of its history, education research and scholarship was moored to psychology. Thus, "real" research was that which followed a psychometric paradigm. Only that scholarship that was "neutral" and "objective" was considered valid and valuable. We had to be able to observe, measure it and quantify it for a phenomenon to be so. Thus, the experience of racism was seen as purely subjective. We could talk about a test as having "adverse impact" because it regularly and systematically excludes Black people but it can be extremely difficult to prove that the same test is "biased."

CRT allows scholars to pull on a variety of scholarly traditions to make sense of experiences and epistemological standpoints. For example, CRT scholars may create "chronicles" that are constructed narratives in which they embed evidence and other forms of data. In a presentation I did some years ago (Ladson-Billings, 2001) I created a chronicle that described the way aggressive urban renewal (now called city revitalization or the new urbanization) programs made city living more attractive for wealthy Whites while continuing to exploit the labor of poor Black and Brown residents. The chronicle explains the way city politicians and corporate leaders colluded to gather more property and power while systematically disadvantaging poor people of color. The chronicle ends with a discussion of the draconian methods the city fathers attempt to employ to control the schools. At the time of the presentation everything I wrote in the chronicle seemed speculative. However, I drew inferences from the events and actions that were occurring as well as the history of urban renewal and displacement of poor communities of color:

> The economy was finally turning around. New construction was sprouting up everywhere and with that construction came more jobs. For the first time in many years the city could begin to compete with the suburbs for new businesses and manufacturing. People were growing tired of long and arduous commutes to the suburbs. If only, the city was safer, cleaner, with good housing, and good schools.
>
> The mayor, some select city council people, and corporation heads met to decide how to make the city a more attractive place. "Well, first we have to get ready those pesky homeless people!" came one voice. "Not a problem," said the Mayor. "We just have to pass some ordinances that make panhandling, loitering, and sleeping on the streets illegal." "But won't that get the churches and do-gooders up in arms?" "Perhaps, but we have to sell this as an initiative for safe and attractive streets. I mean,

we'll keep the shelters open and point out to the public how hard we're working to get these people into them for their own safety." "Yes, but the shelters aren't really safe and we don't have nearly enough to house all of the homeless people." "That's ok. As long as we look like we're trying to help people will support us. You watch, the word will get out in the homeless community that they don't stand a chance in this city and we'll force them out of the central city. They'll relocate to a less desirable part of town or better yet a neighboring town and our problems will be solved."

"Next we have to start recruiting businesses back to the city," said one of the corporate heads. "Not to worry," chimed in a councilperson. "We'll put together tax breaks and incentives for the business community that will make it impossible for them to resist moving back downtown." "Sure, we can make sure that businesses get prime real estate, property tax exemptions, and tax credits for hiring as few as 5% of their workforce from among the 'disadvantaged'." That comment bought a huge burst of laughter. Businesses had no trouble hiring low-income and working class people. There was always some low level, menial job to be done—janitors, clerks, cooks, cafeteria workers, messenger and delivery people. All of these people could be hired on limited and part-time bases and employers could avoid paying living wages or providing any benefits.

With the streets clear and the businesses returning to the city, the next thing that had to be accounted for was housing. The city's movers and shakers could not be expected to leave their lavish suburban mansions to live in the inadequate housing the city currently offered. Then the owner of a major construction firm perked up. "Hey, here's an ingenious plan. What if we run the old 'urban renewal' scheme? We talk up the dangers and inadequate condition of the current public housing. The mayor can start talking about how inhumane it is to crowd that many people in those buildings and get the ball rolling for their demolition. They are awful and even the people who live in them can attest to that. Get some single mothers or elderly people who live over there in front of a TV camera to talk about how terrible living there is. In fact, we could get the local TV news to do a weeklong expose on the conditions inside public housing. We could generate so much support that we could have a 'demolition day' where the Mayor comes out to flip the switch. We'll have the entire city cheering the destruction of those awful places. But, now here's beauty. We replace the public housing with luxury apartments and condominiums—nothing under $200 thousand." "But, what happens to the poor people who were in public housing," asks one of the people seated at the table? "Simple," replied the construction firm owner. "Our research indicates that without adequate resources, poor people just drift on to the next poor community. In Chicago, they started drifting south to Gary and north to Milwaukee. In New York they headed to New Jersey and to the outer boroughs. Don't worry, the poor are like cockroaches. They'll survive."

The Mayor began to smile. The whole plan was coming together nicely. It could be a major campaign that boosted one's political star. "I can see it now," thought the Mayor. "Our town's coming back. Will you be there?" However, after a moment the Mayor began to frown. "What's the matter, Mayor?" asked a city hall lackey. "Hmmm," said the Mayor. "I can see how we can clean up the streets, welcome back the businesses and build high-end housing, but what are we going to do about these awful schools? Nobody is going to want to leave their beautiful suburban schools for the city's schools, especially when that means going to school with *those* kids!"

At that moment the plan seemed lost. The room was deadly quiet. Finally, one of the corporate heads who had seen this plan work in another city spoke up. "The schools don't have to be the problem. All you have to do is take a get-tough, law-and-order type approach to the schools, offer a bunch of specialty programs for your target population, and we can transform the public schools to serve only the kids we want."

"Well what does a get-tough school program look like?" asked one of the council people. "Ok, here's how it goes," said the corporate head. "Like with the housing project, you have to point out to everyone how terrible the schools are. You will have an easy time getting consensus on that, even though most people think their own local school is fine, they are quick to condemn schools in general. Next, you have to start talking about how we have to hold the schools accountable. The best way is by using a rigid testing system. You see, you require one test across all schools. You set a cut off score for passing the test. The kids who don't pass the test don't get promoted. And even though we know that educational research is not that great, one solid piece of educational research is that retention is the biggest predictor of school drop out. We all know who's not going to pass the test and that's exactly who will drop out. You can also institute a "Zero Tolerance" policy that on the surface argues for school safety, but in reality serves as a way to weed out the 'undesirables.' Now, on the upside of the equation, you start creating choice and charter programs that release the middle class from the poor conditions of the regular public schools. You can even comply with federal desegregation laws without losing your White, middle class community."

"How is that possible?" asked one of the business people. "Easy," came the reply. "When we examine what happens in school desegregation we see that schools often re-segregate the students within the schools. Take a look at which students are selected for Gifted and Talented Programs. See who ends up in special education classes. Check the suspension and expulsion rates. Look at who's in the orchestra versus a basic reading class. Heck, I was in a magnet school in San Jose that was set up for the performing arts. The building's top two floors that housed the magnet program was lily white. The bottom floors that maintained the so-called regular program were almost all Black and Brown. It was like two separate schools. When I was in Buffalo, the school district offered the White community free after-school and special enrichment programs. Get this, in a high school in East Palo Alto, California the district offered free ski and camping trips to kids as an inducement for White kids to attend the school. Of course, everyone was permitted to go on the trips but you know who already had ski and camp equipment and you know who would rather do those activities. It's a beautiful plan. I've seen it work over and over."

The construction firm owner broke into a big grin. "Yeah! This could work. And, when these kids can't pass tests and drop out of school we can hire them into those low-paying jobs we talked about. If they don't want those jobs and start doing anti-social things like drug dealing or stealing we can make a pitch for more and bigger prisons. I can build state-of-the-art super prisons out in the suburbs. That will provide a steady stream of state employment for the White working class. Indeed, we will need to manufacture prisoners to keep them employed and it won't be hard to manufacture these prisoners as long as we perpetuate an inferior education for the city's poorest students."

"Does it matter to anyone that the people who are going to get the shaft in our plan are mostly going to be Black and Brown?" came one timid voice in the corner of the room. The Mayor looked up and said, "Well, as my teenagers say, "Duhhh." The entire room exploded into laughter. The die was cast and the plan was put in motion. (excerpted from Ladson-Billings, 2001)

Today, five years after I wrote that chronicle, everything I speculated on in the chronicle has come to pass. The point is not to suggest that I have clairvoyant abilities but rather to demonstrate that CRT scholars are not making up stories—they are constructing narratives out of the historical, socio-cultural and political realities of their lives and those of people of color. The job of the chronicle is to give readers a context for understanding the way inequity manifests in policy, practice, and people's experiences.

In the third section of this volume the scholars begin to move CRT in education in new ways similar to those of CRT in legal scholarship. In addition to race, the scholarship takes on other forms of oppression dealing with class, gender, sexuality, language and ability. Thus, we begin to see son (and daughter) of CRT in the scholarship of Latinas/os (LatCrit), feminists and queer theorists who push the boundaries of CRT to new and exciting heights. In an attempt to describe this expanded use of CRT I argued that CRT could serve as a heuristic for new understandings of multicultural education (Ladson-Billings, 2005). I argued that rather than think of race as positivist social scientists do, CRT scholars were working to deploy "race and racial theory as a challenge to traditional notions of diversity and social hierarchy" (p. 57).

This work looks at the way race continues to operate as a sliding signifier that can be invoked to mean any number of things. For example, during the height of what the U.S. saw as its terrorist threat (following the September 11, 2001 attacks) people from Middle Eastern and Muslim backgrounds became the "new Blacks"*. This moving threat has occurred throughout U.S. history. This is not merely about creating an enemy or opponent but rather about creating a despised Other to validate a construction of normality that resides solely in the identity and embodiment of the dominant group. This attempt to get at multiple social significations other than race is not a sleight of hand designed to instantiate notions of "colorblindness." Rather, this work is designed to remind us how difficult it is to "get past race" when it remains constitutive of what it means to be American.

In its adolescence CRT also takes on an international dimension. Although common knowledge suggests that race is the local invention and problem of the U.S., the global nature of U.S. culture makes race, racism and White privilege exportable and recognizable in international contexts. The evidence of racial strife in places like the UK and the suburbs of Paris suggest that race remains a potent symbol of difference, inequity and oppression. Thus, CRT is becoming a mature and vibrant epistemological stance that scholars throughout the world can employ to understand persistent inequity, injustice and oppression.

The authors in this volume represent a new generation of CRT scholars—those who have come to know CRT in their education classrooms and have made use of it in their scholarly pursuits. They move CRT into its adolescence and, like teenagers, their work is sometimes brash, loud and brutally frank—less concerned with being polite and conformity. Their work is challenging and provocative. It dares us to keep looking at those things we would rather turn from. It makes us grapple with the dirty underside of social phenomenon and events like Hurricane Katrina. Rather than fixate on the weather catastrophe and the breakdown of the social and political infrastructure, new CRT scholars in education look squarely at the way race was prefigured in the midst of the storm. They knew before one drop of rain fell that "they're trying to wash us away; they're trying to wash us away."

---

* I am using polite terminology here. The more common vernacular referred to these people as the "new niggers."

References

Bell, D. (1992). *And We Are Not Saved: The Elusive Quest for Racial Justice*. New York: Basic Books.

Dwyer, J. and Drew, C. (2005, September 29). Fear exceeded crime's reality in New Orleans. *New York Times*, pp. A1, A22.

Ladson-Billings, G. (2001). The Chronicle of the Sacrificed Black Children, Part II. Paper presented at the 2nd annual Let's talk Race Conference, University of North Carolina-Chapel Hill.

Ladson-Billings, G. (2005). New Directions in Multicultural Education: Complexities, Boundaries and Critical Race Theory. In J.A. Banks and C.M. Banks (eds.) *Handbook of Research on Multicultural Education*, pp. 50–65. San Francisco: Jossey Bass.

Ladson-Billings, G. and Tate, W. F. (1995). Toward a Critical Race Theory of Education. *Teachers College Record*, 97(1), 47–68.

Lee, S.M. (1993). Racial Classification in the U.S. Census: 1890–1990, *Ethnic and Racial Studies*, 16, 75–94.

Lieber, J. and Edd-Wheeler, B. (1967). *Jackson*. Bexhill Music, Jerry Lieber Music/Quartet Music.

Newman, R. (1974). *Lousiana 1927*. Song lyrics. Available at www.lyricsdepot.com/randy_newman/louisiana-1927.html.

Winant, H. (2001). *The World Is a Ghetto: Race and Democracy since World War II*. New York: Basic Books.

Introduction

All God's Children Got a Song
I got a song, you got a song
All God's children got a song;
When I get to heaven, gonna *sing a new song,*
Gonna sing all over God's heaven!

—African American spiritual

It was a long time before the masters learned, if they ever did, that the slaves used their songs as a means of communication; giving warning, conveying information about escapes planned and carried out, and simply uplifting the spirit and fortifying the soul. It was even longer before the Spirituals were recognized as theology in song, a new interpretation of Christianity, one far closer to the original than that practiced by those who hoped the Bible would serve as a tool of pacification, not enlightenment.

—Derrick Bell (1995, p. 909)

According to Derrick Bell (1995), there are several similarities between critical race theory (CRT) and African American spirituals. For example, he argues that both CRT and spirituals have as their essence the communication of "understanding and reassurance to needy souls trapped in a hostile world" (p. 910). Another similarity is "the use of unorthodox structure, language, and form to make sense of the senseless" (p. 910). Given the persistence of racism in this "unfriendly world," the similarities between CRT and the spirituals are not surprising. Although these connections appear obvious to us, we point to these similarities to help the novice CRT scholar understand the nature of this "new" song.

What would we want those new to CRT to understand? First, CRT scholars challenge the dominant stories of a racist U.S. society. In the lines of the spiritual quoted at the start of this chapter, the assertion that "all God's children got a song" was a challenge to the dominant, dehumanizing message of the time (Jones, 1993). Another verse of the same song declares:

I got a robe, you got a robe
All God's children got a robe;
When I get to heaven, gonna put on my robe,
Gonna shout all over God's Heaven, Heaven, Heaven!
Everybody talkin' about Heaven ain't going there,
Heaven, Heaven.
Gonna shout all over God's Heaven!

This radical declaration that, at least in heaven, all will be equal was a belief that stood in stark contrast to the attitudes of white slaveholders. The song-writer pointed to this contrast and to the hypocrisy of white Christian slave-holders with the assertion that "everybody talkin' about Heaven ain't going there" (Jones, 1993). In this way, the songwriter offered an alternative vision—a counterstory to the dominant attitudes of the time. CRT offers a similar challenge to the stories of the majority.

A second point that is instructive to those new to CRT is the importance of historical context. Bell (1995) argues that spirituals conveyed messages not only about a transcendent future in heaven but also about immediate events on earth. For example, singing "Steal Away to Jesus" is thought to have been a signal for slaves to assemble for a secret meeting (Cone, 1972; Jones, 1993). Cone (1972) notes similar double meanings of other songs for those who were enslaved. In the historical context of slavery and the possibility of escape, Canaan could signify the North or Canada. Crossing the Jordan could rep-resent crossing the Ohio River. A heavenly chariot could refer to a means or method of escape. In this context, the meaning of the songs can be viewed in a different light:

> I looked over Jordan, an' what did I see
> Comin' for to carry me home?
> A band of angels comin' after me,
> Comin' for to carry me home.

On one level, the song speaks of the promise of heaven after death. For the enslaved, the words could also describe escape to an earthly "home" in the freedom of the North, an escape facilitated by the "angels" of the Underground Railroad (Cone, 1972). As this example illustrates, a full understanding of the multiple levels of meaning in spirituals is lost when we fail to situate them his-torically. In the same way, CRT argues for the need to examine contemporary events with the historical context in mind.

Another similarity between CRT and the spirituals is the combination of struggle and hope. Cone (1972) notes that despair in the spirituals was "usu-ally intertwined with confidence and joy that 'trouble don't last always'" (p. 57). Many spirituals reflect the despair and suffering of life under slavery (e.g., "Sometimes I feel like a motherless child" and "I've been 'buked and I've been scorned"). However, there were also songs (even phrases within the very songs of despair) that asserted hope in the midst of the struggle (e.g., "There is a balm in Gilead"). According to Jones (1993), such songs reflected the "ten-sion between awareness of painful oppressive circumstances and the simul-taneous envisioning of a hopeful future" (p. 127). The same combination of struggle and hope is found in the writings of CRT. CRT scholars acknowledge the permanence of racism while, at the same time, arguing that this recogni-tion should lead not to despair and surrender but to greater resolve in the struggle. This is an important point for those new to CRT to keep in mind. The assertion that racism is a permanent and pervasive part of the American landscape is not a defeatist position. It is an acknowledgment of the "trouble of the world," but it is coupled with a vision of hope for the future.

This struggle for a better future is reflected in the theme of liberation found in many of the spirituals. As Cone (1972) notes, the liberation referred to in song was not only a spiritual liberation from sin. It was also a physical liberation from earthly bondage:

> O freedom! O freedom!
> O freedom over me!
> An' befo' I'd be a slave,
> I'll be buried in my grave and go
> home to my Lord and be free.

According to Jones (1993), the meaning of heaven in the spirituals "interacted actively with religious faith and hopes for freedom as well as with actions in the service of earthly liberation in the present" (p. 89). He further argues that one of the distinguishing features of the spirituals is the balance between inner faith and social action. This balance is one that CRT scholars also seek. There is a focus in CRT on praxis, a commitment not only to scholarship but also to social action toward liberation and the end of oppression.

The final aspect of CRT that we seek to highlight for CRT novices is the need to "listen" to this song with a new ear. Bell (1995) notes that

> at some point, white scholars must have heard the Spirituals. It is easy to imagine their reaction. Even the most hostile would have had to admit that the sometimes joyous and often plaintive melodies had a surface attraction. The scholars would have concluded, though, that the basically primitive song-chants were not capable of complex development and were certainly too simplistic to convey sophisticated musical ideas. The music, moreover, was not in classical form, likely deemed a fatal defect. ...Whatever they were, the critics would conclude, these songs were not art. (p. 909)

As Bell asserts, the spirituals cannot be heard and fully appreciated with a classical ear. Moreover, it is not only the melody but also the words that require a different level of "hearing." According to Cone (1972), the songs reflect a "complex world of thought" that requires analysis for full understanding. In fact, he asserts that there are important theological insights reflected in the spirituals. However, these insights are not ones that can be understood from a traditional theological perspective (Cone, 1972). Hence, to "hear" the spirituals in the fullness of their beauty and meaning, the listener must abandon preconceptions based on classical European musical paradigms. The same can be said of CRT. If readers are not willing or able to put aside preconceptions and traditional paradigms and "hear" the counterstories and challenges to the dominant discourse reflected in this work, they are likely to miss the point.

It is clear that, in many ways, critical race theory does not represent a "new" song—if we think of "new" in a chronological sense. In fact, it is a very old song, one that originated centuries ago during the enslavement of African Americans in this country. Over one hundred years ago, the songwriter challenged the superiority of white slaveholders by offering a different perspective on heaven and on who would be there, affirming that "*All* God's children got a song." Insofar as the perspectives and experiences of persons of color are *still* challenges to the dominant discourse, CRT represents a "new"—as in "different"—song. As will be demonstrated in the chapters of this volume, it is necessary for scholars in education to sing a different song. Racism is still a pervasive part of the American landscape. It is, therefore, important for CRT scholars in education to tell these counterstories to challenge the story of white supremacy. Thus, despite roots that go back to the origins of this country, we are still singing a new song.

Critical Race Theory: The "New" Song

The "new" song of CRT was transposed from legal studies into the study of education in the mid-1990s. Although the legal basis of critical race theory is outlined in greater detail elsewhere in this volume,* it is important for those new to CRT in education to recognize its legal antecedents. Scholarship in CRT in legal studies generally reflects six common themes, several of which were described earlier in this introduction: (1) CRT recognizes that racism is a pervasive and permanent part of American society; (2) CRT challenges dominant claims of objectivity, neutrality, colorblindness, and merit; (3) CRT challenges ahistoricism and insists on a contextual/historical analysis of the law; (4) CRT insists on recognition of the experiential knowledge of people of color in analyzing law and society; (5) CRT is interdisciplinary; and (6) CRT works toward eliminating racial oppression as part of the broader goal of ending all forms of oppression (Matsuda, Lawrence, Delgado, and Crenshaw, 1993). While CRT in legal studies is an eclectic movement encompassing a wide range of scholarship (Crenshaw, Gotanda, Peller, and Thomas, 1995), the foundation of the theoretical perspective rests on these six themes (Matsuda et al., 1993).

In 1994, Gloria Ladson-Billings and William Tate presented a paper at the annual meeting of the American Educational Research Association (AERA) in which they demonstrated the relevance of these six themes to education. They asserted that race remains a salient factor in U.S. society in general and in education in particular. They argued, however, that race at that time was under-

---

* See, for example, the chapters by Ladson-Billings and Tate, Dixson and Rousseau, and Yosso.

theorized in education. To begin to fill this theoretical gap, they proposed that CRT could be employed to examine the role of race and racism in education. In particular, building on the work of Bell and others, they detailed the intersection of race and property rights and the ways this intersection could be used to understand inequity in schools and schooling (Ladson-Billings and Tate, 1995). Since that time, other scholars in education have also begun to use CRT to explore the role of race and racism in the production of inequality.

Critical Race Theory in Education: All God's Children Got a Song was born out of our desire to explore where we in education have come as a field with CRT in the ten years since Ladson-Billings and Tate introduced it. Moreover, we were interested in examining where we might go with CRT in the future. It is important to note that the impetus for this book was a symposium at the 2004 annual meeting of the American Educational Research Association. The goals of the symposium were (1) to outline how CRT has been used in educational scholarship over the past decade, (2) to provide examples by both new and established scholars of current work on CRT in education, and (3) to offer an opportunity for the authors of the original paper on CRT in education to reflect upon where the theory had come in the decade since its introduction and to suggest future directions for CRT scholarship in education. We assembled a panel of scholars at various stages of their professional careers to help us both to examine the state of CRT in education and to illustrate the potential power of an analysis that places race at the center. Most notable was the presence of Gloria Ladson-Billings and William F. Tate IV, who served as discussants, and of Daniel Solórzano, who presented a paper with Tara J. Yosso. All three of these scholars—Ladson-Billings, Tate and Solórzano—have been at the forefront of engaging CRT and pushing its boundaries in education. The contributors to this book are indebted to them and their germinal work in CRT and its use in education. The chapters in this book represent the outgrowth of the intellectual roots that these scholars established.

In the chapter "And We Are Still Not Saved: Critical Race Theory in Education Ten Years Later," we (Dixson and Rousseau) trace the development of CRT scholarship in education over the past decade. Within a few years of Ladson-Billings and Tate's 1994 AERA presentation, several scholars in education had begun to describe their work as reflecting a CRT framework. In an edited volume on CRT in education, however, Tate (1999) cautioned those who would describe their work as illustrative of this theory. He asserted that such scholarship should "build on and expand beyond the scholarship found in the critical race legal literature" (p. 268). Both Ladson-Billings (1999) and Tate (1997) have argued that the established literature on CRT in legal studies must serve as the foundation for work in education. For this reason, we chose to limit the work reviewed for this chapter to that which clearly draws upon or connects to constructs taken from CRT scholarship in legal studies. Thus, this chapter is intended not to be an all-inclusive retrospective but rather to focus on work that can trace its lineage back to the legal foundation of critical race theory. This heritage was at times reflected in the analysis of legal cases or court decisions, but it also manifested itself through the application of constructs from the CRT legal literature to the problems of inequity in education (e.g., the property value of Whiteness, interest convergence, restrictive versus expansive views of equality, the problem of colorblindness). Through examining works of both types, this review aims to understand the extent to which CRT scholarship in education is truly building upon its foundation and employing the analytical tools offered by CRT scholarship in the law.

In Section Two of this volume, the contributors have taken up the challenge laid down by Ladson-Billings (1999) and Tate (1997) to ground CRT scholarship in education within the legal literature that preceded it. The authors build upon constructs from legal studies to examine issues of importance in education. The use of story in this section also reflects the traditions of CRT in legal studies. In particular, the section is introduced with a story modeled after the "chronicles" of Derrick Bell (1987, 1992). This fictional story is used not only as an example of CRT storytelling, but also as an introduction to the CRT constructs that are discussed in greater depth in subsequent chapters of the section. Through the use of story and the various constructs, these chapters reflect an effort to remain true to the legal origins of CRT.

The chapters in Section Three take a slightly different but closely related approach to CRT. We characterize these chapters as the second generation of CRT scholarship in education. The authors here draw heavily upon the interdisciplinary nature of CRT scholarship, pulling from a range of disciplines to inform scholarship on race in education. While their work in many ways represents the new frontier of CRT in education, it also clearly traces its lineage back to the origins of CRT in legal studies. For example, Tara Yosso traces the genealogy of CRT from its beginning in legal studies to its more recent application to education. She engages in the CRT practice of challenging the neutrality and objectivity of educational theory through her critique of Bourdieu's notion of cultural capital, which has been used to construct communities of color as lacking or deficient. In place of this dominant perspective, Yosso posits a theory of the cultural wealth of communities of color. This model of community cultural wealth builds on tenets of CRT through its valuing of the experiential knowledge and cultural assets of persons of color.

The next chapter in this section also pushes the boundaries of CRT scholarship in education while still retaining its connection to the intellectual roots of the movement. Garret Duncan's chapter, "Critical Race Ethnography in Education: Narrative, Inequality, and the Problem of Epistemology," uses an examination of time to frame the consideration of broader epistemological issues related to CRT. Specifically, he considers historical and contemporary cases of *allochronism* in education. In these cases, African American students have been denied the opportunity to experience *coevalness* (the sharing of the present time). This examination then leads to a discussion of the centrality of storytelling in CRT, as Duncan addresses the critiques of this focus on narrative and argues that the allochronism of the dominant discourse can be disrupted only through the stories of people of color.

Like Duncan, Adrienne Dixson examines epistemic considerations with respect to CRT scholarship. In her chapter, "The Fire *This* Time: Jazz, Research and Critical Race Theory," Dixson outlines the potential of a "jazz methodology" for empirical research centered in CRT. She argues that specific characteristics of jazz make it a powerful way to conceptualize research involving the dynamics of race and racism. Like the previous two chapters, Dixson's contribution uses an interdisciplinary perspective to push the boundaries of CRT scholarship in education while remaining true to the origins of the CRT project.

The chapters in Section Four reflect the ever-broadening scope of CRT scholarship in education. Whereas the preceding chapters illustrate the use of CRT as a tool to analyze educational inequity in the United States, the two chapters in this section reflect its use in other spheres. In particular, the chapter by David Stovall reflects the potential of CRT to operate not only as an analytical tool but also as a curricular foundation. Stovall describes the use of CRT as the basis for a high school class. The chapter's subtitle, "CRT Goes to High School," reflects the shift from analysis to praxis in the classroom. The final chapter in this section also reflects the expanding significance of CRT scholarship: David Gillborn provides an international perspective on the role of CRT, arguing that CRT has important implications for the antiracist movement in the United Kingdom. Through his examination of the potential impact on the antiracist movement, Gillborn demonstrates how far CRT has come in education over the past decade.

Finally, William Tate closes the volume with thoughts on the future direction of CRT scholarship in education. As one of the authors of the original paper, his contribution brings this examination of CRT in education full circle and simultaneously points us toward the future.

We believe that each chapter illustrates certain key characteristics of CRT. The authors work from the premise that racism is prevalent in American society in general and in education in particular. They question dominant claims and discourses. The chapters are historically grounded, acknowledging the importance of context. They are interdisciplinary, drawing from a range of literatures including education, law, anthropology, and sociology. And the authors take the experiences and perspectives of persons of color as their focal point. Moreover, all the chapters are grounded in the legal literature on CRT. Each of these characteristics is important to demonstrate the theoretical or analytical potential of CRT. Furthermore, it is through this type of analysis of race and racism in schooling that we seek to meet the ultimate goal of CRT— social transformation. This social transformation in education demands that we not only analyze but also change the structures that prevent all children from receiving the same opportunities to learn and succeed. Just as the "new" song of the spirituals was a call for freedom and justice in an unjust world, CRT not only puts in front of us the image of a "heaven" in which *all* God's children are able to sing their song. It also demands that we find a way to get there.

References

Bell, D. (1987). *And We Are Not Saved: The Elusive Quest for Racial Justice*. New York: Basic Books.

Bell, D. (1992). *Faces at the Bottom of the Well*. New York: Basic Books.

Bell, D. (1995). Who's Afraid of Critical Race Theory? *University of Illinois Law Review* 1995(4): 893–910.

Cone, J. (1972). *The Spirituals and the Blues*. Maryknoll, NY: Orbis.

Crenshaw, K., Gotanda, N., Peller, G., and Thomas, K. (eds.) (1995). *Critical Race Theory: The Key Writings That Formed the Movement*. New York: Routledge.

Jones, A. (1993). *Wade in the Water: The Wisdom of the Spirituals*. Maryknoll, NY: Orbis.

Ladson-Billings, G. (1999). Just What Is Critical Race Theory, and What's It Doing in a "Nice" Field Like Education? In L. Parker, D. Deyhle and S. Villenas (eds.), *Race Is ... Race Isn't: Critical Race Theory and Qualitative Studies in Education*, 7–30. Boulder, CO: Westview.

Ladson-Billings, G., and Tate, W. (1995). Towards a Critical Race Theory of Education. *Teachers College Record* 97(1): 47–68.

Matsuda, M., Lawrence, C., Delgado, R. and Crenshaw, K. (eds.) (1993). *Words That Wound: Critical Race Theory, Assaultive Speech, and the First Amendment*. Boulder, CO: Westview.

Tate, W. (1997). Critical Race Theory and Education: History, Theory, and Implications. In M. Apple (ed.), *Review of Research in Education*, vol. 22. Washington, DC: American Educational Research Association.

Tate, W. (1999). Conclusion. In L. Parker, D. Deyhle and S. Villenas (eds.), *Race Is ...race Isn't*, 251–271. Boulder, CO: Westview.

I
Critical Race Theory and
Education in Context

1

Toward a Critical Race
Theory of Education

GLORIA LADSON-BILLINGS AND WILLIAM F. TATE IV

The presentation of truth in new forms provokes resistance, confounding those committed to accepted measures for determining the quality and validity of statements made and conclusions reached, and making it difficult for them to respond and adjudge what is acceptable.

Derrick Bell, *Faces at the Bottom of the Well*

I am not included within the pale of this glorious anniversary! Your high independence only reveals the immeasurable distance between us. The blessings in which you this day, rejoice, are not enjoyed in common. The rich inheritance of justice, liberty, prosperity and independence bequeathed by your fathers, not by me.

Frederick Douglass, *My Bondage and My Freedom*

In 1991 the social activist and education critic Jonathan Kozol delineated the great inequities that exist between the schooling experiences of white middle-class students and those of poor African American and Latino students. Although Kozol's graphic descriptions may prompt some to question how it is possible that we allow these "savage inequalities," in this chapter we suggest that they are a logical and predictable result of a racialized society in which discussions of race and racism continue to be muted and marginalized.[1]

In this chapter we attempt to theorize race and to use it as an analytic tool for understanding school inequity.[2] We begin with a set of propositions about race and property and their intersections. We situate our discussion in an explication of critical race theory and attempt to move beyond the boundaries of the educational research literature to include arguments and new perspectives from law and the social sciences. In doing so, we acknowledge and are

This chapter originally appeared in *Teachers College Record* 97(1), Fall 1995, pp. 47–68.

indebted to a number of scholars whose work crosses disciplinary boundaries (see, e.g., Collins, 1991; King and Mitchell, 1990; and Williams, 1991).

We conclude by exploring the tensions between our conceptualization of critical race theory in education and the educational reform movement identified as multicultural education.

Understanding Race and Property

Our discussion of social inequity in general, and of school inequity in particular, is based on three central propositions[3]:

1. Race continues to be a significant factor in determining inequity in the U.S.
2. U.S. society is based on property rights.
3. The intersection of race and property creates an analytic tool through which we can understand social (and, consequently, school) inequity.

In this section we expand on these propositions and provide supporting "meta-propositions" to make clear our line of reasoning and relevant application to educational or school settings.

Race as a Factor in Inequity

The first proposition—that race continues to be a significant factor in determining inequity in the United States—is easily documented in the statistical and demographic data. Hacker's (1992) look at educational and life chances such as high school dropout rates, suspension rates, and incarceration rates echoes earlier statistics compiled by the Children's Defense Fund (Edelman, 1987). However, in what we now call the postmodern era, some scholars question the usefulness of race as a category. Omi and Winant (1993) argue that popular notions of race as either an ideological construct or an objective condition have epistemological limitations. Thinking of race strictly as an ideological construct denies the reality of a racialized society and its impact on "raced" people in their everyday lives. On the other hand, thinking of race solely as an objective condition denies the problematic aspects of race: How do we decide who fits into which racial classifications? How do we categorize racial mixtures? Indeed, the world of biology has found the concept of race virtually useless. The geneticist L. L. Cavalli-Sforza (1991) asserts that "human populations are sometimes known as ethnic groups, or 'races.' ... They are hard to define in a way that is both rigorous and useful because human beings group themselves in a bewildering array of sets, some of them overlapping, all of them in a state of flux."

Nonetheless, even when the concept of race fails to "make sense," we continue to employ it. According to the Nobel laureate Toni Morrison:

Race has become metaphorical—a way of referring to and disguising forces, events, classes, and expressions of social decay and economic division far more threatening to the body politic than biological "race" ever was.

Expensively kept, economically unsound, a spurious and useless political asset in election campaigns, racism is as healthy today as it was during the Enlightenment. It seems that is has a utility far beyond economy, beyond the sequestering of classes from one another, and has assumed a metaphorical life so completely embedded in daily discourse that it is perhaps more necessary and more on display than ever before. (Morrison, 1992, p. 63)

Despite the problematic nature of race, we offer as a first meta-proposition that race, unlike gender and class, remains untheorized.[4] Over the past few decades, theoretical and epistemological considerations of gender have proliferated (e.g., Chodorow, 1978; de Beauvoir, 1961; Gornick, 1971; Hartsock, 1979; Jagger, 1983). Though the field continues to struggle for legitimacy in academe, interest in and publications about feminist theories abound. At the same time, Marxist and neo-Marxist formulations about class continue to merit consideration as theoretical models for understanding social inequity (e.g., Bowles and Gintis, 1976; Carnoy, 1974; Apple, 1988; Wexler, 1987). We recognize the importance of both gender-based and class-based analyses while at the same time pointing to their shortcomings vis-à-vis race. Roediger (1991) points out that "the main body of writing by White Marxists in the United States has both 'naturalized' whiteness and oversimplified race."

Omi and Winant have done significant work in providing a sociological explanation of race in the United States. They argue that the paradigms of race have been conflated with notions of ethnicity, class, and nation because "theories of race—of its meaning, its transformations, the significance of racial events—have never been a top priority in social science. In the U.S., although the "founding fathers" of American sociology ... were explicitly concerned with the state of domestic race relations, racial theory remained one of the least developed fields of sociological inquiry" (1994, p. 9).

To mount a viable challenge to the dominant paradigm of ethnicity (which claims that we are all ethnic and, consequently, must assimilate and rise socially the same way European Americans have), Omi and Winant offer a racial formation theory that they define as "the sociohistorical process by which racial categories are created, inhabited, transformed and destroyed. ... [It] is a process of historically situated *projects* in which human bodies and social structures are represented and organized." Further, they link "racial formation to the evolution of hegemony, the way in which society is organized and ruled." Their analysis suggests that "race is a matter of both social structure and cultural representation" (1994, p 56).

By arguing that race remains untheorized, we do not mean that other scholars have not looked carefully at race as a powerful tool for explaining social inequity; rather, we suggest that the intellectual salience of this theorizing has not been systematically employed in the analysis of educational inequality. Thus, like Omi and Winant, we are attempting to uncover or decipher the social-structural and cultural significance of race in education. Our work owes an intellectual debt to both Carter G. Woodson (1933) and W. E. B. Du Bois (1989), who, although marginalized by the mainstream academic community, used race as a theoretical lens for assessing social inequity.

Both Woodson and Du Bois presented cogent arguments for considering race as *the* central construct for understanding inequality. In many ways, our work is an attempt to build on the foundation laid by these scholars.[5] Briefly, Woodson, as far back as 1916, began to establish the legitimacy of race (and, in particular, of African Americans) as a subject of scholarly inquiry (Franklin, 1988). As the founder of the Association for the Study of Negro Life and History and editor of its *Journal of Negro History*, Woodson revolutionized thinking about African Americans from that of pathology and inferiority to multitextured analysis of the uniqueness of African Americans and their situation in the United States. His most notable publication, *The Mis-education of the Negro*, identifies the school's role in structuring inequality and demotivating African-American students:

> The same educational process which inspires and stimulates the oppressor with the thought that he is everything and has accomplished everything worthwhile depresses and crushes at the same time the spark of genius in the Negro by making him feel that his race does not amount to much and never will measure up to the standards of other peoples. (Woodson, 1933, p. xiii)

Du Bois, perhaps better known than Woodson among mainstream scholars, profoundly impacted the thinking of many identified as "other" by naming a "double consciousness" felt by African Americans. According to Du Bois, the African American "ever feels his two-ness—an American, A Negro; two souls, two thoughts, two unreconciled strivings"(1989, p. 5).[6] In a recent biography of Du Bois, David L. Lewis details the intellectual impact of this concept:

> It was a revolutionary concept. It was not just revolutionary; the concept of the divided self was profoundly mystical, for Du Bois invested this double consciousness with a capacity to see incomparably further and deeper. The African-American—seventh son after the Egyptian and Indian, the Greek and Roman, the Teuton and Mongolian—possessed the gift of "second sight in this American world," an intuitive faculty (prelogical, in a sense) enabling him/her to see and say things about American society that possessed a heightened moral validity. Because

he dwelt equally in the mind and heart of his oppressor as in his own beset psyche, the African American embraced a vision of the common-weal at its best. (Lewis, 1993, p. 281)

As a prophetic foreshadowing of the centrality of race in U.S. society, Du Bois reminded us that "the problem of the twentieth century is the problem of the color line" (1989, p. 1).

The second meta-proposition which we use to support the proposition that race continues to be significant in explaining inequity in the United States claims that class-based and gender-based explanations are not powerful enough to explain all of the differences (or variance) in school experience and performance. Although both class and gender can and do intersect with race, as stand-alone variables they do not explain all of the educational achievement differences apparent between whites and students of color. Indeed, there is some evidence (e.g., Cary, 1991; Oakes, 1985) that even when we hold constant for class, middle-class African American students do not achieve at the same level as their white counterparts. Although Oakes reports that "in academic tracking ... poor and minority students are most likely to be placed at the low-est levels of the school's sorting system" (1985, p. 67), we are less sure which factor—race or class—is causal. Perhaps the larger question of the impact of race on social class is the more relevant one. Space limitations do not permit us to examine that question.

Gender bias also figures in inequitable schooling (American Association of University Women, 1992). Females receive less attention from teachers and are counseled away from or out of advanced mathematics and science courses, and although they receive better grades than their male counterparts, their grades do not translate into advantages in college admission and the work-place (Sadker, Sadker and Klein, 1991).

But examination of class and gender, taken alone or together, does not account for the extraordinarily high rates of school dropout, suspension, expulsion, and failure among African American and Latino males.[7] In the case of suspension, Majors and Billson (1992) argue that many African American males are suspended or expelled from school for what they term "non-contact violations"—wearing banned items of clothing such as hats and jackets, or wearing these items in an "unauthorized" manner such as back-wards or inside out. The point we strive to make with this meta-proposition is not that class and gender are insignificant, but rather, as West (1993) suggests, that "race matters," and, as Smith (1993) insists, "blackness matters in more detailed ways."

The Property Issue

Our second proposition, that U.S. society is based on property rights, is best explicated by examining legal scholarship and interpretations of rights. To develop this proposition, it is important to situate it in the context of critical race theory. Monaghan (1993) reports that "critical race legal scholarship developed in the 1970s, in part because minority scholars thought they were being overlooked in critical legal studies, a better-known movement that examines the way law encodes cultural norms." However, Delgado argues that despite the diversity contained within the critical race movement, there are some shared features:

> an assumption that racism is not a series of isolated acts, but is endemic in American life, deeply ingrained legally, culturally, and even psychologically; a call for a reinterpretation of civil-rights law "in light of its ineffectuality, showing that laws to remedy racial injustices are often undermined before they can fulfill their promise"; a challenge to the "traditional claims of legal neutrality, objectivity, color-blindness, and meritocracy as camouflages for the self-interest of dominant groups in American society"; an insistence on subjectivity and the reformulation of legal doctrine to reflect the perspectives of those who have experienced and been victimized by racism firsthand; the use of stories or first-person accounts. (quoted in Monaghan, 1993, p. A7)[8]

In our analysis we add another aspect to this critical paradigm which disentangles democracy and capitalism. Many discussions of democracy conflate it with capitalism, despite the fact that it is possible to have a democratic government with an economic system other than capitalism. Discussing the two ideologies as if they were one masks the pernicious effects of capitalism on those who are relegated to the economy's lowest ranks. Traditional civil rights approaches to solving inequality have depended on the "rightness" of democracy while ignoring the structural inequality of capitalism (Marable, 1983). However, democracy in the U.S. context was built on capitalism. In the early years of the republic, *only* capitalists enjoyed the franchise. Two hundred years later, when civil rights leaders of the 1950s and 1960s built their pleas for social justice on an appeal to civil and human rights, they were ignoring the fact that the society was based on *property rights* (Bell, 1987). An example from the 1600s underscores the centrality of property in the Americas from the beginning of European settlement:

> When the Pilgrims came to New England they too were coming not to vacant land but to territory inhabited by tribes of Indians. The governor of the Massachusetts Bay Colony, John Winthrop, created the excuse to take Indian land by declaring the area legally a "vacuum." The Indians, he said, had not "subdued" the land, and therefore had only a "natural" right to it, but not a "civil right." A "natural right" did not have legal standing. (Zinn, 1980, p. 13)

Bell (1987) examined the events leading up to the Constitution's development and concluded that there exists a tension between property rights and human rights. This tension was greatly exacerbated by the presence of African people as slaves in America. The purpose of the government was to protect the main object of society—property. The slave status of most African Americans (as well as the similarly restricted rights of women and children) resulted in their being objectified as property. A government constructed to protect the rights of property owners lacked the incentive to secure human rights for the African American (Tate, Ladson-Billings and Grant, 1993). According to Bell, "the concept of individual rights, unconnected to property rights, was totally foreign to these men of property; and thus, despite two decades of civil rights gains, most Blacks remain disadvantaged and deprived because of their race" (1987, p. 239).

The grand narrative of U.S. history is replete with tensions and struggles over property in its various forms. From the removal of Indians (and later Japanese Americans) from the land, to military conquest of the Mexicans (Takaki, 1993), to the construction of Africans as property (Franklin, 1988), the ability to define, possess, and own property has been a central feature of power in America. We do not suggest that other nations have not fought over and defined themselves by property and landownership.[9] However, the contradiction of a reified symbolic individual juxtaposed to the reality of "real estate" means that emphasis on the centrality of property can be disguised. Thus, we talk about the importance of the individual, individual rights, and civil rights while social benefits accrue largely to property owners.[10]

Property relates to education in explicit and implicit ways. Recurring discussions about property tax relief indicate that more affluent communities (which have higher property values, hence higher tax assessments) resent paying for a public school system whose clientele is largely nonwhite and poor (see, e.g., Wainer, 1993; Houston, 1993). In the simplest of equations, those with "better" property are entitled to "better" schools. Kozol illustrates the disparities: "Average expenditures per pupil in the city of New York in 1987 were some $5,500. In the highest spending suburbs of New York (Great Neck or Manhasset, for example, on Long Island) funding levels rose above $11,000, with the highest districts in the state at $15,000" (1991, pp. 83–84).

Property differences manifest themselves in other ways as well. For example, curriculum represents a form of "intellectual property."[11] The quality and quantity of the curriculum varies with the "property values" of the school. The use of a critical race story (Delgado, 1990) appropriately represents this notion.

The teenage son of one of the authors of this article was preparing to attend high school. A friend had a youngster of similar age who also was preparing to enter high school. The boys excitedly pored over course offerings in their respective schools' catalogues. One boy was planning on attending school in an upper-middle-class white community. The other would be attending school in an urban, largely African American district. The difference between the course offerings as specified in the catalogues was striking. The boy attending the white, middle-class school had his choice of many foreign languages—Spanish, French, German, Latin, Greek, Italian, Chinese, and Japanese. His mathematics offerings included algebra, geometry, trigonometry, calculus, statistics, general math, and business math. The science department at this school offered biology, chemistry, physics, geology, science in society, biochemistry, and general science. The other boy's curriculum choices were not nearly so broad. His foreign language choices were Spanish and French. His mathematics choices were general math, business math, and algebra (there were no geometry or trig classes offered). His science choices were general science, life science, biology, and physical science. The differences in electives were even more pronounced, with the affluent school offering courses such as film as literature, Asian studies, computer programming, and journalism. Very few elective courses were offered at the African American school, which also had no band, orchestra, or school newspaper.

The availability of "rich" (or enriched) intellectual property delimits what is now called "opportunity to learn" (see, e.g., Stevens, 1993a, 1993b; Winfield and. Woodard, 1994)—the presumption that along with providing educational "standards"[12] which detail what students should know and be able to do, they must have the material resources that support their learning. Thus, intellectual property must be undergirded by "real" property: science labs, computers and other state-of-the-art technologies, and appropriately certified and prepared teachers. Kozol (1991) demonstrated that schools that serve poor students of color are unlikely to have access to these resources and, consequently, their students will have a much reduced opportunity to learn despite the attempt to mandate educational standards.

Critical Race Theory and Education

With this notion of property rights as a defining feature of the society, we proceed to describe the ways in which the features of critical race theory mentioned in the previous section can be applied to our understanding of educational inequity.

Racism as Endemic and Ingrained in American Life

If racism were merely isolated, unrelated, individual acts, we would expect to see at least a few examples of educational excellence and equity together in the nation's public schools. Instead, those places where African Americans do experience educational success tend to be outside the public schools.[13] Some might argue that poor children, regardless of race, do worse in school, and that the high rate of poverty among African Americans contributes to their dismal school performance; however, we argue that the cause of their poverty in conjunction with the condition of their schools and schooling is institutional and structural racism. Thus, when we speak of racism we refer to Wellman's definition: "culturally sanctioned beliefs which, regardless of the intentions involved, defend the advantages Whites have because of the subordinated positions of racial minorities" (1977, p. xviii). We must therefore contend with the "problem facing White people [of coming] to grips with the demands made by Blacks and Whites while at the same time *avoiding* the possibility of institutional change and reorganization that might affect them" (Wellman, 1977, p. 42).

A Reinterpretation of Ineffective Civil Rights Law

In the case of education, the civil rights decision that best exemplifies our position is the landmark *Brown v. Board of Education of Topeka, Kansas*. We have the utmost respect for the work of Thurgood Marshall and the National Association for the Advancement of Colored People (NAACP) legal defense team in arguing the *Brown* decision, but with forty years of hindsight we recognize some serious shortcomings in that strategy. Today students of color are more segregated than ever before (see, e.g., Orfield, 1988; Bell, 1983; Hawley, 1988; Schofield, 1989). Although African Americans represent 12 percent of the national population, they are the majority in 21 of the 22 largest (urban) school districts (Banks, 1991). Instead of providing more and better educational opportunities, school desegregation has meant increased white flight (Taeuber, 1990), along with a loss of African American teaching and administrative positions (King, 1993; Irvine, 1988). In explaining the double-edged sword of civil rights legislation, Crenshaw argues that

> the civil rights community ... must come to terms with the fact that antidiscrimination discourse is fundamentally ambiguous and can accommodate conservative as well as liberal views of race and equality. This dilemma suggests that the civil rights constituency cannot afford to view a antidiscrimination doctrine as a permanent pronouncement of society's commitment to ending racial subordination. Rather, antidiscrimination law represents an ongoing ideological struggle in which occasional winners harness the moral, coercive, consensual power of law. Nonetheless, the victories it offers can be ephemeral and the risks of engagement substantial. (Crenshaw, 1988, p. 1335)

An example of Crenshaw's point about the ambiguity of civil rights legislation comes from a high school district in Northern California. Of the five high schools in the district, one was situated in a predominantly African American community. To entice white students to attend that school, the district funded a number of inducements, including free camping and skiing trips. Even though the trips were available to all students, they were attended largely by the white students, who already owned expensive camping and skiing equipment. However, these inducements were not enough continuously to attract white students. As enrollment began to fall, the district decided to close a school. Not surprisingly, the school in the African American community was closed, and all its students had to be (and continue to be) bused to the four white schools in the district.

Lomotey and Staley's (1990) examination of Buffalo's "model" desegregation program revealed that African-American and Latino students continued to be poorly served by the school system. The academic achievement of African American and Latino students failed to improve while their suspension, expulsion and dropout rates continued to rise. On the other hand, the desegregation plan provided special magnet programs and extended day care of which whites were able to take advantage. What, then, made Buffalo a model school desegregation program? In short, the benefits that whites derived from school desegregation and their seeming support of the district's desegregation program. Thus, a model desegregation program becomes defined as one which ensures that whites are happy (and do not leave the system altogether), regardless of whether African American and other students of color achieve and remain.

Challenging Claims of Neutrality, Objectivity, Colorblindness, and Meritocracy

A theme of "naming one's own reality" or "voice" is entrenched in the work of critical race theorists. Many of them argue that the form and substance of scholarship are closely connected (Delgado, 1989). These scholars use parables, chronicles, stories, counterstories, poetry, fiction, and revisionist histories to illustrate the false necessity and irony of much of current civil rights doctrine. Delgado suggests that there are at least three reasons for naming one's own reality in legal discourse: "(1) much of reality is socially constructed; (2) stories provide members of outgroups a vehicle for psychic self-preservation; and (3) the exchange of stories from teller to listener can help overcome ethnocentrism and the dysconscious conviction of viewing the world in one way" (Delgado, 1989, p. 2073).[14]

The first reason for naming one's own reality is to demonstrate how political and moral analysis is conducted in legal scholarship. Many mainstream legal scholars embrace universalism over particularity (notions of universalism prevail in much of social science research, including educational research). According to Williams (1991), "theoretical legal understanding" is characterized, in Anglo-American jurisprudence, by the acceptance of transcendent, acontextual, universal legal truths or procedures. For instance, some legal scholars might contend that the tort of fraud has always existed and that it is a component of the universal system of right and wrong. This view tends to discount anything that is nontranscendent (historical), contextual (socially constructed), or nonuniversal (specific) with the unscholarly labels "emotional," "literary," "personal," or "false."

In contrast, critical race theorists argue that political and moral analysis is situational: "truths only exist for this person in this predicament at this time in history" (Delgado, 1991, p. 111). For the critical race theorist, social reality is constructed by the formulation and the exchange of stories about individual situations (e.g., Williams, 1991; Matsuda, 1989). These stories serve as interpretive structures by which we impose order on experience and it imposes order on us (Delgado, 1989).

A second reason that critical race theory addresses the theme of naming one's own reality is its goal of the psychic preservation of marginalized groups. One factor contributing to the demoralization of marginalized groups is self-condemnation (Delgado, 1989). Members of minority groups internalize the stereotypic images that certain elements of society have constructed around those minorities in order to maintain their own power (Crenshaw, 1988). Historically, storytelling has been a kind of medicine to heal the wounds caused by racial oppression (Delgado, 1989). The story of one's condition leads to realizing how one came to be oppressed and subjugated and allows one to stop inflicting mental violence on oneself.

Finally, naming one's own reality with stories can affect the oppressor. Most oppression does not seem like oppression to the perpetrator (Lawrence, 1987). Delgado argues that the dominant group justifies its power with stories—stock explanations—which construct reality so as to maintain their privilege (Delgado et al., 1989). Thus oppression is rationalized, causing little self-examination by the oppressor. Stories by people of color can catalyze the necessary cognitive conflict to jar dysconscious racism.

The "voice" component of critical race theory provides a way to communicate the experience and realities of the oppressed, a first step on the road to justice. As we attempt to forge links between critical race theory and education, we contend that the voices of people of color are required for a complete analysis of the educational system. Delpit (1988) argues that one of the tragedies of education is the way in which the dialogue of people of color has been silenced. An example from her conversation with an African American graduate student illustrates this point:

> There comes a moment in every class when we have to discuss "The Black Issue" and what's appropriate education for Black children. I tell you, I'm tired of arguing with those White people, because they won't listen. Well, I don't know if they really don't listen or if they just don't believe you. It seems like if you can't quote Vygotsky or something, then you don't have any validity to speak about your own kids. Anyway, I'm not bothering with it anymore, now I'm just in it for a grade. (Delpit, 1988, p. 280)

A growing number of education scholars of color are raising critical questions about the way that research is being conducted in communities of color.[15]

Without the authentic voices of people of color (as teachers, parents, administrators, students, and community members) it is doubtful that we can say or know anything useful about education in their communities.

The Intersection of Race and Property

In the previous sections we argued that race is still a significant factor in determining inequity in the United States, and that the society is based on property rights rather than on human rights. In this section we discuss the intersection of race and property as a central construct in understanding a critical race theoretical approach to education.

Harris (1993) argues that "slavery linked the privilege of Whites to the subordination of Blacks through a legal regime that attempted the conversion of Blacks into objects of property. Similarly, the settlement and seizure of Native American land supported White privilege through a system of property rights in land in which the 'race' of the Native Americans rendered their first possession right invisible and justified conquest." But more pernicious and long-lasting than the victimization of people of color is the construction of whiteness as the ultimate property: "Possession—the act necessary to lay the basis for rights in property—was defined to include only the cultural practices of Whites. This definition laid the foundation for the idea that whiteness—that which Whites alone possess—is valuable and is property" (Harris, 1993, p. 1721).

Because of space constraints, it is not possible fully to explicate Harris's thorough analysis of whiteness as property. However, it is important to delineate what she terms the "property functions of whiteness," which include (1) rights of disposition, (2) rights to use and enjoyment, (3) reputation and status property, and (4) the absolute right to exclude. How these rights apply to education is germane to our discussion.

Rights of disposition. Because property rights are described as fully alienable—that is, transferable—it is difficult to see how whiteness can be construed as property (Radin, 1987). However, alienability of certain property is limited (e.g., entitlements, government licenses, professional degrees or licenses held by one party and financed by the labor of the other in the context of divorce). Thus, whiteness, when conferred on certain student performances, is alienable (Fordham and Ogbu, 1986). When students are rewarded only for conformity to perceived "white norms" or sanctioned for cultural practices (e.g., dress, speech patterns, unauthorized conceptions of knowledge), white property is being rendered alienable.

Rights to use and enjoyment. Legally, whites can use and enjoy the privileges of whiteness. As McIntosh (1990) has explicitly demonstrated, whiteness allows for specific social, cultural, and economic privileges. Fuller (1994) further asserts that whiteness is both performative and pleasurable. In the school setting, whiteness allows for extensive use of school property. Kozol's description of the material differences in two New York City schools can be interpreted as the difference between those who possess the right to use and enjoy what schools can offer and those who do not: "The [white] school serves 825 children in the kindergarten through sixth grade. This is approximately half the student population crowded into [black] P.S. 79, where 1,550 children fill a space intended for 1,000, and a great deal smaller than the 1,300 children packed into the former skating rink" (1991, p. 93).

This right of use and enjoyment is also reflected in the structure of the curriculum, writes Kozol:

> The curriculum [the white school] follows "emphasizes critical thinking, reasoning and logic." The planetarium, for instance, is employed not simply for the study of the universe as it exists. "Children also are designing their own galaxies," the teacher says. ... In my [Kozol's] notes: "Six girls, four boys. Nine White, one Chinese. I am glad they have this class. But what about the others? Aren't there ten Black children in the school who could *enjoy* this also?" (Kozol, 1991, p. 93; emphasis added)

Reputation and status property. The concept of reputation as property is regularly demonstrated in legal cases of libel and slander. To damage someone's reputation is to damage some aspect of his or her personal property. In the case of race, to call a white person "black" is to defame him or her (Harris, 1993, p. 1735). In the case of schooling, to identify a school or program as non-white in any way is to diminish its reputation or status. For example, despite the prestige of foreign language learning, bilingual education as practiced in the United States as a nonwhite form of second language learning has lower status (Spener, 1988). The term "urban," the root word of "urbane," has come to mean "black" in certain well-understood contexts. Thus, urban schools (located in the urbane, sophisticated cities) lack the status and reputation of suburban (white) schools, and when urban students move to or are bused to suburban schools, these schools lose their reputation (Bissinger, 1994).

The absolute right to exclude. Whiteness is constructed in this society as the absence of the "contaminating" influence of blackness. Thus, "one drop of black blood" constructs one as black, regardless of phenotypic markers (Bell, 1980). In schooling, the absolute right to exclude was demonstrated initially by denying blacks access to schooling altogether. Later it was demonstrated by the creation and maintenance of separate schools. More recently it has been demonstrated by white flight and the growing insistence on vouchers, public funding of private schools, and schools of choice.[16]

Within schools, absolute right to exclude is demonstrated by resegregation via tracking (Oakes, 1985), the institution of "gifted" programs, honors programs, and advanced placement classes. So complete is this exclusion that black students often come to the university in the role of intruders who have been granted special permission to be there.

In this section we have attempted to draw parallels between educational equity and the notion in critical race legal theory of whiteness as property. In the final section we relate some of the intellectual and theoretical tensions that exist between critical race theory and multicultural education.

The Limits of the Multicultural Paradigm

Throughout this chapter we have argued that a critical race theoretical perspective is needed to cast a new gaze on the persistent problems of racism in schooling because of the failure of scholars to theorize race. We have drawn parallels between the way critical race legal scholars understand their position vis-à-vis traditional legal scholarship and the ways critical race theory applied to education offers a way to rethink traditional educational scholarship. We also have referred to the tensions that exist between traditional civil rights legislation and critical race legal theory. In this section we identify a necessary tension between critical race theory in education and what we term the "multicultural paradigm."

Multicultural education has been conceived as a reform movement designed to effect change in the "school and other educational institutions so that students from diverse racial, ethnic, and other social-class groups will experience educational equality" (Banks, 1993, p. 3). In more recent years, multicultural education has expanded to include issues of gender, ability, and sexual orientation. Although one could argue for an early history of the "multicultural education movement" as far back as the 1880s, when George Washington Williams (1882–1883) wrote his history of African Americans, much of current multicultural education practice seems more appropriately rooted in the intergroup education movement of the 1950s, which was designed to help African Americans and other "unmeltable" ethnics become a part of America's melting pot (Cook and Cook, 1954; Traeger and Yarrow, 1952). The latter's goals were primarily assimilationist through the reduction of prejudice. However, after the civil rights unrest and growing self-awareness of African Americans in the 1960s, the desire to assimilate was supplanted by the reclamation of an "authentic black personality" which did not rely on acceptance by white America or on its standards. This new vision was evidenced in the academy first in the form of black studies and later, when other groups made similar liberating moves, ethnic studies (see, e.g., Harding, 1970; Blassingame, 1971; Banks, 1973; Gay, 1971)

Current practical demonstrations of multicultural education in schools often reduce it to trivial examples and artifacts of cultures, such as eating ethnic or cultural foods, singing songs or dancing, reading folktales, and other less than scholarly activities substituted for pursuing the fundamentally different conceptions of knowledge or quests for social justice (Banks, 1973). At the university level, much of the concern over multicultural education has been over curriculum inclusion.[17] However, another level of debate emerged over what became known as "multiculturalism."

Somewhat different from multicultural education in that it does not represent a particular educational reform or scholarly tradition, multiculturalism came to be viewed as a political philosophy of "many cultures" existing together in an atmosphere of respect and tolerance.[18] Thus, outside the classroom multiculturalism represented the attempt to bring both students and faculty from a variety of cultures into the school (or academy) environment of "diversity," a term used to denote all types of "difference"—racial, ethnic, cultural, linguistic, ability, gender, or sexual orientation. Thus, popular music, clothes, media, books, and so forth reflect a growing awareness of diversity or multiculturalism. Less often discussed are the growing tensions which exist between and among various groups that gather under the umbrella of multiculturalism—that is, the interests of groups can compete, or their perspectives can be at odds.[19] We assert that the ever-expanding multicultural paradigm follows the traditions of liberalism—allowing a proliferation of difference. Unfortunately, the tensions between and among these differences are rarely interrogated, and scholars assume a "unity of difference"—that is, that all difference is both analogous and equivalent (Torres-Medina, 1994).

To make parallel the analogy between critical race legal theory and traditional civil rights law and that of critical race theory in education and multicultural education, we need to restate the point that critical race legal theorists have "doubts about the foundation of moderate/incremental civil rights law" (Delgado, 1991). The foundation of civil rights law has been in human rights rather than in property rights. Thus, without disrespect to the pioneers of civil rights law, critical race legal scholars document the ways in which civil rights law is regularly subverted to benefit whites (Bell, 1987).

We argue that the current multicultural paradigm functions in a manner similar to civil rights law. Instead of creating radically new paradigms which ensure justice, multicultural reforms are routinely "sucked back into the system"; and just as traditional civil rights law is based on a foundation of human rights, the current multicultural paradigm is mired in liberal ideology that offers no radical change in the current order (McCarthy, 1994; Olneck, 1993). Thus, critical race theory in education, like its antecedent in legal scholarship, is a radical critique of both the status quo and the purported reforms.

We make this observation of the limits of the current multicultural paradigm not to disparage the scholarly efforts and sacrifices of many of its proponents, but to underscore the difficulty (indeed, impossibility) of maintaining the spirit and intent of justice for the oppressed while simultaneously permitting the hegemonic rule of the oppressor.[20] Thus, as critical race theory scholars we unabashedly reject a paradigm that attempts to be everything to everyone and consequently becomes nothing for anyone, allowing the status quo to prevail. Instead, we align our scholarship and activism with the philosophy of

Marcus Garvey, who believed that the black man was universally oppressed on racial grounds, and that any program of emancipation would have to be built around the question of race first (Martin, 1976). In his own words, Garvey speaks to us clearly and unequivocally: "In a world of wolves one should go armed, and one of the most powerful defensive weapons within the reach of Negroes is the practice of race first in all parts of the world" (quoted in Martin, 1976, p. 22).

Notes

1. For further discussion of our inability to articulate issues of race and racism see Morrison (1992), West (1992), and Tatum (1992).
2. Throughout this article the term "race" is used to denote the polar opposites of "conceptual whiteness" and "conceptual blackness" (King, 1994). We do not mean to reserve the sense of "otherness" for African Americans; rather, our discussion attempts to illuminate how discussions of race in the United States positions *everyone* as either "white" or "nonwhite." Thus, despite the use of African American legal and educational exemplars, we include other groups who have been constructed at various time in their history as nonwhite or black. Readers should note that the leading legal scholars in the critical race legal theory movement include those of Latino and Asian American as well as African American heritage.
3. These propositions are not hierarchical. Rather, they can be envisioned as sides of an equilateral triangle, each equal and each central to the construction of the overall theory.
4. This assertion was made forcefully by the participants of the Institute NHI (No Humans Involved) at a symposium entitled "The Two Reservations: Western Thought, the Color Line, and the Crisis of the Negro Intellectual Revisited," sponsored by the Department of African and Afro-American Studies at Stanford University, March 3–5, 1994.
5. Our decision to focus on Woodson and Du Bois is not intended to diminish the import of the scores of African American scholars who also emerged during their time, such as George E. Haynes, Charles S. Johnson, E. Franklin Frazier, Abram Harris, Sadie T. Alexander, Robert C. Weaver, Rayford Logan, Allison Davis, Dorothy Porter, and Benjamin Quarles. We highlight Woodson and Du Bois as early seminal thinkers about issues of race and racism.
6. Other people of color, feminists, and gay and lesbian theorists all have appropriated Du Bois's notion of double consciousness to explain their estrangement from mainstream patriarchal, masculinist U.S. culture.
7. Hacker (1992) puts the dropout rate for African American males in some large cities at close to 50 percent.
8. For a more detailed explication of the first item in the list, see Bell (1992).
9. Clearly, an analysis of worldwide tensions reinforces the importance of land to a people—Israel and the Palestinians, Iraq and Kuwait, the former Soviet bloc, Hitler and the Third Reich all represent struggles over land.
10. Even at a time when there is increased public sentiment for reducing the federal deficit, the one source of tax relief that no president or member of Congress would ever consider is denying home (property) owners their tax benefits.
11. This notion of "intellectual property" came into popular consciousness when television talk show host David Letterman moved from NBC to CBS. NBC claimed that certain routines and jokes used by Letterman were the intellectual property of the network and, as such, could not be used by Letterman without permission.
12. The standards debate is too long and detailed to be discussed here. For a more detailed discussion of standards see, for example, Apple (1992) and National Council of Education Standards and Testing (1992).
13. Some urban Catholic schools, black independent schools, and historically black colleges and universities have demonstrated the educability of African American students. As of this writing, we have no data on the success of urban districts such as Detroit or Milwaukee which are attempting "African Centered" or "Africentric" education. See also Shujaa (1994).

14. On dysconsciousness, see King (1991, p. 135). King defines dysconsciousness as "an uncritical habit of mind (including perceptions, attitudes, assumptions, and beliefs) that justifies inequity and exploitation by accepting the existing order of things as given. ... Dysconscious racism is a form of racism that tacitly accepts dominant White norms and privileges. It is not the *absence* of consciousness (that is, not unconsciousness) but an *impaired* consciousness or distorted way of thinking about race as compared to, for example, critical consciousness."
15. At the 1994 annual meeting of the American Educational Research Association in New Orleans, two sessions entitled "Private Lives, Public Voices: Ethics of Research in Communities of Color" were convened to discuss the continued exploitation of people of color. According to one scholar of color, our communities have become "data plantations."
16. We assert that the current movement toward African-centered (or Africentric) schools is not equivalent to the racial exclusion of vouchers, or choice programs. Indeed, African-centeredness has become a logical response of a community to schools that have been abandoned by whites, have been stripped of material resources, and have demonstrated a lack of commitment to African American academic achievement.
17. In 1988 at Stanford University, the inclusion of literature from women and people of color in the Western Civilization core course resulted in a heated debate. The university's faculty senate approved this inclusion in a course called Cultures, Ideas, and Values. The controversy was heightened when then Secretary of Education William Bennett came to the campus to denounce this decision.
18. In the "Book Notes" section of the *Harvard Educational Review* 64 (1994): 345–47, Jane Davagian Tchaicha reviews Donaldo Macedo's *Literacies of Power* (Boulder: Westview, 1994) and includes two quotes, one from the noted conservative Patrick Buchanan and another from Macedo on multiculturalism. According to Buchanan, "Our Judeo-Christian values are going to be preserved, and our Western heritage is going to be handed down to future generations, not dumped into some landfill called multiculturalism" (p. 345). Macedo asserts that "the real issue isn't Western culture versus multiculturalism, the fundamental issue is the recognition of humanity in us and in others" (p. 347).
19. In New York City, controversy over the inclusion of gay and lesbian issues in the curriculum caused vitriolic debate among racial and ethnic groups who opposed their issues being linked to or compared with homosexuals. Some ethnic group members asserted that homosexuals were not a "culture," while gay and lesbian spokespeople argued that these group members were homophobic.
20. We are particularly cognizant of the hard-fought battles in the academy waged and won by scholars such as James Banks, Carlos Cortez, Geneva Gay, Carl Grant, and others.

References

American Association of University Women (1992). *How Schools Shortchange Girls: A Study of Major Findings on Gender and Education.* Washington, DC: AAUW and National Education Association, 1992.
Apple, Michael W. (1988), Redefining Inequality: Authoritarian Populism and the Conservative Restoration. *Teachers College Record* 90: 167–184.
Apple, Michael W. (1992). Do the Standards Go Far Enough? Power, Policy, and Practices in Mathematics Education. *Journal for Research in Mathematics Education* 23: 412–431.
Banks, James A. (ed.) (1973). *Teaching Ethnic Studies.* Washington, DC: National Council for the Social Studies.
Banks, James (1991). Teaching Multicultural Literacy to Teachers. *Teaching Education* 4: 135–144.
Banks, James A. (1993). Multicultural Education: Historical Development, Dimensions, and Practice. In L. Darling-Hammond (ed.), *Review of Research in Education, vol. 19,* 3. Washington, DC: American Educational Research Association.
Bell, Derrick (1980). *Race, Racism, and American Law.* Boston: Little, Brown.
Bell, Derrick (1983). Learning from Our Losses: Is School Desegregation Still Feasible in the 1980s? *Phi Delta Kappan* 64 (April): 575.
Bell, Derrick (1987). *And We Are Not Saved: The Elusive Quest for Racial Justice.* New York: Basic Books.
Bell, Derrick (1992). *Faces at the Bottom of the Well.* New York: Basic Books.

Bissinger, H. G. (1994). When Whites Flee. *New York Times Magazine*, 29 May, pp. 26–33, 43, 50, 53–54, 56.

Blassingame, J. (ed.) (1971). *New Perspectives in Black Studies*. Urbana: University of Illinois Press.

Bowles, Samuel and Gintis, Herbert (1976). *Schooling in Capitalist America*. New York: Basic Books.

Carnoy, Martin (1974). *Education and Cultural Imperialism*. New York: McKay.

Cary, Lorene (1991). *Black Ice*. New York: Alfred A. Knopf.

Cavalli-Sforza, Luigi Luca (1991). Genes, People and Languages. *Scientific American*, November 1991, p. 104.

Chodorow, Nancy (1978). *The Reproduction of Mothering*. Berkeley: University of California Press.

Collins, Patricia Hill (1991). *Black Feminist Thought*. New York: Routledge.

Cook, L. A. and Cook, E. (1954). *Intergroup Education*. New York: McGraw-Hill.

Crenshaw, Kimberle Williams (1988). Race Reform, and Retrenchment: Transformation and Legitimation in Antidiscrimination Law. *Harvard Law Review* 101: 1331–1387.

de Beauvoir, Simone (1961). *The Second Sex*. New York: Bantam.

Delgado, Richard (1989). Storytelling for Oppositionists and Others: A Plea for Narrative. *Michigan Law Review* 87: 2411–2441.

Delgado, Richard (1990). When a Story Is Just a Story: Does Voice Really Matter? *Virginia Law Review* 76: 95–111.

Delgado, Richard (1991a). Brewer's Plea: Critical Thoughts on Common Cause. *Vanderbilt Law Review* 44: 11.

Delgado, Richard (1991b). Enormous Anomaly? Left-Right Parallels in Recent Writing about Race. *Columbia Law Review* 91: 1547–1560.

Delgado, Richard, et al. (1989). Symposium: Legal Storytelling. *Michigan Law Review* 87: 2073.

Delpit, Lisa (1988). The Silenced Dialogue: Power and Pedagogy in Educating Other People's Children. *Harvard Educational Review* 58: 280.

Du Bois, W. E. B. (1989 [1903]). *The Souls of Black Folks*. New York: Penguin.

Edelman, Marian Wright (1987). *Families in Peril: An Agenda for Social Change*. Cambridge, MA: Harvard University Press.

Fordham, Signithia and Ogbu, John (1986). Black Student School Success: Coping with the Burden of "Acting White." *Urban Review* 18: 1–31.

Franklin, John Hope (1988). *From Slavery to Freedom*. 6th ed. New York: Alfred A. Knopf.

Fuller, Laurie (1994). Whiteness as Performance. Unpublished preliminary examination paper, University of Wisconsin–Madison.

Gay, Geneva (1971). Ethnic Minority Studies: How Widespread? How Successful? *Educational Leadership* 29: 108–112.

Gornick, Vivian (1971). Women as Outsiders. In V. Gornick and B. Moran (eds.), *Women in Sexist Society*, 70–84. New York: Basic Books.

Hacker, Andrew (1992). *Two Nations: Black and White, Separate, Hostile, Unequal*. New York: Ballantine.

Harding, Vincent (1970). *Beyond Chaos: Black History and the Search for a New Land*. Black Paper No. 2. Atlanta: Institute of the Black World.

Harris, Cheryl I. (1993). Whiteness as Property. *Harvard Law Review* 106: 1721.

Hartsock, Nancy (1979). Feminist Theory and the Development of Revolutionary Strategy. In Z. Eisenstein (ed.), *Capitalist Patriarch and the Case for Socialist Feminism*. London and New York: Monthly Review Press.

Hawley, Willis D. (1988). Why It Is Hard to Believe in Desegregation. *Equity and Choice*, February 1988, pp. 9–15.

Houston, Paul (1993). School Vouchers: The Latest California Joke. *Phi Delta Kappan* 75: 61–66.

Irvine, Jacqueline (1988). An Analysis of the Problem of Disappearing Black Educators. *Elementary School Journal* 88: 503–513.

Jagger, Alison (1983). *Feminist Theory and Human Nature*. Sussex, UK: Harvester.

King, Joyce (1994). Perceiving Reality in a New Way: Rethinking the Black/white Duality of our Time. Paper presented at the annual meeting of the American Educational Research Association, New Orleans, April.

King, Joyce E. (1991). Dysconscious Racism: Ideology, Identity and the Miseducation of Teachers. *Journal of Negro Education* 60: 135.

King, Joyce and Mitchell, Carolyn (1990). *Black Mothers to Sons: Juxtaposing African American Literature and Social Practice*. New York: Peter Lang.

King, Sabrina (1993). The Limited Presence of African American Teachers. *Review of Educational Research* 63: 115–149.

Kozol, Jonathan (1991). *Savage Inequalities*. New York: Crown.

Lawrence, Charles (1987). The Id, the Ego, and Equal Protection: Reckoning with Unconscious Racism. *Stanford Law Review* 39: 317–388.

Lewis, David Levering (1993). *W. E. B. Du Bois: Biography of a Race, 1868–1919*. New York: Henry Holt.

Lomotey, Kofi and Statley, John (1990). The Education of African Americans in Buffalo Public Schools. Paper presented at the annual meeting of the American Educational Research Association, Boston.

Majors, Robert, and Billson, Janet (1992). *Cool Pose: The Dilemmas of Black Manhood in America*. New York: Lexington.

Marable, Manning (1983). *How Capitalism Underdeveloped Black America*. Boston: South End.

Martin, Tony (1976). *Race First: The Ideological and Organizational Struggles of Marcus Garvey and the Universal Negro Improvement Association*. Dover, MA: Majority Press.

Matsuda, Mari (1989). Public Response to Racist Speech: Considering the Victim's Story. *Michigan Law Review* 87: 2320–2381.

McCarthy, Cameron (1994). After the Canon: Knowledge and Ideological Representation in the Multicultural Discourse on Curriculum Reform. In C. McCarthy and W. Crichlow (eds.), *Race, Identity and Representation*. New York: Routledge.

McIntosh, Peggy (1990). White Privilege: Unpacking the Invisible Knapsack. *Independent School*, Winter 1990, pp. 31–36.

Monaghan, Peter (1993). "Critical Race Theory" Questions the Role of Legal Doctrine in Racial Inequity. *Chronicle of Higher Education*, 23 June, pp. A7, A9.

Morrison, Toni (1992). *Playing in the Dark: Whiteness and the Literary Imagination* Cambridge, MA: Harvard University Press.

National Council of Education Standards and Testing (1992). *Raising Standards for American Education: A Report to Congress, the Secretary of Education, the National Goals Panel, and the American People*. Washington, DC: Government Printing Office.

Oakes, Jeannie (1985). *Keeping Track: How Schools Structure Inequality*. New Haven: Yale University Press.

Olneck, Michael (1993). Terms of Inclusion: Has Multiculturalism Redefined Equality in American Education. *American Journal of Education* 101: 234–260.

Omi, Michael and Winant, Howard (1993). On the Theoretical Concept of Race. In C. McCarthy and W. Crichlow (eds.), *Race, Identity, and Representation in Education*, 3–10. New York: Routledge.

Omi, Michael and Winant, Howard (1994). *Racial Formation in the United States from the 1960s to the 1990s*. 2nd ed. New York: Routledge.

Orfield, Gary (1988). School Desegregation in the 1980s. *Equity and Choice*, February 1988, p. 5.

Radin, Margaret (1987). Market-Inalienability. *Harvard Law Review* 100: 1849–1906.

Roediger, David (1991). *The Wages of Whiteness*. London: Verso.

Sadker, Myra, Sadker, David, and Klein, Susan (1991). The Issue of Gender in Elementary and Secondary Education. In G. Cerant (ed.), *Review of Educational Research in Education*, vol. 19, 269–334. Washington, DC: American Educational Research Association.

Schofield, Janet Ward (1989). *Black and White in School: Trust, Tension, or Tolerance?* New York: Teachers College Press.

Shujaa, Mwalimu J. (ed.) (1994). *Too Much Schooling, Too Little Education: A Paradox of Black Life in White Societies*. Trenton, NJ: Africa World.

Smith, David Lionel (1993). Let Our People Go. *Black Scholar* 23: 75–76.

Spener, David (1988). Transitional Bilingual Education and the Socialization of Immigrants. *Harvard Educational Review* 58: 133–153.

Stevens, Floraline (1993a). *Opportunity to Learn: Issues of Equity for Poor and Minority Students*. Washington, DC: National Center for Education Statistics.

Stevens, Floraline (1993b). Applying an Opportunity-to-learn Conceptual Framework to the Investigation of the Effects of Teaching Practices via Secondary Analyses of Multiple-case-study Summary Data. *Journal of Negro Education* 62: 232–248.

Taeuber, Karl (1990). Desegregation of Public School Districts: Persistence and Change. *Phi Delta Kappan* 72: 18–24.

Takaki, Ronald (1993). *A Different Mirror: A History of Multicultural America*. Boston: Little Brown.

Tate, William; Ladson-Billings, Gloria; and Grant, Carl (1993). The *Brown* Decision Revisited: Mathematizing Social Problems. *Educational Policy* 7: 255–275.

Tatum, Beverly Daniel (1992). Talking about Race, Learning about Racism: The Application of Racial Identity Development Theory in the Classroom. *Harvard Educational Review* 62: 1–24.

Torres-Medina, Shirley (1994). Issues of Power: Constructing the Meaning of Linguistic Difference in First Grade Classrooms. Ph.D. dissertation, University of Wisconsin–Madison.

Traeger, H. G. and Yarrow, M. R. (1952). *They Learn What They Live: Prejudice in Young Children.* New York: Harper.

Wainer, Howard (1993). Does Spending Money on Education Help? *Educational Researcher* 22: 22–24.

Wellman, David (1977). *Portraits of White Racism.* Cambridge: Cambridge University Press.

West, Cornel (1992). Learning to Talk of Race. *New York Times Magazine*, 2 August, pp. 24, 26.

West, Cornel (1993). *Race Matters.* Boston: Beacon.

Wexler, Philip (1987). *Social Analysis and Education: After the New Sociology.* New York: Routledge & Kegan Paul.

Williams, George Washington (1882–1883). *History of the Negro Race in America from 1619–1880: Negroes as Slaves, as Soldiers, and as Citizens.* 2 vols. New York: G. P. Putnam.

Williams, Patricia (1991). *The Alchemy of Race and Rights: Diary of a Law Professor* Cambridge, MA: Harvard University Press.

Winfield, Linda and Woodard, Michael D. (1994). Assessment, Equity, Diversity in Reforming America's Schools. *Educational Policy* 8: 3–27.

Woodson, Carter G. (1933). *The Miseducation of the Negro.* Washington, DC: Association Press.

Zinn, Howard (1980). *A People's History of the United States.* New York: Harper & Row.

2

And We Are Still Not Saved: Critical Race Theory in Education Ten Years Later

ADRIENNE D. DIXSON AND CELIA K. ROUSSEAU

This is the story of a school. Within this school, there were two separate academic programs that differed in several ways. Class size was one of the most obvious differences. Students in Program A were often in classes of no more than 15. In contrast, classes of 25 students or more were not uncommon in Program B. Program A's classes were not only smaller but were also staffed by the most highly qualified teachers in the school. These classes were "protected" from teachers who were perceived to be less well qualified. In contrast, Program B's classes were often the last to be assigned teachers. Those responsible for making the assignments confessed that they sometimes subscribed to the "warm body" approach when more qualified teachers were not available. It is probably not surprising to those who are familiar with how these things work that the student populations of the two programs also differed substantially. Classes in Program A were often approximately 80% white and 20% African American. In contrast, classes in Program B were sometimes as much as 80% African American. Moreover, the programs also differed in where they sent their students after graduation. The students from Program A were more likely to graduate and go on to some of the "best" schools in the area, while the Program B graduates often went to the local schools with poor reputations.

Introduction

In 1995 *Teachers College Record* published an article by Gloria Ladson-Billings and William Tate entitled "Toward a Critical Race Theory of Education," reprinted as Chapter 1 of the present volume. The authors asserted that race remains a significant factor in society in general and in education in particular. Yet, according to Ladson-Billings and Tate, at that time race remained undertheorized as a topic of scholarly inquiry in education. To begin to address this theoretical void, they proposed that critical race theory (CRT), a framework developed by legal scholars, could be employed to examine the role of race and

This chapter originally appeared in *Race, Ethnicity and Education* 8(1), March 2005, pp. 7–28.

racism in education. In particular, they detailed the intersection of race and property rights and how this construct could be used to understand inequity in schools and schooling.

Their analysis built on the work of the legal scholar Cheryl Harris, employing her construct of "whiteness as property." According to Harris (1993), although the popular conception of property is in terms of some tangible object—a home or car, for example —many theorists hold that, historically within U.S. society, property is a *right* rather than a physical object. When property is conceived of in this way, it is possible to examine the property value (in terms of rights) of whiteness. Harris proposes that the core characteristic of whiteness as property is "the legal legitimation of expectations of power and control that enshrine the status quo as a neutral baseline, while masking the maintenance of white privilege and domination" (p. 1715). Beyond this general definition, Harris also contends that whiteness meets the more specific functional criteria of property. According to Harris, "the law has accorded 'holders' of whiteness the same privileges and benefits accorded holders of other types of property" (p. 1731).

One of these privileges and benefits of property is the absolute right to exclude. Ladson-Billings and Tate outlined the manifestations of this property function of whiteness in education:

> In schooling, the absolute right to exclude was demonstrated initially by denying blacks access to schooling altogether. Later, it was demonstrated by the creation and maintenance of separate schools. More recently it has been demonstrated by white flight and the growing insistence on vouchers, public funding of private schools, and schools of choice. Within schools, absolute right to exclude is demonstrated by resegregation via tracking. (1995, p. 60)

Thus, tracking can be viewed as one of the current means through which the property right of whiteness is asserted in education. African American and Latino students are disproportionately placed in the lowest tracks and afforded fewer educational opportunities as a result (Darling-Hammond, 1997; Oakes, 1995; Oakes, Muir, and Joseph, 2000). The story included as the prologue to this article could be viewed as an example of the property value of whiteness through the operation of a two-track system characterized by de facto segregation.

Whiteness as property is but one of the theoretical constructs outlined in the legal literature on critical race theory. Much as Ladson-Billings and Tate (1995) described a theoretical void in their discipline, the founders of the movement in legal studies characterize the emergence of CRT as part of the search for a new vocabulary. They needed a vocabulary to name the race-related structures of oppression in the law and society which had not been adequately addressed in existing scholarship (Crenshaw, Gotanda, Peller, and

Thomas, 1995). This effort, which began in the 1970s, has produced a substantial body of legal scholarship seeking to provide this critical vocabulary (for a review of the origins and development of CRT in legal studies, see Tate, 1997). According to Matsuda and colleagues, there are six unifying themes that define the movement:

1. Critical race theory recognizes that racism is endemic to American life.
2. Critical race theory expresses skepticism toward dominant legal claims of neutrality, objectivity, colorblindness, and meritocracy.
3. Critical race theory challenges ahistoricism and insists on a contextual/historical analysis of the law … Critical race theorists … adopt a stance that presumes that racism has contributed to all contemporary manifestations of group advantage and disadvantage.
4. Critical race theory insists on recognition of the experiential knowledge of people of color and our communities of origin in analyzing law and society.
5. Critical race theory is interdisciplinary.
6. Critical race theory works toward the end of eliminating racial oppression as part of the broader goal of ending all forms of oppression. (Matsuda et al., 1993, p. 6)

It was upon this framework outlined in legal studies that Ladson-Billings and Tate (1995) built in their article. Since its publication, several other scholars have written about the application of CRT to education. However, in the midst of the burgeoning CRT movement, both Ladson-Billings (1999a) and Tate (1999) have warned critical race scholars in education against moving too quickly away from the foundation provided by legal studies. In fact, Tate (1999) argues that one criterion for CRT scholarship in education is that it should "build on and expand beyond the scholarship found in the critical race legal literature" (p. 268). The purpose of this chapter is to examine the literature on CRT in education that has developed over the past decade, keeping this criterion in mind. We seek to assess the progress made in educational scholarship with respect to CRT and to suggest where we might go from here.

Using the keywords "critical race theory in education" and "critical race theory and education," we conducted a search in several education, social science and legal databases—ERIC, Education Abstracts, Wilson Social Science and Lexis-Nexis. We limited our search to literature published between 1995 and 2003. Given that the article by Ladson-Billings and Tate was published in 1995, it was unlikely that work on CRT in education would appear before that time. The search with the descriptor "critical race theory in education" revealed 44 hits in ERIC and Wilson and 125 hits in Lexis-Nexis. "Critical race theory and education" revealed 38 hits in ERIC and Wilson and 125 hits in Lexis-Nexis. Not surprisingly, there was a great deal of overlap between the two searches. Several scholars did not draw explicitly on constructs outlined in CRT scholarship in the law, although most of the articles in some manner alluded to the legal antecedents of CRT. For this reason, we have not incorporated into this review all of the articles found in our search. Rather, we have included articles that built on or were clearly tied to the legal literature and tenets of CRT in education as suggested by Ladson-Billings and Tate. It is important to note, however, that the articles found in the Lexis-Nexis search are law review articles wherein legal scholars examine educational issues within a CRT framework. Hence, the articles selected from the Lexis-Nexis search represent the ways in which legal scholars use CRT to analyze educational issues, as distinguished from the work of CRT scholars in education or scholars in education who utilize CRT. Thus, we describe two slightly different but closely related bodies of literature in this chapter—one from education and the other from law.

In the first section of the review, we introduce the reader to legal constructs that have been used in educational scholarship. For the sake of clarity, we address each construct separately, describing how the construct was defined originally in the legal literature and how it has subsequently been employed to understand educational inequity. However, we acknowledge that the separation of these constructs is more for the sake of organization than representative of clear distinctions. The constructs that we describe are, in fact, overlapping and supporting. In the second section, we attempt to illustrate the interrelated nature of these ideas by returning to the legal literature for an examination of cases relevant to education. Specifically, we examine CRT scholarship on the *Brown v. Board of Education* decision, as well as more recent legal cases involving affirmative action in higher education. The analyses of these cases draw on the roots of CRT scholarship in the law and, therefore, provide an image of the theoretical structure on which Ladson-Billings and Tate (1995) argued that scholarship in education should build. Finally, as part of our review of CRT scholarship, we also address critiques of the perspective. Many of these critiques arose in response to CRT scholarship in legal studies. However, insofar as CRT in education builds on its legal roots, these concerns regarding the legal scholarship should also be considered with respect to the study of education.

Critical Race Theory in Education
Voice

One of the central tenets of CRT demands the "recognition of the experiential knowledge of people of color" (Matsuda et al., 1993, p. 6). This recognition is the basis of the theme of "voice" that runs throughout CRT in legal studies. Calmore (1995) describes CRT as tending "toward a very personal expression that allows our experiences and lessons, learned as people of color, to convey the knowledge we possess in a way that is empowering to us, and, it is hoped, ultimately empowering to those on whose behalf we act" (p. 321).

This, then, is the essence of "voice"—the assertion and acknowledgment of the importance of the personal and community experiences of people of color as sources of knowledge. In this way, CRT scholars argue, we should "shift the frame" (Crenshaw, 1989) or "look to the bottom" (Matsuda, 1995) and begin to value the knowledge of people of color. "Those who have experienced discrimination speak with a special voice to which we should listen" (Matsuda, 1995, p. 63). Thus, CRT scholars believe and utilize personal narratives and other stories as valid forms of "evidence" and thereby challenge a "numbers only" approach to documenting inequity or discrimination, which tends to certify discrimination from a quantitative rather than a qualitative perspective.

We should make clear, however, that the use of the term "voice" in the singular does not imply that there exists a single common voice for all persons of color. The stories of individuals will differ. However, Delgado (1990) suggests that, although there is not one common voice, there is a common experience of racism that structures the stories of people of color and allows for the use of the term "voice."

One important function of voice and stories in CRT scholarship is to counteract the stories of the dominant group (Delgado, 1989). The dominant group tells stories designed to "remind it of its identity in relation to outgroups and provide a form of shared reality in which its own superior position is seen as natural" (Delgado, 1989, p. 240). One function of voice scholarship is to subvert that reality. According to Lawrence (1995), "We must learn to trust our own senses, feelings, and experiences, to give them authority, even (or especially) in the face of dominant accounts of social reality that claim universality" (p. 338). Thus, voice scholarship provides a "counterstory" to counteract or challenge the dominant story.

Much of the literature on critical race theory in education has focused on this particular element of the CRT legal literature. In fact, according to Parker and Lynn (2002), a main goal of CRT is to use storytelling and narrative to examine race and racism. Similarly, Solórzano and Yosso (2002) have outlined what they call a "critical race methodology"—a methodology that focuses on the stories and experiences of students of color. They propose that the counterstories offered by students of color can be used as a "tool for exposing, analyzing, and challenging the majoritarian stories of racial privilege" (p. 32).

This attention to voice has been employed in educational research in various ways. For example, Fernandez (2002) presents the counterstory of Pablo, a Latino college student reflecting on his experiences in a Chicago high school. His account of his experiences at the predominantly Latino school includes descriptions of low expectations on the part of teachers, a school-wide focus on discipline, and a lack of academic rigor in the curriculum, even for college-bound students. Similarly, Teranishi's (2002) study of Filipino students in California includes accounts of negative stereotypes, lowered expectations on the part of teachers, and tracking into vocational rather than college prep courses. Although these studies are not unique in their focus on the views and perspectives of students of color (e.g., Fine, 1991), they are of note here because the authors' attention to the experiences of these students is set within a CRT framework. According to Teranishi, "CRT was instrumental in providing a voice for students who are otherwise not heard, thus allowing students to provide their own perspectives on their educational experiences" (p. 152).

Similar studies have been conducted with students of color in higher education. For example, Solórzano (2001) examines the campus climate experienced by African American students at three "Predominantly White Research I" (PWI) universities. The stories recounted by the students of their classroom experiences include feelings of invisibility, low expectations expressed by both students and faculty, and assumptions by others about how they entered the university. The students' stories also depict their struggle with self-doubt and isolation as a result of the daily "microagressions"—subtle, automatic or unconscious racial insults—that they experienced.

The stories of these students were similar in many ways to those of Chicana and Chicano graduate students also studied by Solórzano (1998). The students in Solórzano's study of Ford Fellows describe feeling out of place in graduate school. Their descriptions reflect a lack of "voice" insofar as they felt that their experiences and perspectives were ignored and invalidated. They also describe lowered expectations—"expectations that resulted in stigmatization and differential treatment" (p. 130). As Solórzano (2001) notes, these students' stories serve to counter the dominant discourse. "Their descriptions of racial microaggressions challenge the anti-affirmative action ideology of college as an equal, colorblind, and race-neutral institution" (p. 72).

Another use of voice in the CRT literature has involved examining the experiences of scholars of color in higher education. For example, Delgado Bernal and Villalpando (2002) describe what they call an "apartheid of knowledge" in which the dominant discourse within the mainstream research community devalues the scholarship of faculty of color. Through a form of "epistemological racism," the scholarship of faculty of color is relegated to the margins (Villalpando and Delgado Bernal, 2002). Because the scholarship of faculty of color often focuses on issues related to race and ethnicity, Delgado Bernal and Villalpando contend that it is deemed by the academy to be "illegitimate, biased, or overly subjective" (p. 171). Similarly, Tate (1994) recounts his experience with colleagues who have judged voice scholarship to be "problematic" for its perceived lack of neutrality or objectivity. However, despite this tendency on the part of the academy to silence the voices of scholars of color, Tate contends that attention to voice is important:

Remarks about our experiences as people of color will not be seriously considered in academic circles ... However, for those scholars of color dedicated to improving the experience of African American children in urban schools, there is no choice. We must continue the battle to have our experiences and voice heard in academic discourse. Our voices provide stories that help others think in different ways about complex, context-dependent domains like schools and communities. (Tate, 1994, p. 264)

Thus, the construct of "voice" has been used in various ways in the educational literature. Some scholars have focused on the voices of students of color, describing their perceptions and experiences at both the K–12 and university levels. This literature reveals both individual-level "microaggressions" in the form of lowered teacher expectations and more macro-level forms of institutional racism in which school-wide programs lack the courses and rigor necessary for students to succeed in higher education. A second line of scholarship has focused on how the voices of scholars of color are silenced in the academy.

Both these lines of work are important for what they reveal about the micro and macro systems of inequity in education; but we would argue that, in some cases, scholarship in education has only begun to scratch the surface in terms of the use of the full explanatory power of CRT. The construct of voice is important. As Ladson-Billings and Tate (1995) argue, "the voice of people of color is required for a complete analysis of the educational system. ...Without authentic voices of people of color it is doubtful that we can say or know anything useful about education in their communities" (p. 58). However, we submit that it is not enough simply to tell the stories of people of color. Rather, the educational experiences revealed through those stories must then be subjected to deeper analysis using the CRT lens. Furthermore, CRT mandates that social activism should be a part of any CRT project. To that end, the stories must move us to action and to the qualitative and material improvement of the educational experiences of people of color.

Duncan's (2002a) ethnographic study of black male students at City High School provides an example of such an analysis. His attention to the stories of black male students can be understood as an example of voice scholarship. However, he also includes the perspectives of others in the school. This makes it possible to juxtapose the dominant discourse represented in the voices of other students and faculty with the counterstory told by the black male students.

Duncan (2002a) then uses the CRT literature to analyze these differences and the condition of the black male students at City High School. He builds on the legal scholarship of Richard Delgado (1995), specifically Delgado's conception of certain groups as being "beyond love." According to Delgado, "Blacks, especially, the black poor, have so few chances, so little interaction with majority society, that they might as well be exiles, outcasts, permanent black sheep who will never be permitted into the fold. Majority society has, in effect, written them off" (p. 49). They are "beyond love." Duncan uses this same construct to describe the status of black male students in his study, noting that other students and faculty at the school have written off black males in the same manner. The exclusion and marginalization of black male students from the school is taken not as a cause for concern but as a "predictable, albeit unfortunate, outcome of a reasonably fair system" (p. 134). In this way, Duncan's use of the CRT legal literature to go beyond simply reporting students' stories creates a powerful analysis of the schooling conditions of students in his study. In sections that follow, we outline other constructs from the legal literature that could be used similarly.

Restrictive versus Expansive Views of Equality

According to Crenshaw (1988), there are two visions of equality—the restrictive and the expansive—present in antidiscrimination law. Crenshaw defines the two views:

> The expansive view stresses equality as a result, and looks to real consequences for African Americans. It interprets the objective of anti-discrimination law as the eradication of the substantive conditions of Black subordination and attempts to enlist the institutional power of the courts to further the national goal of eradicating the effects of racial oppression. The restrictive view, which exists side by side with this expansive view, treats equality as a process, downplaying the significance of actual outcomes. The primary objective of anti-discrimination law, according to this vision, is to prevent future wrongdoing rather than to redress present manifestations of past injustice. "Wrongdoing," moreover is seen primarily as isolated actions against individuals rather than as societal policy against an entire group. (pp. 1341–1342)

She goes on to point out that the tension between the two visions is present throughout antidiscrimination law.

Within education, Rousseau and Tate (2003) have used the restrictive versus expansive constructs to examine the beliefs of high school mathematics teachers about the nature of equity. When asked about their response to the needs of an increasingly diverse student population, the teachers in the study universally described "treating students equally" as their approach to ensuring equity. Rousseau and Tate argue that this approach represents a restrictive understanding of the nature of equity, viewing equity as equality of treatment rather than outcomes. The teachers did not connect the concept of equity to the achievement of students of color in their classes (achievement which was substantially lower on average than the achievement of white students in the same classes). Rousseau and Tate posit that it was, in part, the teachers' restrictive view of the nature of equity that prevented them from reflecting deeply on their instructional practices and on the differential effects of those practices on students of color. Because the teachers viewed equity as equal treatment, inequitable results were not a catalyst for reflection. As long as the teachers believed that they had treated students equally, they did not question the disproportionately negative outcomes for students of color.

The contrast between the restrictive and expansive visions can be an important framework for analyzing the nature of equity and inequity in education. We will return to this construct in a subsequent section when we examine the impact of the *Brown* decision. At this point, we simply note that, as indicated in Rousseau and Tate's (2003) study, the distinctions between equality of process and equality of outcome can call into question many practices of teachers in schools. In particular, a focus on achieving an expansive vision of equality would render problematic the ideal of colorblindness.

The Problem with Colorblindness

Crenshaw et al. (1995) note that integration, assimilation, and colorblindness have become the official norms of racial enlightenment. The dominant discourse positions colorblindness as an ideal. The writings of several scholars within CRT in legal studies seek to problematize this construction of colorblindness.

> CRT indicates how and why the contemporary "jurisprudence of colorblindness" is not only the expression of a particular color-consciousness, but the product of a deeply politicized choice. ... The appeal to colorblindness can thus be said to serve as part of an ideological strategy by which the current Court obscures its active role in sustaining hierarchies of racial power. (Crenshaw et al., 1995, p. xxviii)

Like Crenshaw et al.,Gotanda (1991) also asserts that the colorblind ideal in the law serves to maintain racial subordination. In his analysis, Gotanda proposes that the Supreme Court uses the concept of race in different ways. One of those ways is what Gotanda refers to as "formal-race":

> Formal-race refers to socially constructed formal categories. Black and white are seen as neutral, apolitical descriptions reflecting merely "skin color" or country of origin. Formal-race is unrelated to ability, disadvantage, or moral culpability. Moreover, formal-race categories are unconnected to social attributes such as culture, education, wealth, or language. This "unconnectedness" is the defining characteristic of formal-race. (Gotanda, 1991, p. 4)

Gotanda goes on to suggest that colorblind analyses of the law use "race" to mean formal-race. Because formal-race is disconnected from social realities, a colorblind analysis "often fails to recognize connections between the race of an individual and the real social conditions underlying litigation or other constitutional dispute" (p. 7). He notes that this disconnection to social realities places severe limitations on the possible remedies for injustice and thereby maintains a system of white privilege. Thus, the lack of historical or social context is one of the mechanisms through which colorblindness can support inequity.

Within the literature in education, Taylor's (1999) analysis of the Tennessee State University (TSU) desegregation case illustrates the disconnected nature of the court's treatment of race. According to Taylor, TSU was deemed a problem with respect to desegregation as a result of its historically black student population, whereas the status of the predominantly white state schools was left unquestioned. He argues that this focus on TSU as the crux of the desegregation process represents a failure to consider the historical context. "By ... refusing to act on the full ramifications of certain social and economic realities faced by blacks in Tennessee for hundreds of years, the court reveals no contextualized picture" (p. 196). Using the principles of neutrality and choice to buttress its position, the court applied the formal-race definition described by Gotanda (1991).

A similar manifestation of "formal-race" colorblindness can be seen in Rousseau and Tate's (2003) study of high school mathematics teachers. The teachers in their study demonstrated a similar acontextual view of race. In particular, the teachers refused to acknowledge race-related patterns in achievement and the potential role of racism in the underachievement of students of color. They either denied that race-related differences in achievement existed in their classrooms or asserted that the reasons for any differences were related to socioeconomic status rather than to the impact of systemic racism in the school and school district. The authors argue that this colorblind stance, in conjunction with a view of equality as a process, prevented the teachers from reflecting on their own practices and their role in the production of the underachievement of their students of color.

The pernicious impact of colorblindness is also evident in subtle microaggressions against students of color. Patricia J. Williams, another founding member of the CRT movement, examines how this notion of colorblindness manifests in seemingly innocent schooling discourse, and the ways in which this ideology covertly pathologizes students of color. Williams retells an incident that occurred at her son's preschool. His teachers reported to her that they suspected her son had a problem with his vision and suggested that she take him to an ophthalmologist. According to his teacher, her son was unable to identify colors. Williams recalls that in conversations with her son in which she asked him to identify the colors of various objects, his persistent response was indeed "I don't know," or, "What difference does it make?" After careful reflection and observation of his behavior at school, Williams realized that, with only one African American child attending the preschool, his teacher had commented about "color" (meaning skin color) being unimportant, with the pat liberal statement that "it didn't matter ... whether a person is black or white, or red or green or blue," when the white children argued over whether African Americans could play "good guys" (p. 3). The irony, as Williams points out, is that her son's teacher had interpreted his internalization of her own colorblind discourse as a physical malady. The fact that he refused to acknowledge color (as he had been taught, both explicitly and implicitly) had essentially become *his* problem. Williams suggests that the larger discourse on race and the insistence on colorblindness is not necessarily for purely benevolent reasons. Rather, race, within the scheme of whiteness, is seen as a malady. That is, if we accept the notion of whiteness as normal, then any person who is *not white* is abnormal. Thus, within polite, middle class mores, it is impolite to *see* when someone is *different*, abnormal, and thus, *not white*. Hence it is better to ignore, or become colorblind, than to notice that people of color have the physical malady of skin color, or *not whiteness*. Similarly, Thompson (1998) points out that "politely pretending not to notice students' color makes no sense unless being of different colors is somehow shameful" (p. 524). When students begin to internalize this shame or sense of abnormality, colorblindness can become a form of microaggression.

The critique of colorblindness can be viewed as a part of a larger critique of liberalism that is characteristic of CRT. According to Ladson-Billings (1999b), "the liberal discourse is deeply invested in the current system. It relies on the law and the structure of the system to provide equal opportunity for all" (p. 231). CRT calls into question this faith in the system as an instrument of justice. In addition to the challenge to the liberal ideal of colorblindness, this critique of the liberal paradigm is reflected in the literature on CRT in education in various ways.

For example, Ladson-Billings and Tate (1995) have questioned the efficacy of multicultural education as a means of obtaining justice for students of color. They argue that "the multicultural paradigm is mired in liberal ideology that offers no radical change in the current order" (p. 62). Their critique of multiculturalism is similar to CRT scholars' critique of incremental civil rights law. Thus, one of the commonalities between CRT in law and education is a critique both of the inequities of the status quo and of a liberal ideology that fails to advance the cause of justice for people of color. It is important to note that Ladson-Billings and Tate's critique of multiculturalism should be seen as a "call to action" rather than a dismissal of the import of and need for more inclusive schooling. That is, what has often been presented as multicultural education has generally been a superficial "celebration of difference" through "foods and festivals" activities rather than an examination of how "difference" serves to disadvantage some and advantage others.

Duncan's (2002b) CRT analysis of his experiences teaching an undergraduate methods course provides another example of a critique of liberalism. Duncan argues that the students in his class (who were all white) demonstrated a "false empathy" for the African American children at the field site. False empathy occurs when "a white believes he or she is identifying with a person of color, but in fact is doing so only in a slight, superficial way" (Delgado, 1996, p. 12). According to Delgado (1996), this paternalistic form of empathy is a common characteristic of white liberals. Duncan argues that the students in his class held this attitude toward the children at the field site. His students "understood their work as helping a group of unfortunate, underprivileged children take advantage of the offerings of a fundamentally just society" (p. 91). Having identified this false empathy as one of the factors blocking students' reflection, Duncan changed the organization of the course and the nature of the experiences he provided for his students. Beyond a merely theoretical critique of liberalism, the analysis of his experiences provided the basis for a change in practice.

Summary

In the first section of this chapter, we reviewed scholarship in education that has employed critical race theory in an effort to understand the nature of inequity in schools and schooling. The articles discussed in this first section were chosen because they reflect a direct link (or at least a clear potential connection) to the legal literature in which critical race theory originated. The body of literature that has developed in education over the past ten years has drawn on a variety of constructs from legal studies, including the property value of whiteness, voice, restrictive versus expansive visions of antidiscrimination law, and the problem of colorblindness. In the second section of this article, we shift the focus back to the roots of CRT as we examine how this framework can be used to analyze legal cases related to education.

Critical Race Theory in the Law: an Examination of Legal Cases Affecting Education

Brown v. Board of Education

With the recent commemoration of the fiftieth anniversary of the Supreme Court's decision in *Brown v. Board of Education*, it seems appropriate to examine this landmark desegregation case through the lens offered by critical race theory. In 1954, the Supreme Court ruled that the "separate but equal" doctrine that had been legally established in the 1896 *Plessy v. Ferguson* case could no longer be used to justify segregated schools for African American and white children. While the *Brown* decision is one of the best-recognized U.S. Supreme Court rulings, and one with a far-reaching impact on education, critical race theorists (and others) have come to question the nature of the effects of the *Brown* decision on the educational experiences of African American students. Rather than viewing *Brown* as a move to establish racial equality and bring about greater racial justice, critical race scholars have examined both the factors influencing the decision itself and the structures of racial inequity that *Brown* served to reconfigure rather than dismantle.

Derrick Bell (2004) has described Brown as a "magnificent mirage"—an example of the "unfulfilled hopes for racial reform." In order to understand those unfulfilled hopes, it is important to examine briefly the current status of schooling for students of color. Fifty years after the *Brown* decision to end de jure school segregation, reports indicate that growing numbers of African American and Latino students attend predominantly minority schools. For example, during the 2001–2002 school year, nearly 63 percent of black students in Michigan attended schools that were 90 to 100 percent minority (Orfield and Lee, 2004). The picture of increased segregation is even more pronounced in urban school districts. On the eve of the fiftieth anniversary of *Brown*, a Memphis newspaper reported that nearly 75 percent of Memphis city schools were at least 90 percent African American, and over half were at least 99 percent African American (McKenzie, 2004). Latino students are also attending increasingly segregated schools. According to Orfield and Lee (2004), over 58 percent of Latino students in the state of New York attended highly segregated schools (90–100 percent minority) during the 2001–2002 school year. Moreover, this racial segregation in schooling is tied to differential educational opportunity. "The vast majority of intensely segregated minority schools face conditions of concentrated poverty, which are powerfully related to unequal educational opportunity. Students in segregated minority schools face conditions that students in segregated white schools seldom experience" (Orfield and Lee, 2004, p. 2). In fact, according to Bell (2004), "the statistics on resegregation ... painfully underscore the fact that many black and Hispanic children are enrolled in schools as separate and probably more unequal than those their parents and grandparents attended under the era of 'separate but equal' " (p. 114).

What, then, can account for the failure of *Brown* to live up to the vision of equal educational opportunity? Part of the answer lies in the factors contributing to the *Brown* decision. Derrick Bell (1980) has described *Brown* as a prime example of the "interest convergence" principle. According to Bell (2004), the principle of interest convergence has two parts. First, "the interest of blacks in achieving racial equality will be accommodated only when that interest converges with the interests of whites in policy-making positions. This convergence is far more important for gaining relief than the degree of harm suffered by blacks or the character of proof offered to prove that harm" (2004, p. 69).

A second rule of interest convergence holds that "even when the interest-convergence results in an effective racial remedy, that remedy will be abrogated at the point that policy makers fear the remedial policy is threatening the superior societal status of whites" (2004, p. 69). Bell refers to these tacit agreements that occur when interests converge as "silent covenants." He argues that *Brown* represents an example of a silent covenant based on interest convergence insofar as *Brown*'s ostensible move toward racial equality and civil rights for African Americans was only possible as the result of a confluence of domestic and international factors. Specifically, Bell argues that policy makers at the time of *Brown* were motivated by their own self-interest rather than by a desire for racial justice. In the midst of the Cold War, policy makers believed there was a need to improve the image of U.S. democracy, which had been tarnished internationally by pictures of racial injustice. Dismantling U.S. apartheid was an important means to the end of negotiating and working internationally, particularly in newly independent African nations. Furthermore, given the United States' opposition to communism, and its contentious and hostile relationship with communist nations like Cuba, the Soviet Union and China, the fact that democracy and freedom was not enjoyed by *all* citizens of the United States was highly problematic for a government attempting to position itself against those "red" nations. Bell argues that the *Brown* decision was one way to accomplish the desired positioning within the international arena. Thus, the basic civil rights represented in *Brown* were conferred because they converged with the self-interests of U.S. foreign policy.

Interest convergence offers an explanation not only for the *Brown* decision itself but also for the effects of the desegregation efforts that followed the ruling. According to Morris (2001), the St. Louis desegregation plan illustrates the operation of interest convergence. Under the desegregation plan, African American students in St. Louis were offered the option of attending schools in the surrounding, predominantly white county districts. At the same time, magnet programs were provided in the St. Louis district to entice white students to return to city schools. These between-district transfers were intended to provide greater racial balance in both city and county schools. However, although many African American students took advantage of the transfers offered to county schools, far fewer white students went to the magnet schools in the city.

The St. Louis example actually provides evidence for both parts of Bell's interest convergence principle (Morris, 2001). In particular, Morris notes that the white county schools have been the primary beneficiaries of the desegregation plan through increases in overall revenue. In this way, the self-interest of the largely white school systems was served by taking in African American students. Moreover, the relative failure of the city magnet schools to draw large numbers of white students illustrates the second rule of interest convergence—the impact of a threat to the social status of whites:

> Although the integration of Black students into predominantly White county schools might have represented to African Americans a step toward greater social and educational justice, many White families hesitated to disrupt their status by sending their children to the city's

magnet schools just so that racial balancing can occur. For these parents, racial balance and equality are secondary to ensuring a quality education for their children. (Morris, 2001, p. 592)

In conjunction with its origins in white self-interest, Tate, Ladson-Billings, and Grant (1993) argue that *Brown* failed to substantively improve the education of African American students because it represented a restrictive rather than expansive view of equality. Building on Crenshaw's (1988) constructs, Tate and colleagues suggest that *Brown* reflected a restrictive view, focusing on numerical equivalency and equality of process rather than on the actual educational outcomes for students of color. Insofar as the Supreme Court equated desegregation with equal educational opportunity, an expansive vision, attending to the actual educational results for students, was not pursued. By focusing strictly on the process of physical desegregation, the *Brown* court neglected other strategies with the potential to achieve truly equitable educational outcomes for all students. "What was needed was a vision of education that challenged the fundamental structure of schools that reproduced the same inequitable social hierarchies that existed in society" (Tate et al., 1993, p. 267). That the *Brown* decision failed to disrupt these structures is evidenced by the enduring inequities in the educational system.

Specifically, according to Harris (1993), Brown failed to challenge the property value of whiteness. According to Harris, Brown's

dialectical contradiction was that it dismantled an old form of whiteness as property while simultaneously permitting its reemergence in a more subtle form. White privilege accorded as a legal right was rejected, but de facto white privilege not mandated by law remained unaddressed. In failing to clearly expose the real inequities produced by segregation, the status quo of substantive disadvantage was ratified as an accepted and acceptable baseline—a neutral state operating to the disadvantage of Blacks long after de jure segregation has ceased to do so. In accepting substantial inequality as a neutral baseline, a new form of whiteness as property was condoned. (1993, p. 1753)

Thus, Harris argues that part of Brown's "mixed legacy" was its failure to dismantle the structures that had produced and supported school segregation in the first place. An example of this failure can be seen in the St. Louis desegregation plan described by Morris (2001). Morris argues that the effects of the property value of whiteness are demonstrated by white parents' reluctance to send their children to St. Louis magnet schools. Despite the quality of the city's magnet schools, the fact that they were predominantly African American reduced the perceived value of the education that they offered. For white parents, "their children's attendance at predominantly Black schools, despite a particular school's quality, would have represented a loss of 'White' status" (Morris, 2001, p. 593). Moreover, by promoting an image of the superior education provided in county schools, the advertising used to draw African American students to the county districts reified this perception that the "property" of city schools was of lower educational value. This devaluing of the predominantly black city schools served to uphold the perceived value of the educational "property" that belonged primarily to whites.

While the goal of desegregation was ostensibly to provide more equitable educational opportunities for all students, the questionable success of such policies is related, at least in part, to the ongoing salience of racism and white privilege. Bell (2004) argues that the Brown decision "substituted one mantra for another: where separate was once equal, 'separate' would be now categorically unequal. ... By doing nothing more than rewiring the rhetoric of equality, the Brown court foreclosed the possibility of recognizing racism as a broadly shared cultural condition" (p. 197). Thus, the property value of whiteness was maintained, and the promise of substantive change in the education of students of color remained unfulfilled.

Affirmative Action

A similar analysis involving the property value of whiteness has been employed to examine the status of affirmative action in higher education. Legal challenges to race-based admission policies generally focus on "unfair" advantages given to students of color in the admissions process. Filed by white students who were not granted admission, these challenges use the rhetoric of "merit" to argue that policies giving admission points to students of color violate the Equal Protection Clause of the U.S. Constitution and lead to "less qualified" applicants (i.e., applicants with lower test scores or grade point averages) being admitted ahead of the white plaintiffs. However, it is noteworthy that the plaintiffs in such cases do not challenge the admission of other white students with lower test scores and GPAs, nor do they question admission points given for other factors (legacy, high school quality, geographic location, etc.) that are more likely to benefit white applicants. Rather, the action to file suit based on racial discrimination in essence served to protect the property value of whiteness by challenging opportunities provided to people of color—opportunities that were perceived to threaten that which was due to whites. Harris (1993) contends that such suits are based on the premise that "the expectation of white privilege is valid, and that the legal protection of that expectation is warranted. This premise legitimates prior assumptions of the right to ongoing racialized privilege and is another manifestation of whiteness as property" (p. 1769).

According to Harris (1993), the protection of the property interest of whiteness in affirmative action cases is accomplished through appeal to the colorblind norm. In *Hopwood vs. Texas*, for example, a panel of the Fifth Circuit Court found that "considering race or ethnicity in admissions decisions is always unconstitutional, even when intended to combat perceived effects of a hostile environment, to remedy past discrimination, or to promote diversity" (Bell, 2004, p. 145). Pursley (2003) writes that the disavowal of the use of race in *Hopwood* was a quintessential example of the application of colorblindness. By refusing to allow universities to "consider" race, the court was attempting to establish a "race-neutral" approach to college admissions. However, CRT scholars have argued that the appeal to colorblindness is far from racially neutral and in the best interests of persons of color; instead, it supports the operation of white privilege (Crenshaw et al., 1995; Gotanda, 1991). For example, in examining the backlash in Washington state against affirmative action, Taylor (2000) notes that the colorblind approach in fact masks the centrality of white privilege—"the multitude of benefits extended to the majority population by virtue of group membership." He argues that the insistence on race-neutral language negates the social and historical context and leaves unchallenged the privileged and oppressive position of whiteness.

Critiques of CRT

Given its focus on contentious issues of race and racism, it is not surprising that CRT has been the subject of criticism by scholars and others (see Tate's chapter in this volume for an additional description of reactions to CRT). In particular, scholars in the legal field have criticized two major tenets of CRT: storytelling and racial realism (Farber and Sherry, 1993; Posner, 1995; Powell, 1993; Tushnet, 1992). While mainstream legal scholars acknowledge that legal storytelling can be a persuasive explanatory device, they have been critical of "outsider" narratives (i.e., stories by CRT scholars and scholars of color) as taking liberties with "truth." Moreover, critics of CRT's use of storytelling in the law argue that these "outsider" narratives lack intellectual rigor, which makes evaluating them difficult (Farber and Sherry, 1993; Posner, 1995; Tushnet, 1992). Although these critiques are in response to legal storytelling, they are important to acknowledge in the examination of CRT scholarship in education. As Ladson-Billings (in this volume) notes, the stories that we tell in education should serve to situate issues in "more robust and powerful contexts." We should not use storytelling just for the sake of telling a story.

Another aspect of CRT in legal studies that has fallen under scrutiny is Bell's (1992) Racial Realism Theory, which contends that racism is permanent, and that racial equality is not a realistic goal. John A. Powell (1993) responds with an insightful critique of this view. Powell finds Bell's claim that equality for African Americans is not quickly on the horizon probable and worth serious consideration, but he argues that Bell's abandonment of the possibility of equality is a message of despair (p. 550). At first glance, Powell's critique of Bell seems appropriate. When he wrote the article in 1993, the United States was just a year into Bill Clinton's first term, and racial equality and opportunity seemed promising indeed. However, two events during Clinton's presidency suggest that Bell's Racial Realism Theory was not far off base: Clinton's nomination of Lani Guinier as head of the Civil Rights Division of the Department of Justice and his subsequent withdrawal of the nomination in 1993; and the administration's silence and lack of response during the Rwanda genocide in 1994. More recently, the tragedy in New Orleans after Hurricane Katrina highlights the extent to which racism affects even "natural" disasters. Thus, while racial equality on the surface appears to be something that we should hope will come to fruition, the reality is that it has not.

Finally, Darder and Torres (2002) offer a thought-provoking examination of race and racism in their book, edited with Marta Boltadano, *The Critical Pedagogy Reader* (2002). In their chapter, "Shattering the 'Race' Lens: Toward a Critical Theory of Racism," Darder and Torres critique what they describe as an "overwhelming tendency" among social scientists and progressive scholars to focus on "notions of race" (p. 246). They suggest that a "critical language and conceptual apparatus that makes racism the central category of analysis in our understanding of racialized inequality while simultaneously encompassing the multiple social expressions of racism" is more useful than focusing solely on race (p. 260). Certainly it is important to consider the complexity of racism as beyond phenotype; however, one limitation of their critique is that it reduces discussions and examinations of "race" to analyses that attribute racialized inequality entirely to skin-color differences. In doing so, their critique misses the important work of CRT scholars—in both education and the legal field—who examine the ways in which the social construction of race is deployed in "liberal" and "race-neutral" educational policies and practices. This is a critical point, given that a central tenet of CRT is to examine how whiteness as property as an ideological and oppressive construct perpetuates inequality through ostensibly "colorblind" policies and practices. In this sense, CRT goes beyond race and racism as a product of skin color and phenotype to analyze how ways of being, knowledge construction, power, and opportunity are constructed along and conflated with "race."

Conclusion

We have sought in this review to examine the literature that has developed over the past decade on critical race theory in education. At the same time, however, we have attempted to remain grounded in the legal literature from which CRT originated. As a result, we have intentionally not tried to delineate clearly where the legal literature ends and the educational scholarship on CRT begins (in some cases, such distinctions would be impossible). As we seek to assess where we in education should go from here with respect to critical race theory, we must now highlight some differences between CRT scholarship in the law and the work that has been done thus far in education.

In some ways, the scholarship in education that has been described here is very consistent with the legal scholarship on CRT. Several of the tenets of CRT outlined by legal scholars are reflected in the work reviewed in this chapter. The educational scholarship we have described positions race at the center of analysis and reflects the recognition of racism as endemic to U.S. society. It questions mainstream discourse centered on neutrality, objectivity, color-blindness and merit. It insists on historical and contextual analyses. And it values the voices of people of color. With respect to these elements, there is a clear connection between CRT scholarship in education and its antecedents in legal studies. However, the other two tenets outlined by Matsuda et al. (1993) have been less clearly articulated in CRT scholarship in education.

One of the six characteristics of CRT in legal studies is its interdisciplinary nature. According to Matsuda et al. (1993), "this eclecticism allows critical race theory to examine and incorporate those aspects of a methodology or theory that effectively enable our voice and advance the cause of racial justice" (p. 6). We would argue that this quality of CRT scholarship in legal studies should not be overlooked in the application of CRT to education. Much of the literature on CRT in education has focused on the theory's application to "qualitative" research. Qualitative methodologies, such as ethnography, are certainly consistent with particular elements of CRT. However, CRT is probably more accurately described as a problem-centered rather than qualitative approach. Within the problem-centered approach, the problem determines the method, not the other way around (Tate and Rousseau, 2002). As Matsuda and colleagues suggest, the goal of using any method is to further the cause of racial justice. In this sense, CRT scholarship in education is neither inherently qualitative nor quantitative. Rather, such scholarship should employ any means necessary to address the problem of inequity in education.

The sixth tenet outlined by Matsuda et al. (1993) states that "critical race theory *works* toward the end of eliminating racial oppression as part of the broader goal of ending all forms of oppression" (p. 6; emphasis added). One of the core values of the movement, as described in the legal literature, is the theme of active struggle. This theme recurs throughout writings on CRT. Crenshaw et al. (1995) describe one of the common interests that cut across critical race scholarship as the "desire to not merely understand the vexed bond between law and racial power but to *change* it" (p. xiii; emphasis in original). Matsuda et al. (1993) describe CRT as "work that involves both action and reflection. It is informed by active struggle and in turn informs that struggle" (p. 3). In fact, Lawrence (1992) suggests that this relationship between reflection and social action is so symbiotic that if one is sacrificed, the other immediately suffers. For example, CRT founder Derrick Bell received national attention for his two-year protest of Harvard Law School's lack of women of color on its faculty. In this way, active struggle against inequity is an integral part of CRT. This is not simply a theoretical stance. There is a commitment to change and to action inherent in the theoretical position. Calmore (1995) states that CRT "finds its finest expression when it ... serves as 'fuel for social transformation.' In that sense, our efforts must, while directed by critical theory, extend beyond critique and theory to lend support to the struggle to relieve the extraordinary suffering and racist oppression that is commonplace in the life experiences of too many people of color" (p. 317).

This element of CRT in legal studies must be translated into CRT in education. According to Ladson-Billings (1999a), "adopting and adapting CRT as a framework for educational equity means that we will have to expose racism in education *and* propose radical solutions for addressing it" (p. 27; emphasis in original). Thus, in addition to uncovering the myriad ways that racism continues to marginalize and oppress people of color, identifying strategies to combat these oppressive forces and acting upon those strategies is an important next step within CRT. However, in our review of the CRT literature in education, we found that scholars have not yet implemented this aspect of CRT.[1]

Although a number of CRT scholars in education offer recommendations for changes in educational policy and practice, the extent to which these recommendations are carried out, either by the recommender or others, is not clear. Our call to action must move beyond mere recommendations. However, dismantling years of inequitable schooling practices and policies with a large constituency (or constituencies) takes a concerted, organized effort. CRT scholars in education have yet to organize even among ourselves. Perhaps a first step would be for CRT scholars in education to come together as our colleagues in the legal field have done and to plan strategies that address the persistent and pernicious educational inequity in our communities.

The work of ensuring equity in schools and schooling involves continued study of the legal literature and careful thought about its application to education (Ladson-Billings, 1999a; Tate, 1999). That we have made progress toward a critical race theory of education is evident from a review of the scholarship published since 1995. However, that the legal literature still offers much in the way of a framework on which to build is illustrated by the CRT analyses of the *Brown* decision and the affirmative action cases. We assert that constructs such as interest convergence and the property value of whiteness are powerful explanatory tools for analyzing and understanding these legal issues related to education. Despite the powerful analytical lens that they provide, we would argue that the constructs outlined in CRT scholarship in the law have yet to be used to their full potential in education. For example, some scholars have examined whiteness as a construct of privilege, but not as an idea that manifests in tangible ways that affect schooling—through curricula, school choice, and even standards for "normal" and "acceptable" student behavior (see, e.g., Marx and Pennington, 2003; Thompson, 2003). Thus, while the examination of whiteness (and whiteness as a function of racism) is certainly central to a CRT analysis, examining the material effects of whiteness and the manner in which it is deployed and maintained materially, hence as an aspect of property, has yet to be fully pursued by CRT scholars in education. Morris's (2001) work, reviewed earlier in this article, is one exception. Another exception, perhaps, is Michael Vavrus's (2002) text on transforming the multicultural education of teachers. Vavrus uses a CRT analysis and the notions of colorblindness and white privilege to examine the discursive practices within multicultural education that are an obstacle to preparing teachers to address educational inequity in any substantive way. We urge other CRT scholars in education to continue to pursue analyses that build upon these underutilized but neverthe-less powerful tools.

The continued relevance of these constructs to educational scholarship can be illustrated by a return to the story recounted at the start of this article. Ten years ago, Ladson-Billings and Tate (1995) argued that the "intersection of race and property [is] a central construct in understanding a critical race theoretical approach to education" (p. 58). We suggested earlier that one way to view the opening story was as an illustration of tracking as a manifestation of the absolute right to exclude, because tracking was one of the examples provided by Ladson-Billings and Tate of this property function of whiteness. However, the story was not, in fact, about tracking in the traditional sense. It was based not on the curricular structure of a middle or high school, but on the teacher education programs offered by an institution of higher education. The schools that the students moved on to after graduation were not the high schools or colleges in which they would become students, but the elementary and middle schools in which they would become teachers. The students in Program A most often went on to become teachers in largely white subur-ban districts or private schools, while the students from Program B gener-ally went on to largely minority schools in the city. Thus, the story illustrates the second-generation, or inherited, effects of the property value of white-ness. The impact of larger classes and less qualified instructors on students in the teacher education programs would be passed along to the students they would later teach. We offer this "true" story to reiterate the point made by Ladson-Billings and Tate a decade ago. The CRT legal literature offers a neces-sary critical vocabulary for analyzing and understanding the persistent and pernicious inequity in education that is *always already* a function of race and racism. Thus, while CRT in education must necessarily grow and develop to become its own entity, there is much support and needed nourishment yet to be gained from the legal roots of CRT. In this way, the direction forward with respect to CRT in education requires, in some sense, a return to the place where we started.

In 1987, Derrick Bell published *And We Are Not Saved: The Elusive Quest for Racial Justice*. He prefaced the book by reminding the reader of the unful-filled promise of *Brown v. Board of Education*. At that time, thirty years had passed since *Brown*, yet the Supreme Court ruling and other apparent civil rights victories had failed to bring about the lasting harvest of racial equality that many people anticipated. The title of Bell's book, taken from the biblical book of Jeremiah, is a poignant reminder of those unmet expectations. Our adaptation of this title is both a reference to the work of one of the founders of CRT in legal studies and a comment on the of yet-unfulfilled promise of CRT in education.

Note: One exception to this general observation is the involvement of CRT scholars in legal proceedings related to education. For example, both Solórzano and Ladson-Billings have been called as expert witnesses in cases that address educational inequity. Solórzano served as an expert witness in *Gratz vs. Bollinger* (the University of Michigan affirmative action case). Ladson-Billings served as an expert witness in a case against a rural school district in South Carolina. In this way, CRT scholars in education have taken action in the struggle against racial inequity.

References

Bell, D. (1980). *Brown v. Board of Education* and the Interest-Convergence Principle. *Harvard Law Review* 93: 518–533.

Bell, D. (1987). *And We Are Not Saved: The Elusive Quest for Racial Justice.* New York: Basic Books.

Bell, D. (2004). *Silent Covenants: Brown v. Board of Education and the Unfulfilled Hopes for Racial Reform.* New York: Oxford University Press.

Calmore, J. (1995). Critical Race Theory, Archie Shepp, and Fire Music: Securing an Authentic Intellectual Life in a Multicultural World. In K. Crenshaw et al. (eds.), *Critical Race Theory* 315–329. New York: New Press.

Crenshaw, K. (1988). Race, Reform, and Retrenchment: Transformation and Legitimation in Antidiscrimination Law. *Harvard Law Review* 101: 1331–1387.

Crenshaw, K. (1989). Foreword: Toward a Race-Conscious Pedagogy in Legal Education. *National Black Law Journal* 11: 1–14.

Crenshaw, K.; Gotanda, N.; Peller, G.; and Thomas, K. (eds.) (1995). *Critical Race Theory: The Key Writings That Formed the Movement.* New York: New Press.

Darder, A.; Torres, R. D.; and Baltodano, M. (eds.) (2002). *The Critical Pedagogy Reader.* New York: Routledge/Falmer.

Darling-Hammond, L. (1997). *The Right To Learn: A Blueprint for Creating Schools That Work.* San Francisco: Jossey-Bass.

Delgado, R. (1989). Storytelling for Oppositionists and Others: A Plea for Narrative. *Michigan Law Review* 87: 2411–2441.

Delgado, R. (1990). When a Story Is Just a Story: Does Voice Really Matter? *Virginia Law Review* 76: 95–111.

Delgado, R. (1995). *The Rodrigo Chronicles: Conversations about America and Race.* New York: New York University Press.

Delgado, R. (1996). *The Coming Race War? And Other Apocalyptic Tales of America after Affirmative Action and Welfare.* New York: New York University Press.

Delgado Bernal, D. & Villalpando, O. (2002). An Apartheid of Knowledge in Academia: The Struggle over the "Legitimate" Knowledge of Faculty of Color. *Equity and Excellence in Education* 35(2): 169–180.

Duncan, G. (2002a). Beyond Love: A Critical Race Ethnography of the Schooling of Adolescent Black Males. *Equity and Excellence in Education* 35(2): 131–143.

Duncan, G. (2002b). Critical Race Theory and Method: Rendering Race in Urban Ethnographic Research. *Qualitative Inquiry* 8: 85–104.

Farber, D. & Sherry, S. (1993). Telling Stories out of School: An Essay on Legal Narratives. *Stanford Law Review* 45: 807–855.

Fernandez, L. (2002). Telling Stories about School: Using Critical Race Theory and Latino Critical Theories To Document Latina/Latino Education and Resistance. *Qualitative Inquiry* 8: 45–65.

Fine, M. (1991). *Framing Dropouts: Notes on the Politics of an Urban High School*. Albany, NY: SUNY Press.

Gotanda, N. (1991). A Critique of "Our Constitution Is Color-blind." *Stanford Law Review* 44: 1–68.

Harris, C. (1993). Whiteness as Property. *Harvard Law Review* 106: 1707–1791.

Ladson-Billings, G. (1999a). Just What Is Critical Race Theory and What's It Doing in a Nice Field like Education? In L. Parker, D. Deyhle, and S. Villenas (eds.), *Race Is ... Race Isn't: Critical Race Theory and Qualitative Studies in Education* 7–30. Boulder, CO: Westview.

Ladson-Billings, G. (1999b). Preparing Teachers for Diverse Student Populations: A Critical Race Theory Perspective. In A. Iran-Nejad and P. Pearson (eds.), Review of Research in Education, vol. 24, 221–247. Washington, DC: American Educational Research Association.

Ladson-Billings, G. & Tate, W. (1995). Toward a Critical Race Theory of Education. *Teachers College Record* 97: 47–68.

Lawrence, C. (1992). The Word and the River: Pedagogy as Scholarship as Struggle. *Southern California Law Review* 65: 2231–2298.

Lawrence, C. (1995). The Word and the River: Pedagogy as Scholarship as Struggle. In K. Crenshaw et al. (eds.), *Critical Race Theory* 336–351. New York: New Press.

Matsuda, M. (1995). Looking to the Bottom: Critical Legal Studies and Reparations. In K. Crenshaw et al. (eds.), *Critical Race Theory* 63–79). New York: New Press.

Matsuda, M.; Lawrence, C.; Delgado, R.; and Crenshaw, K. (eds.) (1993). *Words That Wound: Critical Race Theory, Assaultive Speech, and the First Amendment*. Boulder, CO: Westview.

McKenzie, K. (2004). Schools Emerge Worlds Apart, Seeking an Ideal. *Commercial Appeal* 16 May, pp. A1, A19.

Morris, J. (2001). Forgotten Voices of Black Educators: Critical Race Perspectives on the Implementation of a Desegregation Plan. *Educational Policy* 15: 575–600.

Oakes, J. (1995). Two Cities' Tracking and Within-School Segregation. *Teachers College Record* 96: 681–690.

Oakes, J.; Muir, K.; and Joseph, R. (2000). Coursetaking and Achievement in Mathematics and Science: Inequalities That Endure and Change. Madison, WI: National Institute of Science Education.

Orfield, G. & Lee, C. (2004). Brown at 50: King's dream or Plessy's nightmare?Cambridge, MA: Civil Rights Project at Harvard University.

Parker, L., & Lynn, M. (2002). What's Race Got To Do with It? Critical Race Theory's Conflicts with and Connections to Qualitative Research Methodology and Epistemology. *Qualitative Inquiry* 8: 7–22.

Posner, R. A. (1995). *Overcoming Law*. Cambridge, MA: Harvard University Press.

Powell, J. A. (1992). Racial Realism or Racial Despair? *Connecticut Law Review*. Winter: 533–551.

Pursley, G. (2003). Thinking Diversity, Rethinking Race: Toward a Transformative Concept of Diversity in Higher Education. *Texas Law Review* 82: 153–199.

Rousseau, C. & Tate, W. (2003). No Time Like the Present: Reflecting on Equity in School Mathematics. *Theory into Practice* 42: 211–216.

Solórzano, D. (1998). Critical Race Theory, Race, and Gender Microaggressions, and the Experience of Chicana and Chicano scholars. *International Journal of Qualitative Studies in Education* 11: 121–136.

Solórzano, D. (2001). Critical Race Theory, Racial Microaggressions, and Campus Racial Climate: The Experiences of African American College Students. *Journal of Negro Education* 69: 60–73.

Solórzano, D. & Yosso, T. (2002). Critical Race Methodology: Counter-Storytelling as an Analytical Framework for Education Research. *Qualitative Inquiry* 8: 23–44.

Tate, W. (1994). From Inner City to Ivory Tower: Does My Voice Matter in the Academy? *Urban Education* 29: 245–269.

Tate, W. (1997). Critical Race Theory and Education: History, Theory, and Implications. In M. Apple (ed.), *Review of Research in Education*, vol. 22, 195–247. Itasca, IL: F. E. Peacock.

Tate, W. (1999). Conclusion. In L. Parker et al. (eds.), *Race Is ... Race Isn't: Critical Race Theory and Qualitative Studies in Education*, 251–271. Boulder, CO: Westview.

Tate, W.; Ladson-Billings, G.; & Grant, C. (1993). The Brown Decision Revisited: Mathematizing Social Problems. *Educational Policy* 7: 255–275.

Tate, W. & Rousseau, C. (2002). Access and Opportunity: The Political and Social Context of Mathematics Education. In L. English (ed.), *Handbook of International Research in Mathematics Education* 271–299. Mahwah, NJ: Lawrence Erlbaum.

Taylor, E. (1999). Critical Race Theory and Interest Convergence in the Desegregation of Higher Education. In L. Parker et al. (eds.), *Race Is ... Race Isn't: Critical Race Theory and Qualitative Studies in Education* 181–204. Boulder, CO: Westview.

Taylor, E. (2000). Critical Race Theory and Interest Convergence in the Backlash against Affirmative Action: Washington State and Initiative 200. *Teachers College Record* 102: 539–560.

Teranishi, R. (2002). Asian Pacific Americans and Critical Race Theory: An Examination of School Racial Climate. *Equity and Excellence in Education* 35: 144–154.

Thompson, A. (1998). Not the Color Purple: Black Feminist Lessons for Educational Caring. *Harvard Educational Review* 68: 552–554.

Tushnet, M. (1992). The Degradation of Constitutional Discourse. *Georgetown Law Review* 81: 1151–1193

Vavrus, M. (2002). *Transforming the Multicultural Education of Teachers: Theory, Research and Practice.* New York: Teachers College Press.

Villalpando, O. and Delgado Bernal, D. (2002). A Critical Race Theory Analysis of Barriers That Impede the Success of Faculty of Color. In W. Smith, P. Altbach, and K. Lomotey (eds.), *The Racial Crisis in American Higher Education* 243–270. New York: SUNY Press.

II
Critical Race Theory Constructs

3

The First Day of School: A CRT Story

CELIA K. ROUSSEAU AND ADRIENNE D. DIXSON

The First Day of School

On the first day of the new school year, parents all around the city woke children up, got them dressed, and put them on yellow school buses. At first it appeared to be a very normal first day, but it soon became clear that this was a first day of school unlike any other.

The students at Frederick Douglass High School noticed it as soon as they came through the doors. The crumbling school building with broken windows, collapsing ceiling tiles, and moldy basement classrooms had been transformed, at least on the interior, into a modern facility in which everything worked and all necessities were available, including toilet paper and soap in the restrooms. Students found new computers in each classroom. Two brand new science laboratories had been outfitted with all the necessary equipment. Students had previously been able only to read descriptions of experiments; now they could actually perform them in the lab. A new library was stocked with current encyclopedias (both electronic and text versions) and books that the students really wanted to read—a dramatic change from the antiquated library materials that the students had left the previous spring. School officials had also replaced the dilapidated, outdated textbooks that students had been forced to share the previous year with new textbooks that came with a range of supplementary materials.

The students at Frederick Douglass noticed other changes as well. For example, there were new course offerings. In recent years, the highest mathematics course offered to high school students had been trigonometry. Students who had taken algebra I in the eighth grade had no math class available to take as seniors. Now, the students were offered a full complement of college preparatory courses such as advanced placement calculus and statistics.

The students also noticed differences in their teachers. Usually there had been little instruction during the first two weeks of school, but these teachers began teaching the curriculum on the first day. What the students understood intuitively, even if they had no official confirmation, was the strength of the teachers' content and pedagogical knowledge. These were not people hired just to fill vacant positions. These were "real" teachers. The students did not know it, but each of the teachers had a full teaching license; none was in the school on an emergency permit or waiver.

When the students got home that afternoon, they told their families about the changes in the school. The adults were surprised, but very pleased. Many parents and grandparents even called the superintendent to congratulate him on an excellent job. With each call, the superintendent expressed his pleasure at the students' positive experiences. But he ended the call by asking for the parents' support when the controversy erupted.

The superintendent was correct that trouble was brewing. Not all parents were pleased about the changes in the school district. For example, students at Jefferson High School went to school on the first day and found conditions much worse than those they had left a few months before. While the façade looked roughly the same, the interior was unquestionably neglected. Water fountains did not work. There were leaks in the ceiling. Air conditioning units did not work, and fans were in short supply. Computers in the lab either did not work or had been stolen over the summer. The science lab had been dismantled. The materials in the library were either outdated or damaged by water or mold.

In addition, the Jefferson students found that course offerings had changed. In many cases, students who had been enrolled in gifted and talented programs learned that such classes were no longer available. Students who had intended to take college preparatory classes discovered there were no teachers qualified to teach those courses. In addition, electives that students had planned to take, such as Japanese, music theory and art history, were no longer offered.

The "tough" teachers who had challenged the students in the past had been replaced by permanent substitutes who did little more than have their classes do exercises out of dilapidated textbooks. Students who asked questions quickly discovered that their teachers were unwilling or unable to assist them. The students found that they were "on their own" with respect to their learning.

There was an uproar when the Jefferson parents heard about the changes at the school. The superintendent's phone rang off the hook, and his e-mail was overwhelmed. Within a few days, the board of education scheduled a special meeting to discuss the situation. When the time for the meeting arrived, the auditorium was packed. The chairman of the board opened the meeting and went through the formalities quickly. He then gave the superintendent the floor.

"I know that this room is divided into two groups—those who are strongly in favor of the changes and those who are strongly opposed to those same changes." The superintendent had to pause, interrupted by cheers and jeers from the audience.

"The chairman has allowed me the opportunity to stand up here and explain myself. Following that explanation, I know that the decision is out of my hands. But I appreciate the opportunity to share my thinking with you.

"Each year for the past several years, we have had board meeting after board meeting in which we pored endlessly over the achievement data and tried to figure out what to do about the disgraceful achievement gap that we have in this district. We have implemented a few programs that appeared to help, but none came anywhere close to eliminating that gap. The commissioners have long agreed that the system itself plays a large role in the creation and maintenance of these disparities. However, with that said, we have not made substantive changes to that system. We fiddled with a few components here and there, but have not made the wholesale changes that we know would make a difference for those students who have traditionally been at the bottom. That is precisely what I was trying to do. I wanted to give the students who have had the least qualified teachers, the worst facilities, the fewest resources, and the most limited course offerings a chance to have what other students in this district have always had. My research suggests that it would take a maximum of three years (possibly less) to completely eliminate the achievement gap in this district under my plan. If we are truly committed to achieving equity, this is the approach that we must take.

"Over the past few days, many of you have expressed a commitment to equity while at the same time questioning the means I have proposed to achieve it. The unfortunate reality is that we have limited financial and human resources in this district. We know that certain schools have always received more of these resources. And the students from these schools have traditionally done better. In order to reverse that trend and eliminate the gap, we must compensate for the past inequities in the system. The outcomes for this year are related to the opportunities of the past several years. So, in this case, we must give more to those schools that have always had less in order to achieve equitable outcomes. And that is what I have heard this board say was its goal—that all students, regardless of the school attended, would experience equitable outcomes. Ideally, all schools would have the human and material resources to achieve excellence. That is not our reality right now. The resources are limited. I am only proposing to redistribute them in a way that will lead to equal outcomes in three years."

The room was quiet until one member of the audience spoke up. "For those of you who don't know me, my name is Anthony. I am a senior at Frederick Douglass. I have always received good grades. I thought that I would be able to go to college next year at State University. I went last month to tour the campus and meet with the people in the engineering department, because I really wanted to be an engineer. When they looked at my transcript and at my SAT scores, they asked me if I played a sport. I told them that I didn't, and they told me that it was unlikely that I could get admitted. They said that, although my grades are good, my SAT score was low, and I would not have the courses necessary to get into the engineering program. They were very nice about it, but they basically said that I was not ready. They said that they have had several students from Douglass who did not last through the first year. They told me that I could take remedial courses at the community college and then transfer. But I can't really afford to be in school for that long. I could not understand why they didn't think that I could go to college, because I have always made A's at Douglass. But when I went to school for the first day this year, I understood. I know what I have been missing all these years. I have learned more in three days than I did in a semester last year. I actually did a chemistry experiment yesterday, for the first time. I am reading real literature by authors like James Baldwin, Zora Neale Hurston, even Shakespeare. My teachers expect me to come to class with my homework completed. We have to answer questions and discuss things. They are really pushing me. If this is what college is like, I can understand why they told me that I am not ready. If I had more classes like I have now, I would probably be ready for college. So I don't know how I would feel if I was at Jefferson. To be honest, I would probably be upset. But I want a chance to go to college. So I think that the superintendent did a good thing."

Another member of the audience stood up. "But what about my child? She is a senior at Jefferson and cannot take AP Calculus or AP Physics because there is no one who is qualified to teach them. What about her? She should have the right to a good education. If this plan is not overturned, I will move her to a private school. Or my family will have to move out to the suburbs so she can go to a good school." There were several shouts of agreement.

The meeting went on for hours, with parents and community members on both sides of the issue expressing their opinions of the superintendent's plan. It was almost midnight when the chairman called for order. "I have been listening to the comments at this meeting and in the community. We have been skirting around the racial issue since this whole thing started. The gap that the superintendent is trying to address is between white students and students of color in our district. He took resources that have been going to the predominantly white schools and moved them to the schools that are predominantly black and Latino. In my conversations with white parents, they have said that they are in favor of equality, but they don't think that their children should have to pay the price for it. I think that every member of this board is committed to achieving equity in our school system, but we also have heard the concerns of the parents who think that it is not in their child's best interests to achieve it in this way. At the same time, we recognize the concerns of the African American and Latino parents with respect to the quality of the schools in their communities. It is a very tough problem to try to solve, and we applaud the superintendent's intentions, if not his means of going about it."

The parents and community members did not know it, but the board members had already worked out a compromise solution. Small groups of board members had met or spoken by phone several times since the first day of school. They had discussed in detail the ramifications of various scenarios and decided to propose a plan involving equalization of resources. Under this plan, the funding to each school would be equalized. Each school would have comparable facilities, course offerings, and resources, including technology. Teachers would be distributed so that all the schools had equal numbers of the most qualified teachers. On the surface, it appeared to be an important move toward equity in the district, but one that would also prevent the schools from losing large numbers of white students.

Following the chairman's speech, one of the board members put forward the board's compromise plan. Motions were made and seconded. Votes were taken. And the superintendent's plan was rejected in favor of the board's equalization plan.

The next day, the new plan was put into place. Resource equalization was implemented across the district. At first, things appeared to be going as expected. The African American and Latino schools had better conditions than in the past (although not as good as the first few days of school). Conversely, the predominantly white schools were better off than they had been at the beginning of the school year, but were still substantially worse off than in previous years.

However, it did not take long for changes to surface at some schools. Long-term substitutes or teachers on waivers had replaced the qualified teachers who had been moved from the predominantly white schools under the equalization plan. At first, this meant that all of the schools had equal proportions of licensed teachers. By November, however, those proportions had changed. The numbers of licensed teachers in the predominantly white schools gradually began to increase as new teachers were recruited from out of the area. Similarly, many of the courses that had been taken out of the predominantly white schools under the equalization plan began to reappear as second semester offerings. Newer computers and state-of-the-art equipment were installed. By January, the predominantly white schools were on par with their status in previous years.

A reporter at the local newspaper decided to investigate these changes. She discovered what the members of the board of education had already anticipated when they designed the equalization plan: equalization of resources from the district did little to change the status of schools with other sources of revenue. The reporter found that the parent organizations of the predominantly white schools had reacted to the shift in district resources with aggressive fundraising campaigns on behalf of their schools. They had been able to leverage resources to more than make up for the cuts from the district. With these additional resources, the principals had been able to make the changes necessary to bring the schools back up to the level of previous years.

At the end of the school year, reviews of the plan were mixed. Achievement results reflected noticeable gains for the black and Latino students in the district. However, the gap between these students and the white students in the district had narrowed only slightly. Some lauded the board's efforts to equalize resources as an important step toward equity. Others pointed to the failure to close the gap to argue that the schools had little to do with why some students were persistently at the bottom. Still others, including the former superintendent, recognized the board's plan for what it was, a shrewd move to preserve the status quo.

Using Stories in Critical Race Theory

There are several reasons for including this story as part of our introduction to this section. First, we want to give readers an example of the "unorthodox" forms that CRT scholars employ to understand race and racism in America (Bell, 1995). The use of narrative is a prominent theme within the CRT literature. "Among the most characteristic approaches in the Critical Race Theory genre are storytelling, counterstorytelling, and analysis of narrative" (Delgado, 1995a). There are several examples in this book of stories told by persons of color about their own experiences, but we also wanted to highlight one other form of storytelling in CRT.

Legal scholars have used fictionalized stories effectively to highlight key points with respect to race (Bell, 1992, 1995, 1996, 1998; Delgado, 1995b). Some of these stories contain fantasy elements, such as Bell's (1992) use of aliens in his story "The Space Traders." In fact, throughout his series of books, Bell repeatedly uses fantasy to shed light on reality. Although Bell "tells stories that are not true ... readers will recognize the realness in them" (Scheppele, 1989). Lawrence notes that Bell is part of a larger tradition in which

> African Americans have ... used fiction to mask their most radical thoughts and aspirations. From the Negro spirituals that disguised their own quest for freedom in the stories of Old Testament heroes to the Brother Rabbit stories to the contemporary work of Toni Morrison and Alice Walker, blacks have often told their most compelling truths in fiction. (1992, pp. 2273–2274)

According to Lawrence, this use of storytelling is not simply a rhetorical device employed by CRT scholars. Rather, stories (both fiction and nonfiction) can play an important role in scholarship. Lawrence argues that narrative is a way to provide context: "Human problems considered and resolved in the absence of context are often misperceived, misinterpreted, and mishandled" (1992, p. 2281). Because the stories of people of color are not part of the dominant discourse, it is this group that is most likely to suffer under the acontextual approach of traditional legal analysis. He also claims that narrative can serve as a source of data, as a "rich evidentiary record for analysis and assessment of complex social processes" (p. 2283). A third role for narrative is to give authority to imagination. Lawrence writes that "imagination is the key to our deepest insights and sympathies" (p. 2285). These uses of narrative are important features of CRT.

A second reason for sharing this story is to briefly introduce the reader to the ideas from CRT that will be discussed in greater detail in the following chapters of this section. For example, the specific type of storytelling done by scholars in CRT often fits within the category referred to by Delgado (1989) as "counterstorytelling." "Counterstories" are narratives told by members of outgroups (Delgado, 1989). Because members of our society who have traditionally been silenced tell these stories, they serve to counteract the stories, or the grand narratives, of the dominant group and to challenge the status quo. Counterstories can destroy the mindset that allows the dominant group to subordinate people of color. Counterstories can "open new windows into reality, showing us that there are possibilities for life other than the ones we live" (Delgado, 1989, p. 2414). The story of the two high schools is intended to illustrate the idea of counterstorytelling in two ways. First, it imagines a reality in which those who have traditionally been underserved by schools have the tables turned and receive the best that the school system has to offer. In addition, Anthony's account of undereducation represents a counterstory within the larger story. Other scholars employing CRT have documented similar counterstories representing the perspectives of students of color (Duncan, 2002; Teranishi, 2002). These counterstories point to the inequities of the system through the experiences of the students. In this section, Thandeka Chapman offers yet another example of a counterstory as she chronicles how parents of color fought for equitable education in the Rockford public schools. Insofar as her account demonstrates the commitment and involvement of parents of color, it serves to counter the dominant stories that portray these same parents as uninvolved in their children's education.

Another key construct from CRT reflected in the story is the idea of whiteness as property. The predominantly white schools in the story had well-kept facilities, computers, laboratory equipment, library materials, qualified teachers, and advanced coursework. The schools that served students of color had far fewer of these same resources. Although this is a fictionalized account, there are many examples of similar disparities between actual schools (Darling-Hammond, 1997; Ferguson, 1991; Kozol, 1991; Oakes, Rogers, Silver, Horng, and Goode, 2004). In the story, this inequitable distribution of resources is deemed natural, compared to the unnatural redistribution accomplished under the superintendent's plan. The fact that this distribution is viewed as a "right" of the white students illustrates the property value of whiteness. The students' access to the most qualified teachers, the most advanced courses, and the best facilities and equipment are all examples of the property rights of whiteness (Ladson-Billings and Tate, 1995). The value of this property is further exemplified in the ability of the parent organizations at the white schools to raise the capital to compensate for the loss of resources at those schools. In addition to the examples provided in the story, the idea of whiteness as property is further explicated in Jessica DeCuir-Gunby's chapter in this section. She uses the case of Josephine DeCuir to illustrate the different dimensions of the property value of whiteness. Although the case is not directly related to education, as DeCuir-Gunby notes, it has implications for a growing population of students. Moreover, the different aspects of the property value of whiteness illustrated in the chapter have direct correlates in schools.

One characteristic of whiteness as property is the institutionalization of this property right. It does not depend on the racist attitudes or actions of individuals (although such acts or attitudes are certainly related to the premise of white supremacy). Rather, the property value of whiteness has been institutionalized in systems. This recognition of the systemic nature of racism is closely related to another idea put forward in the legal literature on CRT: the material aspects of subordination (Delgado, 2001). The story "The First Day of School" does not concentrate on individual racist acts, nor does it attend to symbolic manifestations of white supremacy. Rather, the focus of the story is on the inequitable distribution of material resources. Moreover, the salience of material resources is reflected in the independence of the predominantly white schools from the funding allocations of the district. The capacity of these schools to generate additional resources and the impact of those resources on schooling outcomes highlight the material dimension of inequality in education. Rousseau further explores the significance of material subordination in her chapter in this section, examining several resource disparities in an actual district.

Finally, the story illustrates the principle of interest convergence. Bell (1980) has argued that the interests of persons of color in the search for equity will be met only when they converge with the self-interest of whites. Further, he notes that whites will not agree to any measure aimed at social justice if that measure threatens their own status. The board's compromise position in the story clearly illustrates the operation of interest convergence. The board needed a plan that appeared to make progress toward greater equity without jeopardizing the enrollment of white students in the system. As implied in the story, the board recognized that the equalization of resources would have little practical impact on the status of the predominantly white schools. Thus, even though the equalization plan gave the appearance of justice, it did not threaten the superior status of the white students. This is one (admittedly fictional) illustration of the interest convergence principle. The operation of this principle is discussed in further detail in Jerome Morris's chapter in this section, where he uses it as a lens through which to examine school desegregation policies in St. Louis. Jamel Donnor also examines the implications of the interest convergence principle in education. He employs interest convergence to understand the nature of parental involvement in the educational lives of African American student athletes.

The story "The First Day of School" takes "real" conditions of schools and reverses those conditions for a brief fictional moment. In the reversal process, the injustice of the standard operating procedure is highlighted. This is a common characteristic of CRT scholarship. Scholars often focus on highlighting and analyzing the racist structures inherent in taken-for-granted systems and conditions. The constructs from the legal literature that serve as the focus of this section are parts of a powerful analytical lens that can focus laser-sharp attention on the mechanisms of subordination. One goal of this book is to take that same analytical lens and shift the focus from the law to education. In other words, we have the analytical tools from legal studies. We now need to apply them to education. The chapters in this section provide examples of how this can be accomplished.

References

Bell, D. (1980). Brown v. Board of Education and the Interest-Convergence Principle. *Harvard Law Review* 93: 518–533.

Bell, D. (1992). *Faces at the Bottom of the Well*. New York: Basic Books.

Bell, D. (1995). Who's Afraid of Critical Race Theory? *University of Illinois Law Review* 1995: 893-910.

Bell, D. (1996). *Gospel Choirs: Psalms of Survival in an Alien Land Called Home*. New York: Basic Books.

Bell, D. (1998). *Afrolantica Legacies*. Chicago: Third World.

Darling-Hammond, L. (1997). *The Right To Learn: A Blueprint for Creating Schools That Work*. San Francisco: Jossey-Bass.

Delgado, R. (1989). Storytelling for Oppositionists and Others: A Plea for Narrative. *Michigan Law Review* 87: 2411–2441.

Delgado, R. (1995a). *Critical Race Theory: The Cutting Edge*. Philadelphia: Temple University Press.

Delgado, R. (1995b). *The Rodrigo Chronicles*. New York: New York University Press.

Delgado, R. (2001). Two Ways to Think about Race: Reflections on the Id, the Ego, and Other Reformist Theories of Equal Protection. *Georgetown Law Review* 89: 2279, 2283–2285.

Duncan, G. (2002). Beyond Love: A Critical Race Ethnography of the Schooling of Adolescent Black Males. *Equity and Excellence in Education* 35: 131–143.

Ferguson, R. (1991). Paying for Public Education: New Evidence on How and Why Money Matters. *Harvard Journal of Legislation* 28: 465–498.

Kozol, J. (1991). *Savage Inequalities: Children in America's Schools*. New York: Crown.

Lawrence, C. (1992). The Word and the River: Pedagogy as Scholarship as Struggle. *Southern California Law Review* 65: 2231–2298.

Oakes, J.; Rogers, J.; Silver, D.; Horng, E.; & Goode, J. (2004). Separate and Unequal 50 years after Brown: California's Racial "Opportunity Gap." Los Angeles: Institute for Democracy, Education, and Access.

Scheppele, K. (1989). Foreword: Telling Stories. *Michigan Law Review* 87: 2073–2098.

Teranishi, R. (2002). Asian Pacific Americans and Critical Race Theory: An Examination of School Racial Climate. *Equity and Excellence in Education* 35: 144–154.

4

Pedaling Backward: Reflections of *Plessy* and *Brown* in Rockford Public Schools' De Jure Desegregation Efforts

THANDEKA K. CHAPMAN

Introduction

Much of the education scholarship on urban children and families proposes ways to increase involvement among parents of color and poor parents
(Comer, 1991; Edwards, 1993; Finders and Lewis, 1994). Scholars suggest various ways for teachers and administrators to invite urban parents to participate
in their children's formal schooling experiences (Comer, 1991; Finders and
Lewis, 1994). These suggestions, which presuppose a current and historical
lack of involvement among parents of color, range from traditional parent–
teacher associations and volunteer work to staff support services that provide
resources for parents.

However, Lopez (2003) problematizes these parent–school interactions as
reifications of white middle-class norms and ways of interacting with schools:

> In this regard, the discourse surrounding parental involvement con-
> structs a racial division whereby marginalized parents are viewed as
> lacking the abilities and skills necessary for educational success. Policy
> solutions, therefore, suggest that parents need to adjust their behavior in
> order to mimic/emulate mainstream modes of appropriate home–school
> interactions. (Lopez, 2003, p. 74)

Parents who do not fit the more traditional modes of interaction are seen
as less involved and less concerned about the academic progress of their children. Moreover, Villenas and Deyhle (1999) assert that "parents are really
'kept out' of schools by the negative ways in which they are treated, by insen-
sitive bureaucratic requirements, and by the ways in which school conceived
parent involvement programs disregard Latino knowledge and cultural bias"
(p. 415). Parents are not credited for the ways in which they believe themselves
to be contributing to the success of their children; these contributions include
taking care of children's physical and emotional needs at home, helping them

This chapter originally appeared in *Race, Ethnicity and Education* 8(1), March 2005, pp. 29–44.

as much as possible to complete homework and prepare for school, and providing the teacher with support when they are directly asked to intervene (Fernandez, 2002; Villenas and Deyhle, 1999).

Lopez (2003) suggests that in order for the contributions of urban parents to be recognized and valued, other forms of parental activism must be documented:

> In order to move away from this dominant/hegemonic involvement discourse, we must look for practices that stand outside traditional involvement configurations. By identifying these subaltern epistemologies, ways of knowing, and forms of involvement, we can broaden this seemingly racialized discourse and move beyond narrowly defined understandings of how parents and other family members are- and can be-involved in the educational lives of their children. (Lopez, 2003, p. 87)

In keeping with Lopez's charge to expand the vision of parental activism, I propose that the roles played by urban parents of color who have chosen to use the U.S. court system and social activism to gain equity in public schools should be credited as the ultimate level of parental activism. Parents of color, in their efforts to secure equitable education opportunities for their children through desegregation initiatives, have attempted to hold public school districts accountable for educating their children. Over the past fifty years, parents of color looked to the U.S. district, state, and federal court systems to help them acquire equity and equality in education. In many cases, the federal plans and challenges to the court-ordered reforms have continued for decades and cost taxpayers millions of dollars (Green v. County School Board of New Kent County, 1968; Manning v. The School Board of Hillsborough County, Florida, 2001; Missouri v. Jenkins, et al., 1995). Given the time, money, and commitment parents needed to mount a case against a district, hire representation, and continue these battles for decades, this form of involvement is the pinnacle display of parents' desire to give the best education possible to their children. *Brown v. Board of Education* is possibly the most famous example of parental activism concerning the constitutional rights of children of color. While the outcomes of *Brown* are much debated (Grant, 1995), parents who pursued legal action and won changed the structures of schools and opened the door for other civic action and social justice school reforms (Gay, 2004).

As the United States continues to reflect on the results of *Brown v. Board of Education*, it is important to recognize that this decision and other federal court decisions concerning desegregation were acted upon in various ways by northern and southern states and produced differing policy results. Many northern cities in the United States share similar patterns, events, and conflicts as part of their desegregation processes (Rury and Cassell, 1993). Parents in northern cities such as Boston, Detroit, and Milwaukee have fought for and against desegregation initiatives for more than fifty years. Parents of color repeatedly insisted that they wanted their neighborhood schools to be reformed and given equal resources so that their children would receive a fair amount of district funds, veteran teachers, and competent staff. However, the battles for equity most often highlighted in the aftermath of *Brown* were those waged around the issue of mandatory cross-town busing as a means to integrate schools racially.

Scholars note that the *Brown* decisions of 1954 and 1955 had the fastest and greatest effect on southern states where overt segregation could be easily identified (Orfield and Lee, 2004; Patterson, 2001; Pearsons, 1996). The complexities of segregated housing and red-line districting in the north allowed northern cities to fly under the federal radar much longer before school desegregation became a major court issue there. Patterson (2001) explains: "Brown took direct aim only at the South and those border regions where segregation was *de jure*- sanctioned explicitly in laws. The decision did not challenge the North or threaten it with costs of any kind. It did not affect de facto racial segregation, which was widespread, especially in housing and schooling in the North." (p.xx). The tenuous line between de jure segregation, which was imposed by law, and de facto segregation, created by social practices and individual choices, made it difficult for northern urban parents to prove intended harm and to put pressure on districts.

The city of Rockford, Illinois is a microcosm that exemplifies the socio-political events that took place in many cities in the northern United States. Parents of color in Rockford have been engaged in court action against the Rockford Public School District 205 since 1968 (*Quality Education for All Children v. School Board of School District 205 of Winnebago County, Illinois, 1973*). Their efforts to eradicate racist practices in the school were unsuccessful for almost thirty years. During that twenty-six-year period, parents attended school board meetings, held rallies, sponsored political candidates, and took their district to court repeatedly in their search for justice.

In 1968 parents threatened to boycott classrooms in response to a one-way busing program for Lincoln Park Elementary School students (Salsbury Will Continue Plans for Transfer, 1973). In 1972 parents formed a coalition to boycott desegregation meetings until parents of color were granted representation on all steering committee groups. The *Rockford Register Star* (*RRS*), the most widely read paper in Rockford, reported:

> A coalition of minority groups carried out their threat to boycott Thursday night's organizational meeting of a community committee studying ways to end segregation in Rockford's schools.
>
> Of the 80 to 100 attending the meeting, about 15 persons were either black or members of the Latin American community, who later left the meeting.
>
> Outside Wilson Middle School where the meeting was held, pickets carried signs asking for equal representation on the steering committee to

coordinate community involvement in Rockford's plan to meet desegregation guidelines. (Minority Groups Boycott First Desegregation Meeting, 1972, p.1A)

Ultimately, seats were given to African American and Latino parents on
all subcommittees involved with the desegregation plan. In addition, parents
attended informational meetings to better understand the state requirements
for desegregated schools. "The meeting was informational as white and blacks
[from 12 of the 14 schools cited as being noncompliant with racial balancing]
watched a movie which explored some of the psychological questions involved
in desegregation and listened to various desegregation plans explained"
(Desegregation Plans Aplenty Cause Confusion, 1973, p.1A). During this time,
various community coalitions worked together to elect African American and
Latino community members to the school board. After two decades of community involvement failed to alter academic outcomes for students of color in
Rockford, a parent coalition called The People Who Care (People Who Care v.
Rockford Board of Education, School District 205, 1997) successfully proved
de jure segregation practices and forced the district to reform institutional
structures on all levels of schooling when they were able to. Taylor and Alves
summarize the three decades of district manipulation that eventually led to a
verdict against the district:

> Although the district professed to have operated a racially neutral
> "neighborhood" system of student assignments, the Court found that
> RSD intentionally segregated students between schools by race and
> resisted making changes that would have alleviated the patterns of
> racial isolation.
>
> When RSD did change its student assignment patterns, the Court
> found that they placed a disparate burden on African American and
> Hispanic students. More specifically, the Court found that the RSD
> gerry-mandered neighborhood school attendance boundaries in order
> to create and maintain a racially segregated school system; maintained
> a neighborhood schools policy for white students and deliberately bur-
> dened minority students with one-way busing by closing schools in
> minority neighborhoods; and manipulated school enrollment capacities
> in order to force minority students into predominantly white schools
> while giving white students the opportunity to voluntarily attend high
> status alternative programs in predominately minority schools. (Taylor
> and Alves, 1999, p.18)

The plaintiffs were able to prove deliberate racism by using the district's documented accounts, policies and extensive testimony from administrators,
teachers and staff. Unfortunately, their victory lasted a mere ten years, until

a judge decided that the district had done enough and, more important, had paid enough money to erase the vestiges of discrimination.

Rockford's history of desegregation mirrors that of many northern cities' battles to prove that neighborhood schooling initiatives are thinly disguised veils over de jure segregation systems. Several northern and Midwestern cities such as Milwaukee, Kansas City, Oklahoma City, St. Louis, Detroit and Chicago share similar narratives of extensive court desegregation trials that have recently ended through remanded court orders (Irons, 2002; Orfield and Lee, 2004; Patterson, 2001). When filing a joint lawsuit with parents from Peoria, Illinois, one NAACP organizer observed: "We have been deeply involved in the desegregation of northern schools since 1970. The Midwest seems to be an area that is very resistant to school desegregation. The voluntary adoption of desegregation plans has not been very successful" (Grievances behind Deseg Suit Specified, 1975). These words, spoken thirty years ago, continue to ring true for desegregation policy in northern cities. Each of their stories involves decades of successful battles among the courts, parents, school boards, and students that began with *Brown* and have ended unsuccessfully with a return to segregated systems much like the ones created under *Plessy v. Ferguson* (Orfield and Lee, 2004). For example, eight of the twelve schools on Rockford's original 1975 list of segregated schools which were out of racial compliance because they held 50 percent or more African American students remain on the "out of compliance" list today.

The reasons for the full-circle return to segregated schools in urban districts like Rockford are both complex and simple. The changing political climate, the attack on social science research, the inability to measure racism and its eradication, the pervasive deficit model of students of color and their families, and the economic deterioration of urban centers are interconnected explanations of why urban school districts have become even more segregated than they were fifty years ago. Using Rockford as a representation of northern urban districts, this chapter reveals how the socio-political forces listed have led to the reinstantiation of segregated systems and the elimination of the federal courts as a viable alternative to school reform from within.

Although this chapter focuses on court dealings and political implications, it also serves as a critical race theory (CRT) counternarrative of parental involvement in which parents and students are actually on the front lines in these battles to reform their schools. Scholars such as Fernandez (2002), Villenas and Deyhle (1999), Duncan (2002), and others (Solórzano and Bernal, 2001; Solórzano and Yosso, 2002) have used CRT to tell the stories of students and parents of color that often go untold. When these stories defy conventional stereotypes and ways of depicting people of color, they become *counterstories* or *counternarratives* which document the feelings, beliefs, events, and practices of people who have been marginalized in academic discourses (Delgado, 1995). Therefore, the untold and unexamined actions of urban parents of color and their perseverance in urban school reform serves as a counternarrative to scholarship that poses urban parents of color as absent in the education of their children (Lopez, 2003). Additionally, in keeping with CRT tenets (Tate, 1997), which assert the need for a contextualized, historicized portrait of events and people, newspaper articles will be used in conjunction with legal documents and academic scholarship to demonstrate how Rockford's parents of color have attempted to advocate for their children but have been denied equity.

Why Desegregation Now?

Derrick Bell (1995) and Mary Dudziak (2000) have argued that the *Brown v. Board* decision was largely a reflection of America's need to show a more democratic façade to Europe. Given the fact that Brown was not the first desegregation case to appear before the courts, timing was the major motive for the Supreme Court's decision. At a time when the United States wanted to expand its global interests with the support of European nations, the *Brown* decision demonstrated its supposed dedication to equity and equality of all U.S. citizens. There is great debate about the actual gains produced by the *Brown* decision; however, the number of African American children in integrated school settings has significantly increased and has remained relatively constant in southern states (Orfield and Lee, 2004). In northern states, unfortunately, limited gains have been made and those gains have sometimes been reversed owing to the remand of desegregation initiatives (Frankenberg, Lee and Orfield, 2003).

The different challenges faced by parents and school districts in the northern and southern states were due in part to the ways in which urban areas developed and later declined. In the 1950s and 1960s, white and black schools in northern and southern areas had an array of successful and unsuccessful schools (Bell, 1983). Siddle Walker (2000) asserts that there were high-quality segregated African American schools that often academically outperformed their segregated white counterparts. During the 1950s and the early 1960s, urban areas were enjoying economic booms that benefited both whites and blacks. African Americans continued to migrate into metropolitan areas in large numbers as the industrial job market declined rapidly in the late 1960s (Rury and Cassell, 1993). Urban schools were hailed as landmark institutions of learning that had better resources and teachers than their rural counterparts. Only after urban areas began to experience severe economic decline and the 1964 Civil Rights Act was passed did African American parents in the north begin to take aggressive action against urban school districts (Patterson, 2001).

Rockford's history of desegregation efforts follows this pattern of economic decline during the late 1950s and parental action in the late 1960s. Rockford is a small city in the Midwest of the United States that is topographically, racially, and economically divided by the Rock River, which runs north–south through the city. Rockford's white population comprises the majority of residents (86 percent). It is one of the more diverse cities in the state because of the African American (7.7 percent) and Hispanic (4.7 percent) populations. Historically, 70 percent or more of the white families have lived on the east side, and 70 percent of African American families reside on the west side of town. Latino families are split more evenly between the two sides, with 60 percent living on the west side of the river. The families on the east side enjoy more efficient public transportation, closer access to the shopping mall, direct access to the main street with other diverse shops, larger grocery stores and food warehouses, hotels, and easy access to the two interstate highways bordering the city. Because jobs and transportation to jobs are more easily found on the east side, African American and Latino residents living on the west side have great difficulty coordinating their living arrangements with their job opportunities.

Socio-economically, there is a gap between middle-income families who own their homes and low-income families of all ethnic backgrounds who rent apartments and houses. This disparity in income levels is illustrated through a few local statistics. In the year 2000, the per capita personal income in Rockford was $23,523. The median household income for the same year was $35,172, with a mean of $61,410. These differences reflect a small percentage of wealthy residents at one end of the economic spectrum and a larger number of residents below the poverty line at the other end. For example, 11.5 percent of Rockford's households make less than $10,000 per year, and 3 percent make over $100,000 per year. The largest portion of households (32 percent) have a yearly income between $30,000 and $49,000.

The second-largest city and the third-largest school district in Illinois, Rockford began feeling dramatic economic depression in the late 1960s as a result of massive downsizing of factories and industrial plants in the area. A predominantly working-class city, Rockford's continued loss of employment opportunities for citizens with only a high school diploma and a vocational trade had a significant impact on the district's ability to maintain the schools in the city. In times of financial hardship, the school board's first response to solving financial problems has been to close schools on the west side of town, where the population is predominantly African American, and further to limit the resource funds allotted to the remaining west side schools. Following suit with other parent coalitions formed after the Civil Rights Act, Rockford parents took their complaints to the court system to find relief from unjust practices (Quality Education for All Children v. School Board of School District 205 of Winnebago County, Illinois, 1973).

De Facto versus De Jure

The greatest obstacle Rockford parents and other citizen coalitions in segregated metropolitan areas faced was proving that urban school boards had purposefully participated in maintaining segregated schools. Northern school districts were given a "unitary" status by the courts if they could prove that their current school assignments were the result of de facto housing patterns and were not influenced by district policies to maintain segregated schools. School districts also had to show that they were working toward the alleviation of unequal situations, such as unequal distributions of resources, physical plant upkeep and qualified teachers.

The history of neighborhood schooling in urban areas made it extremely difficult for plaintiffs of desegregation cases to prove intent. In the 1960s and 1970s, majority white school boards asserted that neighborhood schools were pillars of their communities that functioned as more than places of instruction. Other reasons for maintaining neighborhood schools were that "parents were closer in case of emergencies and more able to take part in school functions; children could meet both during and after school to form closer friendships; students could more easily engage in after-school activities" (Patterson, 2001).

While white residents in Rockford were willing to concede that segregated housing existed in the city and that many of them chose their homes with regard to school reputations, they were unwilling to connect housing patterns to the reach of the schools. A white principal stated: "Some of the problems of segregation are outside the schools. You can't put all the blame on the schools for segregation" (Other Integration Plans Proposed, 1971, p.1A). The RRS further explained: "Rockford's schools are not responsible for the city's housing patterns, although some advocates of neighborhood schools are quick to point out they selected their homes in neighborhoods where they were told 'good' schools were nearby" (Other Integration Plans Proposed," 1971). Twenty years later, Rockford continued to stand by its neighborhood schools position. The RRS reported:

> ROCKFORD—A city where most black families live in one part of town and most whites live in others. A city dedicated to neighborhood schools …. A city where families who have the time and money invest in their neighborhood schools. Those premises are part of the School District's defense in the ongoing court trial to determine whether Rockford public schools intentionally discriminated against black and Hispanic children. (A Case for the District, 1993)

In Rockford, as in other Midwest metropolitan areas, such as Milwaukee, Chicago, and Detroit, the defending school boards asserted that they could not be held responsible for where people chose to live; therefore, they could not desegregate the schools and maintain their policy of neighborhood schools (Patterson, 2001).

Housing patterns in Rockford formed a key plank of the district's defense, along with a commitment to neighborhood schools:

"That's a consistent thread over 40 years," Scarino [district's attorney] said. "School boards kept neighborhood schools intact as much as possible, and differences in the neighborhoods, not in school policy made the differences in quality of the schools. (A Case for the District, 1993, p. 4A)

Rockford plaintiffs and other plaintiffs against northern schools had to prove that the districts used segregated housing patterns to maintain the segregation that was initially beyond their control. This assertion held strong in Rockford through two court battles and eventually was proven false in the 1989 trial. However, given the continued patterns of housing segregation in the United States, this effective defense strategy was successfully used again in the later 1990s, when the courts decided to end ongoing desegregation remedies.

Rockford's first lawsuit in 1968 (Quality Education for All Children v. School Board of School District 205 of Winnebago County, Illinois, 1973), filed by 63 parents and five community organizations, was denied because the district was able to show a good faith effort toward eliminating discrimination in the district without disrupting the much-valued neighborhood schools in white areas. The lawsuit was filed primarily by parents of color because of the district's plans for rezoning the district in order to close west side schools and build more schools on the east side of the city. Instead of granting an injunction to stop the school board from rezoning the school district, the court allowed the district to implement a limited "voluntary" busing agenda. African American students would be bused to the east side of town only if the students did not have a neighborhood school to attend or if their school was overpopulated (Quality Education for All Children v. School Board of School District 205 of Winnebago County, Illinois, 1973). This first "voluntary" busing involved elementary schools with homogeneous African American populations being closed and parents being forced to enroll their children in white schools across town because other, nearby African American schools were overcrowded.

Rockford's parents of color and white parents opposed busing African American children to the east side. In response to the school board's initial plans to implement busing, 3,477 parents signed a petition against this measure (Segregation in Rockford Schools Charged by 4 Negro Speakers, 1968). Parents of color also attended school board meetings to express their concerns about the impact white teachers—whom they perceived to be racist—would have on their children. The RRS reported:

Salsbury [the school superintendent] was shouted down as he attempted to tell [black] parents school spending was the same throughout the district and pointed to the target school program as evidence of school officials' concerns for the quality of education on the west side.

"We're not interested in integration, we're interested in education for our kids," shouted one man. (Salsbury Will Continue Plans for Transfer, 1973)

Concerns voiced by African American parents regarding their children's welfare fell on the deaf ears of the majority white school board. Rockford parents accused the board of unequal spending for the two sides of town and said the board was using African American children as "political footballs" (Salsbury Will Continue Plans for Transfer, 1973).

Black parents continuously demanded that schools on the west side be improved. These parents saw integration as a last resort to bring resources to the neighborhood schools as well as to gain access to white schools. The following excerpts demonstrate the mixed feelings of Rockford's black community with regard to busing:

> Black parents said they shared the concern of many white parents about the busing of children, but felt as long as their children were kept in one section of the school district, the students' education would be ignored (Busing Is Supported at 3 Mass Meetings, 1973).
>
> "I emphasize that we are not for busing any more than anyone else. … But if busing is to be used, we're going to make it a two-way thing. One-way busing won't help any of us. The blacks in the community don't see the desegregation issue as mainly an issue for or against busing, however, they see it as a way their children can get better quality education." [response from minority committee representative on the school desegregation committee](Blacks View Quality Education as Issue Rather Than Busing, 1973)
>
> "What we want is quality education in the minorities' schools. We want these schools upgraded. We want more black teachers and administrators in the schools." [chairman of the Rockford Ministerial Fellowship of black ministers] (Blacks View Quality Education as Issue, 1973)

The desire to fix existing schools was expressed by Latino community members as well. One representative explained the various issues involved for Latinos and busing:

> The issue of desegregation might compound the problem if Rockford's 5,000 Latins' special needs aren't taken into consideration.
>
> They [Latino parents] are against massive busing because this would spread Latin children all around town, making them a tiny minority everywhere, breaking into the tight, cohesive Latin community, and creating somewhat of an identity problem.
>
> They are against massive busing because if adequate bilingual and bicultural programs and courses aren't instituted in all schools, all Latin students will continue to have difficulties in communicating and hearing.

They oppose massive busing because the social atmosphere might be strained for Latin students going to school with white students, who may not include them in their parties and other social events.

This puts a heavy kind of pressure on the Latin child. I do think we would be better off if we integrated with the overall community, but like most minority groups, people tend to socialize with their own. ("Only 68 of Every 100 Latin Americans Get to 8th Grade," 1973)

In this instance, Latino parents' concerns for the welfare of their children foreshadow the damage done to students of color forced to attend majority white schools. In her reflection on *Brown*, Gay (2004, p. 196) recognizes that "operational conditions existed in early desegregation efforts that perpetuated educational inequality even as it was struck down in principle, law, and policy" (). Thus, students who were forced into harmful learning environments paid a heavy price for the continuation of social activism.

Despite parental concerns, the voices of community advocates, and the recommendation of the school desegregation committee, the Rockford School Board closed the west side's Muldoon Elementary School and began their "voluntary" busing program. Because there was little change in the educational landscape of white communities, white families remained relatively silent about the limited busing of African American students across town. However, as more political pressure came to bear upon northern districts that were not implementing full-scale district reforms and as Rockford's later K–12 plans for "voluntary" busing began to affect white students, white parents became more vocal and active in the school integration process.

Because of the financial sanctions attached to the Civil Rights Act for those districts out of compliance, urban white communities began to be affected by issues of busing and resource allocation (Butler, 1996). In 1971 the Illinois superintendent of public instruction, Michael J. Balkalis, announced specific guidelines for school district compliance with *Brown* and the Civil Rights Act. Although these were rarely enforced, Illinois attached financial consequences in addition to federal sanctions for those districts that failed to comply. Balkalis attempted to apply pressure to those school districts, including Rockford, which were grossly out of compliance with desegregation measures. To comply with the state, Rockford and other districts were expected to produce a comprehensive plan to desegregate the schools. The plan could include, but was not limited to, student busing. Although most Illinois districts that were out of compliance were given a set period to submit their plans, the larger districts—such as Rockford, Peoria, and Chicago—were not given deadlines and thus felt little incentive to abide by the state's mandates. However, with the threat of financial sanctions looming over the district, Rockford implemented an ambitious mandatory busing program that affected both white and

African American children in its most segregated areas. This move had serious consequences for the district.

Rockford's bold implementation of mandatory cross-town busing for all elementary students in the most racially segregated schools and an open enrollment policy for high school students who wished to transfer increased white flight out of the city and resulted in the creation of suburban developments in what had been small farming towns nearby. White families in urban areas such as Rockford, Detroit, Milwaukee and St. Louis relocated to these small towns because the *Milliken I* federal court decision made it impossible for urban districts to cross district lines and force busing to include neighboring suburbs (Patterson, 2001, p.178). The loss of white middle-class families lowered both the tax base of Rockford's schools and the district's achievement scores and created a "'white noose' of suburban development" (Patterson, 2001) around the city. As a result of the city's pervasive economic woes and declining school system, the number of Rockford's middle-class white and black homeowners continues to decline and the number of elderly homeowners and low-income renters continues to rise.

During the 1970s and 1980s, Rockford and other large urban districts tried to retain their dwindling white middle-class populations by doing the minimum to meet state and federal demands for desegregation. Although the school boards were threatened by the state a number of times during the 1970s and 1980s, the voting power of these large districts made politicians avoid pushing the districts into compliance. For over two decades, various community boards and alliances of parents of color met with their local school boards to design feasible solutions to create greater equity for students of color. In the case of Rockford, the desegregation steering committee's initial recommendation to integrate the schools between 7 and 21 percent by 1975 was supplanted by a motion of the board to permit zero to 29 percent (Desegregation Efforts Called Hollow, 1993). The decision to ignore the recommendations of the steering committee led the NAACP to file a joint lawsuit in 1975 with Peoria, Illinois that was later dismissed owing to the school board's limited but visible efforts to desegregate the schools.

A third lawsuit brought by parents and concerned citizens was successful when a second wave of west side school closings began in 1989. The ill-advised closing of the only high school on the west side lead to a full investigation and the subsequent documentation of Rockford's institutionalized racist practices. Mirroring the downfall of other districts, such as Indianapolis *(United States of America v. Board of School Commissioners of the City of Indianapolis, et al.,*1997), the Rockford school board's decision to build new schools in highly segregated white areas and close old schools on zone borders and in predominantly African American and Hispanic areas raised a red flag for the courts.

Following the filing of the 1989 lawsuit by The People Who Care, the school board once again began bargaining with the African American community to avoid losing in court. Two interim orders were implemented before Judge Mahoney's 1993 ruling in favor of the plaintiffs. Each of these plans incorporated more reforms to appease minority parents and show good faith to the courts, as the board had done in the early 1970s. Despite the district's attempts to bypass another court ruling, Rockford was found liable on eleven counts of willful discrimination through (a) student tracking and ability grouping, (b) within school segregation, (c) student assignment, (d) faculty and equipment disparities, (e) employment disparities, (f) staff assignment, (g) transportation, (h) extracurricular activities, (i) bilingual education, (j) special education, and (k) composition of the board of education (Rockford Public Schools, 1997).

During the trial in 1989, the documented accounts of systematic racism were so profuse and profound that the district unsuccessfully sought to have the proceedings closed to the public. Former superintendents testified about the favoritism extended to white students:

> Shaheen [former superintendent] testified that black children were sent to older schools with less equipment and dated books, and taught by less experienced and educated teachers. Staff expected less of them and punished them more often, all of which contributed to lower academic achievement. (Boards Fought Integration, 1993, p.1A)

African American and white teachers and counselors testified:

> Discipline was more instructive than punitive for white kids … . Black kids were not disciplined early on for minor things. Those things would build up because no controls were set. Then they would set over the line, although it was never clear what the line was, and they would get suspended. (Witness Tells of Faculty Bias, 1993, p. 1A)

Parents testified at length about injustices that they had either witnessed or experienced. One white woman with white and biracial children testified concerning the treatment of her white children: "Teachers would absolutely not allow them [white children] to fail. If they were having difficulty, we were contacted and some plan was devised to make them become successful." In contrast, her biracial children "almost seemed to be invisible to the teachers. When they were having difficulty in schools, we weren't contacted enthusiastically by their teachers" (School Board's Move Implies Guilt, 1993, p. 1B)

Her testimony and others like it, along with profuse archival documentation, proved too substantial for Judge Mahoney to ignore. His decision to call for a Comprehensive Remedial Order (CRO) was based on thirty years' research on other desegregation orders and their subsequent outcomes. In his 539-page opinion, Mahoney stated: "The stigmatizing effect on the students is considered by this court to be a cruel act perpetuated by the district on its students" (Schools Played Numbers Game, 1993, p. 1B). Mahoney's multifaceted plan targeted the elimination of all vestiges of segregation that Rockford's minority populations had endured and aimed to close the achievement gap between students of color and white students by 50 percent (Hendrie, 1996). Elements of this plan included school choice, a parent information center, new school construction, reopening some neighborhood schools, limited tracking, racial balancing of classes and extracurricular sports, and comprehensive curricular reforms. The comprehensive nature of Mahoney's reforms reflected the *Green* standard *(Green v. County School Board of New Kent County, 1968))* put in place thirty years earlier. This standard was created by the U.S. Supreme Court and explicated in the *Green v. New Kent County* verdict; the justices sought to erase all areas of institutional racism that were directly or indirectly linked to the power and control of the school district.

When Is Enough Enough?

Mahoney's decision stands as an anomaly in respect to the timing of his verdict. One reason for the short-lived, heavily appealed and contested decision may be the changing political climate and federal sympathies in the United States during the last decade of the twentieth century. In the 1990s, district and federal courts were less apt to rule in favor of plaintiffs in school desegregation suits (Irons, 2002; Orfield and Lee, 2004; Patterson, 2001). However, issues concerning the gains of desegregation were contested well before the 1990s. In the early 1980s, a House of Representatives subcommittee held hearings to discuss the merits of desegregation and busing for school districts. Under attack in these hearings were the intrinsic worth of the social science research used in the *Brown* decision and the conflicting social science data that had accumulated in the following decades. These hearings and their subsequent reports did not provide clear-cut answers to questions about the outcomes of desegregation initiatives, but they served to discredit research that was not considered rigorous or reliable (Scott, 2003). The failure of researchers to reach a consensus and provide indisputable evidence for positive or negative effects of integration made it even more difficult for plaintiffs to convince the courts to enforce the court-ordered plans.

However, the plaintiffs in the 1989 *Rockford* case were able to make use of certain social science research which provided reliable evidence of racist practices. Jeanie Oakes was asked to examine the tracking practices in the district. She found that race related to the ways students interacted with teachers and played a large part in student assignments. Oakes said that she had not seen such subjective measures used to evaluate students in 50 other school systems she studied. She cited district data that showed that achievement test scores often were disregarded in deciding whether students would be in high-, middle- or low-ability classes (Tracking Called a Sham, 1993, p.1B). Oakes gave key examples of how the tracking system denied blacks and Latinos educational opportunities, which affected their learning and potential for future success.

A second key witness for the plaintiffs, Michael Stolee, gave further evidence of intentional discrimination. Stolee described 30 cases involving district practices and policies that maintained or propagated segregated schools. These cases involved various redistricting and school closing plans that forced students of color to be transferred to east side schools after school closings near their neighborhoods (Witness Cites 30 Cases of Bias, 1993). Supporting his testimony were Rockford administrators and faculty. One principal stated that the school system was "kind of a shipping society" in which black students were continually transferred to fill empty seats in classrooms (School Called 'Shipping Society', 1993). Stolee's multi-case study and Oakes's comprehensive evaluation of the district were valued because both scholars were able to document their assertions with empirical, unequivocal data. Such data are often unavailable to those attempting to measure or place value on the outcome of integration initiatives.

Although social science research played an important role in the *Rockford* case, its usefulness in desegregation cases has come into question. The most rigorous attacks on social science research have questioned the ways in which the elimination of vestiges of segregation was being measured and documented in order for school districts to be considered "unitary" (Scott, 2003). In his dissent of the *Dowell* decision, which was the first Supreme Court verdict remand, Justice Thurgood Marshall expressed his frustration over the lack of measures available to determine if the "root and branch" of segregation had been eliminated in a system *(Board of Education of Oklahoma City, Oklahoma v. Robert L. Dowell et al.,* 1991). Ironically, while leading the charge to remand the St. Louis Missouri verdict, Chief Justice William Rehnquist voiced similar dissatisfaction with the lack of evidence that could be presented to prove or disprove the elimination of racism. However, Justice Rehnquist's displeasure with the fact that the plaintiffs had no way to measure the positive effects of decades of desegregation on children of color led him to give the benefit of the doubt to the district instead of the plaintiffs. (*Missouri vs. Jenkins, et al.,* 1995). To further complicate discussions of the place of social science research in court rulings, Justice Clarence Thomas openly referred to the initial research used in *Brown* as "questionable social science research" (as cited in Patterson, 2001) and attacked the very premise of the research as a defamation of African Americans.

These questions surrounding the value of social science research forced the courts to look back on their decisions and seek other ways to examine de jure and de facto discrimination in public schools. As more districts appealed standing verdicts and sought to regain control of their schools, the courts were met with a task outside their scope—that of measuring racial progress. In response to the political climate and the distrust of previously used social science measurements, the courts looked for new ways to measure a district's compliance. These boiled down to three main measures: money spent, good faith on the part of the school board, and length of time in the court system.

Money Spent

The total amount Rockford spent on reform measures, including responses to both interim orders and the Comprehensive Remedial Order, was over $238 million. In his delivery of the court opinion remanding the 1993 Comprehensive Remedial Order, Judge Richard Posner rationalized: "Hundreds of millions of dollars have been poured into the construction and renovation of schools and into programs designed to extirpate the traces of lawful segregation" (People Who Care, 2001). He stated that despite the enormous depletion of funds, Rockford's students of color had not made significant identifiable gains since the CRO was implemented. Moreover, he echoed the political sentiments of those who opposed the desegregation order on the basis of a failure to provide concrete documentation linking the achievement gap between white and minority students to segregation practices. Posner stated: "Four years ago almost to the day we noted the absence of evidence that the gap in scholastic achievement between white and minority students in Rockford is any greater than the gap between white and minority students in school districts that have not been found to have discriminated against their black and Hispanic students. 111F. 3d at 537" (People Who Care, 2001).

Posner's normalization of the achievement gap as a given certainty because of its pervasive nature is problematic for many reasons. The fact that the achievement gap between white students and African American and Hispanic students exists throughout the United States should not be a reason for not combating it in a given city. His willingness to let this stand as an unchangeable entity reflects the *Plessy* decision's discourse of social and racial stratification as normal and socially intransmutable. Moreover, Patterson suggests that the propagation of the racial achievement gap does a disservice to people of color in three ways: (1) it has negative long-range social and economic consequences for students of color if people continue to see them as cognitively less capable; (2) it reinscribes white parents' belief that their children are smarter than children of other races; and (3) it refocuses arguments for social justice from societal causes to deficit models of people of color and their communities (Patterson, 2001). To add further offense, Posner suggested that communities of color look to themselves for the reasons that students of color do not achieve at the same levels as their white counterparts. This suggestion implies that the students' communities are deficient and primarily at fault for the gap in achievement.

Posner's reasons for remanding the *Rockford* court order are consistent with the language used by Chief Justice Rehnquist in his decisions on the cases of *Jenkins, Dowell,* and *Freeman.* Orfield and Lee (2004) state that these three cases opened the gates for school districts to challenge their court-imposed desegregation procedures. In each of these verdicts, Rehnquist mentioned that outstanding amounts of tax dollars were spent to obtain "unitary" status. In her review of the *Jenkins* case in St. Louis, Missouri, Pearsons (1996) states: "The tone of the majority opinion leaves little doubt that the justices were greatly impressed by the sum of money [$600 million] spent by the State of Missouri in this desegregation case" (p. 24). Therefore, money became a tangible measure in place of conflicting social science research.

Good Faith Efforts

Districts with a solid history of court compliance also impressed the Supreme Court and served as a measure for the courts. As part of his decision to remand the three court orders, Chief Justice Rehnquist leveraged the fact that each of the districts appeared faithfully to attempt to implement court-ordered reforms. Other districts, including those represented in the three major Supreme Court rulings on *Jenkins*, *Dowell*, and *Freeman*, demonstrated that they had done all that they could to desegregate their schools, even when some schools in their districts remained very segregated. Moreover, when challenged to provide reasons for the continued segregation in their districts, school board defendants again claimed that they were not responsible for where people chose to live. The *Green* standard, which had been a friend to plaintiffs seeking equity schools in the past, was now used against those same coalitions. School board defendants used the *Green* standard to show that they had worked to the limits of their power and could do no more to erase discrimination because some vestiges of segregation, particularly housing patterns, were not under their control.

Had Rockford's board shown a better façade of compliance with the CRO, the remediation period might have been even shorter than the eight years it was in place. Unlike other districts that were allowed to regain control of their schools through a show of good faith, the Rockford school board had a history of defiance and conflict with the courts. In his summary of his denial of the Rockford school board's seven collective appeals in 1999, Judge Posner called those instances in which the school board openly defied the court's orders and sought to delay the implementation of reforms "guerrilla warfare tactics" (People Who Care v. Rockford Board of Education, District 205, 1999). However, in his later remand of the CRO, Posner drew technical lines between compliance and compliance in good faith and dismissed the school board's blatant measures to balk at obeying the CRO. He wrote, "State and local officials are under no duty to love the chains that federal judges, however justifiably, fasten upon them" (People Who Care, 2001). Instead of continuing to hold the board accountable for injustice, Posner urged the plaintiffs to look at societal factors beyond the control of the board and the scope of the *Green* standard.

Echoes of Justice Henry Billings Brown's rendering of the *Plessy* decision in 1896 can be heard in Posner's focus on societal factors beyond the control of the courts and schools. Brown stated: "When the government, therefore, has secured to each of its citizens equal rights before the law, and equal opportunities for improvement and progress, it has accomplished the end for which it was organized, and performed all of the functions respecting social advantages with which it is endowed" (Plessy v. Ferguson, 1896). Further, Brown asserted, "If one race be inferior to the other, socially, the constitution of the United States cannot put them upon the same plane." Therefore, the law cannot be responsible for changing racial attitudes; it can only be held responsible for seeing that equitable treatment is given to all parties.

Judges such as Posner were likely to grant districts' petitions to resume local control based on the same reasoning applied by Brown. Using similar language to assert his position, Posner argued:

> The board has no legal duty to remove those vestiges of societal discrimination for which it is not responsible. Insofar as the factors that we have mentioned, rather than unlawful conduct by the Rockford school board in years past, are responsible for lags in educational attainment by minority students, the board has no duty that a federal court can enforce to help those students catch up. It may have a moral duty; it has no federal constitutional duty. (People Who Care, 2001)

Posner pointed to other societal issues as reasons for the achievement lag among Rockford's minority students: poverty, unequal educational attainment, parents' education and employment, family size, parental attitudes and behavior, prenatal and neonatal care, child health care, peer group pressures, and ethnic culture (People Who Care, 2001). By focusing on these factors, he condemned the minority communities as perpetrators of the achievement gap and reified deficit notions of communities of color. Using statistical correlations from social science research which rationalized poor achievement among minority students, Posner, much like Brown, pointed an accusing finger at the victims and liberated the schools from accountability.

How Long? Apparently, Long Enough

Posner's ruling to overturn the CRO in Rockford also mirrored lower and higher court rulings in which judges based their decisions on a school district's time spent combating parents through the courts. In his ruling, Posner began by noting that African American parents had pursued court action against Rockford for over 25 years, and the district had been under court supervision for over a decade. Posner did not mention this lengthy battle to praise the resilience of the parents, but only to point out, as Chief Justice Rehnquist did in his *Dowell, Jenkins,* and *Freeman* opinions, that the courts "are not intended to operate in perpetuity" (Board of Education of Oklahoma City, Oklahoma v. Robert L. Dowell et al., 1991). Many of the 38 districts that received unitary status after the Dowell decision and had extensive records with the courts also reasoned that the courts had interfered in local situations for far too long (Patterson, 2001; Pearsons, 1996).

The lack of significant measures to assess "unitary" status left both the lower and higher courts to use arbitrary calculations of time, money, and good faith to guide their rulings. Posner clarified: "The length of the litigation, the scale of the expenditures, and the achievement of desegregation constitute, against the background of applicable law, compelling arguments to end this litigation" (People Who Care, 2001). Even when these arguments were used to overturn a large number of decisions in the 1990s, judges seemed unsure of the merits of these measurements and readily acknowledged that remnants of discrimination existed in the dealings of the school districts. Posner quoted his opinion from the Indianapolis case to impress upon the plaintiffs that the court recognized the existence of racism but could not further eradicate it through the courts or through Comprehensive Remedial Orders that financially burden taxpayers.

Conclusion

In their various rulings, Posner and Rehnquist both conceded that racism remains firmly entrenched, yet unidentifiable and immobile, in the U.S. public school system. Their concessions mirror Justice Brown's open and accepted acknowledgment of the power and privilege given to whites in the United States when he wrote the *Plessy* decision more than one hundred years earlier. As CRT scholars point out, racism is a persistent and pernicious part of the American social and institutional landscape. This racial reality is reflected in the *Rockford* case and similar desegregation cases.

The acknowledgment of and judicial surrender to systemic racism in public schools was a significant blow to African American parents who were hoping for further remediation from the courts. During nearly 30 years of court battles, parents continued to wage war against school boards. In Rockford, open school board meetings concerning the CRO lasted well into the night. Soon the school board began to have closed sessions to keep the room from filling with outraged parents who wanted to voice their opinions. These skirmishes, as well as detailed depictions of the court wins and losses, were relayed by the local media. Parents and students were forced to read and watch their school board wage "guerrilla warfare" at the courts in order to stop students of color from obtaining the same rights and services as white children.

In their study of parents who had pulled their children out of Rockford public schools, Taylor and Alves (2000) noted that fewer than 25 percent of white parents and parents of color believed that the board implemented controlled-choice changes willingly. In their survey, 47 percent of white parents and 64 percent of parents of color believed that the school board was undermining controlled choice in the district, and 68 percent of white parents and 67 percent of parents of color saw the district's actions as harmful to students. Parents' belief that the school board did not act in the best interest of the students is only one effect of Rockford's contentious relationship with parents of color.

When Posner mentioned the length of time African American and Latino parents had been in conflict with the school board as a reason to end the court order, he failed to see the greater impact of 30 years of hostility between the African American and Latino communities and the schools. Since 1968 almost two generations of students have passed through the school system. When discussing unfair proceedings of the school board, 20 years after the first suit was filed, the community activist Leverne Swain called the actions of the school board "business as usual." The *RRS* explained what she meant:

> During a recent interview, the acting president of the Fellowship, Leverne Swain said, "business as usual" means "there's a lot of things that happen under the table that's certainly not for the benefit of people of color" (Black Community Dissatisfied with New Board, 1992, p. 4A)

Swain went on to say that the African American community will not stand for the poor treatment they are receiving in the schools. Thus, parents of color continued to fight for the rights of their children in unacknowledged forms of parental activism.

Parents and activists such as Swain are part of the undocumented history of people of color who refused to stand for the poor treatment of their children in public schools. The account of this case is offered, therefore, as a counter-narrative to the portrayal of parents of color as unconcerned about education. In addition, it provides an alternative framework for understanding the nature of parent involvement. This attention to the ways that parents of color are involved in the education of their children is critical in districts such as Rockford. Although Rockford's populations of color continue to increase, the white teachers and administrators of 30 years ago have remained almost the same. The older generations of activists are now the parents and grandparents of the current students who line the hallways of the Rockford public schools. These guardians of the current students can recall their experiences with apartheid schooling and the pains of integration. In his 1991 dissent (*Board of Education of Oklahoma City, Oklahoma v. Robert L. Dowell et al., 1991*), Justice Marshall pointed out that racism and unjust practice must remain because the people who were cited for these infractions continued to control the schools. Teachers in Rockford average more than 20 years of experience in the district. This average would be even higher were it not for a few new teachers who significantly alter the mean. As a result, the same teachers who were unfair to past students are now charged with being fair to their children. Without examining this parent/teacher dynamic in urban schools, educators cannot ask parents to smile upon entering schools, bringing baked goods, and successfully to advocate on behalf of their children. Given the negative events of the past and these parents' active multiple roles in the history of desegregation, is it any wonder that Rockford's parents, as well as other urban parents, are less likely to re-enter these spaces on still unequal terms?

References

Bell, D. (1983). Learning from Our Losses: Is School Desegregation Still Feasible in the 1980s? *Phi Delta Kappan* 64(8): 572–575.

Bell, D. (1995). Brown v. Board of Education and the Interest Convergence Dilemma. In K. Crenshaw, N. Gotanda, G. Peller, and K. Thomas (eds.), *Critical Race Theory: The Key Writings That Formed a Movement,* 20–45). New York: New Press.

Black Community Dissatisfied with New Board (1992). *Rockford Register Star,* 12 August, p. 4.

Blacks View Quality Education as Issue Rather Than Busing (1973). *Rockford Register Star,* 3 March.

Board of Education of Oklahoma City Public Schools, Independent School District No. 89, Oklahoma County, Oklahoma Petitioner v. Robert L. Dowell et al. U.S. (1991).

Boards Fought Integration (1993) *Rockford Register Star,* 8 April, p. 1.

Busing Is Supported at 3 Mass Meetings (1973). *Rockford Register Star,* 16 February.

Butler, J. S. (1996). The Return of Open Debate. *Society* 33(3): 11–19.

Case for the District (1993). *Rockford Register Star,* 12 May, p. 4.

Comer, J. P. (1991). Parent Participation: Fad or Function? *Educational Horizons* 69(4): 182–188.

Delgado, R. (1995). Legal Storytelling: Storytelling for Oppositionists and Others, a Plea for Narrative. In R. Delgado (ed.), *Critical Race Theory: The Cutting Edge.* (pp. 60–70) Philadelphia: Temple University Press.

Desegregation Efforts Called Hollow (1993). *Rockford Register Star,* 4 April, p. 1.

Desegregation Plans Aplenty Cause Confusion (1973). *Rockford Register Star,* 19 February, p. 1.

Dudziak, M. L. (2000). *Cold War Civil Rights: Race and the Image of American Democracy.* Princeton: Princeton University Press.

Duncan, G. A. (2002). Beyond Love: A Critical Race Ethnography of the Schooling of Adolescent Black Males. *Equity and Excellence* 35: 131–143.

Edwards, P. A. (1993). Before and after School Desegregation: African American Parents' Involvement in Schools. *Educational Policy* 7: 340–369.

Fernandez, L. (2002). Telling Stories about School: Using Critical Race and Latino Critical Theories To Document Latina/Latino Education and Resistance. *Qualitative Inquiry* 8: 43–65.

Finders, M., and Lewis, C. (1994). Why Some Parents Don't Come to School. *Educational Leadership* 51(8): 50–54.

Frankenberg, E.; Lee, C.; and Orfield, G. (2003). A Multiracial Society with Segregated Schools: Are We Losing the Dream? Cambridge, MA: Civil Rights Project, Harvard University.

Gay, G. (2004). Beyond Brown: Promoting Equality through Multicultural Education. *Journal of Curriculum and Supervision* 19: 195–216.

Grant, C. A. (1995). Reflections on the Promise of Brown and Multicultural Education. *Teachers College Record* 96: 707–721.

Green v. County School Board of New Kent County, Va, 391 U.S. 430 (1968).

Grievances behind Deseg Suit Specified (1975). *Rockford Register Star,* 22 October, p. 1.

Hendrie, C. (1996). Racial Quotas Are Ordered for Rockford. *Education Week* 15(39): 1–2.

Irons, P. (2002). *Jim Crow's Children.* New York: Penguin.

Lopez, G. R. (2003). Parent Involvement as Racialized Performance. In G. Lopez and L. Parker (eds.), *Interrogating Racism in Qualitative Research Methodology,* (pp. 71–96). New York: Peter Lang.

Manning v. The School Board of Hillsborough County, Florida, 244 F.3d 927 (11th Cir. 2001).

Minority Groups Boycott First Desegregation Meeting (1972). *Rockford Register Star,* 13 October, p. 1.

Missouri, et al., Petitioners v. Kalmia Jenkins, et al., 93 U.S. 1823 (1995).

Only 68 of Every 100 Latin Americans Get to 8th Grade (1973). *Rockford Register Star,* 13 March.

Orfield, G., and Lee, C. (2004). Brown at 50: King's Dream or Plessy's Nightmare? Cambridge, MA: Civil Rights Project, Harvard University.

Other Integration Plans Proposed (1971). *Rockford Register Star,* 12 December, p. 1.

Patterson, J. T. (2001). *Brown v. Board of Education: A Civil Rights Milestone and Its Troubled Legacy.* New York: Oxford University Press.

Pearsons, G. (1996). Is Racial Separation Inevitable and Legal? *Society* 33(3): 19–25.

People Who Care v. Rockford Board of Education 171 F. 3d 1083 (7th Cir. 1999).

People Who Care v. Rockford Board of Education 246 F. 3d 1073 (7th Cir. 2001).

People Who Care v. Rockford Board of Education 111 F. 3d 528 (7th Cir. 1997).

Plessy v. Ferguson, 163 U.S.537, 210 (1896).

Quality Education for All Children, v. School Board of School District 205 of Winnebago County, 362 F. Supp. 985 (N. D. IL. 1973).

Rockford Public Schools (1997). Remedial Order. Retrieved 2 April 2000, from http://www.rps205.com/remedial/index.html

Rury, J. L., and Cassell, F. A. (eds.) (1993). *Seeds of Crisis: Public Schooling in Milwaukee since 1920.* Milwaukee: University of Wisconsin Press.

Salsbury Will Continue Plans for Transfer (1973). *Rockford Register Star,* 28 May, p. 1.

School Board's Move Implies Guilt (1993). *Rockford Register Star,* 4 May, p. 1.

School Called 'Shipping Society' (1993). *Rockford Register Star,* 24 April, p. 1.

Schools Played Numbers Game (1993). *Rockford Register Star,* 13 December, p. 1.

Scott, R. (2003). Five Decades of Federal Initiative Concerning School Desegretory Effects: What Have We Learned? *Journal of Social, Political and Economic Studies* 28: 177–215.

Segregation in Rockford Schools Charged by 4 Negro Speakers (1968). *Rockford Register Star,* 29 February, p. 4.

Solórzano, D. G., and Bernal, D. D. (2001). Examining Transformational Resistance through a Critical Race and Latcrit Theory Framework: Chicana and Chicano Students in an Urban Context. *Urban Education* 36: 308–342.

Solórzano, D. G., and Yosso, T. J. (2002). A Critical Race Counterstory of Race, Racism, and Affirmative Action. *Equity and Excellence* 35: 155–168.

Tate, W. F. (1997). Critical Race Theory and Education: History, Theory, and Implications. In M. Apple (ed.), *Review of Research in Education,* vol. 22, 191–243. Washington, DC: American Education Research Association.

Taylor, D. G., and Alves, M. J. (1999). Controlled Choice: Rockford, Illinois, Desegregation. *Equity and Excellence in Education* 32(1): 18–30.

Taylor, D. G., and Alves, M. J. (2000). Implementing Controlled Choice and the Search for Educational Equity in the Rockford, Illinois Public Schools: A Survey of Parents Who Withdrew from the Rockford Public Schools after the 1998–99 School Year. *Equity and Excellence in Education* 33(2): 81–94.

Tracking Called a Sham (1993). Rockford Register Star, 17 April, p. 1.

United States v. Board of School Commissioners of the City of Indianapolis, 128 F. 3d. 507 (7th Cir. 1997).

Villenas, S., and Deyhle, D. (1999). Critical Race Theory and Ethnographies Challenging the Stereotypes: Latino Families, Schooling, Resilience, and Resistance. *Curriculum Inquiry* 29: 413–445.

Walker, V. S. (2000). Valued Segregated Schools for African American Children in the South. *Review of Educational Research* 70: 253–286.

Witness Cites 30 Cases of Bias. (1993). *Rockford Register Star,* 22 April, p. 4.

Witness Tells of Faculty Bias (1993). *Rockford Register Star,* 20 April, p. 1.

5

"Proving Your Skin Is White, You Can Have Everything": Race, Racial Identity, and Property Rights in Whiteness in the Supreme Court Case of Josephine DeCuir

JESSICA T. DECUIR-GUNBY

Issues of race, racial identity, and whiteness as property have historically had major impact on all parts of society in the Americas, including the Louisiana Creole* community. The Creole community, like the larger African American community, has been influenced by social rules stemming from the institution of slavery and pervasive, systemic racism, particularly in terms of differential treatment based on individuals' skin tone and hair texture (Martin, 2000). In both the Creole and black communities, skin color and hair texture are assigned values. (This is discussed in more detail later in this chapter.) There is a preference for light skin and "good hair" (straighter and less coarse), and less preference for those who are darker with curlier and coarser hair. Such prejudices have multiplied subdivisions within the Creole community. The lighter Creoles are considered "better" than the darker Creoles, yet darker-skinned Creoles with "not as good hair" are still viewed as "better" than blacks without Creole heritage. Basically, the "whiter" one's features, the more he or she receives acceptance from the Creole community (Barthelemy, 2000). This colorism (color prejudice) is prevalent within the Creole community and can occur within one's own family.

Although viewed as significant, differences in phenotype within the Creole community can be minuscule, as are the differences found in my own Louisiana Creole family. For instance, I have Native American facial features (particularly my nose), a brown complexion, curly hair, and a French surname. Although I am of Creole heritage† from both parents, with French, African,

---

* I have chosen to use the term "Negro" in several places in this chapter to preserve historical context. In other places, I use the term "black" to represent a more recent means of racial identification. In addition, I use the term "Creole" distinctly from "Black," although in some geographical regions, Creoles are considered a subgroup of blacks.

† When asked about my racial identity, I state that I am black although I acknowledge my Creole heritage.

and Native American ancestors, I do not have the valued and often stereotyped Creole characteristics of light skin and straight hair (see Martin, 2000; Barthelemy, 2000). Because of this, I was often treated differently within my family.

I remember that, as a child, many times I went to visit my great-aunts and saw the power they attributed to skin color and hair texture. In particular, I remember their speaking about how we Creoles needed to marry people with nice light skin, and not anybody with dark skin or "bad" hair. They would always talk about black people with "bad" hair and how our hair was so much better; because we were Creoles and had "better" hair, we were seen as better. However, my relatives made a point of complimenting my brother's and sister's hair over my hair. Although my hair was not as "good" as my siblings', it was still seen by my aunts as better than black people's hair. In addition, because I was darker than many of my relatives, including my siblings, I was treated differently. My lighter relatives were given many advantages: more attention, more financial assistance, and more social opportunities. Despite the difference in our skin tones, it was always implied that because we were Creole and not "black," we were better than our black counterparts.

Because I do not have the Creole community's favored phenotypic characteristics, at an early age I became aware of their importance as well as their impact in the Creole community. In addition, I became cognizant of colorism within the black community, specifically between Creoles and blacks. I realized the centrality of race in my life and the power associated with skin tone and hair texture, particularly "whiter" skin tone and hair texture. However, after seriously pondering the various interactions regarding phenotype that I have encountered in the Creole community, I have realized that these exchanges are not actually a result of the Creole community's disliking me personally for my differences in phenotype; rather, they are a result of the historic differential treatment of blacks in American society in general. The problems I have encountered stem from the endemic practices of white supremacy. It is the institution of slavery, a function of the differential treatment based upon race, that helped to create the issues of skin color and hair texture that have historically plagued and continue to divide the black community. Because of this, many Creoles have internalized a hatred for what is African, including skin color and hair texture, and have chosen to identify with the oppressor (Barthelemy, 2000).

My story is just one example of the complexity of race and the politics and power of skin color and hair texture. Another such story is that of Josephine DeCuir, a fellow Creole and distant relative,* who encountered the politics and power of race and phenotype and attempted to use them to her advantage. The case of Josephine DeCuir demonstrates that race and racial identity are complex issues. It exhibits the power of whiteness and its range of influence.

---

* Josephine DeCuir is my fourth-cousin removed ancestor.

Although her case is little known, it has had a significant impact on society. The purpose of this chapter is to examine the case of Josephine DeCuir, specifically by discussing the importance of race, racial identity, and whiteness as property using a critical race theory (CRT) analysis. This chapter includes a discussion of race, whiteness, skin tone and hair texture, as well as of Creole culture; the illustrative story of Josephine DeCuir; and finally, an analysis of DeCuir's case focusing on whiteness as property. The intention is to elucidate how the property rights of whiteness prevented DeCuir from receiving equal treatment. Moreover, the DeCuir case will be addressed in relation to a similar case, *Plessy v. Ferguson*. Inferences will be drawn regarding multiracialism.

The Defining and Meaning of Race

What Is Race?

In an essay entitled "The Conservation of Races," W. E. B. Du Bois (1995 [1897]) posed a pivotal question: "What is race?" He attempted to answer his question by stating that a race is "a vast family of human beings, generally of common blood and language, always of common history, traditions and impulses, who are both voluntarily and involuntarily striving together for the accomplishment of certain more or less vividly conceived ideals of life" (Du Bois p. 21). Although Du Bois asked how to define race and provided an answer in biological terms, his fundamental concern was not necessarily with the definition of race, but with the actual meaning of race and its effect on Negro people. The impetus of his concern was clarified when he posed these additional questions: "What is the real meaning of Race; what has, in the past, been the law of race and development, and what lessons has the past history of race development to teach the rising Negro people?" (Du Bois p. 20). The search for answers to these questions has remained a central focus in the study of race, racial identity, and blacks.

In addition to Du Bois, other scholars have attempted to discover the meaning of race. Several have described the concept of race as a socially and historically constructed ideological system (Du Bois, 2001 [1915]; Du Bois, 1999 [1920]; Frazier, 1957b; Locke, 1992 [1925]; Omi and Winant, 1994; Roediger, 1991; Winant, 1994). For instance, Locke (1992 [1916]) viewed the concept of race as "a fundamental category in social thinking" (p. 1). In addition, he suggested that "race theory … is something that has and must have correlation with our practical ideas of human society … and must reinforce what is currently believed about human society" (p. 7). Similarly, Roediger (1991) stated, "Race is constructed differently across time by people in the same social class and differently at the same time by people whose class positions differ" (p. 7). Likewise, Omi and Winant (1994) defined race as "a concept which signifies and symbolizes social conflicts and interests by referring to different types of human bodies," and racial formation as "the sociohistorical process by which racial categories are created, inhabited, transformed, and destroyed" (p. 55). Winant (1994) added that racial formation is considered a process because "the inherently capricious and erratic nature of racial categories forces their constant rearticulation and reformulation—their social construction—in respect to the changing historical contexts in which they are invoked" (p. 115). However, Frazier (1957b) conceptualized it differently when he stated that racial classification is actually a hierarchical social organization known as a caste system that serves as the "basis of social control," which ensured that people of European ancestry would remain at the top of the hierarchy and those of African descent would remain at the bottom (p. 262). The evolutionary concepts in the definitions of race by these scholars lend credence to the centrality of the role race plays in the development, maintenance, and evolution of social structure. Moreover, this view appreciates the dynamic social construction of race and accentuates its malleability. Differences in social class, historical eras, and the society's prevailing concepts of race can and do vary as the belief systems of a society change.

Although many scholars have discussed race in terms of social construction, many others have discussed it in terms of economics and power (Du Bois, 2000 [1940]; Frazier, 1957a, 1957b, 1968; Locke, 1992 [1916]; Roediger, 1991). Du Bois (2000 [1940]) saw a connection between race and wealth. He contended that economic differences and the maintenance of economic disparities fuel the creation of theories of racial inferiority: "the income-bearing value of race prejudice was the cause and not the result of theories of race inferiority" (Du Bois, 2000 [1940], p.129). Roediger (1991) expanded on this idea by stating that racial attitudes are often functions of economics and politics, and that in order to understand race, one must explore the relationship between race and class: "The most pressing task for historians of race and class is not to draw precise lines separating race and class but to draw lines connecting race and class" (p. 11). Similarly, Locke (1992 [1916]) contended that race can be better understood if described as a political entity. He stated, "The 'dominant' race becomes the 'political' race, the politically [powerful] people who can mold contacts their way," while those "lacking in the capacities for this kind of racial or political dominance ... will come under the more forceful control of what are political or dominant groups" (p. 22). Approaching race from the perspectives of economics and power allows explication of the continuing political dominance of whites and the political subjugation of blacks in the United States. From this perspective, conceptions of racial superiority and inferiority are extensions of economic and political power.

Discussing the meaning of race is an arduous task because race is a convoluted and enigmatic conception. Particularly in the United States, the elements that frame the discussion of race (social class, economic position and political influence) are all subjectively constructed. There may be associative and objective proxies used to approximate these elements of racial construction, but each element is itself a multidimensional construct. In essence, since social class, economics, and politics all help to determine power, it can be argued that race can be viewed as a symbol of power. Race is a socially and historically constructed ideological system that permeates all social, cultural, economic, and political domains, and thus a major determinant of power. Race is especially a determinant of power if one's race is white.

The Meaning of Whiteness

Although race is an important construct that helps to determine various levels of power, racial categories are difficult to define, especially whiteness. Whiteness is socially determined by skin color, facial features, and national origin (Davis, 1991). These subjective categories allow the definition of whiteness to be vague. Despite this, the legal system has not offered an explicit definition of whiteness. Instead, it has implied the meaning of whiteness in two ways: by determining who is not white, and by denigrating those who are not white (see Gotanda, 1995; Lopez, 2000b). As described by Lopez (2000b), according to Supreme Court rulings, whites are "those not constructed as non-White. That is, Whites exist as a category of people subject to a double negative: They are those who are not non-White" (p. 631). In addition, in determining whiteness, the courts declared those labeled nonwhite to be inferior, and those called whites superior. As Lopez (2000b) stated, "Whites exist not just as the antonym of non-Whites but as the superior antonym" (pp. 631–632). In other words, the courts implied that whiteness is "the reification of privilege and superordination" (Gotanda, 1995, p. 264).

Because of the vagueness in defining what it means to be white, whiteness can be defined as "a racial discourse, whereas the category 'white people' represents a socially constructed identity" (Leonardo, 2002, p. 31). That is to say, whiteness is a socially constructed identity based on mutually agreed-upon characteristics. However, whiteness can also be viewed as "a racial perspective or a world-view" (Leonardo, 2002, p. 31). This perspective shapes the interactions and paradigms of its individual members. In particular, this worldview allows whiteness to be defined as "normal" and gives whiteness a sense of privilege. Manglitz (2003) defines white privilege as "the resulting benefits that accrue to those who have been constructed as possessing 'Whiteness' or who are seen as 'White' " (p. 122). In other words, being white creates a sense of entitlement. Being white means viewing whiteness as normalcy and is commensurate with exclusive access to societal resources facilitated by other powerful whites who already utilize this socially inherited racial privilege.

Because whiteness is normalized and creates privilege, it is an enormous source of power. Whiteness allows for the inequitable distribution of resources and power, with whites receiving material goods and opportunities while nonwhites do not (see Shapiro, 2004). In addition, as described by Hernandez (2000), "the ability of Whites not to think of themselves in racial terms at all is another benefit of whiteness, in that whiteness is cognitively viewed as the norm and hence not a race" (p. 72). Through power and privilege, whiteness creates and maintains social, political, and economic support. Whiteness is thus normalized and protected by its members because of the numerous benefits and privileges that are afforded to them (Bell, 2000; Harris; 1995; Leonardo, 2002; Manglitz, 2003). One obtains power and privilege simply by virtue of being white.

Skin Tone and Hair Texture

Whites thus have had "the leisure of not having to think about race at all" (Hernandez, 2000, p. 72). However, this has not been so for blacks. The determining of whiteness as valuable or superior and the simultaneous establishing of blackness as invaluable or inferior helped create a schism within the black psyche. As described by Frazier (1968), "Living constantly under the domination and contempt of the white man, the Negro came to believe in his own inferiority, whether he ignored or accepted the values of the white man's worlds" (p. 239). These feelings of inferiority were often manifested in different ways in different social and economic classes within the black community. One way in which feelings of inferiority were expressed was the emergence of skin color as a determinant of status and worth (Frazier, 1957a, 1968; Gatewood, 2000). Discrimination based on skin tone, known as "colorism," became common among both whites and blacks.

The importance of skin color in the black community is rooted in the racist practice of slavery (Boyd-Franklin, 2003; Russell, Wilson and Hall, 1992). On plantations, blacks were treated differently according to skin color, facial features, and hair texture. Slaves with lighter skin, European facial features, and straight hair were often given better treatment than their darker-skinned counterparts with African features and curlier hair. Lighter-skinned slaves often worked in the homes of their owners while darker-skinned slaves often worked in the fields. Working in the homes of slave owners as maids, butlers and nannies was usually less difficult than being field workers, cultivating the land in all weathers (Quarles, 1987; Huggins, 1977).

Although the slaves viewed this differential treatment as simply a function of skin color, there was often a deeper reason for it. Many lighter-skinned blacks were allowed to work in the homes of their owners because they were the owners' illegitimate children (Byrd and Tharps, 2001). This was a way for slave owners to remain in contact with their children. In doing so, slave owners were able to compensate for the guilt they often felt for having children with slave women. By allowing their black children to work in the house under better conditions, the slave owners could ease their guilty consciences by knowing they were treating their children better than they did those slaves who were not their offspring.

In addition to being subjected to different treatment regarding labor, slaves were also treated differently economically. In general, lighter-skinned slaves were sold at higher prices than darker slaves:

At slave auctions, [slave masters] would pay almost five times more for a house slave than for a field slave, showing they were also more valuable (a field hand could be bought for sixteen hundred dollars, while the going rate for a "fancy" girl was five thousand dollars). (Byrd and Tharps, 2001, p. 19).

Because light-skinned slaves were purchased at higher prices, it was believed by slaves that lighter-skinned blacks were worth more. Thus, light-skinned blacks began to be viewed as more valuable in the slave community.

Although skin tone was most commonly viewed by the slave community as the major determinant of a slave's worth, hair texture also played a significant role (Russell, Wilson and Hall, 1992; Byrd and Tharps, 2001). Because many slaves had light complexions and European facial features and could pass as people of European descent, it was necessary to identify characteristics that would differentiate light-skinned slaves from Europeans. Whites considered the natural hair texture of Africans to be like wool, more animal-like than human-like, unlike the hair texture of those of European descent. Dehumanizing the African by comparing his hair texture to that of an animal made hair texture an important indicator of blackness, in that whites believed that "hair was considered the most telling feature of Negro status, more than the color of the skin" (Byrd and Tharps, 2001, pp. 17–18). A person could have a light skin tone and not be considered light-skinned if he or she also had African facial features, coarse hair, or both. Likewise, a person with a dark skin tone might not be labeled dark-skinned if he or she had European facial features or finer hair texture. This degradation of African heritage further demoralized slaves and created a pathological self-hatred of all that was African—especially physical features. As a result, slaves quickly differentiated between "good" hair (straighter hair without coarse curls and frizz) and "bad" hair (the antithesis of "good" hair) and began to associate light skin with "good" hair and dark skin with "bad" hair. In doing so, the slaves began to internalize that "darker-skinned Blacks with kinkier hair were less attractive, less intelligent, and worth less than their lighter-hued brothers and sisters" (Byrd and Tharps, 2001, p. 19).

In most cases, darker-skinned slaves saw that lighter-skinned slaves got better treatment and were viewed as more valuable. The lighter-skinned slaves were treated less harshly and cruelly and were afforded more opportunities to acquire valuable skills. Because of this differential treatment based on skin color and hair texture, many darker-skinned slaves began to resent the lighter-skinned slaves (Russell, Wilson and Hall, 1992; Byrd and Tharps, 2001). These sentiments continued after slavery, creating a schism in the black community based on skin tone. This was the case with mulattoes, particularly among the Louisiana Creoles discussed earlier.

Creoles

The complexity of the meaning of race and its interrelatedness with skin color and hair texture has had important implications not only for blacks but also for American society in general. As Fields (1982) stated, the determination to maintain the United States as "a white man's country" has allowed the issues of color and race to infiltrate all political, economic and social domains. This white supremacist ideological system influenced the perceived need to main-tain the "purity" of the white race, encouraging drastic measures to ensure this. One result was a nearly universal abhorrence of intermarriage between whites and Negroes (Teo, 2004). Many anti-miscegenation statutes were passed, including the "one-drop rule," declaring that any person with "one drop of Negro blood" was to be considered Negro, regardless of his or her physical appearance (Davis, 1991; Dominguez, 1986; Gotanda, 1995; Russell, Wilson and Hall, 1993). According to this white supremacist belief system, the "one drop" of Negro blood made such a person contaminated and inferior, unworthy of being labeled white.

Although many whites viewed racial mixing as deplorable, there was a large population of racially mixed people, known by the Spanish-derived term "mulattoes." Mulattoes enjoyed a higher socio-economic status than Negroes because of their white ancestry, yet they were considered inferior to whites because of their Negro ancestry (Gatewood, 2000; Schweninger, 1996). This placed mulattoes in a peculiar position; they were not Negro enough to be called Negro, yet not white enough to be called white. Mulattoes' peculiar position helped create a three-tiered social system in which they were placed between whites and Negroes. In the United States, this system was perhaps most prominent in Louisiana, particularly in New Orleans, where the people caught in the middle were known as Creoles.

Creoles, free people of color, or *gens de couleur libre*, as the French called them, are a unique group who resided in southern Louisiana during the Reconstruction period and still live there today. The first Creoles, descendants of Africans from Senegambia, came to Louisiana in the early nineteenth cen-tury (Hall, 1992; Hanger, 1996). The term "Creole," however, evolved over time. In the early eighteenth century, it referred to those locally born and of some African descent. The term "Creole" was later defined as a person born in the Americas of European heritage. By the nineteenth century, Creoles were considered to be people of mixed African and French and/or Spanish ances-try (see Brasseaux, 1996; Hall, 1992; Hanger, 1996; Martin, 2000). Dunbar-Nelson (2000) suggests that Creoles were natives of the southern Louisiana parishes whose ancestors included Spanish, West Indian, or French people. Dunbar-Nelson describes them: "The true Creole is like the famous gumbo of the state, a little bit of everything, making a whole, delightfully flavored, quite distinctive, and wholly unique" (p. 9).

Creoles were a distinctive group of people. They largely spoke French, practiced Catholicism, and made endogamous marriages with fellow Creoles (Dormon, 1996). In addition, they had political, economic, and social opportunities not often available to Negroes. For example, Creoles were able to own businesses and property, to travel abroad (most commonly to France), and to testify against whites in court, even during slavery (Dormon, 1996; Gehman, 2000; Pearson, 2001). Some Creoles even owned slaves (Brasseaux, 1996; Page, 2001; Schweninger, 1996). Creoles were allowed these privileges because of their European and Native American heritage.

Quite frequently, European men, usually of French or Spanish descent, engaged in long-term relationships with Creole women. This partnership was known as *plaçage* (Martin, 2000). Although Europeans could not legally marry Creole women, they would ensure that their mixed-race children and concubines would be emancipated, even if this meant purchasing their family's freedom. Some Europeans would also purchase houses for their Creole families, have their children educated in France, and provide for their children financially (Gehman, 1994; Schweninger, 1996). This demonstrates that many of the Europeans indeed loved their Creole families.

The system of *plaçage* was beneficial for Creole women; being involved with an established European male often ensured that both she and her children would be provided for and would be afforded many rights and opportunities that Negroes did not have. However, the benefits gained by participating in this system were accompanied by many repercussions. *Plaçage* caused many problems both between Creoles and white women and between Creoles and Negroes. White women resented the fact that many European men were involved with Creole women. In addition, many white women were livid if European men took responsibility for the welfare of their illegitimate, mixed-race children. Negroes often resented Creoles because Creoles were treated better, had more rights, and were viewed by whites as superior to Negroes. In addition, many Negroes disliked Creoles because Creoles often denied their African heritage while choosing to emphasize their European heritage (Brasseaux, 1996; Gehman, 1994; Schweninger, 1996).

Being caught in the middle between whites and Negroes caused Creoles great difficulty. Acknowledging their African heritage frequently led to their enduring the same treatment as Negroes. Claiming their European heritage provoked a serious backlash from whites, who took every opportunity to remind Creoles of the fact that they were not white. In addition, claiming their European heritage further alienated them from Negroes. As a result, Creoles found comfort in socializing among the group that was most receptive to them and their unique experiences—fellow Creoles. However, most Creoles longed for upward mobility, wanting more of the civil rights which accompanied being white (Pearson, 2001). This even came at the expense of Negroes (Dormon, 1996). Louisiana's Creoles often took advantage of their political, economic and social power, which allowed them to make their voices heard, even in the legal arena (see Pearson, 2001). This is particularly true of Josephine DeCuir and her court cases: *DeCuir v. Benson* (1875) and *Hall vs. DeCuir* (1878).

Political Context

The late nineteenth century was a period of racial challenge for the entire United States, especially the South, where Reconstruction was dramatically changing the existing economic, political and social systems. Louisiana was the first formerly Confederate state to be affected by these changes, with Reconstruction lasting from the capture of New Orleans in 1862 until the departure of Northern troops in 1877 (Brasseaux, Fontenot and Oubre, 1994; Hanger, 1997). New Orleans became the first Confederate city to undergo the Reconstruction process, with Louisiana being used experimentally to implement federal policies. Louisiana also served as the model other Confederate states were to follow. These radical changes created a schism among the citizens of Louisiana, with many being torn between the old system of white supremacy and the new system of "racial equality." In particular, it was a difficult time for Creoles because they were beginning to lose some of their power and status, particularly their special legal status in Louisiana's three-tiered racial system (Dormon, 1996).

Because of difficulty in establishing a new system of "racial equality," the status of race relations between Negroes and whites during Reconstruction, particularly in New Orleans, was like a pendulum, swinging back and forth between integration and segregation (Blassingame, 1973). It was not uncommon for laws to change dramatically, particularly those that concerned the rights of Negroes. For instance, legislators, including several Negro legislators (for examples, see Hanger, 1997), during the 1867 Constitutional Convention passed the Louisiana Constitution of 1868, which attempted to create a politically and economically egalitarian society. Specifically, Article 13 of the Constitution of 1868 afforded Negroes the right of equal access to public facilities, referring to facilities that required a city, parish, or state license for operation (see LA Const. art. XIII, 1868; Blassingame, 1973; Hanger, 1997).

Although the Constitution of 1868 promoted the idea of an egalitarian society, it was quite difficult to enforce the racial equality laws, especially Article 13 of the Constitution. In an attempt to strengthen Article 13, legislators passed the Civil Rights Act of 1869, allowing violated persons to sue the owners of public facilities that did not abide by the terms of the article (see Blassingame, 1973; Hanger, 1997). The passage of the Civil Rights Act of 1869 impelled many to take legal action. In fact, numerous Negroes who suffered civil rights violations in public places on the basis of race, particularly on trains and steamboats, utilized this act (for examples, see Blassingame, 1973). Josephine DeCuir, in her Supreme Court case *Hall v. DeCuir* (1878), utilized the momentum of the Civil Rights Act of 1869 to take legal action against the owner of a steamboat, the *Governor Allen*, under the premise that her civil rights as a Creole had been violated.

Josephine DeCuir's Story

Josephine DeCuir was a wealthy Creole woman. She had fair skin, European facial features, and no visibly "Negro" physical traits. Josephine experienced a life of affluence through her travels to France and her marriage to Antoine DeCuir, a plantation owner and grandson of Joseph DeCuir, one of the wealthiest plantation owners in Pointe Coupée Parish (see Page, 2001). In addition to marrying into wealth, Josephine had affluent family members of her own. Her brother, Antoine Dubuclet, served as Louisiana state treasurer from 1868 to 1878; he was also the wealthiest free person of color in Louisiana prior to the Civil War. Her cousin Pierre Deslonde served as Louisiana's secretary of state from 1872 to 1876. Josephine DeCuir could be described as a member of Louisiana's privileged Creole class.

Belonging to the privileged class, she and her family often had experiences that were not available to other people of color. This included being able to travel frequently, including overseas to France. However, being able to travel frequently did not mean evading racial difficulties. Josephine DeCuir had such a racial confrontation on a steamboat. On July 20, 1872, DeCuir boarded the *Governor Allen*, which carried both passengers and cargo, in New Orleans en route to her plantation in Pointe Coupée Parish. Upon boarding, she was informed that there were separate accommodations for Negroes and whites, something that she was well aware of because she regularly traveled this route. She then boarded the boat, paying the $5.00 charge reserved for Negroes rather than the $7.00 charge for whites. After boarding the boat, DeCuir insisted on obtaining a berth in the white cabin instead of residing in the "bureau," the Negro section, located below the deck assigned to white passengers. She was denied this request and was also denied the right to eat with the white passengers. Instead of accepting a room in the bureau, DeCuir, out of protest, took a seat in a chair in the recess of the boat, an area located at the rear of the White cabin, refusing to accept a cot when offered one.

Her written testimony describes her experience on the *Governor Allen*:

> [DeCuir] was expressly denied though in ill health at the time the privilege of even a state room in the cabin or a seat at the table to take her meals on said boat. Although due application was made in her behalf to the officers of said boat, she was forced to remain in a small compartment in the rear of said boat which was a public place, without the common conveniences granted to the other passengers on the sole ground

alleged set up and expressly stated by the Captain and Clerk of said boat that she was a colored person. Thus making an illegal discrimination on account of color. [DeCuir] alleges that she was willing and able to pay for and did proper payment for such privileges as the other cabin passengers had, but was denied such privileges. (*DeCuir v. Benson*, 1875, pp. 3–4).

Josephine DeCuir was denied equal access to facilities because she was a person of color; she believed that her civil rights were violated. In her statement, she averred that she was a native of Louisiana and that "her husband was a large land holder in the parish of Pointe Coupée" and that she was "well educated and had resided more than twelve years in the City of Paris, France" (*DeCuir v. Benson*, 1875, p. 5). More specifically::

the treatment [on the *Governor Allen* was] not only a gross infraction of the constitution and laws of [Louisiana] and those of the United States and of this state [Louisiana]—but [was] also a gross indignity to her personally. And for this denial of equal rights and privileges on the part of said officers of the Steamboat *Governor Allen* was such a shock to her feelings and occasioned so much mental pain, shame, and mortification that her mind was affected. That she was exposed to the vulgar conversation of the crew and everyone on said boat (*DeCuir v. Benson*, 1875, pp. 5–6).

As a result, DeCuir sued John G. Benson, the owner of the *Governor Allen*, for $75,000 ($25,000 in actual damages and $50,000 in exemplary damages). Judge E. North Collum of the Eighth District court ruled in her favor, awarding her $1,000 in damages. Benson later appealed this decision. In March 1874, the Louisiana Supreme Court upheld the decision, declaring that such treatment was in direct violation of Article 13 of the 1868 Constitution of Louisiana, which stated:

All persons shall enjoy equal rights and privileges upon any conveyance of a public character; and all places of business or public resort, or for which a license is required by either state, parish, or municipal authority, shall be deemed places of a public character, and shall be open to the accommodation and patronage of all persons without distinction or discrimination on account of race or color. (Louisiana Const. art. XIII, 1868).

However, in 1877, the U.S. Supreme Court overturned both the lower courts' decisions, stating:

We think this statute, to the extent that it requires those engaged in the transportation of passengers among the States to carry colored passengers in Louisiana in the same cabin with Whites, is unconstitutional and void. If the public good requires such legislation, it must come from Congress and not from the States. (See *Hall v. DeCuir*, 1878, LEXIS 2197).

According to the Supreme Court, DeCuir's treatment on the *Governor Allen* was constitutional. Differential treatment based on race was legally protected. The court felt that changing such a law would require federal—rather than state—legislation. As such, the Supreme Court gave Louisiana, as well as the other states, the right to privilege whiteness.

The Decuir Case and the Property Rights of Whiteness

The United States' history of racism created a racial caste system supporting white racial dominance and the subsequent subordination of people of color. Whiteness has remained at the top the racial caste system and has acquired value like that of property (Bell, 2000; Harris, 1995). Viewing whiteness as a form of property is rooted in the notion that race and property rights have been inextricably intertwined since the creation of the United States (see Harris, 1995). The United States' system of slavery facilitated the confluence of racial identity and property rights. Slavery helped to define racial groups and maintained racial distinctions by establishing a racial hierarchy ranging from white as premier to black as inferior. Racial identity was intertwined with property rights in that being white meant having the right to own property while being black meant being considered property. Whites were slave owners and blacks were slaves. Although some blacks did own slaves, as did some Creoles (see Brasseaux, 1996; Page, 2001; Schweninger, 1996), blacks could never own whites. In addition, whiteness did not have a socio-economic requirement for whites. According to Bell (2000), "Even those whites who lack[ed] wealth and power [were] sustained in their sense of racial superiority" (pp. 71–72). Thus, it can be said that "White identity and Whiteness were sources of privilege and protection" as well as power (Harris, 1995, p. 279).

One tenet of critical race theory (CRT) suggests that whiteness can be viewed in the same terms as property (see Harris, 1995). In viewing whiteness in terms of property, the traditional attributes of property are reified. According to Harris (1995), a possessor of whiteness has the same rights associated with other forms of property, including possession, use and disposition. More specifically, these property rights include transferability, the right to use and enjoyment, reputation rights, and the right to exclude others. Transferability means the transference of whiteness from one generation to another. The right to use and enjoyment refers to the maintenance of white privilege and white identity. Reputation rights suggest that white identity is an individual's most salient characteristic and must be protected. And the right to exclude means that white identity gives a sense of entitlement, including the rights to include and exclude others from its privileges.

Because of the power structure during slavery, whiteness was assured high status and power, and simultaneously blackness was relegated to subjugation and powerlessness. This structure extended after slavery and affected all aspects of life, including public transportation. The property rights of whiteness were particularly visible and influential for Josephine DeCuir on the *Governor Allen*. These property rights include the rights of disposition, use and enjoyment, reputation and exclusion.

Rights of Disposition (Transferability)

One important property right is the right of disposition—the right to transfer whiteness. The functions of the rights of disposition or transferability are to ensure the inalienability of whiteness through the guarantee that whiteness can be transferred from one person to another, from generation to generation (Harris, 1995, p. 282). When whiteness is transferred, those receiving it are entitled to all of the rights and privileges held by previous generations.

The defining of race, as discussed earlier in this chapter, has been based on social, cultural and economic ideologies. However, the maintenance of distinct racial groups has depended largely on physical characteristics (see Byrd and Tharps, 2001; Davis, 1991; Russell et al., 1992). Physical characteristics are an important determinant of racial group membership, particularly between whites and Negroes, because each group has traditionally distinctive features. However, racially mixed people like Creoles blurred this distinction. Josephine DeCuir was such a person.

As described by E. North Collum, the presiding judge in *DeCuir v. Benson* (1875), DeCuir was

> ... a lady of color, genteel in her manners, modest in her deportment, neat in her appearance and quite fair for one of mixed blood. Her features [were] rather delicate with a nose which indicate[d] a decided preponderance of the Caucasian and Indian blood. The Blackness and length of the hair, which [was] straight, confirm[ed] this idea. She was never a slave, nor [was] she the descendant of a slave. Her ancestors were always free as herself. She [had] always been respected by those who knew her. (p. 218).

These were not "typical" Negro characteristics. The description implies that DeCuir was not of Negro heritage. As such, it could be assumed that she was entitled to the transfer of whiteness and all its privileges.

However, the description does not cast her as completely white either. DeCuir was somewhere in the middle racially, and her lack of completely white heritage made her Negro and therefore powerless. Any Native American heritage she might have had was not significant because Native Americans were free during slavery and were not considered to be as low in status as Negroes (Lopez, 2000a). Thus, because she was not completely white, she did have nonwhite heritage and was not able to claim all of the rights afforded by whiteness, including the right to ride in the upper cabin. She was not able to claim the rights of disposition from her white heritage because of her non-white heritage.

Right to Use and Enjoyment

Another important property right is the right to use and enjoyment. This refers to asserting white privilege and maintaining white identity. In addition, whiteness is "something that can both be experienced and deployed as a resource" (Harris, 1995, p. 282). This means that whiteness is intangible—something that one does—as well as tangible, something that is reifiable. This often comes in the form of asserting power and using money (material goods), respectively.

The upper cabin of the *Governor Allen* represented the right to use and enjoyment which could be both experienced and deployed as a resource. The upper cabin cost $7, $2 more than that of the Bureau, the Negro section. This difference in price is significant because charging white passengers more meant that they would be entitled to a better steamboat experience as well as better accommodations. Imposing a higher price made it appear as though white passengers were purchasing better services. However, Negroes were not given the option of paying the higher fee and using the better accommodations. White passengers were benefiting from their right to use and enjoyment based upon their whiteness.

DeCuir thought that she should participate in the right to use and enjoyment. As a landowner and a French-educated person, she possessed all of the resources that entitled her to "whiteness" based upon her deployment of resources. Her cousin Deslonde, in his testimony, explained this sense of entitlement:

> I think it is worse now that it was before the war. Before the war, being a rich planter and patronizing boats, we had some kind of comfort. Since the war, generally the planters made very little crops and they do not patronize these boats to a great extent. They travel on the first boat comes. In fact, I can travel just as well as any man on one certain boat on this river. That is all, but not with the proper fare that should be extended to me. (*DeCuir v. Benson*, 1875, p. 194).

Deslonde's statement implies that Josephine DeCuir was from a family accustomed to wealth. It also suggests that because of Deslonde's status (and money), a status that could be extended to DeCuir, they could afford to travel and had the right to travel on certain steamboats, thereby receiving the right to use and enjoy whiteness.

Because of DeCuir's family background, she believed that she was entitled to and had the ability to pay for a seat on the upper deck. In her statement during the *DeCuir v. Benson* trial, as described earlier, "she was willing and able to pay for and did proper payment for such privileges as the other cabin passengers had, but was denied such privileges." However, the right of use and enjoyment was determined based on race, not money and wealth. This meant that a poor, uneducated white person had more right to utilize the upper cabin of the *Governor Allen* than did DeCuir, a wealthy, educated Creole person.

Reputation

The third property right is that of reputation. This means that there is a value for white identity as well as a need to preserve white identity. Preserving white identity involves engaging in self-ownership of who one is in terms of whiteness. The reputation of whiteness must be maintained at all costs. This often includes preserving white identity at the expense of black identity. Constructing and maintaining whiteness as superior requires blackness as its inferior opposite (see Fanon, 1963, 1967). The property rights of reputation in essence involve establishing whiteness as the most socially desirable race and thus the most reputable.

Because the preservation of white identity was essential to maintaining the reputation of whiteness, segregation was necessary. As implied by John Benson, the boat captain, it was imperative that separate cabins be maintained for white and Negro passengers. Benson stated, "They [white people] would not travel on any boat where the white and colored passengers were mixed because there is a public prejudice against associating with colored persons" (*DeCuir v. Benson*, 1875, p. 73). It is this "prejudice" he described that allowed white identity to be maintained. Not wanting to associate with Negro passengers allowed the preservation of white identity and the subsequent degradation of Negro identity.

White passengers would go to drastic measures to ensure the reputation of whiteness. Benson exclaimed: "If any boat was to attempt to mix the white and colored persons in the same cabin, I believe they would lose the white travel altogether" (*DeCuir v. Benson*, 1875, p. 73). This point is crucial because Benson believed that white passengers would choose not to utilize the services of a steamboat in order to avoid sharing a cabin with black passengers, which would damage their reputation as white individuals. As such, DeCuir could not have obtained a place in the white cabin because it would have damaged the racial reputation of the white passengers there.

Right to Exclude

The last property right is the absolute right to exclude. In other words, it is the right to establish a system of exclusivity which withholds or confers opportunities, access and rights based on race. This right concerns the inclusion of those who are white and the absolute exclusion of those who are not white. A basic premise of the right to exclude is white supremacy and the subordination of blacks: "It assumes that black ancestry in any degree, extending to generations far removed, automatically disqualifies claims to white identity, thereby privileging 'white' as unadulterated, exclusive, and rare" (Harris, 1995, p. 283). Thus, the right to exclude extends to all areas where whiteness can conceivably have power.

During the trial of *DeCuir v. Benson* (1875), when asked if the differential treatment of whites and Negroes on steamboats was based on the race of passengers, Deslonde explained:

> It must be on account of color. Because if you [a white person] travel yourself, they will give you all the accommodations necessary. If I travel, there will be a line of demarcation right away. Proving your skin is white, you can have everything. (p. 195)

His statement points out the preferential treatment that occurred based on race on steamboats. White passengers received the best accommodations and treatment. However, sharp distinctions were made for black passengers. They received separate and most often substandard treatment. Deslonde specifically observed the power in whiteness, as well as its right to exclude. He observed that being white gave one access to all rights and privileges on steamboats and beyond. If one was not white, he or she was not afforded those same opportunities.

Deslonde's observations of differential treatment by race were supported by Benson, as alluded to earlier, when he provided a rationale for segregation on steamboats. Benson further explicated the segregation procedures:

> The custom is on boats where they have them is to give colored persons accommodations by themselves in a cabin appropriated to them exclusively and where the boats have no such accommodations it is customary to give them rooms by themselves or with the colored employees of the boat and giving them their meals after the white cabin passengers are through with the cabin crew of the boat. When I speak for this custom, I have reference to colored persons applying for cabin accommodations. They are never mixed with the white cabin passengers to my knowledge. (*DeCuir v. Benson*, 1875, pp. 72–73)

Benson's description demonstrates how whiteness allowed the exclusion of others. This underscores both the complicity of white business owners in helping to maintain the system and the lengths to which they went to participate in it. Only those deemed white were allowed better treatment. The superiority of white identity was reinforced by providing separate accommodations for white and black passengers, allowing black passengers to share rooms with black employees, and having them to eat meals after white passengers had eaten. Throughout all these practices, black identity was further degraded. These practices helped to maintain feelings of white racial superiority and to fuel the right to exclude.

DeCuir and Plessy

Josephine DeCuir was quite insightful in how she viewed the value of whiteness. She saw that whiteness was the key to a life of comfort, respect and opportunity. Being white meant having access to everything and never being denied anything. She saw the importance of race and racial identity, as well as the power they exerted. As such, she attempted to gain access to the property rights of whiteness through her pursuit of a place in the white cabin on the *Governor Allen*.

About 20 years later, another Louisianan experienced similar racial discrimination while attempting to use public transportation. Homer Plessy was denied access to the white section on a train. He attempted to obtain the right to sit in the white section of the train by addressing the influence of race, racial identity, and whiteness as property through his Supreme Court case, *Plessy v. Ferguson*.

Plessy v. Ferguson, 1896

On June 7, 1892, Homer Plessy, a person of mixed racial descent—one-eighth African and seven-eighths European—sat in a vacant seat reserved for white passengers on a train going from New Orleans to Covington, Louisiana. The train officials became aware that Plessy, a Negro by social definition, was sitting in the white section and told him that he had to move to the Negro section or, according to Louisiana law, be imprisoned. Plessy refused and was sent to the parish jail of New Orleans. He was charged with criminally violating the Act of 1890, which clearly stated that passengers on trains were required to be separated by race.

Plessy contended that the Louisiana Act of 1890 was unconstitutional and violated his civil rights. Because the train officials attempted to seat him with the wrong race, his civil rights were abridged. Plessy believed that his Negro heritage was not physically discernible and that he was entitled to all the rights and privileges of whites. Plessy proudly identified as a white person, not a Negro.

On May 18, 1896, the U.S. Supreme Court eventually upheld the Louisiana lower courts' decision to support the Act of 1890 requiring the segregation of races on trains. More interestingly, with this decision the Supreme Court neglected to address the real issue at hand—the definition of race. Plessy was actually more concerned about being legally identified as a white person than with challenging the Louisiana Act of 1890. Instead of making a decision on the definition of race, the Supreme Court decided that this issue should be determined by each state, and furthermore, that it was irrelevant to the specific case in *Plessy*. The Supreme Court used this opportunity to support segregation, establishing the policy of "separate but equal."

Plessy's and DeCuir's cases have a significant relationship. DeCuir's case is a precursor to *Plessy v. Ferguson* (1896) and is in fact referenced in the *Plessy* argument (see *Plessy v. Ferguson*, 1896; Thomas, 1997). Both cases involve incidents that occurred on vessels of transportation in Louisiana. In addition, both cases attempted to address the differential treatment of people of color, which was a result of the property rights of whiteness. However, unlike Plessy, within her lawsuit DeCuir did not attempt directly to address the issue of defining race, particularly in terms of whiteness. Instead, she concentrated on gaining access to the property of whiteness. Her case indirectly addresses whiteness in terms of material resources and wealth through mentioning her socio-economic status and personal privileges (e.g., being an educated woman and a past resident of France, privileges mostly afforded to whites and Creoles during this period). Despite Plessy's and DeCuir's different approaches, race, racial identity, and the property rights of whiteness were central to both cases, further establishing the importance of these issues.

Although defining race was not a significant issue for DeCuir, it was an important issue for Plessy. By neglecting to address the definition of race, the Supreme Court continued to value whiteness and uphold its property rights. The courts could not allow the reputation of whiteness to be destroyed by letting a man with Negro ancestry to be labeled white. Moreover, establishing a policy of "separate but equal," expanded the rights of use and enjoyment, exclusion and disposition. Whites were given more power to use and enjoy better facilities and to exclude people of color from those facilities, as well as the power to transfer all of these rights.

As the cases of Plessy and DeCuir both demonstrate, the issues of race, skin color, and racial identity have played integral roles in American society. However, the telling of history does not emphasize all the implications of their cases. The telling of history neglects to discuss Plessy's desire to address the defining of whiteness as well as DeCuir's acknowledgment of and desire to obtain access to the property rights of whiteness. Both cases emphasize the importance of taking socio-historical context into consideration when investigating race, skin color, and racial identity. The cases indirectly ask a fundamental question about how race is constructed in America: When one is not completely black or white, where is one's appropriate place?

Implications for Multiracialism

The case of Josephine DeCuir evokes many questions about the present-day role of multiracialism. In present-day terms, DeCuir could be classified as multiracial, although Creoles self-identify in various ways, including Creole, black, both Creole and black, or white (Dormon, 1996). However, the question of how to identify racially is not just a dilemma that Josephine DeCuir encountered. It is an issue for many multiracial people, including the Creole community and other individuals with two or more racial heritages. Multiracialism is particularly important in the recent discussion of multiracial identification and the census.

For the first time in history, during the 2000 U.S. Census individuals were given the opportunity to identify multiracially with a new write-in option. According to the Census, in 2000 there were 36,419,434 blacks residing in the United States (McKinnon, 2001). Of that population, 34,658,190 individuals identified monoracially, or claimed only black heritage. The remaining 1,761,244 individuals identified as multiracial. The combination of black and white heritage was the largest multiracial category involving blacks, with 784,764 individuals (Jones and Smith, 2001).

On the surface, the option of choosing multiple races seems positive. The opportunity to express one's various racial and ethnic heritages allows the expression of multiple identities. Beneath the surface, however, listing all racial groups, especially white, is an attempt to access the property rights of whiteness. The multiracial label has been mostly utilized by whites in an attempt to transfer the property rights of whiteness to their multiracial children. As explained by Hernandez (2000), "Those who are mixed-race will logically assert their White ancestry, while downplaying their African ancestry, in order to further themselves in the social structure and flee repression" (p. 72). By writing in that they are white, they are attempting to gain power. Such behavior is problematic because it "reinforces societal White supremacy when society places greater value on White ancestral connections than on non-White connections" (Hernandez, 2000, p. 71). It further supports the fallacy that whiteness is superior.

In addition, when people with white ancestry use the multiracial label, they may overlook and negate the cultural and social heritages of any other racial groups. Thus, the multiracial label opens the door for the denial of the collective histories of nonwhite racial groups. It helps implement the nonrecognition of race (Gotanda, 1995; Hernandez, 2000; Okizaki, 2000). This will further normalize whiteness and encourage whites not to think in terms of race at all. It also limits the legal means by which racial discrimination can be collectively addressed. Thus, it makes even more pervasive the property rights of whiteness.

Although Josephine DeCuir's experience on the *Governor Allen* occurred more than 130 years ago, her case has many implications for modern-day issues of race and racial identity, especially multiracialism. Her case demonstrates the importance of multiracialism including the impact it has on society. More specifically, it forces us to consider the property value of whiteness when considering multiracialism. Her experience compels us to ask: What does having the opportunity to declare multiple races really mean? Who really benefits from declaring a multiple racial heritage? How can multiracial individuals have a voice and not be victimized by the hegemony of whiteness as property?

Significance of the Case of Josephine DeCuir

As my personal experiences in the Creole community show, race and pheno-type are salient issues. However, what the case of Josephine DeCuir especially illustrates is that concerns of race, racial identity, and whiteness as prop-erty have historically had a major impact on all aspects of society. They have affected the highest court in our legal system. Despite its historical signifi-cance, the case of Josephine DeCuir has been largely overlooked. This chapter has been an attempt to correct this oversight. The inclusion of her story in this volume is significant in many ways.

First, this case has enormous historical and legal importance, especially pertaining to the civil rights movement. Her case, which made it to the Supreme Court in 1877, is a precursor to another Louisiana civil rights case, *Plessy*. The *DeCuir* case contributed to the *Plessy* decision by helping set a legal precedent only 19 years earlier, with DeCuir's case concerning the sleeping arrangements on boats and Plessy's concerning the seating arrangements on trains. The exploration of her case demonstrates the importance of demon-strating how history affects the present.

The civil rights violation of Josephine DeCuir also helps to explain how the complexities of race and racial identity have influenced the legal system. As the case demonstrates, issues of race and racial identity have played inte-gral roles in American society. These are important issues mainly because they help to determine power, particularly in deciding who is or is not white. Similarly, the case of Josephine DeCuir helps to show the pervasiveness of the property rights of whiteness and how the power of whiteness is manifested in social arenas as well as supported by the legal system.

Last, by analyzing DeCuir's case from a CRT perspective and focusing on whiteness as property, this chapter adds to the CRT literature in many ways. Instead of focusing on the more commonly used tenets of CRT such as coun-terstorytelling and the permanence of racism, this chapter utilizes whiteness as property, a less frequently employed tenet of CRT (see DeCuir and Dixson, 2004). Like the other tenets of CRT, whiteness as property is useful in explor-ing issues of race, racism, and power. In addition, in taking a CRT approach, this chapter focuses primarily on the legal writings that shaped the CRT movement as well as on a legal case, further centering on the roots of CRT (see Delgado and Stefancic, 2001; Ladson-Billings and Tate, 1995; Tate, 1997). A return to the legal roots of CRT is important to the continued development and expansion of CRT, especially in social science research.

References

Barthelemy, A. G. (2000). Light, Bright, Damn *Near* White: Race, the Politics of Genealogy, and the Strange Case of Susie Guillory. In S. Klein (ed.), *Creole: The History and Legacy of Louisiana's Free People of Color*, 252–275. Baton Rouge: Louisiana State University Press.

Bell, D. (2000). Property Rights in Whiteness: Their Legal Legacy, Their Economic Costs. In R. Delgado and J. Stefancic (eds.), *Critical Race Theory: The Cutting Edge*, 71–79. Philadelphia: Temple University Press.

Blassingame, J. (1973). *Black New Orleans: 1860–1880*. Chicago: University of Chicago Press.

Boyd-Franklin, N. (2003). *Black Families in Therapy: Understanding the African American Experience*. New York: Guilford.

Brasseaux, C. A. (1996). Creoles of Color in Louisiana's Bayou. In J. H. Dormon (ed.), *Creoles of Color of the Gulf South*, 67–86. Knoxville: University of Tennessee Press.

Brasseaux, C. A.; Fontenot, K. P.; and Oubre, C. F. (1994). *Creoles of Color in the Bayou Country*. Jackson: University Press of Mississippi.

Byrd, A. D., and Tharps, L. L. (2001). *Hair Story: Untangling the Roots of Black Hair in America*. New York: St. Martin's.

Davis, F. J. (1991). *Who is Black?: One Nation's Definition*. University Park: Pennsylvania State University Press.

DeCuir, J., and Dixson, A. (2004). "So When It Comes Out, They Aren't That Surprised That It Is There": Using Critical Race Theory as a Tool of Analysis of Race and Racism in Education. *Educational Researcher* 33(5): 26–31.

DeCuir v. Benson, 27 La. Ann. 1 (Fifth District Court of Orleans Parish, 1875).

Delgado, R., and Stefancic, J. (2001). *Critical Race Theory: An Introduction*. New York: New York University Press.

Dominguez, V. R. (1986). *White by Definition: Social Classification in Creole Louisiana*. New Brunswick, NJ: Rutgers University Press.

Dormon, J. H. (1996). Ethnicity and Identity: Creoles of Color in Twentieth-Century South Louisiana. In J. H. Dormon (ed.), *Creoles of Color of the Gulf South*, 166–179. Knoxville: University of Tennessee Press.

Du Bois, W. E. B. (1995 [1897]). The Conservation of Races. In D. L. Lewis (ed.), *W. E. B. Du Bois: A reader*, 20–27. New York: Henry Holt.

Du Bois, W. E. B. (1999 [1920]). *Darkwater: Voices from within the Veil*. Minneola, NY: Dover.

Du Bois, W. E. B. (2000 [1940]). *Dusk of Dawn: An Essay toward an Autobiography of a Race Concept*. New Brunswick: Transaction.

Du Bois, W. E. B. (2001 [1915]). *The Negro*. Minneola, NY: Dover.

Dunbar-Nelson, A. (2000). People of Color in Louisiana. In S. Kein (ed.), *Creole: The History and Legacy of Louisiana's Free People of Color*, 3–41. Baton Rouge: Louisiana State University Press.

Fanon, F. (1963). *The Wretched of the Earth*. New York: Grove.

Fanon, F. (1967). *Black Skin, White Masks*. New York: Grove.

Fields, B. J. (1982). Ideology and Race in American History. In J. M. Kousser and J. M. McPherson (eds.), *Region, Race, and Reconstruction*, 143–177. New York: Oxford University Press.

Frazier, E. F. (1957a). *Black Bourgeoisie*. Glencoe, IL: Free Press.

Frazier, E. F. (1957b). *Race and Culture Contacts in the Modern World*. New York: Knopf.

Frazier, E. F. (1968). *On Race Relations*. Chicago: University of Chicago Press.

Gatewood, W. B. (2000). *Aristocrats of Color: The Black Elite, 1880–1920*. Fayetteville: University of Arkansas Press.

Gehman, M. (1994). *The Free People of Color of New Orleans*. New Orleans: Margaret Media.

Gehman, M. (2000). Visible Means of Support: Businesses, Professions, and Trades of Free People of Color. In S. Kein (ed.), *Creole: The History and Legacy of Louisiana's Free People of Color*, 208–222. Baton Rouge: Louisiana State University Press.

Gotanda, N. (1995). A Critique of "Our Constitution Is Colorblind." In K. Crenshaw et al. (eds.), *Critical Race Theory: The Key Writings That Formed the Movement*, 257–275. New York: New Press.

Hall, G. M. (1992). *Africans in Colonial Louisiana: The Development of Afro-Creole Culture in the Eighteenth Century*. Baton Rouge: Louisiana State University Press.

Hall v. DeCuir, 95 U.S. 485 (1878).

Hanger, K. S. (1996). Origins of New Orleans' Free Creoles of Color. In J. H. Dormon (ed.), *Creoles of Color of the Gulf South*, 1–27. Knoxville: University of Tennessee Press.

Hanger, K. S. (1997). *Bounded Lives, Bounded Places: Free Black Society in Colonial New Orleans*. Durham, NC: Duke University Press.

Harris, C. I. (1995). Whiteness as Property. In K. Crenshaw et al. (eds.), *Critical Race Theory*, 357–383. New York: New Press.

Hernandez, T. K. (2000). "Multiracial" Discourse: Racial Classifications in an Era of Color-blind Jurisprudence. In J. F. Perea et al. (eds.), *Race and Races: Cases and Resources for a Diverse America*, 69–77. St. Paul, MN: West Group.

Huggins, N. I. (1977). *Black Odyssey: The Afro-American Ordeal in Slavery*. New York: Vintage.

Jones, N. A., and Smith, A. S. (2001). *The Two or More Races Population: 2000*. Washington, DC: U.S. Department of Commerce.

Kaba, M. (2001). When Black Hair Tangles with White Power. In J. Harris and P. Johnson (eds.), *Tenderheaded: A Comb-bending Collection of Hair Stories*, 102–108. New York: Washington Square.

Louisiana Const. Art. XIII (1868).

Ladson-Billings, G., and Tate, W. F. (1995). Towards a Critical Race Theory of Education. *Teachers College Record* 97: 47–68.

Leonardo, Z. (2002). The Souls of White Folk: Critical Pedagogy, Whiteness Studies, and Globalization Discourse. *Race, Ethnicity and Education* 5(1): 29–50.

Locke, A. (1992 [1916]). *Race Contacts and Interracial Relations*. Washington, DC: Howard University Press.

Locke, A. (1992 [1925]). *The New Negro*. New York: Athenaeum.

Lopez, I. F. (2000a). The Social Construction of Race. In R. Delgado and J. Stefancic (eds.), *Critical Race Theory: The Cutting Edge*, 163–175. Philadelphia: Temple University Press.

Lopez, I. F. (2000b). White by Law. In R. Delgado and J. Stefancic (eds.), *Critical Race Theory*, 626–634. Philadelphia: Temple University Press.

Manglitz, E. (2003). Challenging White Privilege in Adult Education: A Critical Review of the Literature. *Adult Education Quarterly* 53(2): 119–134.

Martin, J. M. (2000). *Plaçage* and the Louisiana *Gens de Couleur Libre*: How Race and Sex Defined the Lifestyles of Free Women of Color. In S. Kein (ed.), *Creole: The History and Legacy of Louisiana's Free People of Color*, 57–70. Baton Rouge: Louisiana State University Press.

McKinnon, J. (2001). *The Black Population: 2000*. Washington, DC: U.S. Department of Commerce.

Neal, A. M., and Wilson, M. L. (1989). The Role of Skin Color and Features in the Black Community: Implications for Black Women and Therapy. *Clinical Psychology Review* 9: 323–333.

Okizaki, C. L. (2000). "What Are You?": Hapa-Girl and Multiracial Identity. *University of Colorado Law Review* 71: 464–465.

Omi, M., and Winant, H. (1994). *Racial Formation in the United States from the 1960s to the 1990s*. 2nd ed. New York: Routledge.

Page, K. (2001). Defiant Women and the Supreme Court of Louisiana in the Nineteenth Century. In W. M. Billings and M. F. Fernandez (eds.), *A Law unto Itself? Essays in the New Louisiana Legal History*, 178–190. Baton Rouge: Louisiana State University Press.

Pearson, E. H. (2001). Imperfect Equality: The Legal Status of Free People of Color in New Orleans, 1803–1860. In W. M. Billings and M. F. Fernandez (eds.), *A Law unto Itself?*, 191–210. Baton Rouge: Louisiana State University Press.

Plessy v. Ferguson, 163 U.S. 537 (1896).

Quarles, B. (1987). *The Negro in the Making of America*. New York: Macmillan.

Roediger, D. R. (1991). *The Wages of Whiteness: Race and the Making of the American Working Class*. London: Verso.

Russell, K.; Wilson, M.; and Hall, R. (1992). *The Color Complex: The Politics of Skin Color among African Americans*. New York: Anchor.

Schweninger, L. (1996). Socioeconomic Dynamics among the Gulf Creole Populations: The Antebellum and Civil War Years. In J. H. Dormon (ed.), *Creoles of Color of the Gulf South*, 51–66. Knoxville: University of Tennessee Press.

Shapiro, T. M. (2004). *The Hidden Costs of Being African American: How Wealth Perpetuates Inequality*. New York: Oxford University Press.

Tate, W. F. (1997). Critical Race Theory and Education: History, Theory and Implications. In M. W. Apple (ed.), *Review of Research in Education, vol. 22*, 191–243). Washington, DC: American Educational Research Association.

Teo, T. (2004). The Historical Problematization of "Mixed Race" in Psychological and Human-Scientific Discourse. In A. S. Winston (ed.), *Defining Difference: Race and Racism in the History of Psychology*, 79–108. Washington, DC: American Psychological Association.

Thomas, B. (1997). *Plessy v. Ferguson: A Brief History with Documents*. Boston: Bedford.

Ward, J. V. (2000). *The Skin We're In: Teaching Our Children To Be Emotionally Strong, Socially Smart, Spiritually Connected*. New York: Free Press.

Winant, H. (1994). *Racial Conditions: Politics, Theory, Comparisons*. Minneapolis: University of Minnesota Press.

6
Keeping it Real: Race and Education in Memphis

CELIA K. ROUSSEAU

A 2005 headline in the local newspaper in Memphis, Tennessee reads, "Herenton hits racial nerve on schools." The headline refers to a statement by the city's mayor regarding the funding of local schools. The mayor, who was advocating for the consolidation of city and county school districts, told state legislators his view of school funding: "You know when the funding mechanism is going to change—it's when the education of white students in the suburbs begins to suffer" (Sparks and Dries, 2005, p. B1).

As reported in the newspaper, the mayor's statement "whipped up [a] tempest." The mayor of a suburban municipality voiced his outrage: "I am appalled that he would even say that out loud, much less think it … . This racist jargon disgusts me so much. It's about giving children the best possible education no matter their heritage or economic condition" (Sparks and Dries, 2005, p. B1). The chairman of the county school board said that the mayor's comments were "irresponsible, intellectually lazy, and quite frankly, sad" (Sparks and Dries, 2005, p. B1). Printed letters to the editor were similarly critical of the mayor's statement. The author of one letter asserted, "Herenton's comments … prove again that he is a racist" (Gary, 2005, p. B9). Another author wrote: "So it is finally clear. The only way the school system can go forward is when white students start to suffer. Has this man gone completely insane? The only way this system starts to go forward is when the black students start to catch up" (Setliff, 2005, p. B9).

Not all public responses to the mayor's statement were critical, however. One local newspaper columnist, Wendi Thomas, argued that there was truth in the mayor's words. In fact, she suggested, "If the academic performance of city school students and county school students were reversed, suburban folks wouldn't be able to consolidate fast enough" (Thomas, 2005, p. B1). Thomas wrote that the outraged response by local officials to the mayor's statement distracted people from the critical issue—talking about the role of race in consolidation. "If we're as concerned about the education of all children as we say we are, we must confront the fears that make some parents in a mostly white county school district leery of consolidating with a mostly black, largely poor district" (Thomas, 2005, p. B1).

The mayor's statement and the conditions to which he alluded illustrate several of the core propositions of critical race theory (CRT). The mayor's assertion of the significance of race and the reaction of the community to his statement are an example of a "CRT moment," which occurs when the salience of race is highlighted during everyday events. Critical race theory provides a framework with which to understand these situations and the forces that shape them. The purpose of this chapter is to illustrate how the CRT framework can be employed to analyze educational inequity in a large urban district. I use the CRT moment represented in the controversy over school district consolidation as the point of departure for this examination and seek to highlight a particular approach to CRT analysis.

Two Different Approaches to CRT

As outlined in the first chapter of this book by Dixson and Rousseau, an ever-growing body of scholarship in education has developed that draws upon critical race theory. One concern of some CRT scholars has been that the burgeoning movement will move too quickly away from the scholarship in legal studies on which it was founded (Ladson-Billings, 1999; Tate, 1999). The foundation in legal studies offers not only specific constructs that can be employed in a CRT analysis (as illustrated in several chapters of this volume), but also insight into the potential paths that CRT scholarship in education could follow.

Specifically, Delgado (2001) argues that legal scholars in CRT follow two modes of thought. One view, which Delgado describes as "idealist," holds that "racism and discrimination are matters of thinking, attitude, categorization, and discourse" (2001, p. 2282). These scholars focus on discourse analysis as a primary way to examine issues of race and racism. Moreover, the idealist approach suggests that racial discrimination will be eradicated once stereotypes, along with derogatory images and words regarding people of color, are removed from America's social consciousness (Delgado, 2003).

Another approach to CRT analysis in legal studies focuses less on discourse and the attitudes reflected in speech. This approach, which Delgado (2001) refers to as "materialist" or "racial realist," acknowledges the importance of attitudes and words but regards racism as more than stereotypes and images. The realists view racism as a "means by which society [systematically] allocates privilege, status, and wealth" (Delgado, 2001, p. 2283). Therefore, according to the realists, analysis of racism must go beyond a focus on discourse to include attention to material factors.

This focus on the material aspects of subordination was a key characteristic of the early writings on CRT in the law. However, according to Delgado, the focus of legal scholarship on CRT has shifted from a realist to an idealist approach: "Critical race theory, after a promising beginning, began to focus almost exclusively on discourse at the expense of power, history, and similar material determinants of minority-group fortunes" (2003, p. 122). This shift in the nature of CRT scholarship in legal studies is significant, in part, because it offers insight into the direction of CRT in education.

Much like its predecessor in legal studies, CRT in education began with an emphasis on the realist perspective. The first article on CRT in education (Ladson-Billings and Tate, 1995) drew from the materialist roots of CRT in the law. Specifically, the authors examined the property value of whiteness and its structural impact on education. However, following this realist beginning, CRT scholarship in education appears to have made a shift analogous to that which took place in legal studies. According to DeCuir and Dixson (2003), the dominant pattern in recent CRT scholarship in education has been to focus on counterstorytelling/narratives and discourse analysis to illustrate the phenomenon of race, taking a more "idealist" approach with less attention to materialist factors.

Although some might view these distinctions as merely rhetorical, Delgado (2003) argues that these theoretical differences have important implications, insofar as the failure to understand the nature of racism in all its complexity prevents the development of effective strategies to overcome it. For this reason, I have chosen to focus in this chapter on illustrating the use of CRT in the analysis of a large urban school district, and to do so using a realist approach. There is certainly sufficient rhetoric surrounding the case to provide the foundation for a more idealist examination of the discourse (the quotes shared at the start of the chapter represent only a small portion of those available). Such analysis would offer substantial insight into the attitudes and stereotypes of those involved. However, what I seek to illustrate through a materialist analysis is that a focus strictly on attitudes would reveal only part of the picture and provide a limited understanding of the forces affecting the education of students of color in the Memphis area. A more cogent understanding of the role of race in education in Memphis requires attention to the material factors that both create and sustain the conditions to which the mayor's statement refers. Such a materialist/realist approach serves also to highlight several of the core propositions of CRT.

"Race Is an Issue"

In her article on the reaction to the mayor's statement, Thomas asserts that the episode provides "proof that race is an issue" (Thomas, 2005, p. B1). As noted elsewhere in this volume,* the assertion of the salience of race is one of the primary themes of critical race theory. For example, in their 1995 article on critical race theory in education, Ladson-Billings and Tate write: "Race continues to be

---

* See, for example, the chapters by Dixson and Rousseau, DeCuir-Gunby, and Morris.

a significant factor in determining inequity in the United States" (p. 48). With respect to education, they assert that the significance of race is reflected in the differences in school experience and performance between white students and students of color.

Such differences are evident in the two systems the mayor seeks to consolidate. The Memphis City School (MCS) system serves 116,000 students. In 2005 it was 86.4 percent black, 8.9 percent white, 3.4 percent Hispanic, and 1.2 percent Asian. In 2003, 39 percent of the students in grades K–8 scored below "proficient" on the state standardized test. During the same year, 57 percent of high school students scored below "proficient" on the state mathematics examination. The 2003 "grade" given to the system by the state, based upon the three-year average of test scores, was a "D" in K–8 math and an "F" in K–8 reading. In addition to this achievement data, other outcomes for the system include a 60 percent graduation rate in 2004.

In contrast, the Shelby County School system (which encompasses several suburban municipalities around the city) serves 47,000 students. The student population is currently 68.2 percent white, 25.3 percent black, 2.8 percent Hispanic, and 3.2 percent Asian. In contrast to the Memphis City Schools, only 11 percent of the county's K–8 students scored below "proficient" on the state test in 2003. Similarly, only 16 percent of the county's students scored below "proficient" on the high school mathematics exam. The state's grades for the system in 2003 were an "A" in math and a "B" in reading. In contrast to the city's graduation rate, the corresponding rate for the county was 88 percent in 2004.

Thus, the two districts at the center of the mayor's comments and the ensuing "firestorm" have very different racial compositions and very different levels of success with respect to academic achievement outcomes. Yet, despite the differences in outcomes and racial composition, many in the local community deny that race is an issue. Several of the responses to the mayor's statement and to Thomas's column suggest that the reaction of suburban residents to consolidation is not one of racists but of parents who seek to "ensure that their children have a chance at a good education" (Coker, 2005). The implication is clear—a "good" education means one in the county, as opposed to the city, schools.*

In examining this CRT moment, however, it is necessary to place the current situation within its historical context. As a southern city, Memphis has a history of segregated schools. In fact, the rallying cry of "good education" is not a new one there. In the 1960s, the desire for "quality education" accompanied the focus on "neighborhood schools" in the rhetoric of those who sought to ensure the continued segregation of black students (McRae, 1996). A CRT perspective highlights the significance of this history. In particular, those individuals who point to "quality education," rather than race, as the key difference

---

* See the Morris chapter in this volume for another example of this phenomenon.

separating the two systems ignore the historical race-related conditions that have shaped education in Memphis.

The Historical Context: Legacy of a Biracial System

In 1960, lawyers associated with the NAACP Legal Defense Fund filed a complaint against the Memphis Board of Education. The plaintiffs in *Northcross v. Board of Education* sought an injunction to cease the operation of a biracial school system that they asserted was in violation of the Fourteenth Amendment. While the defendants acknowledged that the Memphis schools were separated by race, they denied that the biracial system was compulsory. Rather, they alleged that attendance at separate schools was entirely voluntary, flowing "from the desire on the part of each race to associate and attend school with members of its own race" (McRae, 1996, p. 37).

In 1961, the presiding U.S. District Court judge ruled in favor of the defendant school board, upholding the board's position that the existing system of voluntary transfer met the requirements for creating a desegregated or "unitary" system. However, in 1962, the Sixth Circuit Court of Appeals reversed the original decision, concluding that the Memphis Board of Education was in fact operating two systems—one for white students and another for black students. As a result, the defendants were required to adopt a desegregation plan to create a unitary system. However, "it took more than twelve years for the Board to put into place, involuntarily, a plan which was approved as a unitary plan in accordance with the United States Constitution as interpreted by the U.S. Supreme Court" (McRae, 1996, p. 42).

Although it is beyond the scope of this chapter to detail the entire history of this case, an overview is necessary to provide the backdrop for examination of the current conditions in the Memphis City Schools. The court in *Northcross* determined that the Memphis Board of Education was responsible for the creation and maintenance of the dual system. Whereas the board argued that one-race schools were the result of parental choice and housing segregation, over which the board had no control, the court held that the defendant had in fact made decisions that promoted educational segregation following the 1954 *Brown* decision (McRae, 1996).

Specifically, the board operated to maintain the ongoing segregation of the Memphis school district through the placement and zoning of neighborhood schools. The plaintiffs in the *Northcross* case presented evidence that the board had exerted significant control over what schools students attended through its placement of new schools. In fact, in response to the 1954 *Brown* decision, the president of the board was quoted in the newspaper regarding the expected reaction to the Supreme Court's ban on school segregation: " 'We have been expecting this to happen for a while ... we believe our Negroes will continue using their own school facilities since most of them are located in the center of Negro population areas' " (City Schools, 2004). And, in fact, the year after *Brown,* the board built a new high school in a heavily concentrated black area less than one mile from a large high school attended exclusively by white students. This school placement decision was later cited in *Northcross* to demonstrate the board's use of new school location as a strategy to maintain racial isolation (McRae, 1996).

Another strategy used by the board to maintain segregated schools was zoning. In its 1962 decision, the Sixth District Court of Appeals held that school zone lines in the Memphis district had been gerrymandered to preserve a maximum degree of segregation (McRae, 1996). Almost a decade later, Herenton (1971) compared school zone maps with maps reflecting housing segregation and concluded, "The school district lines in the City of Memphis conform to the generally recognized boundaries between white and Negro residential areas. The result is predominately Negro schools in one district and predominately white schools in an adjacent district" (p. 47). These zoning decisions, in combination with district feeder patterns, served to maintain the segregation of Memphis schools. Although the first black students had "integrated" Memphis schools in 1961, a decade later fewer than 4 percent of black students attended predominantly white schools (Herenton, 1971). Thus, the history of the Memphis City Schools reflects intentional efforts to maintain a dual system of education even after the *Brown* decision was handed down.

It is also important, from a historical perspective, to outline the changes in the district composition over this time period. In 1963, three years after the filing of *Northcross*, the district was still majority white by a slight margin (51 percent white). In 1970, just a few years before the start of busing, the district was 55 percent black. There is some question as to the exact number of white students who left the system in the process of "white flight" (Egerton 1973; McRae, 1996). However, by 1973, just after the start of court-ordered busing, the percentage of white students had dropped substantially to approximately 33 percent (Terrell, 2004). Citizens Against Busing (CAB), an organization interested in avoiding desegregation, hurriedly set up several private schools. These "CAB schools" boasted an enrollment of 8,000 students just after the start of busing (Egerton, 1973). Other students who left the public schools during this time enrolled in already existing private or parochial schools. One author who wrote at the time that busing began characterized the white flight from the Memphis City Schools: "The school system has already lost many thousands of white students, and in all probability it will lose more. The school system is powerless to control that exodus" (Egerton, 1973, p. 34). After a dramatic drop when busing began, the percentage of white students in the Memphis City Schools continued to decrease steadily over the subsequent decades. In 1978, for example, there were approximately 80,000 black students in MCS and approximately 30,000 white students. By 1987, the number of white students had dropped to slightly over 20,000, while the number of black students had remained relatively constant over the 1980s at slightly more than 80,000 (Terrell, 2004). In 2005 there were 12,000 white students in the district, and more than 100,000 black students (Tennessee Department of Education, 2005).

This brief account of the events and processes surrounding desegregation in the Memphis City Schools is intended to provide the background for the discussion that follows. Specifically, I sought to highlight the intentional mechanisms used by the board of education to maintain a dual system, and to describe some of the demographic changes that have taken place in the district. The historical perspective laid out in this section will be critical in the discussion that follows, as I examine the current status of the school district and seek to illustrate, from a materialist perspective, the current dual system in Memphis.

The Property Value of Whiteness and the Maintenance of a Dual System

As noted earlier, Ladson-Billings and Tate (1995) drew heavily from the materialist roots of CRT in legal studies. In particular, they focused on the relationship between property and inequity in education. Drawing on Harris's (1993) concept of whiteness as property, they noted multiple ways in which this property right is asserted (whether overtly or tacitly) in education.

According to Ladson-Billings and Tate (1995), one manifestation of the property value of whiteness in education can be seen in a school's curriculum—a form of intellectual property. They point to the relationship between the proportion of white students in a school and the "richness" of its curriculum. The greater the percentage of white students, the higher the intellectual property value of the curriculum. The relationship between the percentage of white students and the availability of advanced courses has been documented elsewhere (e.g., Oakes, 1990; Oakes, Muir and Joseph, 2000) and is also evident in the Memphis case. For example, thirteen high schools in the MCS district list advanced placement (AP) course offerings on the school website. There is a strong positive correlation between the percentage of white students in a school and the number of AP courses offered. Thus, Union High School* has the highest proportion (60 percent) of white students in the district and also offers the largest number of AP courses (18 different courses are listed on its website). Conversely, Douglas High School, which is 3 percent white, lists only two AP courses on its website. West High School, which is 1 percent white, lists no AP courses.

Moreover, these course differences and the property value of whiteness they reflect can be associated with material consequences. For example, the brochure of Jefferson, an MCS high school, notes that the school offers 17 AP courses. According to the brochure, students at Jefferson have earned as many as 33 hours of college credit before leaving high school. This head start on

---

* All school names are pseudonyms.

college coursework, as well as the boost to weighted high school GPAs, can translate into "property" with clear monetary value. White students in MCS or students attending schools with higher proportions of white students are more likely to have access to this form of property.

High school outcomes also give evidence of the property value of whiteness in the Memphis district. Jefferson High School, for example, is one of the magnet or "optional" schools in the district. According to promotional material for the optional program, "The College Preparatory program prepares its graduates to enter the nation's finest and most demanding colleges and universities ... [Jefferson] has recent graduates enrolled at Duke, Stanford, Harvard, Yale, Princeton, Emory, Northwestern, Columbia, Spelman, Wellesley, Howard, Dartmouth, Rice." Ninety-eight percent of Jefferson graduates enrolled in the optional program attend college. Data available on the state website indicate that the school as a whole is 50 percent white (Tennessee Department of Education, 2005).* This college attendance rate stands in stark contrast to the outcomes at other MCS high schools. For example, in contrast to Jefferson's college attendance rate, the graduation rate at West High School, which is 99 percent black, was only 46 percent.

Certified and prepared teachers are another form of "property" cited by Ladson-Billings and Tate (1995). Several studies have documented the value of whiteness with respect to ensuring the availability of this form of property, indicating that schools with more students of color are less likely to have access to teachers who are licensed to teach in their area of assignment (e.g., Darling-Hammond, 1997; Ingersoll, 1999; Lankford, Loeb and Wyckoff, 2002; Weiss, 1994). The same is true in Memphis. For example, in a recent school year there were 22 Memphis schools in "corrective action" (indicating multiple years of failing to make adequate yearly progress according to the state's accountability system). In an investigation, the district found that these schools had the highest numbers of the least experienced teachers and principals. In addition, the district also discovered that 57 percent of middle and high school mathematics teachers in the corrective action schools were not licensed to teach the subject (Kumar, 2003). That is compared with less than 9 percent for the district as a whole. Not only were the corrective action schools more likely to have uncertified teachers, these schools were also more likely to be all-black than schools not in corrective action.

Not surprisingly, these property differences coincide with differences in achievement. Consider, for example, the cases of two Memphis middle schools. Both schools are part of the MCS district. Jefferson Middle School is 63 percent white. On a recent administration of the state achievement test,

---

* The optional program at Jefferson operates as a school within a school. For this reason, the percentage of white students in the overall population underestimates the proportion in the optional program.

only 7 percent of the tested students scored below "proficient" in mathematics. Four percent scored below "proficient" in reading. In contrast, the scores for Lakeside Middle School students were significantly lower. Forty-six percent of Lakeside students scored below "proficient" in mathematics, and 32 percent scored below "proficient" in reading. Like nearly half of Memphis City schools, Lakeside is nearly 100 percent black (Tennessee Department of Education, 2005). In fact, there is a strong correlation between the percentage of white students in the school and the school's scores on the state test. Moreover, examination of the schools with the lowest levels of achievement indicates that there are few white students in these schools. The average percentage of white students in the middle schools that are currently at the highest priority level in the state accountability system (those who have failed for multiple years to make adequate yearly progress) was less than 2 percent. Moreover, two-thirds of the highest priority schools are less than 1 percent white (Tennessee Department of Education, 2005).

These disparities suggest that Memphis has yet to create a "unitary" system. Rather, with respect to structural elements such as teacher quality and curriculum, MCS still operates as a dual system. Students in schools with higher proportions of white students are more likely to have access to an advanced college preparatory curriculum and qualified teachers. These students are also more likely to have higher achievement and to graduate from high school. Insofar as the property value of whiteness continues to operate in MCS, a dual system remains in place.

As noted in the previous section, the maintenance of a dual system was achieved historically through school location and zoning decisions made by the board of education. The MCS board no longer plays such a clear-cut role in the maintenance of a dual system, yet a biracial system remains. CRT provides a means to understand the continued operation of a dual system, even absent the intentionally discriminatory actions of the school board.

Race and Class in Memphis

It is difficult, if not impossible, to deny that there are very different outcomes for white and black students in Memphis schools. However, some of those who decry the mayor's statement regarding school consolidation offer an alternative explanation for these differences. Specifically, they point to class, rather than race, as the basis for the disparities seen in Memphis. For example, one of the suburban mayors who reacted so strongly to Herenton's race-based comments on consolidation had previously been quoted as stating that it is no longer white flight, but what he called "economic flight," that leads families to leave the city of Memphis (Consolidation, 2005). In other words, people are moving to the suburbs not to escape a majority black city but to get away from the city's poverty. The same perspective is reflected in the media with respect to schooling. As part of a recent retrospective on the impact of the *Brown* decision, for example, one headline in the Memphis newspaper read, "Class is new school segregator" (Dobbs, 2004).

Certainly, a look at the differences between schools in MCS suggests that there is a strong relationship between the socio-economic status of the community and the achievement status of the school. For example, the two MCS middle schools described earlier, Jefferson and Lakeside, serve students from very different economic backgrounds. Twenty-seven percent of Jefferson's student population qualify for free or reduced-cost lunches. The census tract within which the school is located has a median home value of $132,700 and a median household income of $57,448. In contrast, 93 percent of students attending Lakeside qualify for free or reduced-cost lunches. The census tract in which Lakeside is located has a median home value of $45,000 and a median income of $20,630.

Although this theory of socio-economic difference might, on the surface, appear plausible as an explanation of the duality of the Memphis system, a CRT perspective demands a deeper analysis of the historical and contemporary conditions that have created these socioeconomic disparities. The perspective that race is no longer a factor in the distribution of educational resources and outcomes fails to acknowledge the interrelationship of race and class in Memphis. As Thomas (2004) notes, race and class in Memphis "are so intertwined that it's hard to see where one ends and the other begins" (p. A1). For example, the economic differences between Jefferson and Lakeside mirror differences in race. Jefferson is located in a census tract that is 3 percent black. The area surrounding Lakeside is 99 percent black. Continuing residential segregation, such as that evident in these two census tracts, is widespread in the Memphis area. According to one study, only in Detroit do black residents experience more racial isolation than in Memphis (Bronsnan, Covington and Downing, 2001). The average majority black census tract in Memphis is 73 percent black, compared to the national average of 54 percent.

This persistent residential segregation cannot be ignored in an examination of education in the Memphis area. Rather, these two factors are interrelated and belie the view that race is no longer salient. According to Massey and Denton (1993), the type of residential segregation seen in Memphis is "the institutional apparatus that supports other racially discriminatory processes and binds them together into a coherent and uniquely effective system of racial subordination" (p. 8). These authors argue that it is not, in fact, the impartial operation of the free market but the inequitable mechanism of racism that shapes the economic fortunes of African Americans, particularly with respect to residential segregation. Moreover, housing discrimination affects the economic system as a whole. "Not only does discrimination lead to segregation, but segregation, by restricting economic opportunities for blacks, produces interracial economic disparities that incite further discrimination and more segregation" (Massey and Denton, 1993, p. 109). In a similar vein, Shapiro

(2004) highlights the interrelationship between segregated housing and future opportunity, particularly with respect to schooling: "Residential segregation restricts minority households' access to quality schools. Unequal schooling leads to all sorts of educational disparities that generally provide competitive educational disadvantages for blacks" (p. 146). Thus, to separate race from class is to ignore the historical and contemporary role of residential segregation in the economic and educational cycle.

According to Robert McRae, the presiding judge in the *Northcross* case, this same cycle was in operation in Memphis at the time of desegregation. In fact, McRae (1996) argues that the Memphis Board of Education relied on this "discrimination cycle" to maintain a dual system. Schools intended for black students were placed in the center of residentially segregated neighborhoods maintained through housing discrimination. According to McRae,

> the housing discrimination was buttressed by economic discrimination because blacks were unacceptable for most of the higher-paying jobs ....
> The lack of equal educational opportunities in a unitary school system also deprived black students of an education that was needed in order to get the better-paying jobs so they could afford the higher-priced housing area (1996, p. 64).

Thus, fifty years ago, the board took advantage of a discrimination cycle that involved housing, education, and economic opportunity. The board of education is no longer overtly complicit in the continuation of this cycle in the same manner it was fifty years ago, yet the cycle continues and a dual system is still in place.

An examination of the current mechanisms supporting the dual system requires attention to changes in the nature of the subordination of African Americans in the United States. Crenshaw (1988) proposes that black subordination has historically taken on two forms: symbolic and material. According to Crenshaw, "symbolic subordination refers to the formal denial of social and political equality to all Blacks, regardless of their accomplishments" (p. 1377). Jim Crow segregation was one manifestation of symbolic subordination. "Material subordination, on the other hand, refers to the ways that discrimination and exclusion economically subordinated Blacks to whites and subordinated the life chances to Blacks to those of whites on almost every level" (p. 1377). Although, historically, the two types of subordination were closely related, the presence of one did not necessarily guarantee the other (e.g., segregated schools often did not result in material subordination in the form of an inferior education for black students). Similarly, the end of symbolic subordination, as a result of the civil rights movement, did not necessarily lead to the end of material subordination for many African Americans.

Crenshaw (1988) argues that the continuation of material subordination is tied, in part, to the interrelated myths of equal opportunity and meritocracy. Insofar as the symbolic manifestations of subordination have been removed, whites believe that equal opportunity is the rule and that the free market operates fairly and impartially. Therefore, according to this view, material differences between whites and blacks represent differences in merit. According to Crenshaw, "the race neutrality of the ... system creates the illusion that racism is no longer the primary factor responsible for the condition of the Black underclass; instead ... class disparities appear to be the consequence of individual and group merit within a supposed system of equal opportunity" (1988, p. 1383).

This view is relevant with respect to the current explanations of the educational disparities in the Memphis system. The repeated denial of the salience of race and the continued emphasis on class operate to maintain a dual system of education in Memphis. As Crenshaw (1988) points out, the focus on socio-economic status, in conjunction with the myth of equal opportunity, diverts attention from racial subordination while at the same time justifying continuing inequity. The attribution of differences to socio-economic status casts the disparities as a natural phenomenon, not logically subject to intervention. The argument goes as follows: the economic condition of the students explains the differential results of schools. Because we operate in a system of equal opportunity (a system absent the symbolic manifestations of discrimination), the economic condition of the student's family can be attributed to the fair and impartial operation of the free market. Therefore, the differential educational outcomes described previously are not the products of an inequitable system but the natural result of differential inputs. Just as the Memphis Board of Education claimed in the 1960s that segregation was the natural result of housing and affiliation patterns, a dual system is currently justified by economic differences. In much the same mechanism that Noguera (2003) describes in the case of Berkeley, the attribution to class rather than race has made differential outcomes an issue which has "come to be regarded as impossible to solve" (p. 62). Yet failing to acknowledge the mechanisms, such as housing segregation (Massey and Denton, 1993), which undergird ongoing material subordination virtually guarantees the continuation of a dual system.

"Keeping it Real:" A Materialist/Realist Perspective on Education in Memphis

I began this chapter by describing a CRT moment which occurred in a flurry of rhetoric surrounding school funding and consolidation in Memphis. I then attempted to demonstrate how this CRT moment could be used as the starting point of a materialist analysis of the Memphis City Schools.* Although the original statement at the crux of this CRT moment refers to differences between the city and county districts, I focused my examination on the city schools. The failure of the Memphis City Schools to become a unitary system, even fifty years after *Brown*, strongly indicates the forces at work in any discussion of city-county consolidation. The historical record and contemporary conditions give evidence of the roadblocks that would likely be faced in any serious effort to consolidate the two systems.

This intransigence is due in part to a key dynamic highlighted by the mayor's statement —the challenge of interest convergence in this case. The mayor suggested that only when the problems of the city schools begin to affect the education of students in the county would there be a convergence of interests with the potential to change the school funding system. The mayor's statement reflects the reality of what Massey and Denton (1993) refer to as the "chocolate city-vanilla suburbs" pattern of residential segregation. Such segregation, which is entrenched in the Memphis area, "gives white politicians a strong interest in limiting the flow of public resources to black-controlled cities" (1993, p. 158). The statements of suburban mayors in the Memphis area indicate this lack of interest convergence. When asked about the possibility of consolidation, one of the suburban mayors said that her constituents would support more money for schools "if they can see it and touch it and feel it in their own communities." They want to know how "this improves the quality of education for the children of Shelby County" (Consolidation, 2005). Absent that connection to their own interests, consolidation is not a popular option with suburban residents. Thus, as much as the public has decried the Memphis mayor's statement on schools, he has highlighted the difficulty of interest convergence. This difficulty is also related to the other elements of the CRT analysis of this case: the continued salience of race, the need for a historical perspective, and the property value of whiteness. All these elements come together to preserve the system of inequity to which the mayor was referring.

In closing, I argue that the examination of this CRT moment is significant for what it reveals about the power of the realist/materialist perspective. In an article on the distinction between the idealist and realist perspectives, Delgado (2001) offers the following hypothetical:

---

* It is important to acknowledge that this was merely a preliminary analysis of the conditions of the district. Further inquiry is needed into some of the differences revealed in this analysis. For example, while it is clear that the schools with the highest proportions of white students have the highest numbers of AP course offerings, this tells us little about the students in the these classes. Is the student population in the AP program reflective of the school population as a whole? This is one example of several questions raised by this analysis that require further investigation.

Suppose ... extraterrestrials leave behind a ... pill that eliminates unkind thoughts, stereotypes, and misimpressions harbored by some individuals toward persons of other races. Perhaps an enterprising entrepreneur develops "The Ultimate Diversity Seminar," capable of producing the same result. The President's civil rights advisor prevails on all the nation's school system to introduce this seminar into every K–12 classroom, and the major television networks feature it on prime time. *Would life improve very much for people of color?* (p. 2282; emphasis added)

Analysis of the case of the Memphis City Schools illustrates the distinctions described by Delgado (2001). In particular, the answer to the question at the conclusion of Delgado's hypothetical is clearly "no." In this case, the end of symbolic subordination (in the form of de jure segregation) did not bring about significant improvement in the material conditions of African Americans in Memphis, specifically with respect to education. Even in the absence of clear racial discrimination, material subordination in the form of a dual educational system continues from generation to generation. There are those who would deny the contemporary salience of race, but the tools provided by CRT allow for recognition that "race is [still] an issue" and lead to a deeper understanding of the material manifestations of racism.

One set of reactions to Mayor Herenton's comments voiced outrage at the mere mention of race. However, others expressed the opinion that the mayor had, in fact, attempted to "keep it real" in the discussion of school funding. Only if we continue the work of "keeping it real" with CRT is there any chance of changing the material conditions that have created the systems of inequity to which the mayor was referring.

References

Bronsnan, J., Covington, J., and Downing, S. (2001). Races Staying "Isolated" in Memphis, Study Says. *Commercial Appeal*, 5 May.

City Schools Integration Timeline (2005). *Commercial Appeal*, 16 May, p. A18.

Consolidation: The View from the Suburbs (2005). *Commercial Appeal*, 20 February, p. V1.

Coker, J. (2005). Education, Not Race, Motivates Parents [letter to the editor]. *Commercial Appeal*, 19 March, p. B7.

Crenshaw, K. (1988). Race, Reform, and Retrenchment: Transformation and Legitimation in Antidiscrimination Law. *Harvard Law Review* 101: 1331–1387.

Darling-Hammond, L. (1997). *The Right To Learn: A Blueprint for Creating Schools That Work*. San Francisco: Jossey-Bass.

DeCuir, J., and Dixson, A. (2003). "So When It Comes Out, They Aren't That Surprised That It Is There": Using Critical Race Theory as a Tool of Analysis of Race and Racism in Education. *Educational Researcher* 33(5): 26–31.

Delgado, R. (2001). Two Ways To Think about Race: Reflections on the Id, the Ego, and Other Reformist Theories of Equal Protection. *Georgetown Law Review* 89: 2279, 2283–2285.

Delgado, R. (2003). Crossroads and Blind Alleys: A Critical Examination of Recent Writing about Race. *Texas Law Review* 82: 121–152.

Egerton, J. (1973). *Promise of Progress: Memphis School Desegregation 1972–73*. Atlanta: Southern Regional Council.

Gary, J. (2005). Suffering City Needs Change at Top [letter to the editor]. *Commercial Appeal*, , 25 February, p. B9.

Harris, C. (1993). Whiteness as Property. *Harvard Law Review* 106: 1707–1791.

Herenton, W. (1971). A Historical Study of School Desegregation in the Memphis City Schools. Ph.D. dissertation, Southern Illinois University, Carbondale.

Ingersoll, R. (1999). The Problem of Underqualified teachers in American Secondary Schools. *Educational Researcher* 28(2): 26–37.

Kumar, R. (2003). Why Do Some Schools Lag? Warning Signs May Have Been missed. *Commercial Appeal*, 9 December, p. B1.

Ladson-Billings, G. (1999). Just What Is Critical Race Theory and What's It Doing in a *Nice* Field like Education? In L. Parker, D. Deyhle, and S. Villenas (eds.), *Race Is ... Race Isn't: Critical Race Theory and Qualitative Studies in Education*, 7–30. Boulder, CO: Westview.

Ladson-Billings, G., and Tate, W. (1995). Toward a Critical Race Theory of Education. *Teachers College Record* 97(1): 47–68.

Lankford, H.; Loeb, S.; and Wyckoff, J. (2002). Teacher Sorting and the Plight of Urban Schools: A Descriptive Analysis. *Educational Evaluation and Policy Analysis* 24: 37–62.

Massey, D., and Denton, N. (1993). *American Apartheid: Segregation and the Making of the Underclass*. Cambridge, MA: Harvard University Press.

McRae, R. (1996). *Oral History of Deliberate Unconstitutional Separation of Negro Race by Board of Education Memphis City Schools*. Memphis: University of Memphis.

Noguera, P. (2003). *City Schools and the American Dream: Reclaiming the Promise of Public Education*. New York: Teachers College Press.

Oakes, J. (1990). Opportunities, Achievement, and Choice: Women and Minority Students in Science and Mathematics. *Review of Research in Education* 16: 153–222.

Oakes, J.; Muir, K.; and Joseph, R. (2000). *Coursetaking and Achievement in Mathematics and Science: Inequalities That Endure and Change* . Madison, WI: National Institute of Science Education.

Setliff, J. (2005). Suffering City Needs Change at Top [letter to the editor]. *Commercial Appeal*, 25 February, p. B9.

Shapiro, T. (2004). *The Hidden Cost of Being African American: How Wealth Perpetuates Inequality*. New York: Oxford University Press.

Sparks, J., and Dries, B. (2005). Herenton Hits Racial Nerve on Schools. *Commercial Appeal*, 25 February, p. B1.

Tate, W. (1999). Conclusion. In L. Parker et al. (eds.), Race Is ... Race Isn't: Critical Race Theory and Qualitative Studies in Education, pp. 251–271. Boulder, CO: Westview.

Tate, W. (2005). Ethics, Engineering, and the Challenge of Racial Reform in Education. *Race, Ethnicity, and Education* 8: 123–129.

Tennessee Department of Education. (2005). Report Card: 2004. Available at http://www.k-12.state.tn.us/rptcrd04/.

Terrell, J. (2004). "White Flight" from Memphis City Schools. *Commercial Appeal*, 19 May, p. A19.

Thomas, W. (2005). Bartlett Mayor Also Makes It a Race Issue. *Commercial Appeal*, 27 February, p. B1.

Thomas, W. (2004). Separateness as a Choice Opens Even Wider Gaps. *Commercial Appeal*, 16 May, pp. A1, A19.

Weiss, L. (1994). *A Profile of Science and Mathematics Education in the United States: 1993*. Chapel Hill, NC: Horizon Research.

7

Critical Race Perspectives on Desegregation: The Forgotten Voices of Black Educators

JEROME E. MORRIS

Black educators are often excluded from the discussion of educational issues facing African American[1] children and their communities (Edwards, 1996; Foster, 1991; Lomotey, 1989). This chapter highlights the voices of African American educators as a means of responding to the silence of individuals affected both personally and professionally by the historic Supreme Court decision in *Brown v. Board of Education of Topeka, Kansas* (1954) (Edwards, 1996). Emanating from an in-depth analysis of interviews with 21 African American educators in St. Louis, this chapter discusses how these educators' perspectives on the desegregation plan in that city, which was enacted as a result of a settlement in 1983, reflect elements of what is conceptually being defined today as critical race theory (CRT). In many ways, these educators' views reflect their trepidation about the extent to which the desegregation plan could ensure educational equity for black people in St. Louis and their assertion that the plan was implemented in a manner that primarily protected the interests and the superior status of whites in St. Louis.

First, because these educators' perspectives center on essential elements of CRT, I briefly review major aspects of CRT and discuss it as an emerging conceptual framework for examining the intersection of race with educational practices, programs, and policies. To contextualize the educators' perspectives historically, I discuss the exclusion of black educators from the *Brown v. Board of Education* debates and the educational policies that followed this court case during the 1960s and 1970s. I then chronicle events during the 1970s and 1980s which led to the conceptualization and implementation of the St. Louis desegregation plan in 1983. CRT is used as a guiding theoretical framework for analyzing (a) the interviews with these African American educators,[2] (b) the social and historic efforts that led to the formation of the plan, and (c) more recent issues and events surrounding the desegregation plan. In

Major parts of this chapter were originally published in 2001 in Educational Policy, 15(4), 575-600.

a later section, I illustrate how specific elements of CRT were embedded in these educators' analyses of the desegregation plan. Finally, I discuss the plan's status during the 1990s and the issues that surrounded the ending of the plan on March 12, 1999. I conclude with policy and theoretical implications for examining the intersection of desegregation policy with CRT.

Critical Race Theory and Desegregation

Derrick Bell, a former civil rights attorney who played a pivotal role in desegregation court cases, is perhaps most instrumental in advancing CRT as a framework for examining the experiences of black people in America. Specifically, Bell (1987) used story and narrative to analyze how the litigation of *Brown*, which resulted in court-ordered desegregation, affected the education of African American students. For example, in his chapter titled "The Chronicle of the Sacrificed Black Schoolchildren," Bell argues that desegregation measures ignored the fact that legalized segregation was about maintaining white control of education. If desegregation inconvenienced and threatened white people and their superior social status, then implementation would occur in a way that ensured that white people still controlled public education (Bell, 1987). According to Bell (1992), the "analysis of legal developments through fiction, personal experience, and the stories of people on the bottom illustrates how race and racism continue to dominate our society" (p. 144). CRT approaches the analysis of social policies and practices in America with the recognition that racism is natural and permanently etched in the social and cultural order of American society. Consequently, CRT offers a reinterpretation of liberal civil rights practices and laws by examining their limitations in improving the overall quality of life for African Americans and affecting the social status imbalance between white and black Americans. This critique of traditional civil rights practices, policies, and laws is a prominent feature of CRT.

Ladson-Billings and Tate (1995) may be credited with officially introducing CRT to the field of education with their article "Toward a Critical Race Theory of Education." Furthermore, Tate's (1997) exhaustive review of the historical and theoretical foundations of CRT in education highlights two arguments advanced by Bell in understanding CRT: (1) *the interest convergence principle* "is built on political history as legal precedent and emphasizes that significant progress for African Americans is achieved only when the goals of Blacks are consistent with the needs of Whites"; and (2) *the price of racial remedies* asserts that "Whites will not support civil rights policies that appear to threaten their superior social status" (pp. 214–215) The interest-convergence dilemma posited by Bell (1980) results in whites rather than blacks being the primary beneficiaries of civil rights legislation. Examples of such legislation predicated on improving the conditions of African Americans include desegregation plans, that have often involved the disproportionate busing of African Americans into predominantly white schools and the creation of well-funded magnet schools to lure white students back into urban schools, as well as affirmative action hiring policies in which the major beneficiaries have been white women (Guy-Sheftall, 1993, cited in Ladson-Billings, 1998). In this chapter, I will relate this interest-convergence principle to the implementation of the St. Louis desegregation plan.

In doing so, I will apply these concepts in a manner that differs from much of the existing scholarship on CRT in education. Ladson-Billings (1998) has noted her apprehension about trying to introduce a conceptual framework that specifically focuses on race in a "nice field" like education; she cautions that, as with many new ideas or innovations in educational research, "it is very tempting to appropriate CRT as a more powerful explanatory narrative for the persistent problems of race, racism, and social justice" (p. 22). While this is a valid concern, it is also important to note that the CRT discourse in education since the late 1990s has primarily been within theoretical and philosophical contexts (see Ladson-Billings, 1998; Ladson-Billings and Tate, 1995; Lynn, 1999; Parker, 1998; Tate, 1997). Despite Ladson-Billings's (1998) concerns, there are still far too few applications of CRT as an explanatory framework in field-based research studies and educational policy studies (DeCuir and Dixson, 2003; Dixson and Rousseau, 2005). Furthermore, CRT discourse is occurring primarily within academic communities rather than among practitioners involved with the day-to-day education of African American students. Relegated to "safe" intellectual and academic environments, often missed are everyday "nonacademic" analyses of race and racism.[3] Black people in America have historically recognized racism in its many forms, long before the emergence of CRT. It is for this reason, and also because my qualitative data were not collected using CRT as a guiding framework, that I am using what I am calling "critical race perspectives," rather than CRT, to describe the views of some African American educators. Later in this chapter, I illustrate how their views resonate with CRT.

This focus on the perspectives of African American educators is consistent with one of the key components of CRT. The CRT pioneer Richard Delgado (1990) has argued that a critical element of CRT is valuing the voices of people from marginalized racial groups. "Naming one's own," according to Delgado (1988, 1990), is a theme of critical race scholarship because people of color experience a world in which race and racism permeate all of their experiences. Consequently, CRT presents an alternative framework to traditional educational research and policy analysis through its insistence on a contextual historical and social analysis of policies and scholarship. As the review in the following section illustrates, African American educators' voices were forgotten and ignored in the debates and discussions surrounding the implementation of Brown during the 1960s and 1970s. As this chapter later shows, a similar phenomenon occurred with the implementation of the St. Louis desegregation plan in 1983. This chapter privileges the voices of African

American educators in St. Louis to illuminate how the desegregation plan has shaped African American education in that city since 1983.

Brown and Desegregation: Forgotten Voices

Immediately after African American lawyers brilliantly and successfully argued before the Supreme Court the unconstitutionality of maintaining legal segregation in public education, *Brown* became the symbol for eradicating a legacy of legalized segregation in public schools and all aspects of American society. Lawyers, social scientists, and members of various civil rights organizations played an integral role in directing educational policy for African Americans. They offered their perspectives on what were considered the "damaging effects" of black children's attending legally segregated all-black schools. Prior to the civil rights campaigns of the 1950s and 1960s, black educators assumed a major role in shaping the political and social experiences of African Americans (Franklin, 1990). Ironically, the black professionals whose voices were most likely to be heard in the late nineteenth and early twentieth centuries were ignored as policy makers debated how *Brown* would be implemented. Throughout much of the proceedings, analyses, and debates, the potential long-term impact of the implementation of *Brown* on the African American community was often dismissed. Well before *Brown* became law, African Americans vacillated regarding what would be the most effective environment for educating and schooling Black children—separate schools or integrated schools.[4] African Americans never overwhelmingly believed that receiving education in an "integrated" school would resolve the problems associated with inequitable education; they understood how precarious it was to favor one position over the other. If one pushed for black children to attend schools with white children, chances were great that black children and their culture would be totally ignored in the curriculum and the ethos of the school. If they were kept attending predominantly Black schools, concerns remained about the lack of resources, lack of exposure to rigorous academic curricula, and lack of facilities.

Black educators did not differ from the larger African American community on this issue. Before the *Brown* decision, black educators' support for integration was ambivalent. On one hand, they were compelled to support efforts to eradicate legalized segregation in public schools and the broader society, even though this might lead to the end of their careers as black professionals. In fact, many were ultimately displaced, demoted, and dismissed from the teaching profession once courts and school systems began to enforce *Brown* by desegregating public schools (Etheridge, 1979; Haney, 1978). On the other hand, these educators did not wholly embrace the notion that black children would receive the most effective education if black schools were closed and their former students enrolled in predominantly white schools (Du Bois, 1935; Johnson, 1954).[5] Many realized that black children would encounter modified and covert acts of racism in schools that were integrated in student population only, but not in staffs, curricula, and power arrangements. Black educators have always had a finger on the pulse of the African American community because historically, they have been intimately connected with black families and communities (Anderson, 1988; Foster, 1990, 1997; Morris, 1999; Siddle-Walker, 1996). The implementation of the St. Louis desegregation plan in 1983 enables us as researchers, policy makers and educators to begin listening to the voices of African American educators today.

Method

Although I use CRT as an informative framework, the data from which this chapter emanated were collected from 1994 to 1998, before the emergence of a significant body of scholarship that began to use CRT as a conceptual framework for examining the intersection of race and education. The African American educators interviewed were selected from three elementary schools: an African American neighborhood school, a predominantly white county school, and a magnet school. These schools were part of a larger study that focused on how the St. Louis Interdistrict Transfer Plan affected linkages between African American families, communities, and schools (Morris, 1997). The qualitative interview questions were semistructured, which enabled the educators freely to discuss issues beyond the parameters of the study. Examples of interview questions included the following: (a) How has the transfer plan affected connections between African American families, communities, and schools? (b) To what extent has the desegregation plan benefited the various groups involved? (c) What are some consequences of ending the 1983 settlement (desegregation plan) for African American students, schools, and communities?

In qualitative research, the researcher is the primary instrument of data collection (Merriam, 1988). Researchers' identities are essential components of the entire research process (Scheurich and Young, 1997). One cannot discount the possibility that the race, social class or political views of the researcher affect the research process, because researchers bring their own epistemological perspectives—ways of knowing—into the framing of researchable questions, data collection and analysis, and interpretations and conclusions. Rather than minimize this influence, I use my racial identity as an interactional quality to glean theoretical perspectives. For example, the African American educators I interviewed were eager to discuss how race and racism affected the implementation of the desegregation plan. I have come to believe that my focus on how the plan affects African American education, as well as my racial identity as African American, enhanced my ability to secure the interviews and contributed to the African American educators' comfort and willingness to discuss sensitive issues regarding race. On several occasions I was invited into administrators' offices and teachers' classrooms to talk for hours after school had ended. In one instance, I visited a teacher's home and talked with her and her husband until about two o'clock in the morning about her experiences as an African American teacher in St. Louis, the community work they both were involved in, and larger issues surrounding the St. Louis desegregation plan. Of the 21 African American educators interviewed, seventeen were female and four were male; thirteen were classroom teachers, three were teacher assistants, two were principals (male and female), one was an interim principal, and two were instructional coordinators. The county school employed only one African American teacher, indicative of many of the county districts' failures to desegregate their faculty by recruiting African American teachers. With the exception of this female teacher, the other educators were employed in the St. Louis Public School System. Although a few had taught between five and ten years, most had been teaching since the plan began in 1983. Four of these educators—all from the neighborhood all-black school—had been teaching or otherwise involved in education for at least 30 years; one teacher had taught for 42 years.[6] Before highlighting their voices, though, it is necessary to understand how the desegregation plan came into existence.

Conceptualizing and Implementing the Desegregation Plan

In *Liddell v. St. Louis Board of Education* (1975, 1979), African American plaintiffs accused the St. Louis Board of Education of contributing to African American children's receiving a segregated education. In 1979, Judge Meredith, the judge presiding over the case, held that there was not adequate evidence to prove that the board of education of the city of St. Louis purposefully and intentionally discriminated against African Americans. In March 1980, the U. S. Court of Appeals for the Eighth Circuit reversed Meredith's order; it stated there was adequate evidence of discrimination by the board of education of St. Louis and the state of Missouri. In July 1980, African American plaintiffs—including community organizations and the National Association for the Advancement of Colored People (NAACP)—the city of St. Louis, Missouri, and a number of the nearby county school systems approved a voluntary settlement to allow African American students to attend the county schools. This settlement was reached after the plaintiffs and the St. Louis Board of Education accused the county schools of contributing to a mass exodus to the suburbs of white middle-class families. Dissatisfied with the efforts of the settlement, in 1982 the plaintiffs and St. Louis Board of Education sued to gain a court-ordered remedy that would establish a metropolitan systemwide school district.

To avoid a costly trial, one day before the scheduled trial in 1983 lawyers for the black plaintiffs, officials from the 23 county districts, and the St. Louis Board of Education entered into a settlement. The county districts participated in this settlement under threat of litigation and the possible loss of control over how their districts would be desegregated. The settlement comprised five components: (a) the voluntary desegregation of 16 of the 23 county school districts, (b) the voluntary transfer of white county students to city magnet schools, (c) a quality-of-education package for the all-black schools in the city, (d) a capital improvement package to restore the deteriorated conditions of the city schools, and (e) the hiring of minority staff in the county school districts.

The settlement specified that the county school districts accept black students from the city to desegregate the county schools to achieve a 25 percent African American student population. The participating county school districts would receive financial compensation from the state equal to the cost of attendance in the respective county schools. Seven of the 23 county school districts already had an African American student enrollment of at least 25 percent; therefore, they did not have to accept African American transfer students. The transfer plan focused on the remaining 16 districts, which enrolled low percentages of African American students. The enrollment of African American students in the 16 county districts that participated in the plan ranged from 13 to 26 percent. Since the implementation of the settlement plan, only five of the 16 county districts reached their planned goal of 25 percent African American student enrollment. For example, during the 1997–1998 school year, a total of 14,224 students were enrolled in the transfer program between the city and the county school districts. Of these, 12,746 African American students from the city transferred to county schools, whereas 1,478 white students from the 16 participating county districts transferred to magnet schools in St. Louis. As part of the settlement, the court mandated that the composition of magnet schools be at least 40 percent white; during the 1997–1998 school year, the proportion of white students in magnet schools was 46 percent (Voluntary Interdistrict Coordinating Council [VICC], 1998).

From the inception of the transfer plan in 1983, the state of Missouri and the St. Louis Public School Board paid almost $2 billion into the plan. The state of Missouri paid $160 million into the desegregation plan during the 1998–1999 academic year. Approximately $70 million went into funding the St. Louis Public School District's portion of the plan (examples of enhancements included mandating a maximum student:teacher ratio of 20:1). Another $60 million went toward funding the per pupil cost for transfer students into the county schools, and the remaining funds paid for city and county transportation costs. The state wanted to end the desegregation plan by declaring that the city district had achieved unitary status—a legal term meaning that the state and the city have done all that is necessary to eliminate the vestiges of legal segregation and will not return to earlier illegal and discriminatory practices (Perspectives, 1995). On the other hand, lawyers representing the NAACP argued that the transfer plan should continue because resegregation might result if the plan ended. A panel of judges—as requested by the state of Missouri—began hearing the court case in March 1996 to establish a deadline for settlement negotiations. Missing from these hearings and discussions were African American educators' perspectives on the impact of the desegregation plan and the consequences of continuing or ending it. The perspectives of some of these educators from the public school system are highlighted below.

Black Educators: Embracing Critical Race Perspectives

A critical race perspective permeated these educators' views and analyses of the implementation of the transfer plan, as reflected in the following themes that emerged from the interviews: (a) the stigmatizing of black teachers as incompetent and the subsequent stigmatizing of all-black schools as "inferior" institutions, (b) the "creaming" of talented African American students from city schools and students' subsequent disconnection from their neighborhood schools and their community, (c) skepticism about the extent to which transferring into county schools educationally benefited Black children, and (d) the consequences of ending the plan. Each theme is explicated in the following sections.

Stigmatizing Black Teachers and Schools

In the quest to remedy the educational inequities facing black children at the time of the *Brown* decision, the desegregation of public schools drastically affected African American educators. Many were demoted, lost jobs, and were stigmatized in efforts to desegregate public schools (Foster, 1995; Meier, Stewart and England, 1989). According to some African American educators in St. Louis, remnants of the push to desegregate schools continue adversely to affect the perception of African American teachers and educators today. They have been stigmatized as "unqualified" and "incompetent." Mrs. Burroughs, a teacher in a predominantly African American neighborhood school for 42 years, noted how black teachers' competence has been challenged since the initiation of the transfer plan: "I have enjoyed teaching black students. It is bad the way black teachers have been presented. The busing of black children out to the county schools has allowed this thinking about black teachers as incompetent to continue." Mrs. Woodson, an African American female principal in a magnet school and an educator for 25 years, disagrees with both historical and contemporary perceptions of black teachers as "incompetent" professionals: "Differently from the ways it has been presented, I never believed that black teachers were not teaching [well] in St. Louis [before the desegregation plan]. I think black teachers in St. Louis have done that historically in the black schools—and even today."

The comments by these educators are insightful. One important message is their critique of the deep-seated belief in the larger society that black schools before *Brown* employed "inferior teachers" who were not preparing black students properly. This thinking subsequently fueled the notion that black teachers' "inadequacy" in teaching black students disqualified them even more from teaching white students in racially mixed or predominantly white schools (Foster, 1997). The transfer plan's lack of emphasis in recruiting African Americans to teach in the county schools, further illustrated by the employment of only one African American teacher in a predominantly white county school, affirmed this belief by these educators. The low number of African American teachers employed in the county school districts was one of the original concerns that the St. Louis Interdistrict Transfer Plan was to address. However, this aspect of the plan received little emphasis.

Although a significant number of African American students from the city of St. Louis transferred into county schools (VICC, 1998), the focus on a corresponding increase in the numbers of black teachers in the county schools was largely ignored. Closely connected to the historic stigmatizing of black educators was the way in which their places of employment were also perceived by the larger society. The institutions where they worked, even though many of these schools were grossly underfunded, were also deemed inferior because they enrolled all-black student populations and employed black educators. Mr. Steele, the principal of an all-black neighborhood elementary school for 24 years—a school consistently recognized by African American community leaders and the school system for the quality of education provided to students from the surrounding neighborhood (Morris, 1999)—asserted that the belief that all-black schools are inferior, despite some schools' success in educating black children, persists and is buttressed by the methods used to publicize the transfer plan:

> Parents have been sold on the idea, and the school system and the courts have assisted the parents with publicity blitz "school of choice" that the [all-black] schools in St. Louis are not as good as those in the counties. ... There would be signs everywhere such as "Do you want your child to go out to a good school?" This used to be advertised in the buses on the placards. They would have "Do you want your child to have a good education? Send him or her to a county school. Call your Voluntary Interdistrict Coordinating Committee." What kind of message is that to send? If you are hit with that, okay, you are going to buy into it. And that is the reason.

As he continued, Mr. Steele paralleled the thrust to persuade black parents in St. Louis to send their children to the predominantly white county schools with the "doll experiment" by Kenneth and Mamie Clark, well-known husband and wife social scientists whose research was used in the *Brown* case. In this experiment, the Clarks concluded that a handful of black children's negative preference for the black dolls (only 14 percent of the students in the sample made anti-black statements; 86 percent of the students did not) suggested black "self-hate." Kenneth Clark was later an expert witness in the *Brown* case. Thus, the conclusion drawn by the Court was that legally segregated black schools contributed to black "self-hate" (Cross, 1991). Similar to choosing the white doll over the black doll, Mr. Steele believes that black parents and their children are encouraged to choose "white" schools over "black" schools—despite the quality and reputation of schools like his. He clearly distinguished between the way the Clarks used their doll example to help eradicate legalized segregation in America and the psychological conditioning that caused some African Americans to value white over black:

> [It is] the same rationale and mentality in why would a black parent select a predominantly white school. Transform them [the schools] into being dolls. But Kenneth Clark used that argument to say why we need to break it [legal segregation] down. He used it to identify and say this is what's happening. I am only using it the same way to say that this is why parents choose the white schools. It is the same concept when people are going through the same processes, but you are coming to different conclusions. I had a different goal than what he had. He had a goal to integrate schools; mine is to describe why people choose integrated schools.

Finally, Mrs. Collins, a teacher for 22 years and at the time teaching at a magnet school where she was twice named "Teacher of the Year" in the state of Missouri, shared this critical race perspective of the transfer plan. She contended that African American parents bought into the notion that their children would receive a better overall educational experience in the predominantly white county schools. However, she often heard contrary views from black students who described their experiences and considered returning to the schools in the city of St. Louis[7]:

> My own personal opinion is, I think African American parents—this is just my perspective—I think they think they [their children] are getting a better education by white teachers; this is necessarily not true. I think that sometimes in going out there, some of the feedback from students that are involved in deseg [the desegregation plan], and they come back just to visit, they tell me, "Mrs. Collins, it is terrible. It's not what we thought it was going to be." Most of them, after a year or two, either they come back into the city or either they stay; it depends on the parents. So, I have had numerous kids to come back and say, "I'm coming back into the city." They say they just weren't treated fairly. Sometimes the parents think that white is better.

From the perspectives of these African American educators, advertisements for the transfer plan explicitly and implicitly perpetuated the belief that black teachers and the predominantly black schools in the city were "inferior." According to them, the interdistrict transfer plan has been promoted by devaluing the quality of education that African American children might receive from schools in the city. Consequently, they assert that many of the African American parents who send their children into the predominantly white county schools have been bombarded with misleading "pro-transfer" plan advertisements and are therefore misinformed about what really happens to their children in the county schools. From their perspectives, the massive transferring of African American students into the county schools—partly fueled by misleading information—also has dire consequences for the schools and communities in the city.

"Creaming" African American Students From Communities and Schools

African American schools once served as the centers of close-knit communities (Anderson, 1988; Dempsey and Noblit, 1993; Irvine and Irvine, 1983; Siddle-Walker, 1996), and in many instances, desegregation policies adversely affected African American students' and families' connections with their formerly all-black schools. These educators—particularly those from an all-black neighborhood school—asserted that the desegregation plan in St. Louis also disconnected African American students from their communities and the neighborhood schools. They expressed concerns about the extent to which black children participating in the transfer plan were connected to the neighborhood communities where they lived. These educators also stated that often the higher-performing students ended up attending the county schools because of "promises" of a better educational environment. Mrs. Burroughs, a teacher for 42 years at an all-black neighborhood school, described how the ability levels of students at her school were not as strong as in previous years: "I would have mostly higher achieving students and a few lower achieving students. Now, I might only have a handful of students that are higher achieving." She attributes part of the change in average ability level to the "creaming effect" of students' attending magnet and county schools. Another teacher who had taught at the neighborhood African American school for 36 years, Mrs. Hall, painfully described the creaming effect of the transfer plan:

> They pulled our best children. ... They pulled; they took the cream of the crop, basically! So, you know, when a child goes into a magnet school or when he goes into a county school, there are papers that we have to fill out for days and they scrutinize those papers, and if there are things about that child they don't care for, the child shows right back here in public school at Fairmont School [the neighborhood school]. ... We have a lot of good children here now, but all I am saying is if this became a neighborhood school again, I am pretty sure the school population would change, and I think that the students would come back. [There] would be students who left because they would have done well in any environment, in any situation.

The perception that African American students are "creamed" away from their neighborhood all-black schools is not only held by teachers at the neighborhood all-black school; Ms. Mitchell, a teacher for 16 years and the only

African American teacher at the predominantly white county school where she works, shares this view:

> The drawback to the transfer plan is that it takes the African American children out of their neighborhoods. They really don't have a good connection; they really feel isolated being out here. That's what I think, and I really believe in going to your school in your neighborhood; you get to know the people better and you get to know friends.

Ms. Mitchell was originally brought into the county school to direct the School, Home, At-Risk Program (SHARP), funded through a grant from the state of Missouri. The program involved Ms. Mitchell's working with African American transfer students and their families and required her to make visits to the children's homes, to churches, and to Matthew-Dickey's, a neighborhood Boys' Club. The program was terminated because of funding cuts; however, she was eventually hired as a full-time teacher. According to Ms. Mitchell, the focus of SHARP was initially on developing African American transfer students' academic skills, but the program evolved into one that focused on behavioral issues resulting from the black students' difficulty in making the transition into a predominantly all-white school. Yet, although Ms. Mitchell and the other educators note the drawbacks of the plan, the following section examines the extent to which these educators feel the plan has benefited black students.

Benefits for Black Students?

Debates abound regarding the extent to which black children benefit from the transfer plan. For example, a report from the VICC—the office responsible for coordinating the transfer plan—revealed that test scores of African American students who transferred into the county schools were relatively the same as those of African American students who remained in the all-black schools in the city of St. Louis (VICC, 1993-1994 Report).[8] A report by the Citizen's Commission on Civil Rights (1997), an organization based in Washington, DC, concluded that African American students who attended schools in the county had higher graduation rates than African American students who attended schools in the city. However, this report did not control for socioeconomic status, a factor known to affect the school experiences of students. Whereas 94 percent of the black students in the regular city schools receive free or reduced-cost lunches, only 76 percent of the black students transferring into the county schools have family incomes low enough to qualify them for free or reduced-cost meals. Although not noted in the report by the Citizen's Commission, African American students who attend magnet schools have higher graduation rates than African American students from the city who attend the county districts, as well as those students currently enrolled in the schools in the city (Perspectives, 1995).

When asked about the extent to which she perceives that the desegregation plan has been beneficial for black children, Mrs. Woodson, the African American principal of the magnet school, responded:

> I'm probably not the right person to ask that. I know what the district would want me to say. I've never been a proponent of sending black children to sit with white children was going to help them to learn. I've never been a proponent of putting black children on the bus; I've never wanted to teach in South St. Louis.[9] Never wanted to teach in a magnet school. Whether these magnet programs have been beneficial to black children? Yes, they are beneficial to all children. This could have been done in all-black schools; I think any progressive educator would believe that. The former superintendent had a concept such as this. ... We have benefited from capital improvements.

Mrs. Woodson notes that her school has benefited from the transfer plan's financial support of the magnet school, as well as from the quality of teachers that she "has to work with." Her point, however, is that the magnet school support should have originally been designed for the all-black schools in the city, without having to try to "entice" white families from the various counties to send their children to the magnet schools. Mrs. Bethune, the instructional coordinator at the magnet school where Mrs. Woodson is the principal, said that the transfer plan was implemented not solely to have black students "sit next to white children. ... It also was so that white children could be educated with black children. That was the intent, which was good. But somewhere along the line that was forgotten." This intent may have been ignored by white parents in the county, who rarely exercised the option of sending their children to the magnet schools in the city. Only 1,478 white students transferred into magnet schools in St. Louis during the 1997–1998 academic year. This difficulty in desegregating with magnet schools was also experienced by Kansas City schools. For example, in Kansas City, Missouri, desegregation funds focused on turning many inner-city black schools into magnet schools as a way to attract white students back to the city. The plan was abandoned after very few white parents chose to send their children to the schools, and there was no significant change in students' test scores (see *Missouri v. Jenkins*, 1995).

The extent to which black children benefited academically from transferring into the county schools is not clear, even among these educators. The magnet schools are well funded and receive additional resources because they are intended to desegregate student populations. These extra funds also allowed some of the all-black schools in St. Louis to be assured of adequate educational resources. However, the major beneficiaries of the desegregation plan have been the county schools. The impact of the transfer plan on the overall revenue for the county districts cannot be ignored. For example, the county school district where Ms. Mitchell teaches received approximately $68 million by participating in the transfer plan from 1984 through 1993. The county districts receive a per pupil expenditure allowance for each black student transferring into their respective districts, in addition to half-state aid for each county student who transfers to a city magnet school. Consequently, buildings have been constructed and staff and faculty hired using these funds. Although there have been some financial benefits for black students who attend the magnet schools, the predominantly white county districts benefited much more financially by participating in the plan.

Potential Consequences of Ending the Plan

Some desegregation experts and policy analysts strongly encouraged the continuation of the transfer plan because they believed the plan offered African American students from the inner city greater educational opportunities than did the schools in the city, and the plan slowly chipped away at the color line between whites in the suburbs and African Americans in the city (Wells and Crain, 1997). In particular, Gary Orfield's concern is that the "dismantling of desegregation" would result in the resegregation of the city schools and, once again, high concentrations of minority and low-income schools (Orfield and Eaton, 1996). Most of their arguments embrace an assimilationist paradigm as the most effective means of removing the vestiges of segregation and minimizing the educational disparities between African Americans and whites (see Duncan, 1997).[10] Some African Americans, however, questioned the merits of continuing to desegregate by transferring African American students into the county schools. They have been especially critical of the fact that almost $2 billion has gone into financing the plan, with a significant amount going toward transportation and a per pupil expenditure allowance to the county schools for each African American transfer student.

Furthermore, there have been proposals arguing for refocusing the transfer plan. The former mayor of St. Louis, an African American, wanted the state of Missouri to consider funding the schools in the city with the money allotted for the transfer plan. He suggested that funds from the state should be targeted toward further improving the all-black schools in the northern section of St. Louis (Mannies, 1993a, 1993b). Although educators in my study were also critical in their analyses of the desegregation plan, their views varied regarding the direction of the plan. Most believed that, given the necessary financial resources and support, black children can still receive a quality education within primarily African American school environments. Others believed that there is some merit in maintaining racial balance in the schools. It seems ironic that Ms. Mitchell, the only African American teacher at the county school, embraces the former view:

> If the desegregation plan ended today, I think that I would be sad. But to another extent, I would only relish it if the inner-city schools, the

schools were redone, new books were bought, and the conditions were like they should be in any school when they sent them [the African American students] back.

Some of these African American educators expressed concerns about how the material conditions and funding of the city schools, as well as the racial balance of students, would be affected by ending the plan. Mr. Miles, teacher at the neighborhood African American school, stated:

> I think if you end desegregation, you're going to take a lot of money away from a lot of different programs; I think it would. You know, it's not a total waste. It's done some good; there are problems, but it has done some good. I think that a lot of children, if the children are not bused out there, a lot of times they'll never get to mix with the other people—with the other races. I think they need that, because you need to learn how other people react to different things.

In addition to mentioning the funds for the predominantly black schools in the city, Mr. Miles believed that racial balancing was important because of the exposure it provided to children from various racial-ethnic backgrounds. Others were concerned about the logistical problems that might occur if the plan ended, which would involve reopening some of the schools in the city and hiring more faculty and staff. Still, some did not believe that racial balancing is essential for a quality education for black children. They maintain that the black children in St. Louis can receive a quality education in an adequately funded and supported—albeit predominantly black—St. Louis public school. These educators' perspectives resonated deeply with elements of CRT and were the most skeptical of the plan.

Critical Race Theoretical Analyses of Desegregation in St. Louis

Elements of CRT were embedded throughout the interviews with these black educators. The *interest-convergence dilemma*—grounded in the notion that progress for African Americans is achieved only when the goals of blacks are consistent with the needs of whites—was apparent in the educators' talk about how the plan was implemented. In her assessment of the transfer plan, Mrs. Woodson, the magnet school principal, noted that historically, equality of education has been more about black people taking pragmatic steps to ensure that their children have some semblance of an equitable education. For her, black children benefit only when white people take action to make sure that their children are the primary beneficiaries:

> The focus of *Brown* was the right to go where you wanted to go. Many times, black children had to leave their neighborhoods and attend schools in other neighborhoods. People were talking about equal. Before desegregation, they were busing black children to overcome crowding. It

was not my experience that they had all of the things in South St. Louis that people talk about. Yes, people do take care of their own. Black people wanted a decent education. I've got to attach to this to make sure that my children get it because they [white people] are not going to deprive their children.

On the other hand, the county school districts' failure, or difficulty, in hiring a significant number of minority teachers represented a divergence of interests between advocates for diverse faculty and staff in the county schools and some administrators and school personnel in the county schools who had little incentive to recruit black teachers. Unlike the availability of financial incentives for the recruitment of African American students into the county districts, there were no major incentives for hiring minority teachers—other than the ideal of having a diverse teacher workforce in the county schools as well as some black teachers to teach or deal with the growing number of black transfer students (this was the case with Ms. Mitchell, the only African American educator in her county school). This divergence can be attributed to reservations by white parents and school officials about having a significant number of black teachers teaching white students (see Wells and Crain, 1997). Black educators have historically faced this realization when it came to teaching in desegregated or all-white school settings (Foster, 1997). In particular, the school where Ms. Mitchell was employed took no extra measures to ensure that its staff and faculty were diverse. From the school's perspective, this would have represented a financial and logistical inconvenience (Morris, 1997).

A significant number of African American students transferred into the predominantly white county schools, in comparison with the few white students who chose to participate in the city's magnet school program. The disparity between black students' and white students' participation rates, and the settlement's low expected goal that 1,600 white suburban students would transfer into the magnet schools, may be partly explained by Bell's (1980) argument that "Whites will not support civil rights policies that appear to threaten their superior social status." He termed this *the price of racial remedies.* Although the integration of black students into the predominantly white county schools might have represented to African Americans a step toward greater social and educational justice, many white families hesitated to disrupt their status by sending their children to the city's magnet schools just so that racial balancing could occur. For these parents, racial balance and equality are secondary to ensuring a quality education for their children (Bell, 1980).

Whites' reluctance to send their children to the city's magnet schools and African American students' high participation rates in the transfer plan also bring to the fore the notion of "whiteness as property" delineated by Bell (1992), Grant (1995), and Harris (1993). Prior to *Brown* and the eradication of legalized segregation, whites expected their skin color to provide them with tangible and intangible privileges and advantages (Bell, 1992; Grant, 1995). After legalized segregation was overturned, as Harris (1993) asserts, "whiteness as property" was still white people's expectation. Today, white people in America know that their "white skin"—as noted by McIntosh (1998 [1988])—"opens many doors for whites whether or not we approve of the way dominance has been conferred on us" (p. 81). In an unspoken way, many of the white parents in the counties were reluctant to lose this white privilege by associating with institutions and people who did not represent and reify their whiteness— solely to advance civil rights policies. For example, the magnet schools had to entice white parents to send their children into the city schools with the reassurance that these schools were unlike the predominantly black schools that existed in the city. Their children's attendance at predominantly black schools, despite a particular school's quality, would have represented a loss of "white" status. The transfer plan was conceptualized and implemented in such a way that this racial reality was recognized, and the only realistic way that some white parents would consider sending their children to the city schools was to make these schools "exceptional without question".[11] White students' presence in the city schools automatically ascribed a greater value to the St. Louis public school system. Unfortunately, this valuing of "whiteness" resulted in a simultaneous devaluing of "blackness," particularly by the manner in which advertisement practices promoted the county schools to the detriment of the all-black city schools and African American educators.

The settlement in 1983 also represented the convergence of African Americans' continued quest for social and racial justice and equality since the passage of *Brown* with whites' recognition that a long drawn-out court case could result in the loss of property (i.e., all-white schools) and their ability to dictate how desegregation would occur. They feared that litigation would result in the desegregation of their schools under terms dictated by the courts. In the final analysis, their status was not threatened, because the county schools received large financial incentives for participating in the plan, the financial burden was placed on the state's taxpayers, and the arduous task of desegregating rested on the shoulders of African American students who were merely tolerated but rarely welcomed. The 1983 desegregation settlement in St. Louis, framed within CRT, inherently reified the privileging of whiteness, which resulted in black sacrifice and the protection of white self-interest.

Implications for Educational Policy and Theory

The state of Missouri, the plaintiffs, the school board, and other interested parties negotiated for three years the future of the plan under William Danforth, the former chancellor of Washington University in St. Louis. In addition, the Missouri legislature developed a plan to offset the city's loss of court-ordered state funding and to continue its desegregation efforts with a long-term funding remedy—Senate Bill 781—which became law in August 1998. This law revised the state funding formula and required St. Louis voters to pass an additional local tax to support the St. Louis public schools. A three-member "overlay" board was an outgrowth of this law, and it determined that the tax increase should occur in the form of sales taxes, rather than property taxes, so that individuals who use the services of the city would also pay its taxes. The voters in St. Louis approved on February 2, 1999, a two-thirds of 1 percent sales tax. This tax increase raised the sales tax from 6.85 to 7.51 percent on goods and services sold in St. Louis after July 1, 1999.

Had this tax increase not passed, Senate Bill 781 would have been nullified and the case would have returned to the federal court for a ruling. This could have resulted in the declaration of unitary status for the St. Louis school district and in discontinuation of the transfer plan and desegregation resources for the city schools. Consequently, this action could have placed a heavy financial and logistical burden on the St. Louis school district as it was forced to absorb the returning African American students. It also would have resulted in the loss of funds that participating county schools received for each transferring African American student.

On March 12, 1999, the judges on the case signed the order officially ending the 1983 settlement, which resulted in the following: (a) the transfer plan was to continue during the next three years for African American students who wished to transfer into the county schools; at the end of the third year, citizens from each participating suburban school district would vote on whether to continue or to end the plan in their respective school districts; (b) additional state funds went to the St. Louis Public School District from a change in the state funding formula and the tax increase, allowing for the expansion of magnet school opportunities to white and black students in the city; and (c) money was set aside for capital improvement in the city schools during the next ten years. The sales tax was expected to increase local school revenue for St. Louis by approximately $23 million. This amount would be matched by state funds in the amount of $40 million, which would leave the district approximately $7 million short of the amount that it would have normally received from the 1983 settlement.

How to make up for the difference of this financial shortfall is a concern of the district from year to year. Another important question is, why were the suburban districts—which historically participated in creating the entrenched segregated housing and schooling between the suburban communities and the city—never approached about taxing citizens in their districts as a means of financing the new plan? The framers of the new plan might have realized that the county citizens would not consider imposing such a tax on themselves. In essence, African Americans in St. Louis—the original "victims" of legalized segregation—primarily have to foot the bill to remedy the inequities that they did not create.

Overall, the educators I interviewed recognized that the implications of *Brown* extended beyond education and included the dismantling of legalized racism in all aspects of American society. They remind us, however, that desegregation, in the form of racially balancing black and white students, should be seen as only one way to implement *Brown*. For them, desegregation should have been more about African Americans in St. Louis having greater political and economic control of the education of black students. Whereas the political control was possible, the economic control seemed less so because of efforts to ensure that whites' overall economic interests were maintained. These educators' observations point to the need to ensure that black students who decide to participate in the transfer aspect of the new plan are provided with the necessary resources to enable them to adjust academically, psychologically, socially, and culturally to predominantly white school environments. Transferring into a racially and culturally different school creates problems for African American students from the city because many of them are not welcomed (Wells and Crain, 1997). Although sensitizing white educators in the suburban schools is important, training and hiring African American educators to teach and work in these county schools would have a much more positive impact in minimizing the transitional difficulties encountered by African American students. In the interests of black students, this component of the old plan should have had a greater focus, and the necessity that this be incorporated into the new plan cannot be overemphasized.

Furthermore, these African American educators remind us that schools serve a vital function in communities and have historically done so for African American families and communities. Low-income, predominantly black communities especially need stable institutions (Wilson, 1996), and for many urban communities, schools can serve this function (Morris, 1999). This has to be taken into consideration when policy makers conceptualize choice models that transfer African American students away from their communities. Although it is important to increase choices for those parents who do not want their children to attend the city's schools, if city schools are not viewed as viable choices for African American students, it could have dire effects on the role that schools play in predominantly black communities.

Finally, the implications for educational theory of hearing these black educators include the need to foreground race as an indelible factor that affects all aspects of educational policy. It is not that CRT analyses are cynical or pessimistic—they are realistic. CRT analyses of educational policies force academics, researchers and analysts to view desegregation policy within historical contexts by recognizing the wages and privileges of whiteness and the limitations of policies predicated on minimizing the educational disparity between whites and blacks. More often than not, these policies have ultimately protected the overall interests of whites.

Conclusion: Hearing Black Educators' Voices

Judge Robert Carter (1980), who played a major role in school desegregation strategy, states that if he had to reconsider *Brown* today, "instead of looking principally to the social scientists to demonstrate the adverse consequences of segregation, I would seek to recruit educators to formulate a concrete definition of equality in education, and I would base my argument on that definition" (p. 27). The conceptualization and implementation of educational policies—particularly those with serious implications for African American education—are incomplete when they ignore the perspectives of black educators. These educators provide a more inclusive but often neglected voice on educational policy for African American children. When researchers and policy makers begin fully to chronicle and understand the overall implications and ramifications of desegregation policy on black people—which includes hearing the voices of Black educators—then the real promises of *Brown* may become more fully realized.

Notes

1. The terms "African American" and "black" are used interchangeably; both refer to U.S. citizens of African descent or institutions historically associated with their experiences.
2. Pseudonyms are used throughout for the names of the educators and their schools.
3. Derrick Bell reminds us that critical race theory (CRT) is not so much about intellectualizing and trying to find "critical race moments" in education as about being cognizant of how black people in America have always known what racism was—before there was any such thing as CRT. (This information was based on a conversation that I had with Derrick Bell at the annual meeting of the American Educational Research Association in April 2000.)
4. In Boston, Massachusetts, during the early nineteenth century, African American children were allowed to attend Boston public schools, but few parents enrolled their children because of prejudice on the part of white teachers. Separate schools were then established for the African American students. However, some of the African Americans protested the actions of the Boston public school system, which segregated black children from white children. In 1849 a group of African American parents, in a case that became known as *Roberts v. the City of Boston*, fought for integrated education. The African American community was split on this issue.
5. In his polemical essay "Does the Negro Need Separate Schools?" Du Bois (1935) argued that the Negro child in America—because of the persistence and the pervasiveness of racism in America and public schools—could not be assured an effective education in integrated schools. Ironically, Du Bois began as a staunch integrationist and was one of the founders of the National Association for the Advancement of Colored People (NAACP). He broke from the organization in 1934 because of ideological differences. See also Alridge (1999).
6. Almost all of these educators were born and raised in St. Louis and attended the segregated public school system. All except two received their teacher training or certification to teach from either Stowe—a historically all-black teachers college—or Harris-Stowe Teachers College, a 1955 merger of Stowe with a historically all-white teachers college, Harris, a year after *Brown v. Board of Education of Topeka, Kansas* became law (Wright, 1994). These educators' lives and professions were affected by *Brown* at the K–12 and higher education levels.
7. Approximately10 percent of the African American students withdraw from the plan each year.
8. Fleming (1990) and Hilliard (1990) cautioned against using standardized tests solely to measure African American students' achievement.

9. South St. Louis was once a predominantly white community where the predominantly white schools were located. During the 1950s, the St. Louis Board of Education tried to relieve overcrowding in the schools by busing black children to white schools on the south side. These students were in the school on different schedules and in different classrooms. The north side is where African Americans primarily lived and went to school.

10. See Garret A. Duncan's (1997) review of Wells and Crain's (1997) book *Stepping over the Color Line: African-American Students in White Suburban Schools*. Duncan notes that the authors' allegiance to the ideals of integration presents a very biased view of all-black schools in St. Louis.

11. To encourage white parents to participate in desegregation efforts, many school systems in the 1970s and 1980s created magnet schools in response to the mandate of school desegregation. In 1976, incentives to motivate the voluntary transfer of students were approved by two federal courts in the cases *Arthur v. Nyquist* in Buffalo, New York, and *Amos v. Board of Directors of the City of Milwaukee*. In these decisions, the courts relied on magnet schools to desegregate black schools and used majority to minority transfers to desegregate white schools. Today, magnet schools are being introduced in more urban school districts to achieve racial balance in schools and to promote greater choice in the attempt to satisfy parents' interests and priorities (Smrekar and Goldring, 1999).

References

Alridge, D. P. (1999). Conceptualizing a Du Boisian Philosophy of Education: Towards a Model for African-American Education. *Educational Theory* 49: 359–379.

Amos v. Board of Directors of the City of Milwaukee, 408 F. Supp. 765 (1976).

Anderson, J. D. (1988). *The Education of Blacks in the South, 1860–1935*. Chapel Hill: University of North Carolina Press.

Arthur v. Nyquist, 415 F. Supp. 904 (1976).

Bell, D. (1980). Brown v. Board of Education and the Interest-Convergence Dilemma. *Harvard Law Review* 93: 518–533.

Bell, D. (1987). *And We Are Not Saved: The Elusive Quest for Racial Justice*. New York: Basic Books.

Bell, D. (1992). *Faces at the Bottom of the Well: The Permanence of Racism*. New York: Basic Books.

Brown v. Board of Education of Topeka, Kansas, 347 U.S. 483 (1954).

Carter, R. L. (1980). A Reassessment of *Brown v. Board*. In D. Bell (ed.), *Shades of Brown: New Perspectives on School Desegregation*, 20–28. New York: Teachers College Press.

Citizens' Commission on Civil Rights. (1997). *Difficult Choices: Do Magnet Schools Serve Children in Need?* Washington, DC: Citizens' Commission on Civil Rights.

Cross, W. E. (1991). *Shades of Black: Diversity in African-American Identity*. Philadelphia: Temple University Press.

Delgado, R. (1988). Critical Legal Studies and the Realities of race: Does the Fundamental Contradiction Have a Corollary? *Harvard Civil Rights–Civil Liberties Law Review* 23: 407–413.

Delgado, R. (1990). When a Story Is Just a Story: Does Voice Really Matter? *Virginia Law Review* 76: 95–111.

Dempsey, V., and Noblit, G. (1993). The Demise of Caring in an African American community: One Consequence of School Desegregation. *Urban Review* 25(1): 47–61.

DeCuir, J. T., and Dixson, A. D. (2004). "And Nothing of That Had Ever Been Mentioned": Using Critical Race Theory as a Tool of Analysis and Desilencing in Education. *Educational Researcher* 33(5): 26–32.

Dixson, A. D., and Rousseau, C. K. (2005). And We Are Still Not Saved: Critical Race Theory in Education 10 years Later. *Race, Ethnicity and Education* 8(1):.

Du Bois, W. E. B. (1935). Does the Negro Need Separate Schools? *Journal of Negro Education* 4(3): 328–335.

Duncan, G. A. (1997). Review of *Stepping over the Color Line: African-American Students in White Suburban Schools. Journal of Negro Education* 66(3): 345–348.

Edwards, P. A. (1996). Before and after School Desegregation: African American Parents' Involvement in Schools. In M. Shujaa (ed.), *Beyond Desegregation: The Politics of Quality in African American Schooling*, 138–161. Thousand Oaks, CA: Corwin.

Etheridge, S. B. (1979). Impact of the 1954 *Brown vs. Topeka Board of Education* Decision on Black Educators. *Negro Educational Review* 30(4): 217–232.

Fleming, J. (1990). Standardized Test Scores and the Black College Environment. In K. Lomotey (ed.), *Going to School: The African American Experience*, 143–162. Albany: SUNY Press.

Foster, M. (1990). The Politics of Race: Through African American Teachers' Eyes. *Journal of Education* 172(3): 123–141.

Foster, M. (1991). Constancy, Change and Constraints in the Lives of Black Women Teachers: Some Things Change, Most Stay the Same. *NWSA Journal* 3(2): 233–261.

Foster, M. (1995). African American Teachers and Culturally Relevant Pedagogy. In J. A. Banks and C. M. Banks (eds.), *Handbook of Research on Multicultural Education*, 570–581. New York: Macmillan.

Foster, M. (1997). *Black Teachers on Teaching.* New York: New Press.

Franklin, V. P. (1990). They Rose and Fell Together: African American Educators and Community Leadership, 1795–1954. *Journal of Education* 172(3): 39–64.

Grant, C. A. (1995). Reflections on the Promise of *Brown* and Multicultural Education. *Teachers College Record* 96(4): 706–721.

Guy-Sheftall, B. (1993). Black Feminist Perspective on the Academy. Paper presented at the meeting of the American Educational Research Association, Atlanta, GA.

Haney, J. E. (1978). The Effect of the *Brown* Decision on Black Educators. *Journal of Negro Education* 47(1): 88–95.

Harris, C. I. (1993). Whiteness as Property. *Harvard Law Review* 106: 1707–1791.

Hilliard, A. G., III. (1990). Limitations of Current Academic Achievement Measures. In K. Lomotey (ed.), *Going to School: The African American Experience*, 143–162. Albany: SUNY Press.

Irvine, R., and Irvine, J. (1983). The Impact of the Desegregation Process on the Education of Black Students: Key Variables. *Journal of Negro Education* 52: 410–422.

Johnson, C. S. (1954). Some Significant Social and Educational Implications of the United States Supreme Court Decision. *Journal of Negro Education* 23: 364–371.

Ladson-Billings, G. (1998). Just What Is Critical Race Theory and What's It Doing in a *Nice* Field like Education? *Qualitative Studies in Education* 11: 7–24.

Ladson-Billings, G., and Tate, W. F. (1995). Toward a Critical Race Theory of Education. *Teachers College Record* 97(1): 47–68.

Liddell v. Board of Education of the City of St. Louis, 469 F. Supp. 1304 (E.D. Mo. 1979). *Liddell v. St. Louis Board of Education*, 72C 100(1). Consent Judgment and Decree. U.S. District Court, Eastern District of Missouri (1975).

Lomotey, K. (1989). *African American Principals: School Leadership and Success.* New York: Greenwood.

Lynn, M. (1999). Toward a Critical Race Pedagogy: A Research Note. *Urban Education* 33(6): 606–626.

Mannies, J. (1993a). Bosley Remains Firm on Anti-busing Stance. *St. Louis Post-Dispatch*, 29 September, p. 1A.

Mannies, J. (1993b). Mayor Wants To End school Busing: City Neighborhood Suffering, He Says. *St. Louis Post-Dispatch*, 27 September, p. 1A.

McIntosh, P. (1998 [1988]). White Privilege: Unpacking the Invisible Knapsack. In E. Lee, D. Menkart and M. Okazawa-Rey (eds.) *Beyond Heroes and Holidays: A Practical Guide to K–12 Anti-racist, Multicultural Education, and Staff development.* Washington, DC: Network of Educators on the Americas.

Meier, K.; Stewart, J.; and England, R. E. (1989). *Race, Class, and education: The Politics of Second-Generation Discrimination.* Madison: University of Wisconsin Press.

Merriam, S. B. (1988). *Case Study Research in Education: A Qualitative Approach.* San Francisco: Jossey-Bass.

Missouri v. Jenkins, 115 S. Ct. 2038 (1995).

Morris, J. E. (1997). Voluntary Desegregating in St. Louis, Missouri: Impact on Partnerships among Schools, African American families, and Communities. Ph.D. dissertation, Department of Leadership, Policy, and Organizations, Vanderbilt University, Nashville, TN.

Morris, J. E. (1999). A Pillar of Strength: An African American School's Communal Bonds with Families and Communities since *Brown. Urban Education* 33(5): 584–605.

Orfield, G., and Eaton, S. (1996). *Dismantling Desegregation: The Quiet Reversal of* Brown v. Board of Education. New York: New Press and Harvard Project on School Desegregation.

Parker, L. (1998). Race Is ... Race Ain't; An Exploration of the Utility of Critical Race Theory in Qualitative Research in Education. *International Journal of Qualitative Studies in Education* 11: 43–56.

Perspectives of the parties to the *Liddell* case (1995). A collection of presentations made at meetings of the Voluntary Interdistrict Coordinating Council, 1995–1996.

Scheurich, J. J., and Young, M. D. (1997). Coloring Epistemologies: Are Our Research Epistemologies Racially Biased? *Educational Researcher* 25(4): 4–15.

Siddle-Walker, E. V. (1996). *Their Highest Potential: An African American School Community in the Segregated South.* Chapel Hill: University of North Carolina Press.

Smrekar, C., and Goldring, E. B. (1999). *School Choice in Urban America: Magnet schools and the Pursuit of Equity.* New York: Teachers College Press.

Tate, W. F. (1997). Critical Race Theory and Education: History, Theory, and Implications. In Michael W. Apple (ed.), *Review of Research in Education, vol. 22,* 195–247. Washington, DC: American Educational Research Association.

Voluntary Interdistrict Coordinating Council (1998). *Fourteenth Annual Report to the United States District Court, Eastern District Court of Missouri.* Voluntary Interdistrict Coordinating Council for the settlement agreement, January 1998, submitted by William Gussner and Susan Uchitelle.

Wells, A. S., and Crain, R. L. (1997). *Stepping over the Color Line: African-American Students in White Suburban Schools.* New Haven: Yale University Press.

Wilson, W. J. (1996). *When Work Disappears: The World of the New Urban Poor.* New York: Knopf.

Wright, J. A. (1994). *Discovering African American St. Louis: A Guide to Historic Sites.* St. Louis: Missouri Historical Society Press.

8

Parent(s): The Biggest Influence in the Education of African American Football Student-Athletes

JAMEL K. DONNOR

Introduction

African American parental involvement in education is inextricably linked with improving the political and economic standing of their children. In *The Education of Blacks in the South, 1860–1935*, James Anderson (1988) chronicles the efforts of ex-slaves to "establish schools for their own children" (p. 15). According to Anderson (1988), the Negroes' labors were grounded in the "belief that education could help raise freed people to an appreciation of their historic responsibility to develop a better society and that any significant reorganization of the southern political economy was indissolubly linked to their education in the principles, duties, and obligations appropriate to a democratic social order" (p. 28).

Similarly, Siddle-Walker (1996) details black parents' involvement in a high school they helped to establish for their children in North Carolina during the Jim Crow era:

> Negro parents who wanted a child to have an education beyond elementary school were forced to send the child to neighboring cities in other counties, while white children could choose from among three high schools as early as 1924. ... Many Negro parents were not able to make the sacrifices such a move entailed. The parents who rose to assume the initiative in plans to start a high school in Yanceyville [North Carolina], and who continued to assume the initiative leadership roles in the school over the years, may be called 'advocates.' In general, these advocates were parents...who interposed themselves between the needs of the Negro community and the power of the white school board and made requests on behalf of the school. (p. 19)

While the current social context shaping African American parental involvement is not as repressive as slavery or Jim Crow, the reason for participating in their child's education remains constant.

Traditionally, education scholars have categorized the relationship between the secondary education of African American males and their involvement with athletics as inherently beneficial. Highlighting sports' functional characteristics, this popular perspective suggests that student-athletes learn the value of hard work, perseverance and being goal-oriented (Eitzen, 2001 [1997]). Further, the functionalist perspective contends that involvement in athletics increases students' grades, academic aspirations and self-concept. In a study measuring *Sport and Academic Resilience among African American Males*, Braddock et al. (1991) suggest:

> For African-American male students, this [interscholastic sports] adds an academic incentive to other intrinsic incentives already associated with sport involvement. … Athletic participation, then, may be seen as a mechanism that both forces and facilitates academic responsiveness, thus providing both a rationale and tools for academic effort—even in the face of earlier difficulties. (p. 129)

In addition to advancing a static conception of academic success, conventional studies have ignored the contributory role of parents as stakeholders in the education of African American male student-athletes. As a result, athletics' educational value is overstated.

This chapter is a departure from the extant education research on African American males, education and sport. Moreover, it represents my interest in Derrick Bell's (1992 [1980]) "interest-convergence" theory as a framework to interpret the educational experiences of African American athletes (Donnor, 2005).* Utilizing descriptive information derived from a case study project examining the academic preparedness of African American intercollegiate football student-athletes, this chapter discusses the contributory role of parents in a student-athlete's education. Examining the educational experiences of black male student-athletes from this viewpoint, I argue, uncovers how race as an experiential construct informs parental behavior, attitudes, and decisions regarding academic achievement (Ladson-Billings, 1998, 2003; Duncan, 2005; Dixson and Rousseau, 2005).

The goals of this chapter are twofold. The first is to provide a more holistic understanding of the secondary education of African American male student-athletes. The second goal is to enrich the education literature's theorizing on race. This chapter contains five sections. The first discusses the conceptual limitations of popular theories used to examine this topic. Section two explains

---

* Davis (1995) used interest-convergence to explain African American integration into intercollegiate athletics.

the interest-convergence principle and its application to a study exploring the educational experiences of African American student-athletes. The third section explains the research methods used to collect information from 17 black male student-athletes at three Midwestern universities with Division IA football programs. Section four presents ethnographic interview data describing how parents contributed to the college preparedness of African American males talented enough to play Division IA football. Section five, the conclusion, consists of a discussion and analysis of the study's findings in relation to interest-convergence theory.

Traditional Theoretical Approaches

Theoretically, scholars have used either a dialectical (e.g., conflict theory) or social psychological approach to make sense of African American student-athletes' educational experiences and outcomes. Highlighting institutional factors, conflict theorists focus on the structural and cultural dimensions of sport. Specifically, conflict theories explain the extent to which policies and standard operating procedures work to marginalize participants. For example, conflict theorists assert that at the Division IA level, football student-athletes are exploited based on the following determinants: (1) the amount of potential revenue generated by the sport, (2) coaches' salaries, (3) the total time dedicated to sport-related activities compared to academics, and (4) the fact that student-athletes are not permitted to receive a stipend (Gerdy, 2000; Patterson, 2000; Coakley, 2001). Further, conflict theorists contend that African American student-athletes are particularly vulnerable to exploitation because they are more likely to be "specially admitted"* or encouraged to enroll in "Mickey Mouse" courses to maintain athletic eligibility (Eitzen, 1999; Edwards, 1984).

Conversely, social psychologists explore issues encompassing identity formation, informal interactions, and interpersonal relationships in their examinations of student-athletes. According to the social psychological perspective, individuals identified as having athletic talent are "foreclosed" from developing characteristics associated with being a good student to pursue success in sports (Watt and Moore, 2001, p. 340). According to Webb et al. (1998), the "time and psychological commitment to the [social] role of athlete is such that by the time they reach high school, highly successful athletes have internalized the athletic identity, frequently at the expense of other social roles" (p. 340). Consequently, overidentification with the social role of athlete can result in the unintentional perpetuation of the pervasive image of the intellectually deficient athlete (the "dumb jock") (Gerdy, 2002, p. 69; Edwards, 1984).

---

* This term refers to a student, irrespective of athletic status, who has not met a university's conventional requirement for admission. Legacy admissions and early enrollees are examples of special admits.

Social psychologists also contend that student-athletes disproportionately experience conflict between the demands of sport and education. In addition to addressing nonathletic responsibilities, such as developing "personal competencies that will enable them to bring about a greater degree of mastery and control over their environment," student-athletes must "balance" athletic requirements, adapt to a "certain degree of isolation from mainstream activities," and "satisfy multiple relationships" with coaches, parents, friends and the community (Parham, 1993, p. 412). Unlike conflict theorists, social psychologists recognize the interplay among racial, gendered and athletic identities in the education of African American student-athletes. For instance, because the majority of black college football players come from lower socio-economic backgrounds, social psychologists assert that their chances for academic success are less than those of whites (Harris, 2000).*

Though adequate, both strands of thought conceptually restrict education, individual experience, agency and race to the athletic environment. For instance, conflict theorists minimize in-group variance by not accounting for the academic achievement of student-athletes despite the pressure for athletic success. Similarly, the social psychological framework exaggerates the obvious among African American student-athletes. The majority of African American student-athletes who participate in Division IA football come from urban schools. As a result, the social psychological perspective generalizes that all black males' chances for success are poorer because of their background. Stated differently, social psychology does not explore or consider the differences within this group, and how they may be successful *because* of their background. Benson's (2000) work on the academic achievement of African American Division I football players suggests that a reconceptualization is necessary to understand this phenomenon. According to Benson, "marginal academic performance [is] a phenomenon created by a series of interrelated practices engaged by all significant members of the academic setting, including peers, coaches, advisors, teachers/professors, and the student-athletes themselves" (p. 229). I believe that Derrick Bell's (1992 [1980]) interest-convergence principle (ICP) provides the conceptual space necessary to develop a more nuanced explication of the black athlete's educational experience than the aforementioned theories can.

The Interest-Convergence Theory

Interest-convergence is an analytical construct of critical race theory (CRT) that explains the political economics of race in America (Bell, 1992 [1980], 1987; Delgado and Stefancic, 2005; Tate, 2005). Premised on a racial group's "legal history," interest-convergence describes the tensions between legal

---

* The 2005 graduation rates as reported by the National Collegiate Athletic Association (NCAA) supports this.

redress for racism and maintenance of the political and economic status quo. Legal history establishes a social context for understanding the "world as it is rather than how we might want it" (Bell, 1995, p. 22). Bell developed the interest-convergence thesis to explain external societal factors that influenced the U.S. Supreme Court's decision in *Brown v. Board of Education*. According to Bell (1992 [1980]),

> Until *Brown*, black claims that segregated public schools were inferior had been met by orders requiring merely that facilities be made equal. Courts had been willing to substitute their judgments for those of the legislatures as to the wisdom of school segregation policies. The decision in *Brown* to break with its long-held position on these issues, despite the language of the opinion, can't be understood without some consideration of the decision's impact on interests other than those of long-suffering black children and their parents. (p. 640).

Bell (1992 [1980], 2004) hypothesized that as America began to position itself as a "world" leader by advocating that Third World countries adopt democracy and capitalism as political and economic alternatives to communism after World War II, images broadcast internationally of black Americans' sanctioned oppression (i.e., segregation) and physical repression during the civil rights movement hindered America's democracy project. Segregation no longer contributed to the advancement of U.S. domestic and foreign policies.

Conducting a document analysis of formerly confidential Supreme Court memoranda and classified government documents, Dudziak (1988) found:

> Newspapers throughout the world carried stories about discrimination against non-white visiting foreign dignitaries, as well as against American blacks. At a time when the U.S. hoped to reshape the postwar world in its own image, the international attention given to racial segregation was troublesome and embarrassing. The focus of American foreign policy at this point was to promote democracy and to 'contain' communism. However, the international focus on U.S. racial problems meant that the image of American democracy was tarnished. The apparent contradictions between American political ideology and practice led to particular foreign policy difficulties with countries in Asia, Africa and Latin America. U.S. government official realized that their ability to sell democracy to the Third World was seriously hampered by continuing racial injustice at home. (p. 62)

In this instance of social "progress," the Supreme Court was more *interested* in providing "immediate credibility to America's struggle with communist countries to win the hearts and minds of emerging third world people," instead of doing what was morally right (Bell, 1995, p. 23). Further, public schools were selected because they "represented a far more compelling symbol of the evils of segregation and a far more vulnerable target than segregated railroad cars, restaurants, or restrooms" (Bell, 1995, p. 229).

Interest-convergence puts into full view the limitations and contradictions of law and public policy by pointing out how they operate to secure the dominant class's interests. Paradoxically, the rights of oppressed groups are recognized and legitimated only when they further the interests of the dominant class and of society's governing institutions. Moreover, the identification of the motivating factors that guide policy development, as in *Brown*, suggests that the coincidence of a pressing political and/or economic issue is required rather than a commitment to social justice.

For this study, interest-convergence theory provides the conceptual space to explore the educational history of African American student-athletes, including the behavior and motivation of educational stakeholders (e.g., parents, teachers and peers) in the process. Moreover, interest-convergence theory recognizes parents' interests in academic and athletic achievement as external factors that influence student-athletes' academic choices by developing education's and sport's (intrinsic) value. For example, if parents construct sport as the primary mechanism for improving social and economic standing, a student-athlete might be susceptible to selecting nonrigorous classes. Conversely, if academic achievement is promoted and sport is simultaneously deemphasized by parents, a black male athlete may be more likely to enroll in classes that will prepare him for college. Unlike Bell's (1992 [1980]) use of interest-convergence to uncover the ways in which inequity gets recycled under the guise of "equal opportunity" to advantage the privileged, I used ICP to explore factors outside education that contribute to the academic advancement of African American student-athletes.

Methodology

The use of interest-convergence theory required research methods that allow for consideration of: (1) history and current socio-cultural context, (2) experiential knowledge, and (3) the comparison of similar experiences. Case study and ethnographic interviews were selected as data collection methods because of their potential to extract information that is descriptive, interpretive and comparative (Stake, 1995; Merriam, 1998; Yin, 2003; Cohen, Manion and Morrison, 2000). By suggesting that the academic advancement of African American student-athletes is a convergence of interests, I am attempting to examine and define a set of explicit and implicit actions, attitudes and interactions within a specific setting. Moreover, the case study method was chosen because of its ability to "retain the holistic and meaningful characteristics of real-life" (Yin, 2003, p. 2). In addition, case study supports the investigation and reporting of "complex dynamic and unfolding interactions" between student-athletes and parents (Cohen, Manion and Morrison, 2000).

I also used ethnographic interviewing techniques to collect data and make sense of such "operational links," rather than simply measuring for randomness (Merriam, 1998). I grouped the interview questions posed to the black athletes in this study into the following categories: (1) descriptive, (2) structural, (3) contrasting, and (4) interpretive (Spradley, 1979; Merriam, 1998). I designed the descriptive questions to elicit a "large sample of utterances in the informant's native language" (Spradley, 1979, p. 85). An example of a descriptive question I posed was *How would you describe your educational experience before being identified as possessing the athletic ability to play for a major college program in high school?* I adapted structural questions specifically to the particular participant (Spradley, 1979). For example, I asked a structural question like *Who is responsible for ensuring a student-athlete is prepared in high school?* I used contrasting questions to discover variations among participants. An example of a contrasting question is *Do you think there are differences in the way black student-athletes and non-student-athletes are educated?* Finally, interpretive questions allowed for "reliability" because they check for understanding of the informant's responses (Merriam, 1998). An example is *How important would you say parents are in the education of African American student-athletes?*

Sampling

Participants were both purposely and randomly selected. I intentionally sought first-year student-athletes for their ability to provide a rich delineation of whether they were academically prepared for college. I selected sophomore respondents based on their advanced involvement in athletics and education. According to NCAA (2005) policy, a student-athlete must declare an academic major by his or her junior year in college. Thus, sophomores are best situated to reflect on how or if their values as educational stakeholders have shifted because of their continued association with athletics and its effects on education-related choices. Access to the remaining participants was provided through a collegial relationship I had with a professor at an institution. Because of this, I interviewed senior African American student-athletes. This group supplied a comprehensive assessment of their academic preparation by sharing their insights on the impact of the actions and decisions of significant others on their educational careers.

Findings

A major finding of this study is the centrality of parents to the education of African American male student-athletes. According to Chris (this and other names are pseudonyms), a freshman, "They [parents] are huge ... that is where education starts." Likewise, Anthony, a sophomore, stated, "A lot of it [education] falls on the parents whether or not a student-athlete is successful in high school." More specifically, parental interests in the student-athlete's academic advancement were grounded in the larger concept of "wanting me [student-athlete] to have a better life than them." In other words, according to the student-athletes who participated in this study, parents viewed education, and high academic achievement in particular, as essential for improving a student-athlete's overall quality of life.

The participants told about specific activities parents engaged in to ensure their preparation for college. Parental involvement varied from enrolling the participant in private school, to having discussions on race and academic achievement, to deemphasizing sport. The following vignettes provide insight into how the attitudes and actions of specific family members served the black athlete's educational interests.

James, a freshman, spoke of how his parents paid for him to attend private school, with their individual educational experiences serving as a personal template:

> My parents struggled to pay for private school. That showed me where they placed education on their hierarchy. Also, my father was born in Guyana and his family came here [United States] from Guyana when he was ten. They [father's parents] were high on education so he instilled it in me and my sisters. Also, my mother went to UT-Austin and was a 4.0 student. She graduated in three years with a 4.0. All of my life, my parents put a really high emphasis on education.

Leon, a senior, also discussed how his parents sent him to a private high school and how it positioned him for college:

> My parents decided to send me to a private school because I was not making any progress in public school. There is only one public high school in my town. It is also home to the middle school, which means it actually starts from seventh grade whereas a traditional high school begins in the ninth grade. My mother and my father made the decision to send me to another school because they figured that would be the best thing for me. I did not like it at first, but it ended up being the best thing that happened to me. It was not until my senior year, that I realized that if I stayed at my original school, I would not be in the position to be deciding where to go to college.

Robeson, a freshman, discussed his father's political view of the endemic nature of racism in America and the need for black males to be the best:

> My dad is the one who pushed me to get 4.0 every quarter in high school. My dad told me that it is racial, if it's between you and a white person, you always are going to lose because that is society's mindset. They [whites] don't want to give you a chance over them. So that is the mindset I have right now. Anything I do, it can't be close.

Ray, a freshman, talked about his mother as a role model, and her attitude on doing well in high school:

> She led by example because in high school she played sports and was top in her class. She lived in a predominantly white town so she had to deal with a lot more prejudice. … As my athletic ability started to take off, I did not slack off but my grades certainly were not the same. My mom kept telling me you have to get a 4.0, if you do not, you will be attending college right around the corner at a community college because I'm not going to pay a lot of money for you to go somewhere where you would not put forth the effort you could have right now. So my last two years of high school, I got right around a 3.2. I started taking AP classes so my studies would become more difficult.

Steven, a sophomore, acknowledged his father's laser-like focus on education:

> He was always there at the games, and he was always on me about school work. That is the reason why I am where I am now. He would not let me slack off on my grades no matter what was going on. Even though he loves football and knew how important it was to me, he only talked about my grades. Even when my grades were not bad, he would always say you can do better. He was the biggest influence.

As illustrated by these vignettes, parental interests place African American football student-athletes in a better position to have a rewarding education. This study's use of the interest-convergence principle illustrates how African American parents negotiated race, education, and sport. Further, the manner in which race informs the configuring of black parents' attitudes and actions in their child's education is historically consistent (see the introduction). Specifically, ICP illuminates the complexities involving parents, student-athletes, sport, and education by showing how they converge to contribute to the black student-athlete's achievement. For example, Robeson's father's discussion of the life-long significance of education versus athletics supports this assertion:

> The most important thing in your life, always and forever … football is good, but if you blow out your knee and cannot walk again then you are done. … You always got your brain to fall back on. Academics come first, because it is going to be with you for the rest of your life.

Discussion

This chapter contributes to the field of education research in two ways. The first contribution is theoretical. Interest-convergence counters the positivistic perspectives that dominate the field. Unlike traditional studies that suggest an intrinsic connection among African American males, educational success and athletics, the ethnographic interviews from this study suggest parents are the primary factor in the scholastic achievement of African American student-athletes. This is noteworthy because it interrogates the functional viewpoint that involvement in athletics naturally enhances student's academic performance. Sport, for the majority of participants at the secondary level, is inconsequential to academic success. More important, accounts of parental involvement highlight how sport diverges from their educational values.

A second theoretical contribution of this study is the rejection of deficit viewpoints. Benson (2000) asserts that there are significant data that attribute underachievement of intercollegiate African American male football student-athletes to poor high school preparation: "Problems within society at large suggesting that these students' underachievement may be caused in part by the way that schools are structured to maintain the prevailing social and economic order" (p. 223). Rather, this study recognizes the multiple contexts in which African American males, education and sport are positioned. For instance, Steven's father acted to convey a sense of balance between education and athletics, suggesting that student-athletes possess a modicum of control over athletic experience by regulating the demands of academics. Moreover, balance rebuts the social psychological assertion that athletic "over-conformity" conflicts with being a successful student (Webb et al., 1998). Hence, balance provides a tangential benefit to the student-athlete.

The second contribution this chapter makes to the education field is methodological. Case and ethnographic interviews are research methods that provide a clearer understanding of the education of black football student-athletes. A case study supports general understanding, whereas the information obtained from ethnographic interviews provided the "rich" data (details) for this project. The participants' narratives bridge the high school and collegiate settings, which gave me with a more complete understanding of their educational experience. The interviewees' shared and individual "stories" showed how race and competing self-interests contributed to academic performance through a series of interrelated practices involving parents as educational stakeholders. Finally, having the respondents of this study "name their reality" is contributory because it rejects outright the deficit and social reproductive perspectives that dominate this topic.

References

Anderson, J.D. (1988). *The Education of Blacks in the South, 1860–1935*. Chapel Hill: University of North Carolina Press.

Bell, D. (1987). *And We Are Not Saved: The Elusive Quest for Racial Justice*. New York: Basic Books.

Bell, D. (1992 [1980]). *Race, Racism and American Law*. 3rd ed. Boston: Little, Brown.

Bell, D. (1995). *Brown v. Board of Education* and the Interest Convergence Dilemma. In K. W. Crenshaw et al. (eds.), *Critical Race Theory: The Key Writings That Formed the Movement*, 20–29. New York: New Press.

Bell, D. (2004). *Silent Covenants: Brown v. Board of Education and the Unfulfilled Hopes for Racial Reform*. New York: Oxford University Press.

Benson, K. F. (2000). Constructing Academic Inadequacy: African American Athletes' Stories. *Journal of Higher Education* 71(2): 223–246.

Braddock, J. H. II; Royster, D. A.; Winfield, L. A.; and Hawkins, R. (1991). Bouncing Back: Sport and Academic Resilience among African-American Males. *Education and Urban Society* 24(1): 113–131.

Coakley, J. J. (2001). Sport in Society: An Inspiration or an Opiate? In D. S. Eitzen (ed.), *Sport in Contemporary Society*, 20–37. New York: Worth.

Cohen, L.; Manion, L.; and Morrison, K. (2000). *Research Methods in Education.* 5th ed.. London: RoutledgeFalmer.

Delgado, R., and Stefancic, J. (2005). Introduction. In R. Delgado and J. Stefancic (eds.), *The Derrick Bell Reader*, 1–15. New York: New York University Press.

Dixson, A. D., and Rousseau, C. K. (2005). And We Are Still Not Saved: Critical Race Theory in Education Ten Years Later. *Race, Ethnicity and Education* 8(1): 7–27.

Donnor, J. K. (2005). Towards an Interest-Convergence in the Education of African American Football Student Athletes in Major College Sports. *Race, Ethnicity and Education* 8(1): 45–67.

Dudziak, M. L. (1988). Desegregation as a Cold War Imperative. *Stanford Law Review* 41(61): 1–61.

Duncan, G. (2005). Critical Race Ethnography in Education: Narrative, Inequality, and the Problem of Epistemology. *Race, Ethnicity and Education* 8(1): 95–116.

Edwards, H. (1984). The Black "Dumb Jock": An American Sports Tragedy. *College Board Review* no. 131: 8–13.

Eitzen, D. S. (1999). *Fair and Foul: Beyond the Myths and Paradoxes of Sport.* Lanham, MD: Rowman and Littlefield.

Eitzen, D. S. (2001 [1997]). Big-time College Sports: Contradictions, Crises, and Consequences. In D. S. Eitzen (ed.), *Sport in Contemporary Society: An Anthology*, 201–212. 6th ed. New York: Worth.

Gerdy, J. R. (2000). College Athletics as Good Business? In J. R. Gerdy (ed.), *Sports in School: The Future of an Institution*, 42–54. New York: Teachers College Press.

Gerdy, J. R. (2002). *Sports: The All-American Addiction.* Jackson: University of Mississippi Press.

Harris, O. (2000). African American Predominance in Sport. In D. Brooks and R. Althouse (eds.), *Racism in College Athletics: The African American Athlete's experience*, 37–52. Morgantown, WV: Fitness Information Technology.

Hartmann, D. (2000). Rethinking the Relationships between Sport and Race in American Culture: Golden Ghettos and Contested Terrain. *Sociology of Sport Journal* 17: 229–253.

Ladson-Billings, G. (1998). Just What Is Critical Race Theory and What's It Doing in a *Nice* Field like Education? *Qualitative Studies in Education* 11(1): 7–24.

Ladson-Billings, G. (2003). It's Your World, I'm Just Trying To Explain It: Understanding Our Epistemological and Methodological Challenges. *Qualitative Inquiry* 9: 5–12.

Merriam, S. B. (1998). Qualitative Research and Applications in Education. San Francisco: Jossey-Bass.

Parham, W. D. (1993). The Intercollegiate Athlete: A 1990s Profile. *Counseling Psychologist* 21(3): 411–429.

Patterson, C. M. (2000). Athletics and the Higher Education Marketplace. In J. R. Gerdy (ed.), *Sports in School: The Future of an Institution*, 119–127. New York: Teachers College Press.

Siddle-Walker, V. (1996). *Their Highest Potential: An African American School Community in the Segregated South.* Chapel Hill: University of North Carolina Press.

Spivey, D., and Jones, T. A. (1975). Intercollegiate Athletic Servitude: A Case Study of the Black Illini Student-Athletes, 1931–1967. *Social Science Quarterly* 55: 939–947.

Spradley, J. P. (1979). *The Ethnographic Interview.* New York: Holt, Rinehart and Winston.

Stake, R. E. (1995) *The Art of Case Study Research.* Thousand Oaks, CA: Sage.

Tate, W. F. (1999). Conclusion. In L. Parker et al. (eds.), *Race Is ... Race Isn't: Critical Race Theory and Qualitative Studies in Education*, 251–271. Boulder, CO: Westview.

Tate, W. F. (2005). *Brown*, Political Economy, and the Scientific Education of African Americans. *Review of Research in Education* 28: 147–184.

Taylor, E. (1999). Bring in "Da Noise": Race, Sports, and the Role of Schools. *Educational Leadership* 56(7) 75–78.

Watt, S. K., and Moore, J. L., III (2001). Who Are Student Athletes? *New Directions for Student Services* 93: 7–18.

Webb, W.; Nasco, S. A.; Riley, S.; and Headrick, B. (1998). Athletic Identity and Reactions to Retirement from Sports. *Journal of Sport Behavior* 21(3): 338–358.

Yin, R. K. (2003). *Case Study Research: Design and Methods.* 3rd ed. Thousand Oaks, CA: Sage.

III

The Interdisciplinary Nature
of Critical Race Theory

9

Whose Culture Has Capital?
A Critical Race Theory Discussion
of Community Cultural Wealth

TARA J. YOSSO

Introduction

> Theory, then, is a set of knowledges. Some of these knowledges have
> been kept from us—entry into some professions and academia denied
> us. Because we are not allowed to enter discourse, because we are often
> disqualified and excluded from it, because what passes for theory these
> days is forbidden territory for us, it is *vital* that we occupy theorizing
> space, that we not allow whitemen and women solely to occupy it. By
> bringing in our own approaches and methodologies, we transform that
> theorizing space" (Anzaldúa, 1990, p. xxv; emphasis in original).

In the epigraph above, Gloria Anzaldúa (1990) calls on People of Color to
transform the process of theorizing. This call is about epistemology—the
study of sources of knowledge. Scholars such as Gloria Ladson-Billings (2000)
and Dolores Delgado Bernal (1998, 2002) have asked, "Whose knowledge
counts, and whose knowledge is discounted?" Throughout U.S. history, race
and racism have shaped this epistemological debate (Lopez and Parker, 2003;
Scheurich and Young, 1997). Indeed, it has been over a century since W. E. B.
Du Bois (1903, 1989) predicted that racism would continue to emerge as one
of the United States' key social problems. Racism overtly shaped U.S. social
institutions at the beginning of the twentieth century and continues, although
more subtly, to affect U.S. institutions of socialization in the beginning of the
twenty-first century. Researchers, practitioners, and students are still searching for the necessary tools to analyze and challenge the impact of race and
racism in U.S. society.

In addressing the debate over knowledge within the context of social
inequality, Pierre Bourdieu (Bourdieu and Passeron, 1977) argued that the
knowledges of the upper and middle classes are considered capital valuable

This chapter originally appeared in *Race, Ethnicity and Education* 8(1), March 2005, pp. 69–92.

to a hierarchical society. If one is not born into a family whose knowledge is already deemed valuable, one can then access the knowledges of the middle and upper classes and the potential for social mobility through formal schooling. Bourdieu's theoretical insight about how a hierarchical society reproduces itself has often been interpreted as a way to explain why the academic and social outcomes of People of Color are significantly lower than the outcomes of whites. The assumption follows that People of Color "lack" the social and cultural capital required for social mobility. As a result, schools most often work from this assumption in structuring ways to help "disadvantaged" students whose race and class background has left them lacking necessary knowledge, social skills, abilities and cultural capital (see Valenzuela, 1999).

This interpretation demonstrates Anzaldúa's point: "If we have been gagged and disempowered by theories, we can also be loosened and empowered by theories" (Anzaldúa, 1990, p. xxvi). Indeed, if some knowledges have been used to silence, marginalize and render People of Color invisible, then "Outsider" knowledges (Hill Collins, 1986), Mestiza knowledges (Anzaldúa, 1987) and Transgressive knowledges (hooks, 1994) can value the presence and voices of People of Color, and they can reenvision the margins as places empowered by transformative resistance (Delgado Bernal, 1997; hooks, 1990; Solórzano and Delgado Bernal, 2001). Critical race theory (CRT) listens to Du Bois' racial insight and offers a response to Anzaldúa's theoretical challenge. CRT is a framework that can be used to theorize, examine and challenge the ways race and racism implicitly and explicitly affect social structures, practices and discourses.

Following, I discuss the ways CRT centers Outsider, Mestiza and Transgressive knowledges. After outlining the theoretical framework of CRT, I critique the assumption that Students of Color come to the classroom with cultural deficiencies. Utilizing a CRT lens, I challenge traditional interpretations of Bourdieu's cultural capital theory (Bourdieu and Passeron, 1977) and introduce an alternative concept called "community cultural wealth." Then I outline at least six forms of capital that make up community cultural wealth and usually go unacknowledged or unrecognized. In examining some of the underutilized assets Students of Color bring with them from their homes and communities into the classroom, this chapter notes the potential of community cultural wealth to transform the process of schooling.

Critical Race Theory in Education

CRT draws from and extends a broad literature base of critical theory in law, sociology, history, ethnic studies, and women's studies. Kimberlé Crenshaw (2002) explains that in the late 1980s, various legal scholars felt limited by work that separated critical theory from conversations about race and racism. Alongside other "Outsider" scholars (Hill Collins, 1986), Crenshaw was "looking for both a critical space in which race was foregrounded and a race space where critical themes were central" (2002, p. 19). Mari Matsuda (1991)

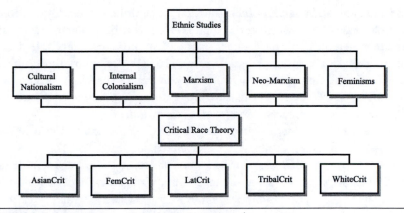

Figure 9.1 An intellectual genealogy of critical race theory.[1]

defined that CRT space as "the work of progressive legal scholars of color who are attempting to develop a jurisprudence that accounts for the role of racism in American law and that work toward the elimination of racism as part of a larger goal of eliminating all forms of subordination" (p. 1331).

In previous work, I have described a genealogy of CRT that links the themes and patterns of legal scholarship with the social science literature (Solórzano and Yosso, 2001). Figure 9.1 represents some of this intellectual history.

In its post-1987 form, CRT emerged from criticisms of the critical legal studies (CLS) movement. CLS scholars questioned the role of the traditional legal system in legitimizing oppressive social structures. With this insightful analysis, CLS scholarship emphasized a critique of the liberal legal tradition as opposed to offering strategies for change. Scholars such as Derrick Bell and Alan Freeman asserted that one reason that the CLS critique of the law could not offer strategies for social transformation was that it failed to incorporate race and racism into the analysis (Delgado, 1995a; Ladson-Billings, 1998). Not listening to the lived experiences and histories of those oppressed by institutionalized racism limited CLS scholarship. This argument had also been taking place in social science and history circles, specifically in ethnic studies and women's studies.

Critical race theorists began to pull away from CLS because the critical legal framework restricted their ability to analyze racial injustice (Crenshaw, 2002; Crenshaw, Gotanda, Peller and Thomas, 1995; Delgado, 1988; Delgado and Stefancic, 2001). Initially, CRT scholarship focused its critique on the slow pace and unrealized promise of civil rights legislation. As a result, many of the critiques launched were articulated in black vs. white terms. Women and People of Color who felt their gendered, classed, sexual, immigrant and language experiences and histories were being silenced challenged this tendency toward a Black/White binary. They stressed that oppression in the law and society could not be fully understood in terms of only Black and White. Certainly, African Americans have experienced a unique and horrendous history of racism and other forms of subordination in the United States. Other People of Color have their own histories that likewise have been shaped by racism and the intersecting forms of subordination (Espinoza and Harris, 1998). By offering a two-dimensional discourse, the Black/White binary limits understanding of the multiple ways in which African Americans, Native Americans, Asian/Pacific Islanders, Chicanas/os, and Latinas/os continue to experience, respond to and resist racism and other forms of oppression.

For example, Latina/o critical race (LatCrit) theory extends critical race discussions to address the layers of racialized subordination that make up Chicana/o and Latina/o experiences (Arriola, 1997, 1998; Stefancic, 1998). LatCrit scholars assert that racism, sexism, and classism are experienced amid other layers of subordination based on immigration status, sexuality, culture, language, phenotype, accent and surname (Johnson, 1999; Montoya, 1994). Indeed, the traditional paradigm for understanding U.S. race relations is often a Black/White binary that limits discussions about race and racism to terms of African American and White experiences (Valdes, 1997, 1998). Like Manning Marable (1992), who defines racism as "a system of ignorance, exploitation, and power used to oppress African-Americans, Latinos, Asians, Pacific Americans, American Indians, and other people on the basis of ethnicity, culture, mannerisms, and color" (p. 5), CRT scholarship has benefited from work addressing racism at its intersections with other forms of subordination (Crenshaw, 1989, 1993).

Over the years, the CRT family tree has expanded to incorporate the racialized experiences of women, Latinas/os, Native Americans, and Asian Americans (see Figure 9.1). For example, LatCrit, TribalCrit and AsianCrit are branches of CRT, evidencing Chicana/o, Latina/o, Native American, and Asian American communities' ongoing search for a framework that addresses racism and its accompanying oppressions beyond the Black/White binary (Brayboy, 2001, 2002; Chang, 1993, 1998; Chon, 1995; Delgado, 1997; Ikemoto, 1992; R. Williams 1997). Women of Color have also challenged CRT to address feminist critiques of racism and classism through FemCrit theory (Caldwell, 1995; Wing, 1997, 2000). In addition, White scholars have expanded CRT with WhiteCrit, by "looking behind the mirror" to expose White privilege and challenge racism (Delgado and Stefancic, 1997).

CRT's branches are not mutually exclusive or in contention with one another. Naming, theorizing, and mobilizing from the intersections of racism need not initiate some sort of oppression sweepstakes—a competition to measure one form of oppression against another. As Cherrie Moraga (1983) writes:

> The danger lies in ranking the oppressions. The danger lies in failing to acknowledge the specificity of the oppression. The danger lies in attempting to deal with oppression purely from a theoretical base. Without an emotional, heartfelt grappling with the source of our own

oppression, without naming the enemy within ourselves and outside of us, no authentic, non-hierarchical connection among oppressed groups can take place. (pp. 52–53)

Indeed, racism and its intersections with other forms of subordination shape the experiences of People of Color very differently from those of Whites (Baca Zinn, 1989; Bell, 1986, 1998; Essed, 1991). Still, the popular discourse in the United States, as well as the academic discourse, continues to be limited by the Black/White binary. CRT adds to efforts to expand this dialogue and to recognize the ways in which our struggles for social justice are limited by discourses that omit and thereby silence the multiple experiences of People of Color (Ellison, 1990).

As a student of Chicana/o studies, I have utilized theoretical models including the Internal Colonial model (Blauner, 2001; Bonilla and Girling, 1973), Marxism (Barrera, 1979; Bowles and Gintis, 1976), Chicana and Black feminisms (Anzaldúa, 1987; Hill Collins, 1998, 2000; hooks, 1990; Hurtado, 1996; Saldivar-Hull, 2000; Zavella, 1991), and cultural nationalism (Asante, 1987). Despite all their strengths, each of these frameworks had certain blind spots that limited my ability to examine racism. Now, as a professor of Chicana/o studies, I work informed by the hindsight of CRT and its genealogical branches. To document and analyze the educational access, persistence and graduation of underrepresented students, I draw on my interdisciplinary training and on theoretical models whose popularity may have waned since the 1960s and 1970s, but whose commitment to speaking truth to power continues to address contemporary social realities.

For the field of education, Daniel Solórzano (1997, 1998) identified five tenets of CRT that can and should inform theory, research, pedagogy, curriculum, and policy[2]: (1) the intercentricity of race and racism, (2) the challenge to dominant ideology, (3) the commitment to social justice, (4) the centrality of experiential knowledge, and (5) the utilization of interdisciplinary approaches.

The intercentricity of race and racism with other forms of subordination: CRT starts from the premise that race and racism are central, endemic, permanent and fundamental in defining and explaining how U.S. society functions (Bell, 1992; Russell, 1992). CRT acknowledges the inextricable layers of racialized subordination based on gender, class, immigration status, surname, phenotype, accent and sexuality (Crenshaw, 1989, 1993; Valdes, McCristal Culp and Harris, 2002).

The challenge to dominant ideology: CRT challenges White privilege and refutes the claims of educational institutions to objectivity, meritocracy, color-blindness, race neutrality and equal opportunity. CRT challenges notions of "neutral" research or "objective" researchers and exposes deficit-informed research that silences, ignores and distorts epistemologies of People of Color

(Delgado Bernal, 1998; Ladson-Billings, 2000). CRT argues that these traditional claims act as camouflage for the self-interest, power and privilege of dominant groups in U.S. society (Bell, 1987; Calmore, 1992; Solórzano, 1997).

The commitment to social justice: CRT is committed to social justice and offers a liberatory or transformative response to racial, gender, and class oppression (Matsuda, 1991). Such a social justice research agenda exposes the "interest-convergence" (Bell, 1987) of civil rights "gains" in education and works toward the elimination of racism, sexism and poverty, as well as the empowerment of People of Color and other subordinated groups (Freire, 1970, 1973; Solórzano and Delgado Bernal, 2001).

The centrality of experiential knowledge: CRT recognizes that the experiential knowledge of People of Color is legitimate, appropriate and critical to understanding, analyzing and teaching about racial subordination (Delgado Bernal, 2002). CRT draws explicitly on the lived experiences of People of Color by including such methods as storytelling, family histories, biographies, scenarios, parables, *cuentos*, *testimonios*, chronicles and narratives (Bell, 1987, 1992, 1996; Carrasco, 1996; Delgado, 1989, 1993, 1995a, 1995b, 1996; Espinoza, 1990; Montoya, 1994; Olivas, 1990; Delgado Bernal and Villalpando, 2002; Solórzano and Delgado Bernal, 2001; Solórzano and Yosso, 2000, 2001, 2002a; Villalpando, 2003).

The transdisciplinary perspective: CRT goes beyond disciplinary boundaries to analyze race and racism within both historical and contemporary contexts, drawing on scholarship from ethnic studies, women's studies, sociology, history, law, psychology, film, theater and other fields (Delgado, 1984, 1992; Garcia, 1995; Gotanda, 1991; Gutiérrez-Jones, 2001; Harris, 1994; Olivas, 1990).

These five themes are not new in and of themselves, but collectively they represent a challenge to existing modes of scholarship. Informed by scholars who continue to expand the literature and scope of discussions of race and racism, I define CRT in education as a theoretical and analytical framework that challenges the ways race and racism affect educational structures, practices and discourses. CRT is conceived as a social justice project that works toward the liberatory potential of schooling (hooks, 1994; Freire, 1970, 1973). This acknowledges the contradictory nature of education, wherein schools most often oppress and marginalize while they maintain the potential to emancipate and empower. Indeed, CRT in education refutes dominant ideology and White privilege while validating and centering the experiences of People of Color. CRT utilizes transdisciplinary approaches to link theory with practice, scholarship with teaching, and the academy with the community (see LatCrit Primer, 1999; Solórzano and Yosso, 2001).

Many in the academy and in community organizing, activism and service who look to challenge social inequality will probably recognize the tenets of CRT as part of what, why and how they do the work they do. CRT addresses the social construct of race by examining the ideology of racism. CRT finds that racism is often well disguised in the rhetoric of shared "normative" values and "neutral" social scientific principles and practices (Matsuda et. al., 1993). However, when the ideology of racism is examined and racist injuries are named, victims of racism can often find their voices. Those injured by racism and other forms of oppression discover that they are not alone; moreover, they are part of a legacy of resistance to racism and the layers of racialized oppression. They become empowered participants, hearing their own stories and the stories of others, listening to how the arguments against them are framed, and learning to make the arguments to defend themselves.

Challenging Racism, Revealing Cultural Wealth

CRT's five tenets provide a helpful lens that can guide and inform research in Communities of Color. Looking through a CRT lens means critiquing deficit theorizing and data that may be limited by their omission of the voices of People of Color. Such deficit-informed research often "sees" deprivation in Communities of Color. Indeed, one of the most prevalent forms of contemporary racism in U.S. schools is deficit thinking. Deficit thinking takes the position that minority students and families are at fault for poor academic performance because (a) students enter school without the normative cultural knowledge and skills, and (b) parents neither value nor support their children's education. These racialized assumptions about Communities of Color often lead schools to default to the "banking" method of education critiqued by Paulo Freire (1973). As a result, schooling efforts usually aim to fill up supposedly passive students with forms of cultural knowledge deemed valuable by dominant society. Shernaz García and Patricia Guerra (2004) find that such deficit approaches to schooling begin with overgeneralizations about family background and are exacerbated by a limited framework to interpret how individual views about educational success are shaped by personal "sociocultural and linguistic experiences and assumptions about appropriate cultural outcomes" (p. 163). Educators most often assume that schools work and that students, parents and communities need to change to conform to this already effective and equitable system.

Indeed, García and Guerra's (2004) research acknowledges that deficit thinking permeates U.S. society, and both schools and those who work in schools mirror these beliefs. They argue that this reality necessitates a challenge of personal and individual race, gender and class prejudices expressed by educators, as well as a "critical examination of systemic factors that perpetuate deficit thinking and reproduce educational inequities for students from nondominant sociocultural and linguistic backgrounds" (p. 155). I believe CRT can offer such an approach by identifying, analyzing and challenging distorted notions of People of Color.

As part of the challenge to deficit thinking in education, it should be noted that race is often coded as "cultural difference" in schools. Indeed, culture influences how society is organized, how school curriculum is developed, and how pedagogy and policy are implemented. In social science, the concept of culture for Students of Color has taken on many divergent meanings. Some research has equated culture with race and ethnicity, while other work clearly has viewed culture through a much broader lens of characteristics and forms of social histories and identities. For my purposes here, "culture" refers to behaviors and values that are learned, shared and exhibited by a group of people. Culture is also evidenced in the material and nonmaterial productions of a people. Culture as a set of characteristics is neither fixed nor static (Gómez-Quiñones, 1977). For example, with Students of Color, culture is frequently represented symbolically through language and can encompass identities around immigration status, gender, phenotype, sexuality and region, as well as race and ethnicity.

Looked at through a CRT lens, the cultures of Students of Color can nurture and empower them (Delgado Bernal, 2002; Delgado-Gaitan, 2001). Focusing on research with Latina/o families, Luis C. Moll, Cathy Amanti, Deborah Neff, and Norma Gonzalez (1992), Carlos Vélez-Ibáñez and James Greenberg (1992), and Irma Olmedo (1997) assert that culture can form and draw from communal *funds of knowledge* (Gonzalez et al., 1995; Gonzalez and Moll, 2002). Likewise, Douglas Foley (1997) notes research revealing the "virtues and solidarity in African American community and family traditions" as well as the "deeply spiritual values passed from generation to generation in most African American communities" (p. 123).

Taken together, the CRT challenge to deficit thinking and understanding the empowering potential of the cultures of Communities of Color leads me to the following description of cultural wealth. I begin with a critique of the ways Bourdieu's (Bourdieu and Passeron, 1977) work has been used to discuss social and racial inequity. In education, Bourdieu's work has often been called upon to explain why Students of Color do not succeed at the same rate as Whites. Bourdieu's term "cultural capital" denotes an accumulation of cultural knowledge, skills and abilities possessed and inherited by privileged groups in society. Bourdieu asserts that cultural capital (education, language), social capital (social networks, connections), and economic capital (money and other material possessions) can be acquired in either or both of two ways—from one's family, and through formal schooling. The dominant groups within society are able to maintain power because access is limited to acquiring and learning strategies to use these forms of capital for social mobility.

Although Bourdieu's work sought primarily to provide a structural critique of social and cultural reproduction, his theory of cultural capital has also been used to assert that some communities are culturally wealthy while others are culturally poor. This interpretation of Bourdieu exposes White, middle-class culture as the standard, and therefore all other forms and expressions of "culture" are judged in comparison to this "norm." In other words, cultural capital is not just inherited or possessed by the middle class, but rather it refers to an accumulation of specific forms of knowledge, skills and abilities that are *valued* by privileged groups in society. For example, middle- or upper-class students may have access to computers at home and therefore can learn extensive computer-related vocabulary and technological skills before arriving at school. These students have acquired cultural capital because computer-related vocabulary and technological skills are valued in the school setting. In contrast, a working-class Chicana/o student whose mother works in the garment industry may bring a different vocabulary, perhaps in two languages (English and Spanish) to school, along with techniques of running errands on the city bus and translating mail, phone calls and coupons for her or his mother (see Faulstich Orellana, 2003). This cultural knowledge is very valuable to the students and their families but is not necessarily considered to carry any capital in the school context. So are there forms of cultural capital that marginalized groups bring to the table but traditional cultural capital theory does not recognize or value? CRT answers "yes."

CRT shifts the center of focus from notions of White, middle-class culture to the cultures of Communities of Color. In doing so, I also draw on the work of the sociologists Melvin Oliver and Thomas Shapiro (1995) to understand how cultural capital is actually only one form of many assets that might be considered valuable. Oliver and Shapiro (1995) propose a model to explain how the narrowing income or earnings gap between Blacks and Whites is a misleading measure of inequality. They argue that one's income over a typical fiscal year focuses on a single form of capital, and that the income gap between Blacks and Whites is narrowing over time. They examine separately the concept of wealth and define it as the total extent of an individual's accumulated assets and resources (e.g., ownership of stocks, money in bank, real estate, or businesses). They then argue that while the income of Blacks may indeed be climbing and the Black/White income gap narrowing, their overall wealth, compared to that of Whites, is declining and the gap is widening (see also Shapiro, 2004).

Traditional Bourdieuean cultural capital theory has parallel comparisons to Oliver and Shapiro's (1995) description of income. Both place value on a very narrow range of assets and characteristics. A traditional view of cultural capital is narrowly defined by White, middle-class values and is more limited than wealth – one's accumulated assets and resources. CRT expands this view. Centering the research lens on the experiences of People of Color in critical historical context reveals accumulated assets and resources in the histories and lives of Communities of Color.

Figure 9.2 demonstrates that community cultural wealth is an array of knowledge, skills, abilities and contacts possessed and utilized by Communities of Color to survive and resist racism and other forms of oppression.[3]

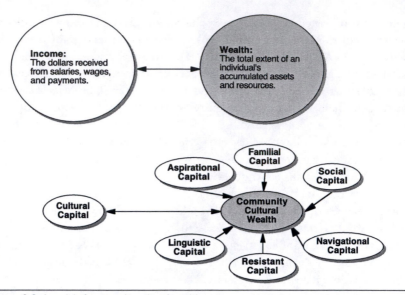

Figure 9.2 A model of community cultural wealth.

Indeed, a CRT lens can "see" that Communities of Color nurture cultural wealth through at least six forms of capital: aspirational, navigational, social, linguistic, familial and resistant capital (see Auerbach, 2001; Delgado Bernal, 1997, 2001; Faulstich Orellana, 2003; Stanton-Salazar, 2001; Solórzano and Delgado Bernal, 2001). These various forms of capital are not mutually exclusive or static, but rather are dynamic processes that build on one another as part of community cultural wealth. For example, aspirational capital is the ability to hold onto hope in the face of structured inequality, and often without the means to make such dreams a reality. Yet aspirations are developed within social and familial contexts, often through linguistic storytelling and advice (*consejos*) that offer specific navigational goals to challenge (resist) oppressive conditions. Therefore, aspirational capital overlaps with each of the other forms of capital—social, familial, navigational, linguistic, and resistant. As Anzaldúa asserts, "In our *mestizaje* theories we create new categories for those of us left out of or pushed out of existing ones" (Anzaldúa, 1990, xxvi; emphasis in original).

Aspirational capital refers to the ability to maintain hopes and dreams for the future, even in the face of real and perceived barriers. This resilience is evident in those who allow themselves and their children to dream of possibilities beyond their present circumstances, often without the objective means to attain those goals. Defining this form of cultural wealth draws on the work of Patricia Gándara (1982, 1995) and others who have shown that Chicanas/os experience the lowest educational outcomes of any group in the United States but maintain consistently high aspirations for their children's future (Auerbach, 2001; Delgado-Gaitan, 1992, 1994; Solórzano, 1992). Their stories nurture a culture of possibility as they represent "the creation of a history that would break the links between parents' current occupational status and their children's future academic attainment" (Gándara, 1995, p. 55).

Linguistic capital includes the intellectual and social skills attained through communication experiences in more than one language and/or style (see Faulstich Orellana, 2003).[4] This aspect of cultural wealth learns from over 35 years of research about the value of bilingual education and emphasizes the connections between racialized cultural history and language (Anzaldúa, 1987; Cummins, 1986; Darder, 1991; García and Baker, 1995; Gutierrez, 2002; Gutierrez, Rymes and Larson, 1995; Macedo and Bartolomé, 1999). Linguistic capital reflects the idea that Students of Color arrive at school with multiple language and communication skills. In addition, most of these children have been engaged participants in a storytelling tradition, which might include listening to and recounting oral histories, parables, stories (*cuentos*) and proverbs (*dichos*). This repertoire of storytelling skills may include memorization, attention to detail, dramatic pauses, comedic timing, facial affect, vocal tone, volume, rhythm and rhyme. Linguistic capital also refers to the ability to communicate via visual art, music or poetry.[5] Just as students can utilize different vocal registers to whisper, whistle or sing, they must often develop and draw on various language registers, or styles, to communicate with different audiences. For example, Marjorie Faulstich Orellana (2003) examines bilingual children who are often called on to translate for their parents or other adults and finds that these youths gain multiple social tools of "vocabulary, audience awareness, cross-cultural awareness, 'real-world' literacy skills, math skills, metalinguistic awareness, teaching and tutoring skills, civic and familial responsibility, [and] social maturity" (p. 6).

Familial capital refers to cultural knowledges nurtured among *familia* (kin) that carry a sense of community history, memory and cultural intuition (see Delgado Bernal, 1998, 2002). This form of cultural wealth engages a commitment to community wellbeing and expands the concept of family to include a broader understanding of kinship. Acknowledging the racialized, classed, and heterosexualized inferences that compose traditional understandings of "family," familial capital is nurtured by our "extended family," which may include immediate family (living or long dead) as well as aunts, uncles, grandparents and friends we might consider part of our *familia*. From these kinship ties, we learn the importance of maintaining a healthy connection to our community and its resources. Our kin also model lessons of caring, coping and providing (*educación*)[6] that inform our emotional, moral, educational and occupational consciousness (Auerbach, 2001, 2004; Elenes, Gonzalez, Delgado Bernal and Villenas, 2001; Lopez, 2003; Reese, 1992). This consciousness can be fostered within and between families, as well as through sports, school, religious gatherings and other social community settings. Isolation is minimized as families "become connected with others around common issues" and realize they are "not alone in dealing with their problems" (Delgado-Gaitan, 2001, p. 54). Familial capital is informed by the work of scholars who have addressed the *communal bonds* within African American communities (Foley, 1997; Morris, 1999), the *funds of knowledge* within Mexican American communities (Gonzalez, Moll, Tenery, Rivera, Rendon, Gonzales and Amanti, 1995; Moll, Amanti, Neff and Gonzalez, 1992; Olmedo, 1997; Rueda, Monzo and Higareda, 2004; Vélez-Ibáñez and Greenberg, 1992), and *pedagogies of the home* that Students of Color bring with them to the classroom setting (Delgado Bernal, 2002).

Social capital can be understood as networks of people and community resources. These peer and other social contacts can provide both instrumental and emotional support to navigate through society's institutions (see Gilbert, 1982; Stanton-Salazar, 2001). For example, drawing on social contacts and community resources may help a student identify and attain a college scholarship. These networks can help a student in preparing the scholarship application itself, while also reassuring the student emotionally that she or he is not alone in the process of pursuing higher education. Scholars note that historically, People of Color have utilized their social capital to obtain education, legal justice, employment and health care. In turn, these Communities of Color gave the information and resources they gained through these institutions back to their social networks. *Mutualistas* or mutual aid societies are an example of how, historically, immigrants to the United States—as well as African Americans, even while enslaved—created and maintained social networks (Gómez-Quiñones, 1973, 1994; Gutman, 1976; Sanchez, 1993; Stevenson, 1996). This tradition of "lifting as we climb" has remained the motto of the National Association of Colored Women's Clubs since its organization in 1896 (see Guinier, Fine and Balin, 1997, p. 167). Concha Delgado-Gaitan's (2001) ethnographic research with the Mexican immigrant community of Carpinteria, California further confirms that "families transcend the adversity in their daily lives by uniting with supportive social networks" (p. 105).

Navigational capital refers to skills of maneuvering through social institutions. Historically, this implies the ability to maneuver through institutions not created with Communities of Color in mind. For example, strategies to navigate through racially hostile university campuses draw on the concept of academic invulnerability, or students' ability to "sustain high levels of achievement, despite the presence of stressful events and conditions that place them at risk of doing poorly at school and, ultimately, dropping out of school" (Alva, 1991, p. 19; see also Allen and Solórzano, 2000; Auerbach, 2001; Solórzano, Ceja and Yosso, 2001). Scholars have examined individual, family and community factors that support Mexican American students' academic invulnerability—their successful navigation through the educational system (Arrellano and Padilla, 1996). In addition, resilience has been recognized as "a set of inner resources, social competencies, and cultural strategies that permit individuals to not only survive, recover, or even thrive after stressful events, but also to draw from the experience to enhance subsequent functioning" (Stanton-Salazar and Spina, 2000, p. 229). Indeed, People of Color draw on various social and psychological "critical navigational skills" (Solórzano and Villalpando, 1998) to maneuver through structures of inequality permeated by racism (see Pierce, 1974, 1989, 1995). Navigational capital thus acknowledges individual agency within institutional constraints, but it also connects to social networks that facilitate community navigation through places and spaces including schools, the job market, and the health care and judicial systems (Williams, 1997).

Resistant capital refers those knowledges and skills fostered through oppositional behavior that challenges inequality (Delgado Bernal, 1997; Giroux, 1983; Freire, 1970, 1973; McLaren, 1994; Solórzano and Delgado Bernal, 2001). This form of cultural wealth is grounded in the legacy of resistance to subordination exhibited by Communities of Color (Deloria, 1969). Furthermore, maintaining and passing on the multiple dimensions of community cultural wealth is also part of the knowledge base of resistant capital. For example, even from within internment camps, Japanese American communities resisted racism by maintaining and nurturing various forms of cultural wealth (Wakatsuki Houston and Houston, 1973).[7] Expanding on this history, Tracy Robinson and Janie Ward's (1991) research shows a group of African American mothers who consciously raise their daughters as "resisters." Through verbal and nonverbal lessons, these Black mothers teach their daughters to assert themselves as intelligent, beautiful, strong and worthy of respect to resist the barrage of societal messages devaluing Blackness and belittling Black women (Ward, 1996). Similarly, Sofia Villenas and Melissa Moreno (2001) discuss the contradictions Latina mothers face as they try to teach their daughters to *valerse por si misma* (value themselves and be self-reliant) within structures of inequality such as racism, capitalism and patriarchy. All these research studies found Parents of Color consciously instructing their children to engage in behaviors and maintain attitudes that challenge the status quo. These young women are learning to be oppositional with their bodies, minds and spirits in the face of race, gender and class inequality. In analyzing students' historical and contemporary efforts to transform unequal conditions in urban high schools, Daniel Solórzano and Dolores Delgado Bernal (2001) reveal that resistance may include different forms of oppositional behavior, such as self-defeating or conformist strategies that feed back into the system of subordination. However, when resistance is informed by a Freirean critical consciousness (1970), or recognition of the structural nature of oppression, and the motivation to work toward social and racial justice, it becomes transformative (see Solórzano and Yosso, 2002b). Therefore, transformative resistant capital includes cultural knowledge of the structures of racism and motivation to transform such oppressive structures (Pizarro, 1998; Villenas and Deyhle, 1999).

Discussion

Recently, the *Journal of African American History* dedicated an entire issue to "Cultural Capital and African American Education" (see Franklin, 2002). In this issue, V. P. Franklin (2002) defines cultural capital as "the sense of group consciousness and collective identity" that serves as a resource "aimed at the advancement of an entire group" (p. 177). Franklin goes on to explain that various forms of cultural capital "became a major resource historically for the funding of African American schools and other educational institutions and programs" (2002, pp. 177–178). This research indicates that "African Americans were willing to contribute their time, energies, and financial and material resources to support these educational institutions because they knew they were important to the advancement of African Americans as a group" (178).

Furthermore, in discussing implications of his ethnographic work with two African American school communities in the U.S. urban South and Midwest, Jerome Morris (2004) explains: "Black people shared their cultural capital with one another and developed their social capital (black social capital) for survival and success in a segregated world bounded by the omnipresent forces of racism and discrimination" (p. 102). This scholarship documenting community mobilization efforts to create access and equity for African Americans in education bolsters the examples of cultural wealth offered above. Such work also demonstrates that the forms of capital composing community cultural wealth are engendered from within the context of a legacy of racism and are thus tied to a larger social and racial justice project (Perea, Delgado, Harris and Wildman, 2000). Morris (2004) asserts, "It is important that social capital theory also consider the agency and sustenance that are characteristic of African American people, culture, and institutions—apart from and in response to oppressive forces" (p. 102). Indeed, the main goals of identifying and documenting cultural wealth are to transform education and empower People of Color to utilize assets already abundant in their communities.

As demonstrated through the concept of cultural wealth, CRT research begins with the perspective that Communities of Color are places with multiple strengths. In contrast, deficit scholars bemoan a lack of cultural capital, which E. D. Hirsch (1988, 1996) terms "cultural literacy," in low-income Communities of Color. Such research utilizes a deficit analytical lens and places value judgments on communities that often do not have access to White, middle- or upper-class resources. In contrast, CRT shifts the research lens away from a deficit view of Communities of Color as places full of cultural poverty or disadvantage, and instead focuses on and learns from these communities' cultural assets and wealth (Solórzano and Solórzano, 1995; Valencia and Solórzano, 1997; Villalpando and Solórzano, 2005).

CRT centers the view of research, pedagogy and policy on Communities of Color and calls into question White middle-class communities as the standard by which all others are to be judged. This shifting of the research lens allows critical race scholars to "see" multiple forms of cultural wealth within Communities of Color. CRT identifies various indicators of capital that have rarely been acknowledged as cultural and social assets in Communities of Color (aspirational, social, navigational, linguistic, resistant, and familial capital). These forms of capital draw on the knowledges Students of Color bring with them from their homes and communities into the classroom. They are not conceptualized for the purpose of finding new ways to coopt or exploit the strengths of Communities of Color.[8] Instead, community cultural wealth involves a commitment to conduct research, teach, and develop schools that serve a larger purpose of struggling toward social and racial justice.

In the epigraph of this essay, Anzaldúa urges the generation of theories based on those whose knowledges are traditionally excluded from and silenced by academic research. She further asserts that beyond creating theories, "we need to find practical application for those theories. We need to de-academize theory and to connect the community to the academy" (Anzaldúa, 1990, p. xxvi). Anzaldúa (2002) also notes, "Change requires more than words on a page—it takes perseverance, creative ingenuity, and acts of love" (p. 574). CRT offers a response to Anzaldúa's challenge by listening to the experiences of those "faces at the bottom of society's well" (Bell, 1992, p. v). These experiences expose the racism underlying cultural deficit theorizing and reveal the need to restructure U.S. social institutions around those knowledges, skills, abilities, and networks—the community cultural wealth—possessed and utilized by People of Color.

Notes

1. Although not exhaustive, the following resources are examples of the different frameworks cited: for ethnic studies, see *Aztlan: A Journal of Chicano Studies*; for, feminist studies, *Frontiers: A Journal of Women's Studies*; for cultural nationalist paradigms, Asante, 1987; for critical legal studies, Kelman, 1989; for Marxist and neo-Marxist frameworks, Bowles and Gintis, 1976, and Barrera, 1979; for internal colonial models, Bonilla and Girling, 1973; for LatCrit, Arriola, 1998, and Valdes, 1997, 1998; for WhiteCrit, Delgado and Stefancic, 1997; for FemCrit, Wing, 1997; for AsianCrit, Chang, 1993.

2. Solórzano and Yosso (2001) note that while each individual tenet of CRT is not "new," synthesizing these tenets into a CRT framework in education is relatively recent. For instance, William Tate's 1994 autobiographical article in the journal *Urban Education*, "From Inner City to Ivory Tower: Does My Voice Matter in the Academy," represents (to my knowledge) the first use of CRT principles in education. A year later, in 1995, Gloria Ladson-Billings and William Tate published "Toward a Critical Race Theory of Education" in *Teachers College Record*. Two years later, Daniel Solórzano's 1997 essay on "Images and Words That Wound: Critical Race Theory, Racial Stereotyping, and Teacher Education" in *Teacher Education Quarterly* applied CRT to a specific subfield of teacher education. Also in 1997, William Tate's "Critical Race Theory and Education: History, Theory, and Implications" in the *Review of Research in Education* furthered our understanding of the history of CRT in education. The field was expanded significantly with the 1998 "Special Issue on Critical Race Theory in Education" of the *International Journal of Qualitative Studies in Education*. The 1999 edited book on *Race Is ... Race Isn't : Critical Race Theory and Qualitative Studies In Education* (Parker, Deyhle and Villenas, 1999) was followed by individual scholars presenting on panels at professional conferences across

the country and publishing their work in various journals. In 2002, the journals *Qualitative Inquiry* and *Equity and Excellence in Education* dedicated a special issue to CRT in education. In 2004, the American Education Research Association conference symposium "And We Are Still Not Saved: Critical Race Theory in Education Ten Years Later" acknowledged the tenth anniversary of the original paper on CRT in education presented at AERA by Ladson-Billings and Tate.

3. As is consistent with the concept of community cultural wealth, this working definition demonstrates an accumulation of collaborative work. Thank you to Daniel G. Solórzano, who originally conceptualized cultural wealth. He shared with me a model in progress and later a collaboratively written piece (with Octavio Villalpando), and asked me to "run with it." Since that time, cultural wealth has taken on multiple dimensions. I also acknowledge the personal and professional experiences, community histories, and students' research projects which have informed this work. I look forward to how cultural wealth will take on new dimensions as others also "run with it."

4. Thanks to Rebeca Burciaga, whose identification of linguistic and familial capital added important dimensions to the discussion of cultural wealth.

5. Thanks to University of California, Santa Barbara, undergraduate students Pablo Gallegos, Moises Garcia, Noel Gomez, and Ray Hernandez, whose research conceptualizing graffiti and hip-hop poetry as unacknowledged sources of community cultural wealth expanded my thinking about linguistic capital.

6. Chicana scholars note, for example, that in Spanish, *educación* holds dual meanings (Elenes, Gonzalez, Delgado Bernal and Villenes, 2001; Delgado-Gaitan, 1992, 1994, 2001). A person can be formally educated with multiple advanced degrees but may still be rude, ignorant, disrespectful or unethical (immoral)—*mal educada*. On the other hand, a person with only a second-grade formal education may be *una persona bien educada* or a well-mannered, kind, fair-minded, respectful (moral) individual.

7. The book *Farewell to Manzanar* (Wakatsuki Houston and Houston, 1973) offers a firsthand account of some ways Japanese internees held onto hope, fostered caring, coping and responsibility, maintained skills of language, poetry, music, social networks and critical navigational skills, and challenged social and racial inequality.

8. I recognize that the notion of capital may be associated with capitalism, which is a system that is exploitative and has historically been an oppressive force against Communities of Color. The concept of schooling itself can be contradictory, given that schools have historically oppressed Students of Color, while still having the potential to be transformative places of empowerment. Similarly, as viewed through mainstream media, hip-hop's contradictory nature offers an example of how historically some aspects of community cultural wealth are coopted and utilized for exploitative purposes (see Spike Lee's film *Bamboozled*, 2000). Still, hip-hop maintains amazing potential to be a revolutionary art form and transformative cultural expression which can inspire and inform social movement. I believe community cultural wealth and forms of capital nurtured in the histories of People of Color holds the same potential.

References

Allen, W. (1993). A Response to a 'White Discourse on White Racism.' *Educational Researcher* 22: 11–13.

Allen, W., and Solórzano, D. (2001). Affirmative Action, Educational Equity, and Campus Racial Climate: A Case Study of the University of Michigan Law School. *Berkeley La Raza Law Journal* 12(2): 237–363.

Alva, S. (1991). Academic Invulnerability among Mexican American Students: The Importance of Protective Resources and Appraisals. *Hispanic Journal of Behavioral Sciences* 13(1): 18–34.

Anzaldúa, G. (1987). *Borderlands/La Frontera: The New Mestiza*. San Francisco: Aunt Lute.

Anzaldúa, G. (1990). *Haciendo Caras/Making Face, Making Soul: Creative and Critical Perspectives by Women of Color*. San Francisco: Aunt Lute.

Anzaldúa, G. (2002). Now Let Us Shift ... the Path of Conocimiento ... Inner Work, Public Acts. In G. Anzaldúa and A. Keating (eds.), *This Bridge We Call Home: Radical Visions for Transformation*, 540–578. New York: Routledge.

Arrellano, A. R., and Padilla, A. M. (1996). Academic Invulnerability among a Select Group of Latino University Students. *Hispanic Journal of Behavioral Sciences* 18(4): 485–507.

Arriola, E. (1997). LatCrit Theory, International Human Rights, Popular Culture, and the Faces of Despair in INS Raids. *Inter-American Law Review* 28(2): 245–262.

Arriola, E. (1998). March! *Chicano-Latino Law Review* 19: 1–67.

Asante, M. K. (1987). *The Afrocentric Idea*. Philadelphia: Temple University Press.

Auerbach, S. (2001). Under Co-construction: Parent Roles in Promoting College Access for Students of Color. Ph.D. dissertation, University of California, Los Angeles.

Auerbach, S. (2004). From Moral Supporters to Struggling Advocates: Reconceptualizing Parent Involvement through the Experience of Latino Families. Paper presented at annual meeting of the American Educational Research Association. San Diego, CA.

Baca Zinn, M. (1989). Family, Race, and Poverty in the Eighties. *Signs: Journal of Woman in Culture and Society* 14: 856–874.

Barnes, R. (1990). Race Consciousness: The Thematic Content of Racial Distinctiveness in Critical Race Scholarship. *Harvard Law Review* 103: 1864–1871.

Barrera, M. (1979). *Race and Class in the Southwest: A Theory of Inequality*. London: University of Notre Dame Press.

Bell, D. (1986). Application of the 'Tipping Point' Theory to Law Faculty Hiring Practices. *Nova Law Journal* 10: 319–327.

Bell, D. (1987). *And We Will Not Be Saved: The Elusive Quest for Racial Justice*. New York: Basic Books.

Bell, D. (1992). *Faces at the Bottom of the Well: The Permanence of Racism*. New York: Basic Books.

Bell, D. (1995). Who's Afraid of Critical Race Theory? *University of Illinois Law Review* 1995: 893–910.

Bell, D. (1996). *Gospel Choirs: Psalms of Survival for an Alien Land Called Home*. New York: Basic Books.

Bell, D. (1998). *Afrolantica Legacies*. Chicago: Third World.

Blauner, B. (2001). *Still the Big News: Racial Oppression in America*. Philadelphia: Temple University Press.

Bonilla, F., and Girling, R. (eds.) (1973). *Structures of Dependency*. Stanford, CA: Stanford Institute of Politics.

Bonilla-Silva, E. (2001). *White Supremacy and Racism in the Post Civil Rights Era*. Boulder, CO: Lynne Rienner.

Bourdieu, P., and Passeron, J. (1977). *Reproduction in Education, Society, and Culture*. London: Sage.

Bowles, S., and Gintis, H. (1976). *Schooling in Capitalistic America: Educational Reform and the Contradictions of Economic Life*. New York: Basic Books.

Brayboy, B. (2001). Toward a Tribal Critical Theory in Higher Education. Paper presented at annual conference of the Association for the Study of Higher Education, Richmond, VA.

Brayboy, B. (2002). Tribal Critical Race Theory in Education. Paper presented at annual conference of the American Educational Research Association, New Orleans, LA.

Caldwell, P. (1995). A Hair Piece: Perspectives on the Intersection of Race and Gender. In R. Delgado (ed.), *Critical Race Theory: The Cutting Edge*, 267–277). Philadelphia: Temple University Press.

Calmore, J. (1992). Critical Race Theory, Archie Shepp, and Fire Music: Securing an Authentic Intellectual Life in a Multicultural World. *Southern California Law Review* 65: 2129–2231.

Calmore, J. (1997). Exploring Michael Omi's 'Messy' Real World of Race: An Essay for 'Naked People Longing To Swim Free'. *Law and Inequality* 15: 25–82.

Carrasco, E. (1996). Collective Recognition as a Communitarian Device: Or, Of Course We Want To Be Role Models! *La Raza Law Journal* 9: 81–101.

Chang, R. (1993). Toward an Asian American Legal Scholarship: Critical Race Theory, Poststructuralism, and Narrative Space. *California Law Review* 81: 1243.

Chang, R. (1998). Who's Afraid of Tiger Woods? *Chicano-Latino Law Review* 19: 223.

Chon, M. (1995). On the Need for Asian American Narratives in Law: Ethnic Specimens, Native Informants, Storytelling and Silences. *UCLA Asian Pacific American Law Journal* 3(4): 4–32.

Crenshaw, K. (1989). Demarginalizing the Intersection of Race and Sex: A Black Feminist Critique of Antidiscrimination Doctrine, Feminist Theory and Antiracist Politics. *University of Chicago Legal Forum* 1989: 139–167.

Crenshaw, K. (1993). Mapping the Margins: Intersectionality, Identity Politics, and the Violence against Women of Color. *Stanford Law Review* 43: 1241–1299.

Crenshaw, K. (2002). The First Decade: Critical Reflections, or "a Foot in the Closing Door." In F. Valdes et al. (eds.), *Crossroads, Directions, and a New Critical Race Theory*, 9–31. Philadelphia: Temple University Press.

Crenshaw, K.; Gotanda, N.; Peller, G.; and Thomas, K. (eds.) (1995). *Critical Race Theory: The Key Writings That Formed the Movement.* New York: New Press.

Cummins, J. (1986). Bilingual Education and Anti-Racist Education. *Interracial Books for Children Bulletin* 17(3/4): 9–12.

Darder, A. (1991). *Culture and Power in the Classroom: A Critical Foundation for Bicultural Education.* New York: Bergin and Garvey.

Davis, P. (1989). Law as Microaggression. *Yale Law Journal* 98: 1559–1577.

Delgado, R. (1984). The Imperial Scholar: Reflections on a Review of Civil Rights Literature. *University of Pennsylvania Law Review* 132: 561–578.

Delgado, R. (1988). Critical Legal Studies and the Realities of Race: Does the Fundamental Contradiction Have a Corollary? *Harvard Civil Rights-Civil Liberties Law Review* 23: 407–413.

Delgado, R. (1989). Storytelling for Oppositionists and Others: A Plea for Narrative. *Michigan Law Review* 87: 2411–2441.

Delgado, R. (1992). The Imperial Scholar Revisited: How To Marginalize Outsider Writing, Ten Years Later. *University of Pennsylvania Law Review* 140: 1349–1372.

Delgado, R. (1993). On Telling Stories in School: A Reply to Farber and Sherry. *Vanderbilt Law Review* 46: 665–676.

Delgado, R. (ed.) (1995a). *Critical Race Theory: The Cutting Edge.* Philadelphia: Temple University Press.

Delgado, R. (1995b). *The Rodrigo Chronicles: Conversations about America and Race.* New York: New York University Press.

Delgado, R. (1996). *The Coming Race War?: and Other Apocalyptic Tales of American after Affirmative Action and Welfare.* New York: New York University Press.

Delgado, R. (1997). Rodrigo's Fifteenth Chronicle: Racial Mixture, Latino-Critical Scholarship, and the Black-White Binary. *Texas Law Review* 75: 1181–1201.

Delgado, R. (1999). *When Equality Ends: Stories about Race and Resistance.* Boulder, CO: Westview.

Delgado, R. (2003). *Justice at War: Civil Liberties and Civil Rights during Times of Crisis.* New York University Press.

Delgado, R., and Stefancic, J. (1992). Images of the Outsider in American Law and Culture: Can Free Expression Remedy Systematic Social Ills? *Cornell Law Review* 77: 1258–1297.

Delgado, R., and Stefancic, J. (1993). Critical Race Theory: An Annotated Bibliography. *Virginia Law Review* 79: 461–516.

Delgado, R., and Stefancic, J. (1994). Critical Race Theory: An Annotated Bibliography 1993, a Year of Transition. *University of Colorado Law Review* 66: 159–193.

Delgado, R., and Stefancic, J. (eds.) (1997). *Critical White Studies: Looking behind the Mirror.* Philadelphia: Temple University Press.

Delgado, R., and Stefancic, J. (2001). *Critical Race Theory: An Introduction.* New York University Press.

Delgado Bernal, D. (1997). *Chicana School Resistance and Grassroots Leadership: Providing an Alternative History of the 1968 East Los Angeles Blowouts.* Ph.D. dissertation, University of California, Los Angeles.

Delgado Bernal, D. (1998). Using a Chicana Feminist Epistemology in Educational Research. *Harvard Educational Review* 68(4): 555–582.

Delgado Bernal, D. (2001). Living and Learning Pedagogies of the Home: The Mestiza Consciousness of Chicana Students. *International Journal of Qualitative Studies in Education* 14(5): 623–639.

Delgado Bernal, D. (2002). Critical Race Theory, LatCrit Theory, and Critical Raced-Gendered Epistemologies: Recognizing Students of Color as Holders and Creators of Knowledge. *Qualitative Inquiry* 8(1): 105–126.

Delgado Bernal, D., and Villalpando, O. (2002). An Apartheid of Knowledge in Academia: The Struggle over the "Legitimate" Knowledge of Faculty of Color. *Equity and Excellence in Education* 35(2): 169–180.

Delgado-Gaitan, C. (1992). School Matters in the Mexican American Home: Socializing Children to Education. *American Educational Research Journal* 29(3): 495–513.

Delgado-Gaitan, C. (1994). Socializing Young Children in Mexican-American Families: An Intergenerational Perspective. In P. Greenfield and R. Cocking (eds.), *Cross-Cultural Roots of Minority Development*, 55–86. New Jersey: Lawrence Erlbaum.

Delgado-Gaitan, C. (2001). *The Power of Community: Mobilizing for Family and Schooling*. Boulder, CO: Rowman and Littlefield.

Deloria, V. (1969). *Custer Died For Your Sins: An Indian Manifesto*. New York: Avon.

Du Bois, W. E. B. (1989 [1903]). *The Soul of Black Folks*. New York: Bantam.

Elenes, C. A.; Gonzalez, F.; Delgado Bernal, D.; and Villenes, S. (2001). Introduction: Chicana/Mexicana Feminist Pedagogies: Consejos Respeto, y Educación. *International Journal of Qualitative Studies in Education* 14(5): 595–602.

Ellison, R. (1990). *Invisible Man*. New York: Vintage.

Espinoza, L. G. (1990). Masks and Other Disguises: Exposing Legal Academia. *Harvard Law Review* 103: 1878–1886.

Espinoza, L. G. (1998). Latino/a Identity and Multi-identity: Community and Culture. In R. Delgado and J. Stefancic (eds.), *The Latino/a Condition: A Critical Reader*, 17–23. New York: New York University Press.

Espinoza, L., and Harris, A. (1998). Embracing the Tar-Baby: LatCrit Theory and the Sticky Mess of Race. *La Raza Law Journal* 10(1): 499–559.

Essed, P. (1991). *Understanding Everyday Racism: An Interdisciplinary Theory*. Newbury Park, CA: Sage.

Faulstich Orellana, M. (2003). *In Other Words: En Otras Palabras: Learning From Bilingual Kids' Translating/interpreting Experiences*. Evanston, IL: School of Education and Social Policy, Northwestern University.

Fay, B. (1987). *Critical Social Science: Liberation and Its Limits*. Ithaca, NY: Cornell University Press

Foley, D. E. (1997). Deficit Thinking Models Based on Culture: The Anthropological Protest. In R. Valencia (ed.), *The Evolution of Deficit Thinking: Educational Thought and Practice*, 113–131. London: Falmer.

Franklin, V. P. (2002). Introduction: Cultural Capital and African American Education. *Journal of African American History* 87: 175–181.

Freire, P. (1970). *Education for Critical Consciousness*. New York: Continuum.

Freire, P. (1973). *Pedagogy of the Oppressed*. New York: Seabury.

Gándara, P. (1982). Passing through the Eye of the Needle: High-Achieving Chicanas. *Hispanic Journal of Behavioral Sciences* 4: 167–179.

Gándara, P. (1995). *Over the Ivy Walls: The Educational Mobility of Low-Income Chicanos*. Albany: State University of New York Press.

Garcia, R. (1995). Critical Race Theory and Proposition 187: The Racial Politics of Immigration Law. *Chicano-Latino Law Review* 17: 118–148.

García, O., and Baker, C. (eds.) (1995). *Policy and Practice in Bilingual Education: A Reader Extending the Foundations*. Philadelphia: Multilingual Matters.

García, S.B., and Guerra, P. L. (2004). Deconstructing Deficit Thinking: Working with Educators To Create More Equitable Learning Environments. *Education and Urban Society* 36(2): 150–168.

Gilbert, M. J. (1982). Los Parientes: Social Structural Factors and Kinship Relations among Second Generation Mexican Americans in Two Southern California Communities. Ph.D. dissertation, University of California, Santa Barbara.

Giroux, H. (1983). Theories of Reproduction and Resistance in the New Sociology of Education: A Critical Analysis. *Harvard Educational Review* 55: 257–293.

Gómez-Quiñones, J. (1973). The First Steps: Chicano Labor Conflict and Organizing 1900–1920. *Aztlan* 3(1): 13–49.

Gómez-Quiñones, J. (1977). *On Culture*. Popular Series 1. Los Angeles: UCLA Chicano Studies Center.

Gómez-Quiñones, J. (1994). *Roots of Chicano Politics, 1600–1940*. Albuquerque: University of New Mexico Press.

Gonzalez, N., and Moll, L. C. (2002). Cruzando el Puente: Building Bridges to Funds of Knowledge. *Educational Policy* 16(4): 623–641.

Gonzalez, N.; Moll, L. C.;. Tenery, M. F.; Rivera, A.; Rendon, P.; Gonzales, R.; and Amanti, C. (1995). Funds of Knowledge for Teaching in Latino Households. *Urban Education* 29(4): 443–470.

Gotanda, N. (1991). A Critique of 'Our Constitution Is Color-Blind'. *Stanford Law Review* 44: 1–68.

Guinier, L.; Fine, M.; and Balin, J. (1997). *Becoming Gentleman: Women, Law School, and Institutional Change*. Boston: Beacon.

Gutierrez, K. (2002). Studying Cultural Practices in Urban Learning Communities. *Human Development* 45(4): 312–321.

Gutierrez, K., Rymes, B. and Larson, J. (1995). Script, Counterscript, and Underlife in the Classroom: James Brown versus Brown v. Board of Education. *Harvard Educational Review*, 65(3), 445–471.

Gutiérrez-Jones, C. (2001). *Critical Race Narratives: A Study of Race, Rhetoric, and Injury*. New York: New York University Press.

Gutman, H. (1976). *The Black Family in Slavery and Freedom, 1750–1925*. New York: Pantheon.

Harris, A. (1994). Forward: The Jurisprudence of Reconstruction. *California Law Review* 82: 741–785.

Hill Collins, P. (1986). Learning from the Outsider Within: The Sociological Significance of Black Feminist Thought. *Social Problems* 33: S14–S32.

Hill Collins, P. (1998). *Fighting Words: Black Women and the Search for Justice*. Minneapolis: University of Minnesota Press.

Hill Collins, P. (2000). *Black Feminist Thought: Knowledge, Consciousness, and the Politics of Empowerment*. 2nd ed. New York: Routledge.

Hirsch, E. D., Jr. (1988). *Cultural Literacy: What Every American Needs To Know*. New York: Vintage.

Hirsch, E. D., Jr. (1996). *The Schools We Need and Why We Don't Have Them*. New York: Doubleday.

hooks, b. (1990). *Yearning: Race, Gender, and Cultural Politics*. Cambridge, MA: South End

hooks, b. (1994). *Teaching To Transgress: Education as the Practice of Freedom*. New York: Routledge.

Hurtado, A. (1996). *The Color of Privilege: Three Blasphemies on Race and Feminism*. Ann Arbor: University of Michigan Press.

Ikemoto, L. (1992). Furthering the Inquiry: Race, Class, and Culture in the Forced Medical Treatment of Pregnant Women. *Tennessee Law Review* 59: 487.

Johnson, K. (1999). *How Did You Get to Be Mexican? A White/Brown Man's Search for Identity*. Philadelphia: Temple University Press.

Kelman, M. (1987). *A Guide to Critical Legal Studies*. Cambridge, MA: Harvard University Press.

Ladson-Billings, G. (1998). Preparing Teachers for Diverse Student Populations: A Critical Race Theory Perspective. *Review of Research in Education* 24: 211–247.

Ladson-Billings, G. (2000). Racialized Discourses and Ethnic Epistemologies. In N. Denzin and Y. Lincoln (eds.), *Handbook of Qualitative Research*, 257–277. 2nd ed. Thousand Oaks, CA: Sage.

Ladson-Billings, G., and Tate, W. (1995). Toward a Critical Race Theory of Education. *Teachers College Record* 97: 47–68.

LatCrit Primer (1999). Fact Sheet: LatCrit. Presented to the 4th Annual LatCrit Conference, "Rotating Centers, Expanding Frontiers: LatCrit Theory and Marginal Intersection" Stanford Sierra Conference Center, Lake Tahoe, Nevada, April 29–May 5, 1999.

Lawrence, C. (1987). The Id, the Ego, and Equal Protection: Reckoning with Unconscious Racism. *Stanford Law Review* 39: 317–388.

Lawrence, C. (1992). The Word and the River: Pedagogy as Scholarship as Struggle. *Southern California Law Review* 65: 2231–2298.

Lawrence, C., and Matsuda, M. (1997). *We Won't Go Back: Making the Case for Affirmative Action*. Boston : Houghton Mifflin

Lawson, R. (1995). Critical Race Theory as Praxis: A View from Outside to the Outside. *Howard Law Journal* 38: 353–370.

Lopez, G. (2003). Parental Involvement as Racialized Performance. In G. Lopez and L. Parker (eds.), *Interrogating Racism in Qualitative Research Methodology*, 71–95. New York: Peter Lang.

Lopez, G., and Parker, L. (eds.). (2003). *Interrogating Racism in Qualitative Research Methodology*. New York: Peter Lang.

Lynn, M. (1999). Toward a Critical Race Pedagogy: A Research note. *Urban Education* 33: 606–626.

Lynn, M., and Adams, M. (eds.) (2002). Special issue: Critical Race Theory in Education. *Equity and Excellence in Education* 35(2): 87–199.

Lynn, M.; Yosso, T.; Solórzano, D.; and Parker, L. (eds.) (2002). Special issue: Critical Race and Qualitative Research. *Qualitative Inquiry* 8(1): 3–126.

Macedo. D., and Bartolomé, L. (1999). *Dancing with Bigotry: Beyond the Politics of Tolerance.* New York: Palgrave.

Marable, M. (1992). *Black America.* Westfield, NJ: Open Media.

Matsuda, M. (1991). Voices of America: Accent, Antidiscrimination Law, and a Jurisprudence for the Last Reconstruction. *Yale Law Journal* 100: 1329–1407.

Matsuda, M.; Lawrence, C.; Delgado, R.; and Crenshaw, K. (1993). *Words That Wound: Critical Race Theory, Assaultive Speech, and the First Amendment.* Boulder, CO: Westview.

McLaren, P. (1994) *Life in Schools: An Introduction to Critical Pedagogy in the Foundations of Education.* 2nd ed. White Plains, NY: Longman.

Moll, L. C.; Amanti, C.; Neff, D.; and Gonzalez, N. (1992). Funds of Knowledge for Teaching: Using a qualitative approach to connect homes and classrooms. *Theory into Practice* 31(2): 132–141.

Montoya, M. (1994). Mascaras, Trenzas, y Grenas: Un/masking the Self While Un/braiding Latina Stories and Legal Discourse. *Chicano-Latino Law Review* 15: 1–37.

Montoya, M. (2002). Celebrating Racialized Legal Narratives. In F. Valdes et al. (eds.), *Crossroads, Directions, and A New Critical Race Theory*, 243–250. Philadelphia: Temple University Press.

Moraga, C. (1983). La Güera. In C. Moraga and G. Anzaldúa (eds.), *This Bridge Called My Back: Writings by Radical Women of Color*, 24–33. 2nd ed. New York: Kitchen Table.

Morris, J. (1999). A Pillar of Strength: An African-American School's Communal Bonds with Families and Community since *Brown. Urban Education* 33(5): 584–605.

Morris, J. (2004). Can Anything Good Come from Nazareth? Race, Class, and African American Schooling and Community in the Urban South and Midwest. *American Educational Research Journal* 41(1): 69–112.

Olivas, M. (1990). The Chronicles, My Grandfather's Stories, and Immigration Law: The Slave Traders Chronicle as Racial History. *Saint Louis University Law Journal* 34: 425–441.

Oliver, M., and Shapiro, T. (1995). *Black Wealth/White Wealth: A New Perspective on Racial Inequality.* New York: Routledge.

Olmedo, I. M. (1997). Voices of Our Past: Using Oral History To Explore Funds of Knowledge within a Puerto Rican Family. *Anthropology and Education Quarterly* 28(4): 550–573.

Parker, L.; Deyhle, D.; Villenas, S.; and Crossland, K. (eds.) (1998). Special issue: Critical Race Theory and Education. *International Journal of Qualitative Studies in Education* 11: 1–184.

Parker, L.; Deyhle, D.; and Villenas, S. (eds.) (1999). *Race Is ... Race Isn't: Critical Race Theory and Qualitative Studies in Education.* Boulder, CO: Westview.

Perea, J.; Delgado, R.; Harris, A.; and Wildman, S. (2000). *Race and Races: Cases and Resources for a Multiracial America.* St. Paul, MN: West Group.

Pierce, C. (1974). Psychiatric Problems of the Black Minority. In S. Arieti (ed.), *American Handbook of Psychiatry*, 512–523. New York: Basic Books.

Pierce, C. (1989). Unity in Diversity: Thirty-Three Years of Stress. In G. Berry and J. Asamen (eds.), *Black Students: Psychological Issues and Academic Achievement*, 296–312. Newbury Park, CA: Sage.

Pierce, C. (1995). Stress Analogs of Racism and Sexism: Terrorism, Torture, and Disaster. In C. Willie et al. (eds.), *Mental Health, Racism, and Sexism*, 277–293. Pittsburgh: University of Pittsburgh Press.

Pizarro, M. (1998). "Chicano Power!" Epistemology and Methodology for Social Justice and Empowerment in Chicana/o Communities. *International Journal of Qualitative Studies in Education* 11(1): 57–80.

Reese, L. J. (1992). Ecocultural Factors Influencing the Academic Success of Young Latino Students. Ph.D. dissertation, University of California, Los Angeles.

Robinson, T., and Ward, J. (1991). "A Belief in Self Far Greater Than Anyone's Belief": Cultivating Resistance among African American Female Adolescents. In C. Gilligan et al. (eds.), *Women, Girls, and Psychotherapy: Reframing Resistance*, 87–103. New York: Haworth.

Rueda, R.; Monzo, L. D.; and Higareda, I. (2004). Appropriating the Sociocultural Resources of Latino Paraeducators for Effective Instruction with Latino Students: Promises and Problems. *Urban Education* 29(1): 52–90.

Russell, M. (1992). Entering Great America: Reflections on Race and the Convergence of Progressive Legal Theory and Practice. *Hastings Law Journal* 43: 749–767.

Saldivar-Hill, S. (2000). *Feminism on the Border: Chicana Gender Politics and Literature.* Berkeley: University of California Press.

Sanchez, G. J. (1993). *Becoming Mexican American: Ethnicity, Culture, and Identity in Chicano Los Angeles, 1900–1945.* Oxford University Press.

Scheurich, J., and Young, M. (1997). Coloring Epistemologies: Are Our Research Epistemologies Racially Biased? *Educational Researcher* 26: 4–16.

Shapiro, T. (2004). *The Hidden Cost of Being African American: How Wealth Perpetuates Inequality.* New York: Oxford University Press.

Solórzano, D. (1989). Teaching and Social Change: Reflections on a Freirean Approach in a College Classroom. *Teaching Sociology* 17: 218–225.

Solórzano, D. (1992). Chicano Mobility Aspirations: A Theoretical and Empirical Note. *Latino Studies Journal* 3: 48–66.

Solórzano, D. (1997). Images and Words That Wound: Critical Race Theory, Racial Stereotyping, and Teacher Education. *Teacher Education Quarterly* 24: 5–19.

Solórzano, D. (1998). Critical Race Theory, Racial and Gender Microaggressions, and the Experiences of Chicana and Chicano Scholars. *International Journal of Qualitative Studies in Education* 11: 121–136.

Solórzano, D.; Ceja, M.; and Yosso, T. (2000). Critical Race Theory, Racial Microaggressions, and Campus Racial Climate: The Experiences of African American College Students. *Journal of Negro Education* 69(1/2): 60–73.

Solórzano, D., and Delgado Bernal, D. (2001). Critical Race Theory, Transformational Resistance, and Social Justice: Chicana and Chicano Students in an Urban Context. *Urban Education* 36: 308–342.

Solórzano, D., and Solórzano, R. (1995). The Chicano Educational Experience: A Proposed Framework for Effective Schools in Chicano Communities. *Educational Policy* 9: 293–314.

Solórzano, D., and Villalpando, O. (1998). Critical Race Theory, Marginality, and the Experience of Minority Students in Higher Education. In C. Torres and T. Mitchell (eds.), *Emerging Issues in the Sociology of Education: Comparative Perspectives,* 211–224. New York: SUNY Press.

Solórzano, D., and Yosso, T. (2000). Toward a Critical Race Theory of Chicana and Chicano Education. In C. Tejeda et al. (eds.), *Charting New Terrains of Chicana(o)/Latina(o) Education,* 35–65. Cresskill, NJ: Hampton.

Solórzano, D., and Yosso, T. (2001). Critical Race and LatCrit Theory and Method: Counterstorytelling Chicana and Chicano Graduate School Experiences. *International Journal of Qualitative Studies in Education* 14(4): 471–495.

Solórzano, D., and Yosso, T. (2002a). A Critical Race Counterstory of Race, Racism, and Affirmative Action. *Equity and Excellence in Education* 35(2): 155–168.

Solórzano, D., and Yosso, T. (2002b). Maintaining Social Justice Hopes within Academic Realities: A Freirean Approach to Critical Race/LatCrit Pedagogy. *Denver Law Review* 78(4): 595–621.

Stanton-Salazar, R. D. (2001). *Manufacturing Hope and Despair: The School and Kin Support Networks of U.S. - Mexican Youth.* New York: Teachers College Press.

Stanton-Salazar, R. and Spina, S. U. (2000). The Network Orientations of Highly Resilient Urban Minority Youth: A Network-Analytic Account of Minority Socialization and Its Educational Implications. *Urban Review* 32(3): 227–261.

Stefancic, J. (1998). Latino and Latina Critical Theory: An Annotated Bibliography. *La Raza Law Journal* 10: 423–498.

Stevenson, B. (1996). *Life in Black and White: Family and Community in the Slave South.* New York: Oxford University Press.

Tate, W. (1994). From Inner City to Ivory Tower: Does My Voice Matter in the Academy? *Urban Education* 29(3): 245–269.

Tate, W. (1997). Critical Race Theory and Education: History, Theory, and Implications. *Review of Research in Education* 22: 191–243.

Tatum, B. D. (1997). *Why Are All the Black Kids Sitting Together in the Cafeteria? And Other Conversations about Race.* New York: Basic Books.

Tierney, W. (1993). *Building Communities of Difference: Higher Education in the Twenty-First Century.* Westport, CT: Bergin and Garvey.

U.S. Bureau of the Census. (2000). *2000 Census of the Population: General Population Characteristics, United States Summary.* Washington, DC: U.S. Government Printing Office.

Valdes, F. (1997). LatCrit Theory: Naming and Launching a New Direction of Critical Legal Scholarship. *Harvard Latino Law Review* 2: 1–501.

Valdes, F. (1998). Under Construction: LatCrit Consciousness, Community and Theory. *La Raza Law Journal* 10(1): 1–56.

Valdes, F.; McCristal Culp, J.; and Harris, A. (eds.) (2002). *Crossroads, Directions, and a New Critical Race Theory.* Philadelphia: Temple University Press.

Valencia, R. (eds.) (1991). *Chicano School Failure and Success: Research and Policy Agenda for the 1990s.* New York: Falmer.

Valencia, R. (ed.) (2002). *Chicano School Failure and Success: Past, Present, and Future.* 2nd ed. New York: Routledge/Falmer.

Valencia, R., and Solórzano, D. (1997). Contemporary Deficit Thinking. In R. Valencia (ed.), *The Evolution of Deficit Thinking in Educational Thought and Practice,* 160–210. New York: Falmer.

Valenzuela, A. (1999). *Subtractive Schooling: U.S.-Mexican Youth and the Politics of Caring.* New York: SUNY Press.

Vélez-Ibáñez, C., and Greenberg, J. (1992). Formation and Transformation of Funds of Knowledge among U.S.-Mexican Households. *Anthropology and Education Quarterly* 23(4): 313–335.

Villalpando, O. (2003). Self-segregation or Self-preservation? A Critical Race Theory and Latina/o Critical Theory Analysis of Findings from a Longitudinal Study of Chicana/o College Students. *International Journal of Qualitative Studies in Education* 16(5): 619–646.

Villalpando, O., and Solórzano, D. (2005). The Role of Culture in College Preparation Programs: A Review of the Literature. In W. Tierney et al. (eds.), *Preparing for College: Nine Elements of Effective Outreach,* 13–28 Albany, NY: SUNY Press.

Villenas, S., and Deyhle, D. (1999). Critical Race Theory and Ethnographies Challenging the Stereotypes: Latino Families, Schooling, Resilience and Resistance. *Curriculum Inquiry* 29(4): 413–445.

Villenas, S., and Moreno, M. (2001). To Valerse por Si Misma between Race, Capitalism, and Patriarchy: Latina Mother-Daughter Pedagogies in North Carolina. *International Journal of Qualitative Studies in Education* 14(5): 671–688.

Wakatsuki Houston, J., and Houston, J. D. (1973). *Farewell to Manzanar: A True Story of Japanese American Experience during and after the World War II Internment.* Boston: Houghton Mifflin.

Ward, J. (1996). Raising Resisters: The Role of Truth Telling in the Psychological Development of African American Girls. In B. Leadbetter and N. Way (eds.), *Urban Girls: Resisting Stereotypes, Creating Identities,* 85–99. New York: New York University Press.

Williams, P. (1991). *The Alchemy of Race and Rights: Diary of a Law Professor.* Cambridge, MA: Harvard University Press.

Williams, P. (1997). Spirit-Murdering the Messenger: The Discourse of Fingerprinting as the Law's Response to Racism. In A. Wing (ed.), *Critical Race Feminism: A Reader,* 229–236. New York: New York University Press.

Williams, R. (1997).Vampires Anonymous and Critical Race Practice. *Michigan Law Review* 95: 741–765.

Wing, A. (ed.) (1997). *Critical Race Feminism: A Reader.* New York: New York University Press.

Wing, A. (ed.) (2000). *Global Critical Race Feminism: An International Reader.* New York: New York University Press.

Zavella, P. (1991). Reflections on Diversity among Chicanas. *Frontiers: A Journal of Women Studies* 2(2): 73–85.

10

Critical Race Ethnography in Education: Narrative, Inequality, and the Problem of Epistemology

GARRETT ALBERT DUNCAN

Introduction

When asked for his definition of "equal," Thurgood Marshall once answered, "Equal means getting the same thing, at the same time and in the same place." Here Marshall established coevalness, or the "sharing of the present time" (Fabian, 2002, p. 32), as a condition of justice. This article also examines a socio-temporal aspect of education and justice to examine schooling and inequality 50 years after Marshall made his remarks on behalf of the plaintiffs in the landmark case *Brown v. Board of Education*. As I discuss in the sections that follow, the unequal material conditions of education before the civil rights movement, as implied by Marshall's answer, were racially inflected expressions of what Johannes Fabian (2002) calls the *allochronism of anthropology* or, in simple terms, the denial of coevalness. As Fabian explains, the denial of coevalness is effected primarily through language or, more specifically, through *allochronic discourses*. Allochronism has a discursive function which shapes racial norms in U.S. society in ways that make them "commonsense" and susceptible to be taken for granted by most individuals. W. E. B. Du Bois alluded to these intricate discursive processes as he reflected on the meaning of his life's work late in his life:

> [N]ot simply knowledge, not simply direct repression of evil, will reform the world. In long, ... the actions of [women and] men which are due not to a lack of knowledge nor to evil intent, must be changed by influencing folkways, habits, customs, and subconscious deeds. (Du Bois, 1997, p. 222)

Given its emphasis on placing at the center of analysis the stories that people of color tell of their experiences, critical race theory (CRT) is an especially useful tool for examining how socio-temporal notions of race inform the naturalization of oppression and the normalization of racial inequality

This chapter originally appeared in *Race, Ethnicity and Education* 8(1), March 2005, pp. 93–114.

in public schools and society. These discursive processes are shorn of the more explicit and formal expressions of power that we typically associate with oppression and inequality (Crenshaw et al., 1995), and the narratives of people of color often bring them into relief with a clarity that is seldom communicated through dominant technologies (Bell, 1999; Collins, 1990; Delgado and Stefancic, 1991; Matsuda, 1996; MacKinnon, 1993; Young, 1990). In the following account, Richard Delgado and Jean Stefancic (1991) describe the purpose and goal of racially-specific narrative intervention in the context of legal studies:

> Legal storytelling is a means by which representatives of new communities may introduce their views into the dialogue about the way society should be governed. Stories are in many ways more powerful than litigation or brief-writing and may be precursors to law reform. They offer insights into the particulars of lives lived at the margins of society, margins that are rapidly collapsing toward a disappearing center. This is not just true of our times. In biblical history, storytellers for oppressed groups told tales of hope and struggle – for example, that of the promised land – to inspire and comfort the community during difficult times. Reality could be better – and perhaps will be. Other storytellers have directed their attention to the oppressors, reminding them of the day when they would be called to account. Stories thus perform multiple functions, allowing us to uncover a more layered reality than is immediately apparent: a refracted one that the legal system must confront. (Delgado and Stefancic, 1997, p. 321)

Against this backdrop, the analysis presented in this article proceeds as follows: In the first section, I frame my larger argument within a critical race analysis of the literature and primary data related to the concepts of time, narrative, and educational inequality. I then examine the implications of narratives in a discussion of their possibilities and limitations of CRT for researching the schooled lives of black children and youth. This discussion takes seriously a major criticism of CRT: that it relies too heavily on storytelling and narrative data. As I explain below, from an epistemological standpoint, criticism is warranted when truth claims are made exclusively on data derived from subjective ontological categories. Along these lines, I propose critical race ethnography as one measure to build around and advance the rich corpus of CRT studies. I conclude with a discussion of the implications of the analysis presented in this article for urban school reform within the contexts of the post-industrial United States and the "runaway world" of globalization (Giddens, 2000).

Time, Justice, and Education

> We measure time according to the movement of countless suns; and they measure time by little machines in their little pockets. Now tell me, how could we ever meet at the same place and at the same time? (Gibran, 1926, p. 7)

As indicated in the introduction, contemporary forms of racial oppression and inequality are expressions of allochronic discourses that inform "ontological blackness," or the blackness that whiteness created as Western civilization began to emerge as a prominent force in the world (Anderson, 1995; Morrison, 1993; Scheurich and Young, 1997; West, 1982). In the United States, this notion of ontological blackness is thoroughly implicated in the contradiction between democracy and capitalism. This contradiction has its origins in the framing of the U.S. Constitution and creates a tension in U.S. society between *property* rights and *human* rights (Bell, 1987; Duncan, 2000; Ladson-Billings and Tate, 1995; Wronka, 1994). The tension was greatly exacerbated by the presence of enslaved Africans in the country, where black people were viewed as commodities to be consumed rather than persons worthy of the civil and political rights granted by the U.S. Constitution (Chin, 2001; Ladson-Billings and Tate, 1995; Mills, 1997). The preservation of material property rights as well as the extension of the notion of property to include skin color has always played out in this country in ways that maintain an unequal distribution of economic, social and political resources, which, in turn, privileges white people over people of color. The intransigent nature of white supremacy in the United States—despite the ratification of the 14th Amendment and Supreme Court rulings such as *Brown v. Board of Education* that uphold it or the passage of civil rights legislation—is in large part attributable to a society which, to a certain degree, recognizes the civil and political rights of people of color but in the main does not affirm their cultural, social and economic rights (Du Bois, 1903; Duncan, 2000; Mills, 1997; Wronka, 1994).

As it relates to the present analysis, the allochronism of anthropology (Fabian, 2002) is useful for explaining why white supremacy is largely accepted and taken for granted, especially in terms of its pernicious effects on black people. Fabian's critique of allochronism, or the denial of coevalness, occurs within a comprehensive analysis of the function of socio-temporal systems in Western scientific discourses. He points to anthropological categories like "primitive," "savage," and "barbaric" to illustrate the allochronism that confounds the ethnographic project. In the ethnographic project, although both the ethnographer and the Other share the present time in terms of objective and, to a lesser extent, subjective states, coevalness is denied in terms of the conventions that regulate how the anthropologist depicts her or his subject. That the denial of coevalness has taken on meaning outside the academy is discernible in the epigraph that opens this section. Gibran's epigram had contemporaneous meanings attached to race, time, and social inequality in the United States during the decades around the turn of the twentieth century. The poet wrote during a period when time as told by "little machines in little pockets" was prominent in mediating the social construction of virtue and vice, especially around the issue of work and how it defined whiteness and its cultural corollary, blackness (Hall, 1983; Roediger, 1991; Smith, 1997).

Allochronism and the Architecture of Early Black Education

During the same period, G. Stanley Hall's (1904) depiction of people of color in his influential writings casts in bold relief the problem of allochronism in Western scientific discourses in the field of education. For example, Hall (1904) observed about African, Native American, and Chinese peoples: "Most savages are children, or because of sexual maturity, more properly, adolescents of adult size" (p. 649). In a related vein, Amanda D. Kemp and Robert Trent Vinson (2000) describe how, in the 1920s, the black nationalist and American-educated president of the African National Congress, James Thaele, employed similar logic to counter discriminatory sentiments and legislation in South Africa. Such views and policy were predicated on the notion that black people were primitive and therefore undeserving of full citizenship rights. In contrast to Hall, though, Thaele sought to subvert the concept of "racial time" that posited that "native subjects" were underdeveloped human beings. Employing the modernist markers of the "new Negroes" that he acquired through his American education, Thaele used himself as evidence to refute the allochronic discourses that impeded the full social acceptance and economic participation of black people in South Africa's multiracial society.

For South African white segregationists, however, "James Thaele symbolized the urgent need to institute segregation, for here was an urban-based, 'detribalized' African who paraded his abundant modernist qualities in order to demand full political and civil rights" (Kemp and Vinson, 2000, p. 148). Similarly, during this period in the United States, white-dominated institutional and bureaucratic forces sought to align the schooling of black students with their view of racial time to guide them slowly toward civilization (Anderson, 1988; Washington, 1989; Watkins, 2001). In this sense, the white architects of black education in the United States echoed the sentiments of a South African prime minister when he observed that it had "taken the white man 2,000 years to become civilized and the black man cannot expect to reach such a standard in 200 years" (Kemp and Vinson, 2000, p. 147); the American architects aligned their educational programs accordingly to ensure that any expectations by black students to the contrary would go unmet. W. E. B. Du Bois's report on the state of public schools in Butte, Montana, published in *The Crisis* in 1918, illustrates how such sentiments translated into disparities in the education provided to black and white students:

What, now, is the real difference between these two schemes [white and black] of education? The difference is that in the Butte schools for white pupils, a chance is held open for the pupil to go through high school and college and to advance at the rate which the modern curriculum demands; that in the colored, a program is being made out that will land the boy at the time he becomes self-conscious and aware of his own possibilities in an educational *impasse*. He cannot go on in the public schools even if he should move to a place where there are good public schools because he is too old. Even if he has done the elementary work in twice the time that a student is supposed to, it has been work of a kind that will not admit him to a northern high school. No matter, then, how gifted the boy may be, he is absolutely estopped from a higher education. This is not only unfair to the boy but it is grossly unfair to the Negro race. (Du Bois, 1995, p. 263)

As illustrated in the passage above, white power interests used the considerable material and political resources at their disposal to impede the academic advancement of black children and youth in ways that all but guaranteed that racial progress in the United States would proceed slowly if at all. As Du Bois's report indicates, in the first decades of the twentieth century, this occurred as white domination over black schooling contributed to inferior curriculum and instruction for black students, especially at the secondary level. For instance, Anderson (1988) observes that, from 1880 to 1930, the expressed objective of the architects of the southern public black high school system was "to meet the needs" of black students by equipping them to "move from unskilled to skilled labor" in preparation for "Negro jobs" (pp. 187–237). In practice, according to Anderson, these schools met the needs of black students by adjusting their expectations to align with their presumed fixed economic station in society. This is illustrated in *The Autobiography of Malcolm X* (Haley and X, 1965), when Malcolm describes how his ambition to become a lawyer was halted in order to "meet his needs." In this instance, his English teacher, Mr. Ostrowski, ostensibly concerned for his emotional wellbeing, advised Malcolm, his top student, to align his expectations with social reality in order to avoid frustration and disappointment later in life:

Malcolm, one of life's first needs is for us to be realistic. Don't misunderstand me, now. We all like you, you know that. But you've got to be realistic about being a nigger. A lawyer – that's no realistic goal for a nigger. You need to think about something you *can* be. You're good with your hands – making things. Everybody admires your carpentry shop work. Why don't you plan on carpentry? People like you as a person – you'd get all kinds of work. (Haley and X, 1965, p. 37)

As Malcolm would recall later in his life, "I was one of his top students, one of the school's top students – but all he could see for me was the kind of future 'in your place' that almost all white people see for black people" (1965, p. 36). Anderson (1988) points out that schools sought to mediate the psychological adjustment of black students to the racial calendar by providing them with curriculum and instruction to make them more proficient, or skilled, at the same menial tasks to which they had been previously relegated to performing and to which white communities would seek to restrict them in the future. Of course, these programmatic features were at variance with the students' expectations that education would facilitate their movement from one occupation to another that demanded better technical training and expertise. Black students' expectations notwithstanding, gross educational injustices, with the support of meritocratic and racist discourses, allowed society to attribute inevitable racial disparities in school and eventually inequalities in society, to natural albeit potentially remediable differences between the races.

Allochronic Discourses in Contemporary Education

In contemporary times, concepts like "inner-city" and "urban" reiterate the "savage," "primitive," and "barbaric" in the present; and the applications of these concepts to certain schools and students indicate the allochronism that informs U.S. public education. For example, in his study of city schools, Pedro Noguera (2003) points out that the ways in which policy makers and others talk about and respond to things designated as "urban" suggest that the appellation refers neither to geographical locations nor to spatial configurations. Rather, Noguera argues that "urban" is typically employed "as a social or cultural construct used to describe certain people and places" (p. 23). Along these lines, in urban classrooms the denial of coevalness inheres in what Ann Arnett Ferguson (2000) calls the "adultification" of black boys in the school she studied. Adultification occurs as the behaviors of boys as young as eleven and twelve foreclose their futures in the eyes of adults, who often identify them as headed for jail. Similarly, in his study of school violence, Ronnie Casella (2003) found that urban school officials were prone to "punishing dangerousness" – punishing not the specific violent behavior of youths but the *possibility* of their violent behavior somewhere off in the future.

In addition, the problem of allochronism in education in the late nineteenth- and early twentieth-century education of black students, illustrated by the examples in the previous section, continues to find expression in urban schools at the turn of the twenty-first century. For example, in the aftermath of the 1992 Los Angeles uprisings, Leilani Pettigrew, a resident of South Central Los Angeles and mother of four school-age children, described an encounter she had at the high school one of her sons attended. Some of her comments allude to the problem of allochronism in urban education:

What the funny part is that they have, they have courses in the school – they have a wood shop. You see no … you have no kind of tool in the woodshop. Okay, you have no wood – nothing. And I walk in the class and said, "this is a wood shop?" And the teacher said, "yes." And I said, "where is the wood? Where're the tools?" I said. "Okay, fine. How are you supposed to grade a child for something that is not even available to them?" (Holland, 1995)

Ms. Pettigrew provides a poignant example of the expression of allochronic discourses in modern-day urban schools and alludes to their disconcerting implications for the prospects of black youth in post-industrial U.S. society. In the above example, students are enrolled in a woodshop course that has neither wood nor equipment. At the same time, students are not only being awarded credit but, in some instances, given grades which indicate mastery of the "hard skills" which they are supposed to acquire in such a course. In the event that students from this course decide to pursue employment or advanced studies in, say, carpentry or woodworking, such a curriculum will land them, to quote Du Bois, at an impasse when they enter the world of work or higher education.

I have found similar evidence of allochronism both in my work as a science teacher in southern California and in my ethnographic research in urban schools in the Midwest. For example, my research indicates that urban schools typically subject students to anachronistic (dated), liminal (suspended), asynchronous (out of sync) and/or dyschronous (context-inappropriate) conditions (Duncan, forthcoming). The following two examples illustrate some of these practices. In the first example, from 1996 through 2000, students at an elementary school were compelled to use model 186 and 286 personal computers despite the fact that updated Internet-ready computers were available throughout the school, including in the room next door to the one where the older computers were housed. Some of these newer computers, including those housed in the "New Millennium Computer Lab," went unused over a span of three years. During this period the school was under academic scrutiny; it was subsequently placed on the district's infamous "school of opportunity" list – a designation which effectively placed the school on academic probation and at risk for being closed. The second case concerns the use of outdated curriculum. In this extreme example, a teacher at the same school used reading materials published in 1965, prepared by a noted textbook publishing company, with his fourth grade class to celebrate Black History Month in 1997.

Examples abound to demonstrate that these practices typically occur not only in this school but also in similar settings across the nation. In addition, allochronic conditions in these schools are exacerbated, and sometimes caused, by another feature of public education: chronic standardized testing. Two examples that illustrate the debilitating effect of chronic testing on the culture of schools and, consequently, on academic achievement follow. A secondary school principal decried what she viewed as the heavy-handed approach of the central office to the issue of testing, complaining: "TEST, TEST, TEST, every staff meeting, beating this dead horse all year long. Our superintendent got up last year and said, 'If teachers can't do it, they can get out.' How dare he? He couldn't do it! We're working against extraordinary odds, and all we get is browbeaten." The level of adult anxiety is often translated into the classroom culture and resonates in the frequent use of war metaphors, such as "attack mode," "under siege," "lockdown," and "triage," to describe instructional approaches to the exam. In another example, a middle school teacher advised his students to "bullshit the white folks," which translates to "To hell with the white people who impose the test on us." In addition, a seventh-grade girl told a tutor that the "crazy white folks just want us to be dumb, so I'm going to draw pictures," and a boy observed that even if "I do well on the test, I still have to come back to the raggedy school with the bootleg table."

These examples also illustrate how the denial of coevalness undermines the conditions for students and teachers to empathize or to connect with one another in the learning process. Empathy is intimately related to notions of time and specifically to synchrony, a form of coevalness bringing together two entities under one rhythm where there had formerly been two or more rhythms moving simultaneously. Along these lines, the critical race theorist Richard Delgado alludes to the need to achieve synchrony in social institutions that are organized to foster human development:

> care-giving and the profit motive are incompatible. The temptation is to cut corners, which is contrary to what's needed.... So, the trick is to draw the right line between the productive sector, which should be governed by aggressive, dog-eat-dog capitalism – the sort of things our conservative friends love – and the care-giving sector, which should be socialized. Model-fitting, as they say. (Delgado, 1995, pp. 38–39)

Here Delgado alludes to the distinction between the role of *polychronic* time of the private sector and the role of *monochronic* time of the public sector in mediating human experiences. As Edward T. Hall (1983) explains, values that are associated with polychronic time (P-time), which means "many things at a time-time," are most amenable to situations that require caregivers to attend to multiple tasks, such as those attendant on the social dimensions of teaching. Values associated with monochronic time (M-time), which means "one thing at a time-time," are most compatible with situations that require order and discipline, such as direct instruction.

Along these lines, the examples provided in the previous sections are also expressions of what I call "dyschronism," or a model-"mis-fitting" of sorts. In these instances, P-time values were imposed upon M-time situations, and M-time values regulated situations where P-time values were more appropriate, in both cases resulting in dysrhythmic conditions that have arresting effects on teaching and learning in urban classrooms. In other words, data indicate that instructional situations that require clarity, order and direction – M-time conditions – were disrupted by anachronistic curricula and materials that contributed to a general sense of inefficacy and confusion on the part of teachers and students and that resulted in academic underperformance. In addition, love, compassion and nurturance – values attendant on P-time settings– were compromised, if not altogether sacrificed, under conditions attributable to the stress of high-stakes testing, resulting in teacher and student resistance and hostility toward the pedagogy being imposed on them.

Critical Race Theory, Narrative, and Epistemology

> We, the blacks, are in trouble, certainly, but we are not doomed, and we are not inarticulate because we are not compelled to defend a morality that we know to be a lie. (Baldwin, 1979, p. 374)

Simply to point out that concepts like "inner-city" and "urban" signify allochronic discursive practices will do little to change the conditions that shape the schooling of black children and youths. In fact, such a critique alone is too easily mistaken for moral posturing or condemnation of those who use these terms. As Fabian (2002) points out, "At least the more clearheaded radical critics know that bad intentions alone do not invalidate knowledge. For that to happen it takes bad epistemology which advances cognitive interests without regard for ideological presuppositions" (pp. 32–33). Following this, the "critical" dimension in the critical race analysis presented in this article emphasizes epistemology; that is, it centers on questions of what and how we know, as opposed to value orientation or political or ideological commitments.

Although moral concerns certainly play a big part in the present analysis, this project seeks to explicate and disrupt the allochronic discourses that give enduring forms of oppression and inequality their appearance of normalcy and naturalness. This is largely a question of epistemology and entails an analysis that moves beyond the reproduction of received "realities" to one that identifies the processes by which the interplay of the different "ontologies" reproduces them (Mills, 1997). The ontological categories, or states of existence, to which I am referring include the following: subjective ontological categories, that refer to existing states of mind and feelings to which only one actor has access; objective ontological categories, that refer to existing objects, conditions, and events to which all people have access; and normative-evaluative ontological categories that refer to existing agreements on the rightness, goodness, and appropriateness of certain states of mind and objects (Carspecken, 1996).

As a discursive force, the problem of allochronism described in the previous sections of this article is primarily a feature of the last ontological category, the normative-evaluative. This is the category that informs our "folkways, habits, customs, and subconscious deeds" (Du Bois, 1997, p. 222). As such, an allochronic discourse, as do many discourses, has a narrative function insofar it presents itself as an exhaustive story, thus concealing the particularity of its perspective and excluding the possibility that other points of view exist. In the process, it obfuscates its material origins as well as the human interests that inhere in them. It follows, then, that the antidote to an allochronic discourse is a counternarrative or counterstory. Thus, CRT privileges the voices of those who bear the brunt of inequalities in society and relies heavily on storytelling, as opposed to analytic means, as the methodology to represent them. This treatment of voice is consistent with a tradition of ethnographic research exemplified by the work of the postcolonial anthropologist John Langston Gwaltney (1993), who posits that the words of ordinary black folk are more than "crude data" to be analyzed by university-trained experts. On the contrary, Gwaltney surmises, the values, systems of logic and worldview that the words of black folk evince "are rooted in a lengthy peasant tradition and clandestine theology" (Gwaltney, 1993, pp. xxvi, xxix).

I regard the stories of people of color as necessary to disrupt allochronic discourses. In particular, they provide potent counterpoints to challenge the existing narratives that shape how we understand the post-civil rights schooling experiences and outcomes of students of color. As various scholars argue, racially particular, culture-centric, standpoint knowledge throws into relief the values, assumptions, categories and concepts that inform racist epistemologies (Collins, 1990; Mills, 1997; Morrison, 1993; Scheurich and Young, 1997; Young, 1990). Racist epistemologies are deeply embedded in the meaning-making structures that inform the naturalization of oppression and the normalization of racial inequality in public schools.

As it relates to the analysis presented in this chapter, I posit that racially signified normative-evaluative notions about the "backwardness" of black children and youth inform the subjective and objective dimensions of their experiences in schools in ways that undermine their capacities. Perhaps nowhere is this relationship more powerfully exemplified than in the words of the young girl and boy quoted in the previous section, which illustrate the capacity of oppressed people to name their realities and warrant the prominence of narrative and storytelling in critical race theory. Along these lines, storytelling differs from conventional scholarship on three points, as succinctly captured by Daniel Farber and Suzanna Sherry (1995):

> First, the storytellers view narratives as central to scholarship, while deemphasizing conventional analytic measures. Second, they particularly value 'stories from the bottom' – stories from women and people of color about their oppression. Third, they are less concerned than conventional scholars about whether stories are either typical or descriptively

accurate, and they place more emphasis on the aesthetic and emotional dimensions of narration. (p. 283)

The centrality of narrative and storytelling in critical race approaches to educational research is consonant with Paulo Freire's (1995) view that changing language "is part of the process of changing the world" (pp. 67–68). Along these lines, proponents of CRT emphasize aesthetic and emotional dimensions in their stories to stimulate the imagination and to inspire empathy to allow others to imagine the mind of the oppressed and to see, and perhaps vicariously experience, the world through their eyes. Such emphasis is also consistent with what I call a spiritual ontological category, which thoroughly imbricates the stories of oppressed people that depict conditions of injustice (Berry and Blassingame, 1982; Clark, 1996; Freire, 1995, 1996, 2002; Gwaltney, 1993; Palmer, 1993). A spiritual state is characterized by concepts such as "courage," "belief," "hope" and "faith" and defies easy placement into purely subjective or objective categories. The source of these concepts is neither our intellectual tradition nor our material reality but rather our spiritual heritage (Palmer, 1993). Cornel West captures this idea when he notes that those of us who are serious about struggle often find ourselves "stepping out on nothing, hoping to land on something" (hooks and West, 1991, pp. 8–9).

In addition, language, through which narratives are conveyed, is not only a reflection and a constituent of reality but also a cultural rope that connects people across generations and even continents. It is the source and the substance of the enduring hope implicit in the struggles of a people who strive to "make a way out of no way." In short, the spiritual ontological category is constituted of a collection of conceptual devices that fall into what Paulo Freire calls "the category of the untested feasibility," or a belief in the possible dream (1995, 1996; see also Freire, 2002). Such a belief is sustained by the view that the stories of the oppressed have the potential to render more vivid and tangible the limit situations that impede social change. Limit situations are the psychological, material, political or social conditions that hinder societal transformation (Freire, 1996). By using the stories of people of color to explicate limit situations, we can rethink our research or pedagogy in accordance with the new knowledge that inheres in them and can act upon it to realize our untested feasibilities.

Critical race theorists' emphasis on storytelling and privileging the voices of people of color has drawn criticism from some quarters. As it relates to the present analysis, critics charge, for instance, that CRT has failed to meet the burden of proof of the existence of fundamental cognitive differences between subjugated and dominant voices that would warrant privileging the former over the latter in the research enterprise (Farber and Sherry, 1995). Instead, they argue that the voice of color and the dominant voice differ primarily on the basis of content. Critics in this vein go further and assert that the voice of color is but another in a long line of epistemological critiques of liberalism; in addition, they charge that the qualities that characterize voices of color – contextualization and groundedness in lived experience as opposed to abstraction (Delgado, 1995; Duncan, 2002a; Matsuda, 1996) – have a strong affinity with pragmatism, a tradition dominated by the very white males that CRT often critiques (Farber and Sherry, 1995). In short, critics charge that CRT claims to a voice of color, especially in legal studies, "often piggyback on feminist scholarship" (Farber and Sherry, 1995, p. 287) and rarely draw on independent social science for support; at best, critics argue, proponents of CRT who posit the existence of a voice of color merely postulate that people of color occupy subordinate status in the U.S. and are so positioned to provide perspectives unavailable or uneasily accessible to those who are privileged in society. However, the critics maintain, critical race theorists have yet to adequately demonstrate how these perspectives are fundamentally different from those underlying traditional scholarship (Farber and Sherry, 1995).

Critics also question whether academics of color can make a claim to represent the plight of the oppressed, especially given their relatively privileged status in society. Critics charge that to do so is tantamount to an essentialism that minimizes the heterogeneous experiences of persons of color and that collapses their diverse opinions into a single unproblematic voice (Farber and Sherry, 1995; Kennedy, 1995). They also charge that the claim of a distinctive racial voice stereotypes scholars of color "whereby the particularity of an individual's characteristics are denied by reference to the perceived characteristics of the racial group with which the individual is associated" (Kennedy, 1995, p. 319). In addition, some critics charge that to confer special status to the black middle class promotes unfairness where those with the greatest privilege continue to gain advantages at the expense of those with the least advantage. For example, Richard Posner, Chief Judge of the United States Court of Appeals for the Seventh Circuit, argues that affirmative action often "transfers wealth or opportunity from people who have not engaged in or benefited from discrimination to blacks who have not been harmed by discrimination, and it tends to benefit the already most advantaged blacks at the expense of the least advantaged whites" (1995, p. 383).

Along these lines, a final general criticism of CRT's reliance on storytelling has to do with the issue of truth claims. In the view of some critics, storytelling in scholarship often fails to render social reality with the balance, nuance and concreteness "that provides a needed antidote to the partial visions furnished by abstract, generalizing social sciences" (Posner, 2000, p. 380). Instead, it fosters onesidedness and encourages a form of empathy that causes one to lose the distance and, by extension, the perspective necessary for judgment. Posner (1995) sums up this line of critique as follows: "The project of empathetic [sic] jurisprudence invites us to choose between achieving a warped internal perspective and an inhumanly clinical detachment: between becoming too hot and too cold" (p. 382). In a related vein, critics raise the question of how we know that one version of events is better or more accurate that other versions of the same event – especially given CRT's tendency to sacrifice detail for aesthetics and to gloss over the heterogeneity of voices of color. And, as critics argue, claiming subordinate status does not prevent one from being inaccurate or from inadvertently omitting relevant information; neither does it make one immune to bias or deceit. Also, as Antonia Darder (2002) points out, people of color, too, are vulnerable to limit situations that may impair how they comprehend their experiences. In addition, as Randall Kennedy (1995) argues, "the mere experience of racial oppression provides no inoculation against complacency. Nor does it inoculate the victims of oppression against their own versions of prejudice and tyranny" (p. 317).

The preceding discussion captures some of the major relevant criticisms of the use of stories in CRT scholarship and warrants consideration in the present analysis. The first critique is that CRT has failed to meet the burden of proof of the existence of a distinctive voice of color, a claim that is predicated largely on the absence of social science research in the field of CRT legal studies. Research in the fields of linguistics and sociology, however, provides strong evidence to support the thesis that voices of color differ from dominant white voices in the United States in significant ways. For instance, a cultural argument posits that features which distinguish black language from the dominant American code is attributable to the former's autochthonous African (i.e., Niger-Congo and Bantu) linguistic heritage (Dillard, 1973; Turner, 1973; Vass, 1979). Other scholars have documented the sociolinguistic and discursive practices this heritage informs (Duncan, 2004; Duncan and Jackson, in press; Gundaker, 1998; Matthews, 1998; Morgan, 1993). The link between the structural and discursive dimensions of black language informs Baldwin's remarks in the epigraph that opens this section and also is taken up in the black literary tradition (e.g., Dash, 1997; Naylor, 1988). In addition, the sociological literature provides support that different discursive practices exist between dominant and subjugated communities in the United States and attributes such distinctions to the relative separation of social groups and to different perspectives on time that each group brings to bear on making meaning (Berry and Blassingame, 1982; Hall, 1983; Shipler, 1998).

A second criticism questions whether scholars of color can represent the plight of the oppressed, especially given their relatively privileged status in society. Criticism that such practices may invoke stereotypes or gloss over the diversity of opinions among people of color is serious, and for epistemological and ethical reasons it cannot be dismissed; however, it is important to note that some of the individuals who raise this critique are actually seeking to make a larger point, one that has political undertones. This argument holds that middle-class black individuals and families, for example, have more in common culturally and economically with their white middle-class counterparts than they do with members of the working-class black community. It follows that the voices of black academics are more akin to those of the white middle class than they are to the black community at large. In support of this contention, critics point to research that suggests that black academics, for instance, are generally more liberal than are members of the black working class (Farber and Sherry, 1995).

However, the relative conservatism that critics imply is characteristic of the black working class may reflect a pragmatic approach to decision making that develops when people are denied multiple good options when making vital decisions about their lives. That many black Americans are forced to choose from among restricted or poor options in society is the result of a conservative American social policy with a severe impact on the capacity of individuals to live self-determined lives (Moses, 2002). Anderson (1988), for example, illustrates how such pragmatism informed the educational decision making of black communities at the turn of the twentieth century. He notes that they often were compelled to make pragmatic choices that resulted in tremendous social and personal losses and to some extent made them complicit in their own oppression. There is also reason to believe that pragmatism rather than conservatism is the basis of black support for contemporary right-wing educational initiatives such as school vouchers (Duncan, 1992).

In addition, the suggestion that the black middle class and white middle class are social equals glosses over the vast advantages that the latter group has over the former in society. Scholars attribute these massive differences to injustices originating in the institution of slavery that led to huge discrepancies in the intergenerational transfer of power and wealth between the two groups (Hacker, 1995; Oliver and Shapiro, 1995; Shapiro, 2004). In addition, educational and sociological research on the black middle class suggests that it differs significantly from the white middle class with respect to culture and to the social universes that they each occupy (Ogbu, 2003; Patillo-McCoy, 1999). To be clear, my intention is not to downplay the diversity among black people but to point out a flaw in the attempt to dismiss the claim that black academics bring a distinct voice vis-à-vis their white peers to bear on their work, on the grounds that they share cultural, social and economic milieus with one another. Along these lines, during a recent class discussion on affirmative action in higher education, an undergraduate student best captured the view that society considers the black middle class intellectually and morally suspect and inferior to their white counterparts. The student, a white male from an affluent background, shared with the class that it was commonly said among family and friends in his circles to "never trust a black physician under forty." As he explained, the implication was that, in the eyes of the people with whom he associates, affirmative action had diminished the qualifications of these professionals.

The last major criticism to be taken up is that CRT storytelling is often one-sided, misleading and tendentious, glossing over the diversity of opinion in communities of color, providing inaccurate versions of events, or both. Certainly, one may find in the CRT literature, as in any other corpus of scholarly writing, evidence to warrant this critique. However, a review of the literature indicates that the goal of using narrative in CRT is to encourage an ethics in scholarship that prompts a kind of multiple consciousness. It is one that goes beyond simply entertaining one or a number of random viewpoints to seriously consider specific viewpoints. It is the kind of multiple consciousness that Mari Matsuda (1996) proposes as a method of inquiry into social reality that includes a deliberate choice to see the world from the point of view of socially subjugated groups. An invitation of this sort does not entail excluding other points of view. In fact, such an invitation is predicated upon a carefully considering other – especially dominant – explanations for social problems, and finding them wanting; the proof of the inadequacy of the latter viewpoints, it may be argued, is in the enduring presence of oppression in society and the inability of these viewpoints to lead to lasting measures of relief.

However, there is a major epistemological concern attendant on this critique that is especially relevant to any discussion that examines the usefulness of counterstories to promote social change. Specifically, such criticism points to an over-reliance on evidence derived from subjective ontological categories. The problem here is that these categories are defined by being accessible to only one actor. It follows that if individuals do not have direct access to the experience around which a claim is being made, they must either accept the version of events told to them or reject it. In the latter instance, individuals are often left without an alternative account or with one based largely on speculation. This is where a critical race ethnography is useful. It follows the lead indicated by proponents of CRT to take the words of people of color seriously and, instead of stopping there, to allow these voices to inform how we approach our examination of the material conditions basic to and inextricably a part of lived experience. In other words, a critical race ethnography seeks to engage the multiple ontological categories that give meaning to lived experience.

Engaging multiple ontological categories entails bringing to bear on our work data from different sources—for example, sociolinguistic, interview, observational, statistical or documentary—to provide stronger warrants for or even more plausible alternatives to the claims that result from our inquiries. In my view, the experiences of oppression that people of color in the United States encounter can be so outrageous and unimaginable to outsiders that it is difficult for even the most openminded and reasonable person to grasp the enormity of some of our claims. A relevant example occurred when I presented a paper that analyzed the two computer labs mentioned in a previous section of this article at a meeting of the American Educational Research Association a few years ago. The discussant for my paper session, a prominent white senior scholar whose research focuses on school equity, declared that, despite the availability of video-taped evidence supporting the claim, she could not imagine a school subjecting children to such conditions and did not believe that the two computer labs existed in the same building, let alone next door to each other. In addition to in effect calling me a liar and accusing me of fabricating data, she disparaged my work to the extent that during the question period, several members of the audience criticized her for being unprofessional.

More generally, I often wonder if some of the more outrageous stories about the harm done to people of color that have been taken up recently in news reports or studies would have been accorded respect if not for the fact that they were exposed and reported by white people, usually at professional and personal risk (e.g., Case, 1998; Jones, 1981; Watkins, 1997; Webb, 1998). For example, in 1997, a white New York police officer, Justin Volpe, brutalized a Haitian immigrant, Abner Louima, in a police station bathroom by repeatedly thrusting the wooden handle of a toilet plunger in his rectum before forcing it into his throat. Volpe pleaded guilty to the assault. It is highly unlikely that Louima would have achieved any measure of justice had it not been for the white nurses and officers who reported the atrocity. Given the racist and homophobic stereotypes that informed the explanations that Louima's violators initially used to explain his injuries, there is little doubt that his version would have been believed or that his story would have seen the light of day had only he or one of his family members reported the act of brutality. This point raises questions about what stories go untold in the absence of voices of color, and what costs we pay when our stories have to be told by others in order to be accorded respect.

These questions also complicate the further question of how we assess evidence, make truth claims, and determine the validity of such claims, especially when they turn on the stories of people of color. Some critical ethnographic traditions address truth claims by drawing on theories of communicative competence, which hold that human beings have the capacity to deliberate and come to a consensus around pressing issues (Carspecken, 1996). However, that view is predicated on the assumption that class mainly shapes social relations in capitalist societies, and that the inequalities attendant on other salient formations, such as race, derive from economic contradictions. Once scholars of color can penetrate the illusion of race, it follows, they will understand that the real problem confronting oppressed people of color is economic exploitation and will redirect their focus from analyzing racial injustice toward forging multiracial alliances to eliminate class domination. For example, addressing the reluctance of educators of color to heed the call of Freire's call to form multiracial alliances, Darder (2002) makes the following relevant point:

[M]any of us could not break loose from our deep-rooted (and objectified) distrust of 'whites,' nor could we move beyond our self-righteous
justification of our sectarianism. These represented two of the limit-sit-
uations that prevented the kind of democratic solidarity or *unity within
diversity* that potentially could generate profound shifts in the political
and economic systems that intensify racism. (p. 41)

Darder's observation, which occurs within a larger discussion that posits capitalism as the root of domination (pp. 38–44), captures the view of many in various
left and critical traditions that chastise critical race theorists for their adher-
ence to "parochial" notions of race. Such loyalties, the critics argue, undermine
the capacity of progressive researchers and educators to come to a consensus
around pressing social issues and to mobilize to produce social change.

In contrast, race-conscious scholars argue that though the contemporary
brand of racial oppression in the United States originated in economic exploitation in the form of the institution of slavery, it has since assumed status
as an autonomous social value in American society. Further, they posit, racism will not be eliminated by the resolution of the class conflicts but instead
"expands and contracts within restrictions established by economic incentives" (Willhelm, 1970, p. 2; see Bell, 2004, for a contemporary discussion of
this thesis as it relates to education). Thus, critical race theorists argue that,
rather than limit situations hampering the ability of race-conscious people
of color to agree with white people around issues that matter, unequal power
relationships between social groups make true consensus virtually unachiev-
able (Bell, 1995a; Delgado, 1995, 1996; Delgado and Stefancic, 2001; Duncan,
2000, 2002b). Such power relations typically marginalize or render mute the
voices of scholars of color. The society at large regularly dismisses the stories
of people of color and typically distorts them in those cases where it does take
them up. In many instances, the stories are incomprehensible to outsiders and
are simply not attended to.

Here, I am describing what is essentially a *différend*. A *différend* is a conflict between two or more parties that cannot be equitably resolved for lack of
terms to which all parties can agree, causing members of the subjugated group
to continue to suffer (Delgado, 1996; Lyotard, 1988). As noted by Delgado and
Stefancic (2001), there is no English word to convey the specific meaning of
the technical term *différend*, and following them I draw upon the work of the
French philosopher Jean-François Lyotard to clarify the problem I raise here.
Lyotard (1988) uses the term to describe "a case of conflict, between (at least)
two parties, that cannot be equitably resolved for lack of a rule of judgment
applicable to both arguments" (p. xi). Lyotard argues that when a conflict
arises between dominant and subjugated group members, the stories of members of the latter group are incommensurable with those of the former group
and are not taken into full account in decision-making processes, causing the

oppressed to continue suffering wrongs at the hands of those who oppress them. Similarly, Richard Delgado and Jean Stefancic (2001) note that the *différend* "occurs when a concept such as justice acquires conflicting meanings for two groups" (p. 44). In most cases, the dominant system of justice deprives subjugated persons of the chance to express their grievances in terms the system will understand. In such cases, the language that subjugated persons use to express how they have been wronged does not resonate with those who are in authority, and consequently, their versions of truth are not accorded full respect when justice is meted out.

To be clear, critics of Lyotard find his idea of incommensurability troubling and point out that such a take on language disputes is epistemologically suspect and leaves no hope for a resolution of the *différend* (e.g., Burbules, 2000). Departing from Lyotard in this respect, Delgado and Stefancic (2001) frame the *différend* as a dialectic and believe that narrative intervention—that is, allowing those who suffer to tell their stories on their own terms—creates the conditions for a resolution that involves both the oppressed and the oppressor. However, these conditions are predicated on ethical considerations as opposed to epistemological ones. Pessimistically, there is little evidence that the broader white society will follow the lead of people of color or respond to their injuries when it is not in its own interests (Bell, 1995b, 2004). Even in public policy, behind-the-scenes brokered deals that benefit white people often all but guarantee that people of color will make involuntary sacrifices that undermine any small measure of relief they are provided (Bell, 2004). However, as indicated previously, the stories of people of color are hopeful, even when our circumstances are not. Thus, in the concluding section, I bring the discussion together to identify the implications of the analysis provided in this article for addressing the problem of allochronism compromising the education of black students, and for changing the quality of their lives in school and society.

Conclusion

The data and analysis presented in this article illustrate the problem of allochronism in the education of black children and youth and offer critical race ethnography, guided by the voices of those most injured, as a means to address it. With respect to the problem of allochronism, deeply embedded, racially signified normative-evaluative notions about the humanity of black children and youth inform the subjective and objective dimensions of their experiences in schools. In the context of a society that relies heavily on imagery and spin, the critical race analysis provided in this article is a useful tool for clarifying some of the challenges that face educators and researchers who nowadays teach and work in what the social theorist Anthony Giddens (2000) calls a "runaway world." Giddens is referring here to postindustrialism and globalization. It is a world that presents us with limitless social, cultural and economic opportunities. To be clear, though, the opportunities brought about by postindustrialism and globalization are meted out unevenly and, so far, this has reinforced relations of dominance along the lines of region, nationality, race, gender, class, age, language and ability.

In my view, critical race approaches are needed now more than ever for appraising what postindustrialism and globalization mean for the education of black children and youth. As Gidden (2000) explains, the world in which we now live is much more complicated than those of the past because of the proliferation of media and other technologies that allow for the unchecked dissemination of information, images and symbols, including those that reinforce allochronic discourses. To grasp the implications of these technologies for our world, consider that "it took 40 years for radio in the United States to gain an audience of 50 million. The same number was using the personal computers only 15 years after the personal computer was introduced. It needed a mere 4 years, after it was made available, for 50 million Americans to be regularly using the Internet" (Giddens, 2000, p. 30). A critical race perspective is required to unravel the effects that the confluence of postindustrial forces has on shaping identity and perceptions, including those that bear on educational practice, as noted throughout this chapter.

Along these lines, critical race approaches allow us to rethink and reconstruct traditional school policy and practices around the insights of the greatest stakeholders—those who experience the brunt of educational injustice. It is crucial for explicating the assumptions and practices that inform the reproductive nature of urban schools. Critical race theory makes the once invisible visible, as does the analysis provided here. For instance, the allochronism pervasive at the schools described above works dialectically to shape how society conceives black youth and urban schools, and how it responds to them in terms of policy and the curriculum and instruction it imposes on them. Framed this way, restoring coevalness allows black youth access not only to the resources that empower them to eliminate material conditions of inequality but also to the means of production to challenge the print and visual media that figure so prominently in reproducing the allochronic discourses at the heart of their oppression. By explicating these mechanisms, knowledge production informed by critical race theory can readily contribute to educational reforms that position black children and youth as change agents to transform their schools and communities in their best interests and in the better interests of the larger society.

References

Anderson, J. (1988). *The Education of Blacks in the South, 1860–1935*. Chapel Hill: University of North Carolina Press.

Anderson, V. (1995). *Beyond Ontological Blackness: An Essay on African American Religious and Cultural Criticism*. New York: Continuum.

Baldwin, J. (1993 [1979]). If Black English Ain't a Language, Then Tell Me What Is? In D. Gioseffi (ed.), *On Prejudice: A Global Perspective*, 372–375. New York: Anchor.

Bell, D. (1987). *And We Are Not Saved: The Elusive Quest for Racial Justice*. New York: Basic Books.

Bell, D. (1995a). Serving Two Masters: Integration Ideals and Client Interests in School Desegregation Litigation. In R. Delgado (ed.), *Critical Race Theory: The Cutting Edge*, 228–238. Philadelphia: Temple University Press.

Bell, D. (1995b). *Brown v. Board of Education* and the Interest Convergence Dilemma. In K. Crenshaw et al. (eds.), *Critical Race Theory: The Key Writings That Formed the Movement*, 20–29. New York: Routledge.

Bell, D. (1999). The Power of Narrative. *Legal Studies Forum* 23(3): 315–348.

Bell, D. (2004). *Silent Covenants:* Brown v. Board of Education *and the Unfulfilled Hopes for Racial Reform*. New York: Oxford University Press.

Berry, M. and Blassingame, J. (1982). *Long Memory: The Black Experience in America*. New York: Oxford University Press.

Burbules, N. (2000). Lyotard on Wittgenstein: The Différend, Language Games, and Education. In P. Dhillon and P. Standish (eds.), *Lyotard: Just Education*, 36–53. London: Routledge.

Carspecken, P. (1996). *Critical Ethnography in Educational Research: A Theoretical and Practical Guide*. New York: Routledge.

Case, C. (1998). *The Slaughter: An American Atrocity*. Asheville, NC: First Biltmore Corporation.

Casella, R. (2003). Punishing Dangerousness through Preventative Detention: Examining the Institutional Link between Schools and Prisons. Paper presented at "The School to Prison Pipeline: Charting Intervention Strategies of Prevention and Support for Minority Students," a conference sponsored by the Civil Rights Project, Harvard University and Institute on Race and Justice, Northeastern University, Cambridge, MA, May 15–16, 2003.

Clark, S. (1996). *Ready from Within: A First Person Narrative*. Trenton, NJ: Africa World.

Chin, E. (2001). *Purchasing Power: Black Kids and American Consumer Culture*. Minneapolis: University of Minnesota Press.

Collins, P. (1990). *Black Feminist Thought: Knowledge, Consciousness, and the Politics of Empowerment*. New York: Routledge.

Crenshaw, K., Gotanda, N., Peller, G., and Thomas, K. (eds.) (1995). *Critical Race Theory: The Key Writings That Formed the Movement*. New York: Routledge.

Dash, J. (1997). *Daughters of the Dust*. New York: Dutton.

Delgado, R. (1995). *The Rodrigo Chronicles: Conversations about America and Race*. New York: New York University Press.

Delgado, R. (1996). *The Coming Race War? And Other Apocalyptic Tales of America after Affirmative Action and Welfare*. New York: New York University Press.

Delgado, R. and Stefancic, J. (1991). Derrick Bell's Chronicle of the Space Traders: Would the U.S. Sacrifice People of Color If the Price Were Right? *University of Colorado Law Review* 62: 321.

Delgado, R. and Stefancic, J. (2001). *Critical Race Theory: An Introduction*. New York: New York University Press.

Dillard, J. L. (1973). *Black English: Its History and Usage in the United States*. New York: Vintage.

Du Bois, W. E .B. (1903). *The Souls of Black Folk*. New York: Bantam.

Du Bois, W. E. B. (1995). Negro Education. In D. L. Lewis (ed.), *W. E. B. Du Bois: A Reader*, 261–269. New York: Henry Holt.

Du Bois, W. E. B. (1997). *Dusk of Dawn: An Essay toward an Autobiography of a Race Concept*. New Brunswick, NJ: Transaction.

Duncan, G. (1992). The Substance of Things Hoped for: Milwaukee Schools and the Education of Black Children [technical report]. Claremont, CA: Claremont Project VISION, Claremont Graduate School.

Duncan, G. (2000). Race and Human Rights Violations in the United States: Considerations for Human Rights and Moral Educators. *Journal of Moral Education* 29(2): 183–201.

Duncan, G. (2002a). Critical Race Theory and Method: Rendering Race in Ethnographic Research. *Qualitative Inquiry* 8(1): 83–102.

Duncan, G. (2002b). Beyond Love: A Critical Race Ethnography of the Schooling of Adolescent Black Males. *Equity and Excellence in Education* 35(2): 131–143.

Duncan, G. (2004). The Play of Voices: Black Adolescents Constituting the Self and Morality. In V. Siddle Walker and J. Snarey (eds.), *Racing Moral Formation: African American Voices on Care, Justice, and Moral Education*, 38–54. New York: Teachers College Press.

Duncan, G. (forthcoming). Schooling and Inequality in the Post-industrial United States: Toward a Critical Race Ethnography of Time. Ms.

Duncan, G. and Jackson, R. (in press). The Language We Cry in: Black Language Practice at a Post-Desegregated Urban High School. *GSE Perspectives on Urban Education*.

Fabian, J. (2002). *Time and the Other: How Anthropology Makes Its Object*. New York: Columbia University Press.

Farber, D. and Sherry, S. (1995). Telling Stories out of School: An Essay on Legal Narratives. In G. Delgado (ed.), *Critical Race Theory: The Cutting Edge*, 283–292. Philadelphia: Temple University Press.

Ferguson, A. (2000). *Bad Boys: Public Schools in the Making of Black Masculinity*. Ann Arbor: University of Michigan Press.

Freire, A. (2002). Paulo Freire and the Untested Feasibility. In J. Slater et al. (eds.), *The Freirean Legacy: Educating for Social Justice*, 7–14. New York: Peter Lang.

Freire, P. (1995). *Pedagogy of Hope: Reliving the Pedagogy of the Oppressed*. New York: Continuum.

Freire, P. (1996). *Pedagogy of the Oppressed*. New York: Continuum.

Gibran, K. (1926). *Sand and Foam*. New York: Alfred K. Knopf.

Giddens, A. (2000). *Runaway World: How Globalization Is Reshaping Our Lives*. New York: Routledge.

Gundaker, G. (1998). *Signs of Diaspora, Diaspora of signs: Literacies, Creolization, and Vernacular Practice in African America*. New York: Oxford University Press.

Gwaltney, J. (1993). *Drylongso: A Self-portrait of Black America*. New York: New Press.

Hacker, A. (1995). *Two Nations: Black and White, Separate, Hostile, Unequal*. New York: Ballantine.

Haley, A. and X. M. (1965). *The Autobiography of Malcolm X*. New York: Grove.

Hall, G. (1904). *Adolescence: Its Psychology and Its Relations to Physiology, Anthropology, Sex, Crime, Religion, and Education*. 2 vols. New York: D. Appleton.

Hall, E. (1983). *The Dance of Life: The Other Dimension of Time*. New York: Anchor.

Holland, R. (producer and director) (1995). *The Fire This Time: Why Los Angeles Burned* [film]. Available from Rhino Home Video, 10635 Santa Monica Blvd., Los Angeles, CA 90025-4900.

hooks, b. and West, C. (1991). *Breaking Bread: Insurgent Black Intellectual Life*. Boston: South End.

Jones, J. (1981). *Bad Blood: The Tuskegee Syphilis Experiment—a Tragedy of Race and Medicine*. New York: Free Press.

Kemp, A. and Vinson, R. (2000). "Poking Holes in the Sky": Professor James Thaele, American Negroes, and Modernity in 1920s Segregationist South Africa. *African Studies Review* 43(1): 141–160.

Kennedy, R. (1995). Racial Critiques of Legal Academia. In G. Delgado (ed.), *Critical Race Theory: The Cutting Edge*, 316–321. Philadelphia: Temple University Press.

Ladson-Billings, G. and Tate, W. (1995). Toward a Critical Race Theory of Education. *Teachers College Record* 97(1): 47–68.

MacKinnon, C. (1993). *Only Words*. Cambridge, MA: Harvard University Press.

Matsuda, M. (1996). *Where Is Your Body? And Other Essays on Race, Gender, and the Law*. Boston: Beacon Press.

Matthews, D. H. (1998). *Honoring the Ancestors: An African Cultural Interpretation of Black Religion and Literature*. New York: Oxford University Press.

Mills, C. (1997). *The Racial Contract*. Ithaca and London: Cornell University Press.

Morgan, M. (1993). The Africanness of Counterlanguage among Afro-Americans. In S. Mufwene (ed.), *Africanisms in Afro-American Language Varieties*, 423–435. Athens: University of Georgia Press.

Morrison, T. (1993). *Playing in the Dark: Whiteness and the Literary Imagination*. New York: Vintage.

Naylor, G. (1988). *Mama Day*. New York: Vintage.

Noguera, P. (2003). *City Schools and the American Dream: Reclaiming the Promise of Public Education*. New York: Teachers College Press.

Ogbu, J. (2003). *Black American Students in an Affluent Suburb: A Study of Academic Disengagement*. Mahwah, NJ: Lawrence Erlbaum.

Oliver, M. and Shapiro, T. (1995). *Black Wealth/White Wealth: A New Perspective on Racial Inequality*. New York: Routledge.

Patillo-McCoy, M. (1999). *Black Picket Fences: Privilege and Peril among the Black Middle Class*. Chicago: University of Chicago Press.

Posner, R. A. (2000). *Overcoming Law*. Cambridge, MA: Harvard University Press.

Roediger, D. (1991). *The Wages of Whiteness: Race and the Making of the American Working Class*. London and New York: Verso.

Scheurich, J. and Young, M. (1997). Coloring Epistemologies: Are Our Research Epistemologies Racially Biased? *Educational Researcher* 26(4): 4–16.

Shapiro, T. (2004). *The Hidden Costs of Being African American: How Wealth Perpetuates Inequality*. Oxford: Oxford University Press.

Shipler, D. (1998). *A Country of Strangers: Blacks and Whites in America*. New York: Vintage.

Smith, M. (1997). *Mastered by the Clock: Time, Slavery, and Freedom in the American South*. Chapel Hill: University of North Carolina Press.

Turner, L. (1973 [1948]). *Africanisms in the Gullah Dialect*. Ann Arbor: University of Michigan Press.

Vass, W. K. (1979). *The Bantu Speaking Heritage of the United States*. Los Angeles: Center for Afro-American Studies, UCLA.

Washington, B. T. (1989 [1902]). *Up from Slavery: An Autobiography*. New York: Carol.

Watkins, S. (1997). *The Black O: Racism and Redemption in an American Corporate Empire*. Athens: University of Georgia Press.

Watkins, W. (2001). *The White Architects of Black Education: Ideology and Power in America, 1865–1954*. New York: Teachers College Press.

Webb, G. (1998). *Dark Alliance: The CIA, the Contras, and the Crack Cocaine Explosion*. New York: Seven Stories.

Willhelm, S. (1970). *Who Needs the Negro?* Cambridge, MA: Schenkman.

Woodson, C. G. (1919). *The Education of the Negro prior to 1861*. Brooklyn, NY: A and B Books.

Wronka, J. (1994). Human Rights and Social Policy in the United States: An Educational Agenda for the 21st Century. *Journal of Moral Education* 23(3): 261–272.

Young, I. (1990). *Justice and the Politics of Difference*. Princeton, NJ: Princeton University Press.

11
The Fire This Time: Jazz, Research and Critical Race Theory

ADRIENNE D. DIXSON

Jazz is merely the Negro's cry of joy and suffering.

"Lewis" in *The Cry of Jazz*, Bland, Hill, Kennedy and Titus (1959)

I do not mean to be sentimental about suffering—enough is certainly as good as a feast—but people who cannot suffer can never grow up, can never discover who they are. That man who is forced each day to snatch his manhood, his identity, out of the fire of human cruelty that rages to destroy it knows, if he survives his effort, and even if he does not survive it, something about himself and human life that no school on earth—and, indeed, no church—can teach. He achieves his own authority, and that is unshakeable.

James Baldwin, *The Fire Next Time* (1963)

My primary jazz professor, the clarinetist Alvin Batiste, spoke frequently about the contradiction in traditional conceptions of Western music theory between what is "correct" theoretically and what is "right" musically. Thus, the task of the jazz musician is not only to understand music theory but also to know when to play music "right." This notion of being "correct" and "right" has been key as I conceptualize a jazz methodology, particularly in light of how a "racial discourse and an ethnic epistemology" might inform my work (Ladson-Billings, 2000). For example, designing research questions, selecting or locating a site for research, identifying participants and gaining access are details that require deliberate thought. These decisions, like the knowledge the research will generate, are not made haphazardly and without consideration of their impact on the field, stakeholders and participants. These ideas are related to the idea of ensemble playing and improvisation. Playing together in front of a live audience influences the creative process differently than playing in a recording studio or an empty rehearsal hall. In qualitative research, the context not only affects the data collection process but also adds to the understanding of the research question. For example, understanding the ways in which "urban" students experience middle school is in many ways contingent on where their school is located. The urban context is meaningful, but only if we unpack what and who constitutes urbanness (Popkewitz, 1998). How does schooling—physically and psychologically—compare with what students experience in their home communities? Furthermore, understanding how language is used at both the meta (body language, gesticulations, personal interactions) and the micro levels (vocabulary, syntax, grammar) is as important as the aesthetic value of the physical location in understanding the context within which students live and attend school. Thus, how the researcher, or "band leader," and the participant, or "band member," understands their relationship greatly influences the music they create. This begs the following questions: (1) What does research look like when the researcher sees herself as part of the community in which she collects data? (2) What can she learn when she is able to ask the intimate, "hard" questions about race and racism? (3) What insight can she bring to the data analysis when, in some ways, she understands that answering those questions is difficult, but necessary?

The jazz musician Art Blakey (personal communication, 1984) generally closed his concerts by saying that music comes "from the Creator, through the musician, to the audience." Blakey suggested that music is in part a manifestation not only of the musician's deeply spiritual relationship with "the Creator" but also of the musician's relationship with the audience. The music could not happen without those key relationships. Similarly, jazz musicians' relationships with one another greatly influence the music they create. Miles Davis felt that having John Coltrane in his band opened up his senses of harmony and improvisation in ways that other musicians did not (Dibb Directions, 2001).

In this chapter, I suggest that a jazz methodology (Dixson, 2005), from an epistemological perspective, might be useful for examining educational issues utilizing a critical race theory (CRT) theoretical and analytical lens. Thus, for this project, I will be discussing a jazz methodology not as a method of collecting data but as an epistemic research complement to the overall project of CRT. In addition, this discussion will draw upon the philosopher Charles Mills's scholarship on alternative epistemologies, Du Bois's (1995 [1903]) notion of double consciousness and Collins's (2000 [1990]) black feminist thought. Drawing on the CRT tenet of storytelling, I will use a semi-fictional narrative to illustrate and argue for the need for this epistemological stance—CRT and jazz methodology—which can help uncover the insidious ways race and racism manifest in "everyday" schooling.

CRT, Jazz and Alternative Epistemologies

> Like jazz music, critical race theory tends "to make the familiar strange and the strange familiar."

John O. Calmore (1999)

The legal scholar John O. Calmore (1992) suggests that jazz is an appropriate metaphor for the aims and goals of critical race theory. He argues that just as jazz as an aesthetic form of resistance was born out of the experiences of black people, so was CRT, an oppositional discourse that critiques and examines the failures of U.S. jurisprudence to redress racism. As scholars both within and outside the legal field attempt to utilize CRT to examine issues and instances of racism, it becomes increasingly important, particularly for scholars who engage in empirical research, to locate a research methodology that can aid in that project. A jazz methodology in the service of CRT brings to fruition "a desire not merely to understand the vexed bond between law and racial power but to change it" (Crenshaw, Gotanda, Peller and Thomas, 1995, p. xiii). Said differently, for CRT scholars in education, a jazz methodology brings to fruition a desire not merely to understand the vexed bond between educational policy and racial power but to change it. Indeed, Calmore offers the following rationale for the jazz–CRT relationship:

> To appreciate both jazz and critical race theory, one must be open and intellectually curious in ways that Eurocentric, assimilationist dictates frustrate. One certainly cannot assume that one has a conceptual corner on the market of "truth," "value," and "reason." Playing against this tendency, jazz musicians are strong-willed and committed to their art in unshakable ways. Over the century, jazz has persisted against the odds and despite popular apathy, misunderstandings, and harsh critique. Like critical race theory, people have always messed with it without even getting it. In many ways jazz and critical race theory are coherent and not at the same time. As Ornette Coleman observes, "you can be in unison without being in unison." (Calmore, 1999, p. 1613)

It is important to note that in offering jazz as a research methodology, I do so drawing on Harding's (1987) distinction between research methodology and research methods. For Harding, the difference between methodology and methods is a matter of theory and pragmatics. That is, methodology is comprised of the theory and analysis that undergird research. Methods, on the other hand, are the ways in which data are collected.

What Is This Thing Called Jazz?

Jazz, as both a musical and cultural concept, can be a powerful way to conceptualize research which examines the dynamics of race and racism. I would argue that most projects that aim critically to examine the ways in which race and racism manifest in educational settings are inherently political, particularly if the goal is to disrupt marginalizing educational practices and policies. Given the development of jazz as an aesthetic expression of protest and opposition, specifically for African Americans, we can think of jazz as always already political. It is important to note that jazz, like most protest genres—especially those developed and nurtured within the African American community—has been coopted and used to advance a capitalist, conservative, apolitical agenda (Calmore, 1999). Examples are replete from jazz, to spoken word to hip-hop.

Most music historians and critics agree that jazz music is a major contribution to the American aesthetic. Many argue that jazz is one of the few truly American art forms (Giddins, 1998). That this music, jazz, is American and is a contribution from African Americans is also significant, not merely because African Americans created the music but particularly because of the experiences of African Americans in the United States, from which the music emerged (Jones, 1999 [1963]; Murray, 2000 [1976]). Jazz music began out of African Americans' resistance to oppression and the struggle for equality. The music epitomizes the political will of black people who toiled for liberation (Jones, 1999 [1963]; Murray, 2000 [1976]). One of the foundations of jazz is the blues. It is beyond the scope of this chapter to give a history of jazz and blues; suffice it to say, the blues is more than just melancholy music. The distinctive harmonic and melodic elements of the blues grew out of the overall aesthetic expression of black people, and jazz is one more outgrowth of that expression. In addition, as a genre of black music, jazz developed or evolved more rapidly and with more complexity than the blues. This is not to disparage blues music or blues musicians. As a form of music, jazz has taken on more complex harmonic, rhythmic and melodic elements than the blues and has developed the elements of the blues more complexly. However, it is important to note the foundation that the blues laid for the development of jazz; many musicians, music critics and historians believe that, without that harmonic and melodic foundation, jazz music would not exist. The literary critic Albert Murray wrote one of the first books to examine the blues as an epistemic expression of blackness, *Stomping the Blues*. Murray (2000 [1976]) asserted that as art, the blues idiom is "the process by which raw experience is stylized into aesthetic statement" (p. v). I would submit that for those of us engaged in examining the nuances of racism and oppression and people's resistance to both, Murray's conception of the blues idiom might also be a helpful way to conceptualize our research, our participants, and ourselves. Furthermore, this look at the blues idiom offers an aesthetic epistemology that may be helpful as we consider jazz methodology and CRT. In addition to the space that the blues idiom offers as an aesthetic epistemology, Charles Mills's (1998) "alternative epistemologies" thesis supports CRT and jazz in research, particularly in relation to suggesting that "outsider" groups have ways of knowing that are shaped in large part by their experiences and positionality within a racialized and gendered U.S. context.

Alternative Epistemologies

Hence, a major theme of Critical Race Theory reflects the colored intellectual's persistent battle to avoid being rendered inauthentic by the pressures of adapting to the white world and, instead, to take an oppositional stance by relying on one's true existential life, which is rooted in a world of color even though not stuck there.

Calmore (1992, p. 2170)

In his chapter "Alternative Epistemologies" from his book *Blackness Visible: Essays on Philosophy and Race* (1998), the philosopher Charles Mills argues for "alternative epistemologies." Mills states that given the limitation and what some describe as the racist and sexist orientation or foundation of "traditional" epistemologies, alternative epistemologies are necessary; dominant perspectives are inadequate to explain how we know and understand the world (Mills, 1998, p. 21). Heretofore, the "knower" has been framed against a Cartesian notion of the abstract individual, disembodied from emotions in the pursuit of "universal knowledge." Mills suggests, however, that the "knower" is not an isolated individual divested of knowledge; rather, what we know, we know in relation to the social context in which we experience that knowledge. He offers a justification for alternative epistemologies, that he argues can benefit from social causation (p. 26). Moreover, white feminist philosophers have challenged the notion of the "autonomous epistemic agent" (Code, 1987). Code offers the "community of knowers" as an alternative to the autonomous agent:

To a much greater extent than the examples commonly taken to illustrate epistemological points might lead one to believe, people are dependent, at a fundamental level, upon other people ... for what they, often rightly, claim to know ... . Far from being autonomous in the senses discussed above, knowledge is an interpersonal product that requires communal standards of affirmation, correction, and denial for its very existence. (as cited in Mills, p. 33, 1998)

Thus, for Code and others arguing for alternative epistemologies, the ability to know comes not in isolation from others but in communion with others. For the researcher committed to examining the racialized impact of phenomena, issues and events, among other things, this notion of social causation, or "knowing in community," is important and supports the premise of jazz methodology. That is, the underlying principle of the jazz methodology is the notion that knowledge construction, like jazz, is communal, dynamic and synergistic. Moreover, this notion of social causation supports the notion that acts of racism and oppression are not isolated. That is, racist acts generally occur within a particular social context in which some people are powerful and others are vulnerable. Furthermore, the way in which marginalized groups make sense of society is through the common experiences of oppression they share through storytelling, testifyin', protest and aesthetic genres (Collins, 2000; Dixson and Rousseau, 2005).

Like CRT's critique of liberalism, Mills cautions against reductionist moves toward a relativistic pluralism which suggests that all perspectives are different and therefore valid. Mills (1998, p. 29) argues that part of what marginalizes alternative epistemologies is the "background hegemonic ideologies" that sustain interpretations of events and denigrate others.

Du Bois and Double Consciousness

Du Bois's (1995 [1903]) notion of double consciousness seems appropriate in relation to the marginal spaces within which members of liminal groups find themselves. Du Bois describes double consciousness thus:

> After the Egyptian and Indian, the Greek and Roman, the Teuton and Mongolian, the Negro is a sort of seventh son, born with a veil, and gifted with second-sight in this American world,—a world which yields him no true self-consciousness, but only lets him see himself through the revelation of the other world. It is a peculiar sensation, this double-consciousness, this sense of always looking at one's self through the eyes of others, of measuring one's soul by the tape of a world that looks on in amused contempt and pity. One ever feels his twoness—an American, a Negro; two warring souls, two thoughts, two unreconciled strivings; two warring ideals in one dark body, whose dogged strength alone keeps it from being torn asunder. ... The history of the American Negro is the history of this strife—this longing to attain self-conscious manhood, to merge his double self into a better and truer self. (p. 45)

In his *University of Miami Law Review* article "Doubting Doubleness, and All That Jazz: Establishment Critiques of Outsider Innovations in Music and Legal Thought" (1997), the legal scholar Peter Margulies contends that "outsider innovators," or the CRT scholars in legal scholarship, had introduced an innovation in legal writing which sought to elucidate the centrality of race and racism in U.S. society in general, and specifically the role that U.S. jurisprudence has played in reifying race and supported racial differences and inequity. Utilizing Du Bois's notion of double consciousness, or what he calls "doubleness," Margulies (1997) identifies three ways in which "outsider innovators have responded to the nearly impenetrable walls of the legal field:

> Doubleness leads outsider innovators to diverge from three dichotomies which are central to the High Modernist analysis...dichotomy of theory versus experience...the elite versus the vernacular ... alienation versus redemption. In each case, High Modernists have sought to maintain dichotomies already bridged by outsider innovators; the High Modernists have monitored boundaries, which outsider innovators have crossed. (Margulies, 1997, p. 1161)

Thus, for both Du Bois and Margulies, this "doubleness" comes with a set of challenges and opportunities. On one hand, the challenge is finding legitimacy within structures and spaces that place one a priori on the margins. On the other hand, being on the periphery allows one to see the limitations, flaws, weaknesses and contradictions of spaces and structures that appear transparent and accessible, but are not. Margulies (1997), making a connection to the relationship between jazz and CRT, offers Duke Ellington and his music an example of the aesthetic manifestation of double consciousness:

> For outsider innovators, form is never merely formal. Instead, it is always rich in metaphors for multiple consciousness. Ellington's view of dissonance illustrates how jazz defies High Modernist paradigms. For High Modernists, dissonance was a crucial element in a hermetic conception of form—an ascetic manifesto of independence from traditional conceptions of tonality. Ellington, in contrast, treated dissonance not as hermetically formal, but instead as a representation of the African-American experience. He noted that, "dissonance is our way of life in America. We are something apart, yet an integral part." Ellington used dissonance to embody that tension between marginalization and belonging which Du Bois defined as double consciousness. (Margulies, 1997, p. 1163)

This notion of dissonance becomes key for the researcher whose work resides within a CRT framework utilizing a jazz methodology. Despite the popularly held belief that racism and racist acts are only those perpetrated by hood-wearing Klansmen or drunken "frat boys" spray-painting racial epithets, CRT maintains that racism is perpetuated subtly and discursively in the ways in which notions of behavior, decorum, intelligence, aptitude, ability, femininity, masculinity and sexuality (among other characteristics) are framed against a normative and ubiquitous whiteness. Thus, the dissonance is in challenging this normative whiteness that purports to be fair, neutral, unbiased and colorblind. Moreover, uncovering the "unintentional" acts of racism that are no less virulent for their subtlety causes a great deal of dissonance, particularly in a political climate premised on and invested in colorblindness as a condition for equal opportunity, meritocracy, rugged individualism and dogged religiosity. While both Mills's notion of alternative epistemologies and Du Bois's double consciousness speak to the experience of "blacks," the obvious limitation, from my perspective, is that both collapse the experiences of black men and black women into a seemingly single experience unmediated by gender, class, sexual orientation and other significant social identities. Thus, although I have argued for a way of conceptualizing research as drawn significantly on a cultural aesthetic way of knowing, it is important that I address my positionality as a woman of color, and specifically as an African American woman. Moreover, as I conceptualize the jazz methodology, I do so fully informed by black feminist theories more generally (Collins, 2000 [1990]; Ladson-Billings, 2000).

Black Feminist Thought

> Only the BLACK WOMAN can say "when and where I enter, in the quiet, undisputed dignity of my womanhood, without violence and without suing or special patronage, then and there the whole ... race enters with me." —Anna Julia Cooper, *A Voice from the South by a Black Woman from the South* (1988 [1892])

In her groundbreaking text *Black Feminist Thought* (2000 [1990]), the sociologist Patricia Hill Collins suggests that black women researchers look for ways to explore the lives, experiences and praxis of other black women as a way to challenge "traditional" research methodologies and epistemologies that have historically pathologized our behaviors or rendered us invisible. Collins also asserts that the ways in which both the African American female researcher and participant determine or validate what is truthful or valid can differ from "realist discourses on epistemology" (Denzin, 1997, p. 70). In particular, within the African American community—and, Collins argues, for African American women specifically—the use of narrative, story, or "testifyin'," wherein one can verify information through personal experience, has been a traditionally valid form of determining truth. Moreover, for Collins and similarly for Sara Lawrence-Lightfoot, knowledge is validated through "voice," "speaking" and "listening" (Collins, 2000 [1990]; Lawrence-Lightfoot and Davis, 1997).

By the same token, Gloria Ladson-Billings (2000) suggests that the field of qualitative research be open to epistemological perspectives, particularly those that are "multiply informed and multiply jeopardized" by race, class, gender, sexuality and other aspects of difference (p. 273). This is not to say that scholars who are situated within marginalized or liminal groups are "burdened" by their race, class, gender or sexuality; rather, these positionalities provide a perspective on both the margin and the center that can "reveal the ways that the dominant perspectives distort the realities of the other in an effort to maintain power relations that continue to disadvantage those who are locked out of the mainstream" (Ladson-Billings, 2000, p. 263). With respect to CRT and jazz, Collins, Lawrence-Lightfoot and Ladson-Billings provide yet another "angle of vision" that takes into account the ways in which gender—among other aspects of difference—helps to elucidate the complexity of race.

When the Wolves Cry Wolf

"He said he was going to hurt her and it scared me!" said Gifted White Boy (GWB), a nine-year-old whom adults at his school describe as "very aware of issues and current events" and "very mature in his view points." GWB came inside from the playground and told his teacher that Any Black Boy (ABB), ten years old, said he was going to hurt Innocent White Girl (IWG). Teachers describe ABB as "impulsive." Mr. Liberal, ABB's teacher, describes him as his "main discipline problem" but says he is also an "articulate" and "capable student" who is "gifted in music."

After hearing GWB's story, his teacher, Miss Bystander, tells Mr. Liberal about the playground incident. Mr. Liberal relays the story to Ms. Colorblind, the school's principal. Ms. Colorblind investigates the story before she talks to ABB. She talks to GWB and two of his friends with whom he shared the story when he came inside from the playground. Satisfied with what the boys have told her, Ms. Colorblind decides that ABB needs to be taught that threatening to kill someone is unacceptable and assigns him to an in-school suspension.

Ms. Colorblind calls over the intercom for ABB to come to the office. ABB is unaware that he has done something wrong, and amid a chorus of "Ooh, ABB what did you do? You're in trouble!" that rings out from his classmates, he tells Mr. Liberal that he is scared. Mr. Liberal tells ABB to "go and deal with it. Make it better." ABB is confused. What did he do?

As he enters the office, ABB sees GWB and his two friends, Confused and Concerned, standing in the waiting area. ABB is still confused himself. What could he have done to Confused and Concerned? He didn't even see them this morning, because his mother drove him to school and he had just enough time to talk to GWB before they had to line up and go inside. None of the boys speaks to him, and GWB gives him an apologetic look. Ms. Colorblind directs ABB into her office and tells him that he will serve an in-school suspension for threatening to kill IWG. ABB is again confused and tells Ms. Colorblind that he did not make such a threat. Ms. Colorblind tells him that he is not being honest and that GWB told her about what happened on the playground. She asks ABB if he had heard about Columbine. He says that he had. She reminds him that making threats is not good, especially since the shootings in Columbine and more recently in California. Again, ABB tells Ms. Colorblind that he didn't make a threat and that GWB must have misunderstood him. Ms. Colorblind tells ABB that he is not being honest, and that his threat scared GWB very much, and that she was proud of GWB for being brave enough to report it to her. Ms. Colorblind tells ABB that she must call his mother to inform her that he will serve an in-school suspension for making a threat against another student. ABB begins to cry. Both of his parents are educators and expect that he and his brother will behave well in school, follow the rules, and be respectful to the teachers. His mother will not be happy that Ms. Colorblind is calling her and that he is going to have an in-school suspension. He is going to be in trouble.

Ms. Colorblind calls ABB's mother, Ms. Black Parent (BP), to inform her of her son's in-school suspension. In the background, Ms. BP hears her son crying. Not accustomed to getting calls from the school about behavior problems, initially she thought that he was injured. In fact, until today's phone call, Ms. BP has not had much communication from the school regarding ABB and behavior problems. There was one incident with this girl, IWG, but it turned out that both ABB and IWG and one of ABB's friends were bothering each other in computer class. Initially, ABB's teacher and the principal were going to give ABB an in-school suspension because IWG accused him of drawing uncomplimentary pictures of her in computer class. It turned out, however, that IWG had initiated the game, and rather than suspend IWG for starting the incident, they decided not to suspend ABB. At any rate, that was an isolated incident, and generally, her conversations with ABB's teacher, Mr. Liberal, centered on ABB submitting his homework on time. Other than that, Mr. Liberal talked about how much he enjoyed having ABB in his class. ABB is a bit of an "old soul" who likes 1970s funk, the music of Mr. Liberal's era. According to Mr. Liberal, he was pleased to have a student who enjoyed Earth, Wind and Fire as much as he.

Focused on her son's crying, Ms. BP doesn't hear Ms. Colorblind's explanation for her call and immediately asks to speak to ABB. Ms. Colorblind continues with her explanation for the call. During Ms. Colorblind's explanation, Ms. BP asks two more times to speak to her son, who is crying loudly, almost wailing. He is obviously quite upset. Ms. Colorblind continues with her story before she allows Ms. BP to speak to her son. Ms. Colorblind states that before school that morning, GWB and ABB were on the playground talking. ABB saw IWG playing a game and asked GWB rhetorically, "Why does she always play that stupid game?" GWB responds, "Why is IWG afraid of you? Are you going to hurt her or something?" According to GWB, ABB made a gesture with his finger as if he was pointing a gun and pulling the trigger and said, "I might." At that point, GWB became afraid that ABB was going to hurt IWG and reported it to his teacher. GWB had just heard about shootings at a school in California, and his parents had told him to report anything he heard that could be a potential problem, no matter how innocent it might seem. Ms. BP explains to Ms. Colorblind that the in-school suspension seems inappropriate for a case of one child's word against another. Ms. Colorblind explains that GWB was obviously upset, and therefore the event must have happened as he reported it. ABB's version is similar, with the exception that in answering GWB's question about why IWG is afraid of him, he shrugged his shoulders because he didn't understand the nature of GWB's question. Why would he ask him about IWG being afraid of him and whether he was going to hurt her?

Ms. BP comes to the school to talk with Ms. Colorblind and clarify the reason for the in-school suspension. Ms. BP explains to Ms. Colorblind that she does not agree with the in-school suspension because GWB and ABB disagree about the nature and content of the discussion. She asks for more than just GWB's word as justification for a suspension. Ms. Colorblind then states that ABB has a "history of harassing" IWG and has been sent to her office a couple of times for "gun play." Ms. BP is surprised because she is unaware of any such incidents. Neither Ms. Colorblind nor Mr. Liberal has ever called her to discuss these incidents. She questions the validity of this "history" Ms. Colorblind describes, and after a lengthy conversation with Ms. Colorblind decides that she should transfer her son to another school. That same day, she transfers ABB to another school in their neighborhood. When Ms. BP comes to the new school to register ABB, Ms. Insightful, the principal, calls her into her office to inform her that Ms. Colorblind called to give her a "heads up." Ms. BP explains the discrepancy between GWB's and ABB's stories and her feeling that ABB would not be treated fairly at his present school. Ms. Colorblind apparently had not only shared the incident with GWB's two friends but also had gone to GWB's classroom and spoken to his entire class, all of whom were unaware that anything had happened on the playground. Ms. Colorblind wanted to make sure that all the students felt safe and knew that ABB was being punished for making threats against another student. She wanted them to know that such behavior would not be tolerated at the school and that students should feel safe to come to her if they thought another student was going to harm someone. Ms. BP is concerned that ABB will be labeled as violent and that Ms. Colorblind has not been fair to him. From Ms. BP's perspective, Ms. Colorblind's phone call to the new principal is confirmation that she intends to harm ABB's character. Ms. Insightful shares that she, too, thinks the phone call and the information Ms. Colorblind shared with her are inappropriate. She assures Ms. BP that ABB will have every opportunity for a fresh start at her school. Ms. BP decides, however, that she needs to file a discrimination complaint against Ms. Colorblind.

Ms. BP filed her complaint through the school district's Equity and Diversity Office, and an investigation ensued. The school district hired an "outside, independent" investigator. Ms. BP questioned the district on how they selected the investigator and whether he could truly be independent, given that he was retained and paid by the district. However, as a graduate student, Ms. BP could not afford to retain an attorney on her own and put her confidence in the investigator. The investigator interviewed Ms. BP, her father, several women who had provided child care for Ms. BP, and parents of ABB's friends. The investigator also interviewed all the teachers involved, including Ms. Colorblind. He did not interview any of the children. All of the parents were concerned that participating in the interviews with the lawyer would make them feel as if they had done something wrong. Ms. BP was particularly concerned that speaking with an attorney hired by the school district would confirm that ABB had done something criminal. She agreed to allow the investigator to speak to him only if she could be present. The investigator would not agree to that condition, so he never spoke to ABB.

The conclusion of the investigator's report said that although Ms. Colorblind had made unwise decisions, had at times fabricated information, and had not followed district procedure with respect to disciplinary matters, he found no evidence of discrimination. Using the precedents of *McDonnell Douglas v. Green* and *Texas Department of Community Affairs v. Burdine*, or the McDonnell Douglas/Burdine paradigm, as a test for discrimination and *St. Mary's v. Hicks* for the relief for the respondent, he found that although the complainant, Ms. BP, made a prima facie case for discrimination, Burdine allows respondents to prevail if they articulate a "legitimate non-discriminatory reason" for their actions. Under *St. Mary's v. Hicks*, the burden is on the complainant to demonstrate that the "legitimate non-discriminatory reason" is a pretext for the real reason, which is discrimination. Rather, he found that Ms. Colorblind was unaware of proper district procedures on how to handle and document disciplinary actions. He recommended that she get training to handle disciplinary paperwork correctly, apply discipline evenhandedly and in assess risk for violence. Moreover, he recommended that "diversity training" be required for Ms. Colorblind and focused specifically on working with African American children and their parents. He also recommended that she be trained in equal rights laws. He offered the following to explain dismissal of Ms. BP's racial discrimination complaint:

> Ms. BP was also angry for reasons for which Ms. Colorblind became the lightning rod. They are reasons of race; unresolved and with which society and school districts in particular have been grappling for years. They are part of a continuing unresolved drama played out in various arenas *and fueled by misperceptions on both sides.* ... Ms. BP used the incident with GWB to draw her own line in the sand and to send her message of, "Enough!" To Ms. Colorblind's dismay, being new to [the school district] she was not only the lightning rod *for Ms. BP's hostility, but did not understand the message, which Ms. BP sought to convey and did not understand where Ms. BP was coming from.* When Ms. BP accused her of treating ABB unfairly and later told her that she "shouldn't be 'criminalizing' children of color," *Ms. Colorblind was mortified. She could not fathom* how that particular incident (taken in isolation) or her actions *could be viewed in such a light,* and she was a loss to explain to herself or to others why Ms. BP *had reacted so strongly.* In the past, Ms. BP had always been a *cooperative, supportive* parent when interacting with

school authorities. Each of the teachers with whom she had interacted ... describe her as *cordial, cooperative and supportive*. ABB's teacher, Mr. Liberal, described his relationship with and interactions with Ms. BP as *"polite"* and *"supportive"* [emphasis mine].

Mr. Liberal called Ms. BP at home to try and persuade her to keep ABB at his school. During the conversation, he shares several stories where ABB had misbehaved in his classroom. Ms. BP asked him why he never contacted her about the incidents. He explained after one incident when ABB was "in trouble," he informed ABB that he was going to call home. ABB began crying and according to Mr. Liberal, said, "Oh, man, I'm going to get in trouble." Mr. Liberal decided to handle things on his own from that point on *because he was afraid that he would be putting ABB in more harm than his misbehaviors were worth.* [emphasis mine].

Through this story, I demonstrate the discursive ways in which people of color are cast as deviant and violent and how those discursive practices help to justify inequity and discrimination. I offer the story to illustrate how particular epistemological stances shape the racialized reality of schooling. Consider the teachers' differing descriptions of the two boys, "Gifted White Boy" and "Any Black Boy." Teachers described GWB as "mature" and "aware of current events" and ABB as "impulsive" and a "discipline problem," although one teacher acknowledges that he is "articulate" and "gifted in music." The absence of the adjective "articulate" for GWB is curious: it suggests that given his "maturity," we should assume that he is articulate. Furthermore, given his awareness of current events, his perspective on the events that transpired on the playground was unimpeachable. ABB, on the other hand, because he was cast as "impulsive," was guilty of threatening to kill the "innocent" young white girl despite the fact that no one close to him knew him to be violent. Thus, unless we accept that ABB has multiple personalities, someone's "reality" is inaccurate. Furthermore, given that both descriptions are so radically different, it would seem impossible for them to coexist. Moreover, given the radically different characterizations of ABB, one question that emerges is: If we accept that ABB has a school persona and a home persona that are quite different from each other, what are the conditions within the school that would encourage or enable a seemingly peaceful child to turn into a violent predator? A jazz methodology situated within a CRT project would examine a school environment that casts African American students as violent predators when they do not display this type of behavior within their home communities.

This story also illustrates Mills's (1998) notion that the perspectives of the dominant group are illusory and hegemonic. These perspectives frame reality and mask the racist and sexist practices that oppress and punish children and their families. Thus, GWB, Mr. Liberal and Ms. Colorblind held a common perspective on ABB that constructed him as violent, impulsive and a discipline problem capable of making deadly threats against an innocent white female student. This contemporary scenario plays dangerously on the fears of whites during the early twentieth century, that cast black men as barbaric predators on young white women. Despite this being based in large part on irrational and unfounded fears, hundreds of black men, young and old, were imprisoned and even lynched for the mere accusation of harming a white woman. In the modern era, especially in schools, young black men are not literally lynched, but far too many are suspended, expelled and otherwise disciplined based largely on mere accusations of impropriety.

Finally, I offer this story to demonstrate the limitations of racial discrimination law that allow for systematic and clandestine racial bonding (in the case of Mr. Liberal, Ms. Colorblind and GWB) masked as "racial naïvete." Ms. Colorblind's extreme response to an unfounded accusation was dismissed as her lack of awareness of the district's discipline code. This seems curious since Ms. Colorblind, although new to the district, had been a principal for nearly 20 years. It seems reasonable that although there is some variation in how school districts handle discipline issues, there is a modicum of common sense when it comes to impeaching a student's character. Furthermore, the investigator failed to consider the fact that most of Ms. Colorblind's experience had been in a rural, monocultural, monoracial school district. By her own admission, Ms. Colorblind had no experience working with students and families of color and was concerned about working in an urban school district. Thus, it is very likely that Ms. Colorblind held stereotypic views of not only ABB but also his mother and perhaps other African American students. Not only was ABB working against the identity that his teacher and GWB had constructed of him, he was also working against the image of African American males Ms. Colorblind held based in large part on her lack of experience working with families and children of color.

The burden placed on complainants by *St. Mary's v. Hicks* is compounded when the pretext is nuanced, subtle and masked by unsubstantiated "histories of behavior." This story further illustrates the need for a way to examine race from an epistemological stance that can account for and critique the discursive practices that justify oppressive and inequitable treatment. Mills (1998) suggests that alternative epistemologies provide an "inversion of perspective" that speaks to and against the experiences of "hegemonic groups." These experiences, states Mills, "characteristically foster illusory perceptions of society's functioning" (1998, p. 28). Thus, the value of alternative epistemologies is that they provide this "inversion of perspective" that illuminates the limitations of society with respect to the experiences and perspectives of people of color and others who may be marginalized. According to Mills, "Subordinate groups characteristically have experiences that (at least potentially) give rise to more adequate conceptualizations" (1998, p.28). However, the challenge for CRT scholars, regardless of discipline or methodology, is finding a forum that will legitimize or at the very least give an audience to these "inverted perspectives."

Finally, it is important to note that this story is a semi-fictionalized rendering of an actual event. ABB, while named as an allegorical character, sadly represents what often happens daily to young African American males. In my own history, my sons have been accused of some form of violence against young white female students at their schools. Fortunately for my oldest son, he was exonerated when the young white girl who accused him of hitting her confessed to lying and identified the young white male who actually hit her. Sadly, before her confession, the principal threatened to suspend my son for five days despite the fact that my son maintained his innocence. The young girl's parents made threats to call the police and have my son arrested for assault. One mother followed my son home from school and yelled obscenities at him; he was only ten years old. His school was located in an upscale neighborhood of homes worth nearly a million dollars. When the young girl finally confessed that she had lied, she gave no reason for doing so. Her "punishment" was to write a letter of apology to my son and me. When I explained to the principal that I thought she should be suspended and likened her behavior to a modern-day lynching, the principal told me that I was being emotional and blowing the incident out of proportion. Unfortunately, my younger son's accuser, GWB, never admitted that he lied. I decided to remove him from that school. Indeed, we had our own "history of behavior" that proved for our family that the school was a psychologically unsafe space for my sons.

CRT, Jazz Methodology and Research

In a jazz methodology situated within this idea of a "racial discourse and an ethnic epistemology," the relationship between the researcher and participant is vital (Ladson-Billings, 2000). Moreover, given the decidedly political intent of a jazz methodology, equitable relationships between the two must be sought. The researcher must see herself as part of and invested in the community in which she is conducting research. It is more than just an opportunity to learn something new. For example, I was invited by a local school district to examine one of their middle schools. This is a relatively large urban school district that several years ago dedicated two schools to be exemplary urban schools. Unfortunately, they have not lived up to their potential. The middle and high school in particular are plagued by high absenteeism, low scores on state standardized tests, student apathy, frustrated teachers, little or no parental involvement and high teacher turnover. In most respects, these schools are not exemplary but stereotypical urban schools.

My invitation to conduct research in the middle school was preceded by the director's interest in professional development opportunities for the teachers on culturally relevant pedagogy. In my first meeting with the director of the urban academies, Dr. Johnson (a pseudonym), we spoke at length about our perspectives on pedagogy, and in particular, pedagogical approaches that might be effective with African American students. From that meeting, the director invited me to accompany her as she did "walk-throughs" of the urban academies, ("Walk-throughs" are the district's formal observational structures for monitoring and evaluating schools, during which observers visit classrooms looking for specific things like time on task, student engagement, classroom management, or teacher's use of the district curriculum.)

Over several months, we had begun to develop a relationship. Through our debriefing sessions after the walk-throughs, we discovered that we shared similar beliefs about the importance of culture and its relationship to pedagogy. Interestingly, her dissertation research had examined the impact of spirituality on the pedagogical beliefs of African American women teachers. This was another point of convergence for us: my dissertation research examined the ways in which the nexus of race, class and gender identities informed the pedagogical practices and philosophies of African American women teachers. These convergences in our pedagogical beliefs, among others, provided a foundation for our relationship.

Holding similar beliefs is certainly not a prerequisite for conducting research, but I would argue that my gaining access is largely attributable to the fact that the director felt comfortable with me. It is important to note that access to the site is not limited to those researchers with whom the director feels a connection, nor is that the only way one can gain access. On the contrary, a number of scholars in the district in which I am conducting research routinely engage in research at request of the district and through their own ingenuity. However, I would argue that the quality of the research is significantly influenced by the relationship between the researcher and the participants. I want to underscore the importance of developing meaningful relationships within particular communities. Given that the tenets of CRT are first and foremost about social change, from my perspective it is essential that CRT researchers take seriously the importance of developing meaningful, reciprocal relationships within the communities in which they do research.

The questions that frame the middle school project came out of my conversations with the director, our observations of the schools and informal conversations with students and teachers. In a sense, we co-constructed the questions: although I had an intellectual interest in the project, I recognized that it must serve the needs of the participants. The middle school project focused on African American students and their academic and social engagement or lack thereof within a particular middle school initially designed to be an exemplary urban school. Asking questions for the sake of asking questions, or asking questions whose answers will not help the participants, is contradictory to a project premised within a CRT framework and a jazz methodology. In light of the racial realism premise of CRT and the fact that schools are a microcosm of U.S. society, the research questions examine the role of race and racism in shaping students' experiences in and perceptions of middle school. Ultimately, the goal of this project is to imagine and enact ways to "reform" urban middle schools to meet the needs of the students they serve. The promise of this project is that these reforms will be organic rather than imposed on the students and their families by the school district, the state or a national association that a posture of speaking for "all" middle school students. Additionally, the project was premised on the CRT notion that scholarship must work toward social change and liberation. In this regard, we also wanted to pay attention to the potential barriers to student engagement with school.

Conclusion

> Such being the nature of the creative process, the most fundamental prerequisite for mediating between the work of art and the audience, spectators or readers, as the case may be, is not reverence for the so-called classics but rather an understanding of what is being stylized plus an accurate insight in to how it is being stylized. Each master work of art, it must be remembered, is always first of all a comprehensive synthesis of all the aspects of its idiom. Thus to ignore its idiomatic roots is to miss the essential nature of its statement, and art is nothing if not stylized statement. (Murray, 2000 [1976], p. 196)

In this chapter I have argued for a jazz methodology in the service of critical race theory. I premise the notion of jazz as a methodology in part on Mills's (1998) notion of "alternative epistemologies," Du Bois' double consciousness and black feminist thought (Collins, 2000 [1990]). I used a story to illustrate the ways in which racial naïveté and white racial bonding occurred within one school to frame an African American boy as violent and impulsive and his mother as racially hypersensitive and to justify inequitable disciplinary actions. I argue that given CRT's assertion that race and racism are endemic to U.S. society, a research methodology that centers on race but draws upon culturally relevant ways of knowing is also needed. Moreover, in arguing for a methodology that can aid in uncovering both the blatant and subtle acts of racism, I suggest that the very nature of research must be conceptualized in ways that allow for the subjective lens of the researcher. Jazz is a communal, synergistic enterprise with its foundation in an oppositional discourse, so it can be a useful methodological heuristic. Moreover, research does not occur in a vacuum, so the notion of relationship building is central to both a jazz methodology and a CRT project. Finally, a project framed around CRT and utilizing a jazz methodology always already works toward social change and liberation.

References

Baldwin, J. (1963/1992). *The Fire Next Time*. London: Vintage.
Bland, E. O. (writer, director and producer); Hill, N. (writer and director); Kennedy, M. (writer); and Titus, E. (writer) (1959). *The Cry of Jazz* [film]. Chicago: Unheard Music Series.

Calmore, J. O. (1992). Critical Race Theory, Archie Shepp, and Fire Music: Securing an Authentic Intellectual Life in a Multicultural World. *University of Southern California Law Review* 65: 2131–2229.

Calmore, J. O. (1999). Random Notes of an Integration Warrior, Part 2: A Critical Response to the Hegemonic "Truth" of Daniel Farber and Suzanna Sherry. *Minnesota Law Review* 83: 1589–1617.

Code, L. (1987). Second Persons. In M. Hanen and K. Neilson (eds.), *Science, Morality, and Feminist Theory*. Suppl. to *Canadian Journal of Philosophy* 13.

Collins, P. H. (2000 [1990]). *Black Feminist Thought: Knowledge, Consciousness, and the Politics of Empowerment*. New York: Routledge.

Cooper, A. J. (1988 [1892]). *A Voice from the South by a Black Woman from the South*. New York: Oxford University Press.

Crenshaw, K.; Gotanda, N.; Peller, G.; and Thomas, K. (eds.) (1995). *Critical Race Theory: The Key Writings That Formed the Movement*. New York: Routledge.

Denzin, N. (1997). *Interpretive Ethnography: Ethnographic Practices for the 21st Century*. Thousand Oaks, CA: Sage.

Dibb Directions (2001). The Miles Davis Story (Videorecording produced for Channel 4 Television). New York: Sony Music Entertainment.

Dixson, A. D. (2005). Extending the Metaphor: Notions of Jazz in Portraiture. *Qualitative Inquiry* 11(1): 106–137.

Dixson, A. D. and Rousseau, C. K. (2005). And We Are Still Not Saved: Critical Race Theory Ten Years Later. *Race, Ethnicity, and Education* 8(1), 7–27).

Du Bois, W. E. B. (1995 [1903]). *The Souls of Black Folks*. New York: Signet.

Giddins, G. (1998). *Visions of Jazz: The First Century*. New York: Oxford University Press.

Harding, S. (1987). *Feminism and Methodology*. Bloomington: Indiana University Press.

Jones, L. (1999 [1963]). *Blues People: Negro Music in White America*. New York: William Morrow.

Ladson-Billings, G. J. (2000). Racialized Discourses and Ethnic Epistemologies. In N. K. Denzin and Y. S. Lincoln (eds.), *Handbook of Qualitative Research*, 257–278. Thousand Oaks, CA: Sage.

Lawrence-Lightfoot, S. and Davis, J. H. (1997). *The Art and Science of Portraiture*. San Francisco: Jossey-Bass.

Lawrence-Lightfoot, S., and Hoffman, J. (1997). The Art and Science of Portraiture.

Margulies, P. (1997). Doubting Doubleness, and All That Jazz: Establishment Critiques of Outsider Innovations in Music and Legal Thought. *University of Miami Law Review* 51: 1155–1194.

Mills, C. W. (1998). *Blackness Visible: Essays on Philosophy and Race*. Ithaca: Cornell University Press.

Murray, A. (2000 [1976]). *Stomping the Blues*. New York: Da Capo.

Popkewitz, T. S. (1998). *Struggling for the Soul: The Politics of Schooling and the Construction of the Teacher*. New York: Teachers College Press.

Solórzano, D. and Yosso, T. (2002). Critical Race Methodology: Counter-storytelling as an Analytical Framework for Education Research. *Qualitative Inquiry* 8(1): 23–44.

12
Where the Rubber Hits the Road: CRT goes to High School

DAVID STOVALL

The radical critics can maintain their innocence because many of them are professors in educational policy studies and foundations departments. Consequently, they have the luxury to write, talk, and dream about schools without having to confront directly the challenges that teachers, student teachers, and students must experience each day.

J. A. Banks (1992)

The quote can be both true and unfortunate. Although it is not a sweeping generalization meant to ridicule faculty in educational policy studies and foundations departments (like myself), many professors who deliver messages of educational critique to pre-service teachers are far removed from the lives of young people. The painful reality is that writing, talking and dreaming can be luxuries in relation to the contested spaces of schools. K–12 teaching can be messy, contradictory, and conflicting, particularly in light of recent developments in urban schools such as high-stakes testing, the privatization of public education, and the gentrification of working-class communities of color by middle-class and affluent residents. Still, because K–12 schools are spaces where we interact with young people, they remain sites of hope in challenging times. They are spaces that offer an alternative reality to the sensibilities of the ivory tower. The following is an account of my experiences in just such a space. I attempted through these experiences to make my writing, talking, and dreaming practical through the use of critical race theory (CRT).

This chapter highlights my experiences with high school students in a course centered in CRT. Through this course, the stories of students of color in high school were legitimated as they engaged with viewpoints that challenged those of the status quo. The legitimation of students' stories is an example of counterstory. Counterstory, as enacted in the course, enabled the participants take as the starting point for analysis the first-hand experiences of those who have intimate knowledge of racism in their lives.

In constructing this course, I attempted to engage with ideas from CRT that resonated deeply with my own perspectives. These ideas included the view that racism is endemic to daily life in the United States and the assertion that there is a unique voice of those who have been marginalized in relationship to the status quo (Crenshaw, Peller, Gotanda and Thomas, 1995). However, what intrigued me most was CRT's call to action in terms of bridging theoretical concepts to practice. According to Yamamoto (1997), justice, as an "experienced" phenomenon, involves grappling with the often "messy and conflictual racial realities" that are almost absent in the current literature (p. 875). In calling for a critical race praxis, Yamamoto pushes those employed in academia to infuse "aspects of critical inquiry and pragmatism" to recast "theory in light of practical experience" (p. 874). The combination of theory and practice (praxis) becomes central in developing CRT's commitment to social justice. This commitment to praxis was one of the characteristics of CRT scholars (Ladson-Billings & Tate, 1995; Lynn 1999; Parker and Lynn, 2002; Skrla and Scheurich, 2004; Solórzano and Villalpando,1997; Solórzano and Yosso, 2000) that drew me to this perspective. One means of developing this praxis is by bringing the concepts of racial justice upheld in CRT.

Schools often operate as spaces where the realities of race and racism go undiscussed, even if understood by the students. We hear the stories of black and Latino/a students being placed in remedial and special education programs, disproportionately recruited to the military, and suspended at alarming rates. These issues have recently entered the larger stage of academic and broad-based public periodicals (e.g., Institute for Democracy Education and Access, 2002; Lipman, 2004; Lynn, 1999; New York Collective of Radical Educators, 2004), but these inequities have represented the lived reality of students of color for years. The experiences described in this chapter represent an attempt to provide a context for the issues and concerns of students and to equip them with the analytical tools and vocabulary to critique the status quo. Continuing work from a previous project (Stovall, 2004), my high school course on race and the media was an attempt to centralize race while making it relevant and practical to high school students.

From Theory to Praxis in a Secondary Classroom

One unique aspect of working in an academic department is that the work often requires a lot of reading, writing and theorizing. Indeed, much of this theorizing greatly influences the work in which I engage with young people. However, it is best actualized when theories are converted to action and praxis is developed. One means of developing that praxis involves engaging in critical reflection on the policies and structures that shape the educational system. While this is often the purview of the ivory tower, it becomes more relevant as we help students develop these same critical perspectives. For example, policies such as No Child Left Behind and school vouchers have important implications for students in schools. However, critical conversations on these policies are impossible to have without considering race, class, gender and sexuality. Those who find the aforementioned policies counterproductive must engage and struggle in a process that identifies the dysfunctional nature of current policies while creating critical and productive spaces for young people to process these structures with respect to their own lives. Coupled with a historical context, the social project of education becomes one that calls upon all parties, including students, to challenge shared assumptions about how things should be.

Understanding that these critical conversations do not take place in the vast majority of urban public schools, I set out to participate in an exemplary project employing an ideology counter to the status quo. As a faculty member at an urban public university and doubling as a high school social studies teacher, I hoped to engage theory from an experiential/participatory standpoint, developing relevance for me and the students. Instead of engaging the "liberal rhetoric" of helping the downtrodden, my idea was to "get my hands dirty" and begin to help myself.

Returning to Yamamoto's (1997) concept of critical race praxis, a sound approach to social justice would be to partner with organizations that concentrate on issues facing communities on a daily basis (e.g., education, health care, employment, criminal justice). Fortunately, my experience with community organizations and school groups over the past twelve years in the Chicago area has placed me in contact with many social justice-oriented individuals and collectives. One such contact provided me the opportunity to work with a program called CORP: Using the City as a Classroom. According to the director of the program, the title is intended to emphasize how using the city as a classroom would develop the group of students into a "corps" to work collectively in their observations and practice. As a guiding premise, the idea was to have young people "question, explore and respond to the world in which they live by participating in the creative opportunities to wrestle with the tangled complexities of self, other and difference." In a segment designed for the second semester, the director's idea was to create a program in which students travel around the city, take classes in nontraditional spaces (e.g., health clinics, public defenders' offices), participate in workshops, and create community presentations that highlight their discoveries and critical assessments. My first year with CORP is documented elsewhere (Stovall, 2004); the course described in this chapter took place in the spring semester of 2004, my second year with the program.

The other instructors in the program were a diverse group, ranging from high school math teachers to Chicago poets. Funded by a number of local nonprofit organizations and two local schools, our class titles didn't fit the "normal" fare in terms of a high school curriculum. Instead of a "world studies" class, the CORP class was called "Fear of a Black Planet." English/Language

Arts became "Poetics to Prose: Reading and Writing in Chicago." My social studies class became "Race, Class, Media and Chicago." Our charge was to create a set of courses that were not only similar to what the students would be taking next year in college, but to center them in a discourse of the intersections of race and power in the city. The courses fit into a ten-week schedule during the spring semester.

The student participants in 2003 came from two high schools on the west side of Chicago (here called Garfield and Pilsen). The 2004 cohort included two additional student groups, one from a small charter school on the south side of Chicago (called Southside) and the other from a private school on the north side of the city (called Northside). The second-year course included 25 students. The group was predominantly African American (7 male, 3 female) and Latino/a (5 male, 6 female), with four white students (3 female, 1 male). Their class backgrounds were mixed, ranging from low-income to very affluent families. Northside was private and affluent. Southside had students from various socio-economic backgrounds. Garfield and Pilsen were both located in working-class neighborhoods, one predominantly African American (West Garfield Park) and the other Latino/a (Pilsen).

Many of the students would not be considered "successful" in the traditional sense of high classroom achievement and test scores. However, despite troubles in earlier schools, the entire class had been admitted to four-year colleges, and the students were engaged in this program to prepare them for what they would encounter when they entered college. The students' interest level was high, and they grilled me with questions about what next year would be like for them, in addition to questions on course content.

The range of student experiences and backgrounds contributed to intense discussions on the intersection of race and class in the city. A goal of the program was that group members from different backgrounds would observe the myriad experiences available in Chicago while making their own decisions concerning the intersections of race, power and class. The process involved a substantial amount of work independent from the classroom. Students were required to create community presentations for parents and other residents of their neighborhoods. In many ways, this was the ultimate laboratory for a larger discussion of CRT to develop context for media analysis. It represented an ideal setting to engage students in "experiential learning."

CRT and the Media

To put CRT at the forefront, I grounded the course in the tenets of critical race theory outlined by Solórzano and Villalpando (1997). These include (1) the centrality of racism, (2) the challenge to dominant ideology, (3) the commitment to social justice, (4) the importance of experiential knowledge, and (5) the use of an interdisciplinary perspective (p. 213). Placing CRT in the forefront allowed the class to deal with race as central to our endeavors.

While discussing the tenets, my class and I were able to unpack their meanings. One that resonated with the students was the assertion of the importance of the experiential knowledge of persons of color. This made a direct connection to their expertise as persons who have intimately experienced racism and observed its effects. Students appreciated being able to speak freely about race without ridicule. In addition, we examined the interdisciplinary nature of CRT as we entered conversations about how sociology, philosophy, legal theory and educational theory could interact to inform our ideas about race and racism.

My goal was to teach a class that examined the intersections of race and power through analysis of images in the media. Returning to their experiential expertise, the media served as a space where race could be discussed and analyzed through a relevant lens. From situation comedies to music videos, young people are immersed in a visceral onslaught of words, images and concepts. Often these spaces are saturated with subtle racial innuendo and conjecture. To critique such spaces, CRT was a valuable framework for discussion of race. As a dialogical and practical exercise, the course was to operate as a site to make sense of what we read, see and hear. I made a concerted effort to make the subject matter relevant while connecting it to theoretical concepts to which they would be introduced in college. As the college professor in the teaching cohort, I was giving the group a "heads-up" about what was in store for them as college freshmen.

Media were loosely defined as electronic, radio and television or print messages that inform our lives through either entertainment or journalism. Media literacy was defined as critical knowledge of such information. This gave us numerous opportunities to engage the various contexts of media and their influences. From there, we discussed the social context of music videos, network television, cable corporate entities, documentary films and various print media. This "curriculum" was not very different from the material I discuss in my CRT course with graduate students.

Rather than beginning with dense theoretical concepts and providing examples, however, I introduced the examples first, using theory as secondary reinforcement. Although we repeatedly referenced the tenets of CRT, we did not operate in a purely theoretical space. Instead, the idea was to develop a "living deconstruction" of the subject matter, placing students' lives at the center. Instead of a textbook, in addition to the writings of the aforementioned CRT scholars, I was able to develop a course packet with authors such as Chomsky (2003) and Coontz (2000). However, text was more a reference than a focal point; the course centered on dialogue.

Rarely do we give young people credit for being experts on their lives. Although they may not articulate their expertise in the same manner as adults, a meticulous understanding is revealed if they are given the proper arena. In fact, if we pay close attention, we will discover a gateway to provide new relevance to our courses and schools. To engage with the knowledge that the students brought, we made student–instructor dialogue a critical element of the class. The course operated as a discussion rather than a didactic lecture with nominal student response. A premise in my classes is to take nothing at face value. Students were expected to challenge ideas and question "truths." At these moments we were able to exchange our views and beliefs, sometimes agreeing to disagree. To give a space where ideas could be explored, it was important for me to step away from leading the discussion and become more of a facilitator, challenging students on their own understandings. Some human interactions are better and more productive than others; however, the ability of our group to engage on such a level promoted a sense of ownership.

CRT in the Classroom

On the first day of class, I asked the students to write on index cards what they expected from the class. Some wanted to enhance their understandings of race and culture. Others wanted to know why everything is "relevant." A few had no expectations at all. The first conversation was on race, media and Chicago. I was the only teacher for the course, and it took place on campus at my university. I began by trying to engage them on the nature of image vs. reality. The first challenge was to deconstruct the concept of "keeping it real." Some of the students explained that it meant not being "fake." I asked them to give me an example of what "fake" was. They got into the concept of being something that they are not. I asked them if they could give me a media example. They talked about current rap videos that displayed scantily clad women and men excessively draped in jewelry. Similar to the issues and concerns brought forth by Kimberle Crenshaw (1993) in a discussion of the rap group 2 Live Crew, we were able to talk about misogyny and patriarchy and concluded that they have negative effects on both women and men.

We then began to investigate media structures. One of our first assignments was to examine an example of a media web. Our model, printed in a 1997 edition of the *Nation*, used the concept of an octopus. The web was a centerfold pullout with four octopi at the top of the page. The head of each octopus had the name of a mega-corporation: General Electric, Time Warner, Disney/Cap Cities, and Westinghouse. The graph connected all four octopi conglomerates with arrows, listing the subsidiary companies each group shared with another. Students were confused by the graph, entitled "The National Entertainment State," upon first sight. However, as we discussed it in the context of their favorite television programs, they began to make connections to how their shows fit into the graph.

The discussion about media conglomerates led us into how a small number of media corporations control the full range of mass media, from television to feature films to radio programming. We began discussing why we enjoy particular television shows and whether those shows reinforce stereotypes. We deconstructed each of the television shows and videos, discussing pervasive stereotypes and whether the images are damaging. At first, the majority of the class was not very concerned about the issue. However, when we got into their favorite shows, our discussion became heated. We watched the Marlon Riggs film on the history of African American stereotypes in entertainment, *Ethnic Notions*. At this point, some students began to dissect the phenomenon of Bert Williams and place it in the context of current media.

Next, our work branched into the nature of diversity and multicultural-ism. When asked about "diversity," many students felt that it meant putting people from different backgrounds in the same place to perform a particular task. They talked about how groups had been historically excluded, and how diversity was a way to include people from marginalized groups. Employment and education were the most cited examples; some students had gone to visit "offices of diversity" or speak with "diversity counselors" at various univer-sities. However, when we analyzed the three major television networks and the top-rated shows for the season, very few contained "diverse" populations. Again, for some students, it was old news, but for others it developed a new take on how television often does not reflect the lives we live.

During the ten-week session, one of the most heated conversations took place when we examined the role of the media in shaping our perceptions. After watching a segment of the documentary "Eyes on the Prize," on slain Black Panther member Fred Hampton, we had a discussion about gangs in Chicago. As a community organizer in the late 1960s, Hampton had the abil-ity to organize scores of former gang members into recreational leagues and community workers. Hampton's story served as the counternarrative to com-monly shared beliefs on the inability of African Americans to organize as a collective. To many of the students the story sounded amazing, but it gave us the opportunity to investigate topics that local news outlets often ignore or rarely report. We discussed how the local news is often inaccurate and reporters seem to locate and interview the most inarticulate people possible to give eyewitness accounts. The conversations in class transitioned to how the public at large can mistake these eyewitnesses for typical representatives of communities of color. By contrasting the televising of crime with crime statistics, the students began to recognize the power of television in reinforc-ing stereotypes.

We then moved to the war in Iraq. This gave us the chance to study the geography of the Middle East and South Asia. In our conversation, we consid-ered the nature of colonial states and how many of the nations in the Middle East, Africa, and South Asia remain critical of the former colonial powers that continue to export their natural resources. From Nigeria to India, we reviewed countless examples of colonial exploitation. One student led the class based on his gathering of alternative news sources on Iraq. Many of the class members began to ask about the nature of economic sanctions and how they work. We referred to an article in *Harper's* that depicted how sanctions operated, with the example of water filtration systems. Students discovered that before Operation Iraqi Freedom, the United States invoked policies that made it illegal to export certain items used for water filtration, arguing that the components doubled for weapons manufacturing. Consequently, the Iraqi government might have a water filtration system that lacked a pump needed to power the machines. Because the pump was one of the targeted components under the sanctions policy, many Iraqi communities did not have the proper water treatment and began to contract waterborne diseases such as cholera and typhoid. From an international perspective, the CRT tenet claiming racism as endemic to daily life became salient. Students had a clear example of contrasting images in the media of the Iraqi people and the situations they face. Because the U.S. media cast Saddam Hussein as a ruthless dictator, this cast the citizens of Iraq as his followers and implied that they also had wanted to destroy the United States since the first conflict in 1991. Providing students a practical example of how stereotypes operate made our discussions relevant to daily news.

The session left the students with a number of opinions. Transitioning from the Black Panther Party to Chicago street gangs to counter-intelligence to the war in Iraq led to an intense session. Media and CRT became the threads by which we intertwined the topics and unpacked our relationships to the various events. As we examined the role of the media, many of the students of color and white students began to contrast their experiences. Through this process, the students discovered a common thread: students from both groups had experiences with omissions of historical and local events from popular outlets. Many African American and Latino/a students used examples of the under-reporting of police brutality in local media. Others used historical events like Japanese internment during World War II and the reign of the Khmer Rouge in Cambodia. These discussions provide evidence of the potential for high school student to develop a critical perspective based on their own experiences or those of others with whom they identify.

Conclusion

The commitment to social justice through CRT calls for those concerned with making substantive change in our communities to develop processes and strategies with those who are currently engaged in this work. Community organizations, student organizations and civic groups are central to engaging issues that complicate communities of color in urban areas. However, part of this engagement must include preparing others, particularly students, to become involved in social justice. In this chapter, I have described my own efforts toward this goal and the role of CRT in that process.

One key feature of this effort was the creation of a space in which students of color felt comfortable and were encouraged to share their perspectives. CRT focuses on the experiential knowledge of persons of color and uses this knowledge to construct counterstories that challenge the discourse of the dominant group. The course offered a space to engage in this process. The experiences and perspectives of students of color were validated. Moreover, the class told its own story of the vast potential of students of color, thus countering the dominant discourse that often portrays these same students in negative ways.

It is important to note, however, that this form of praxis is not easy. Spaces such as the one created in the CORP program are challenging because collective leadership and decision making is a painstaking process. On the classroom level, dialogue and interaction with 25 students isn't always orderly or expedient. It becomes especially difficult if factions of the group are diametrically opposed to a suggestion and deeply invested in their way of looking at and responding to socio-cultural issues. However, it is powerful because everyone is provided the opportunity to engage his or her sense of agency to make decisions.

Moreover, such praxis, particularly in schools, disrupts the status quo. I was reminded through this experience that teaching is never neutral. I knew that the issues and views we were discussing and the ideas to which my students were exposed in the course were far different from the mainstream discourse. As teachers we must be prepared to engage this messy process that is low on accolades and public recognition. In the end, however, if we are serious about the lives of young people and our own, we will continue to challenge, create and discover new ways to change our condition.

Note: Bert Williams was an African American vaudeville performer and silent film star who donned "blackface" makeup while portraying an array of stereotypical characters of the black experience. His characters would often slouch, make exaggerated faces and speak in broken English. Despite the derogatory effect of his performances, Williams was a very wealthy man from his performances in the early twentieth century.

References

Banks, J. A. (1992). African-American Scholarship and the Evolution of Multicultural Education. *Journal of Negro Education* 61: 273–286.

Chomsky, N. (2003). *On Democracy and Education.* New York: Routledge.

Coontz, S. (2000). *The Way We Never Were: American Families and the Nostalgia Trap.* New York: Basic Books.

Crenshaw, K. (1993). Mapping the Margins: Intersectionality, Identity Politics and the Violence against Women of Color, *Stanford Law Review* 43, 1241–1299.

Crenshaw, K.; Gotanda, N.; Peller, g.; and Thomas, K. (eds.) (1995). *Critical Race Theory: The Key Writings That Formed the Movement.* New York: New Press.

http://www.isacs.org. (www.isacs.org/about/news/detail.aap?newsid=39483).

Institute for Democracy, Education, and Access (2002). *IDEA Summer Seminar 2002* (video). University of California, Los Angeles.

Kick, R. (ed.) (2001). *You Are Being Lied To: The Disinformation Guide to Media Distortion, Historical Whitewashes, and Cultural Myths.* St. Paul, MN: Disinformation Company.

Ladson-Billings, G. and Tate, W. A. (1995). Towards a Critical Race Theory of Education. *Teachers College Record* 97(1): 47–68.

Lipman, P. (2004). *High Stakes Education: Inequality, Globalization, and Urban School Reform.* New York: Routledge.

Lynn, M. (1999). Toward a Critical Race Pedagogy: A Research Note. *Urban Education* 33(5): 606–627.

Matsuda, M.; Lawrence, C., III; Delgado, R.; and Crenshaw, K. (eds.) (1993). *Words That Wound: Critical Race Theory, Assaultive Speech, and the First Amendment.* Boulder: Westview.

New York Collective of Radical Educators (2004). Curriculum Guide to Anti-military Recruitment in High Schools.

Parker, L. and Lynn, M. (2002). What's Race Got to Do with It? Critical Race Theory's Conflicts with and Connections to Qualitative Research Methodology and Epistemology. *Qualitative Inquiry* 8(1), 7–22.

Skrla, L. and Scheurich, J. J. (eds.) (2004). *Educational Equity and Accountability: Paradigms, Policies, and Politics.* New York: Routledge.

Solórzano, D. and Villalpando, O. (1997). Images and Words That Wound: Critical Race Theory, Racial Stereotyping, and Teacher Education. *Teacher Education Quarterly* 24(3): 186–215.

Solórzano, D. and Yosso, T. (2000). Critical Race and Latcrit Method: Counterstorytelling Chicana and Chicano Graduate School Experiences. *Qualitative Studies in Education.*

Solórzano, D. G. and Yosso, T. (2001). Critical Race and LatCrit Theory and Method: Counter-Story telling, Chicano and Chicano Graduate School Experiences. *Qualitative Studies in Education* 14(4), 471–495.

Stovall, D. (2004). Take Two on Media and Race. In F. Ibanez-Carrasco and E. Meiners (eds.), *Public Acts: Disruptive Readings on Making Curriculum Public,* 117–134. New York: Routledge.

Tate, W. (1997). Critical Race Theory and Education: History, Theory and Implications. *Review of Research in Education* 22: 195–247.

Yamamoto, E. (1997). Critical Race Praxis: Race Theory and Political Lawyering Practice in Post Civil Rights America. *Michigan Law Review* 95(7): 821–900.

13

Critical Race Theory beyond North America: Toward a Trans-Atlantic Dialogue on Racism and Antiracism in Educational Theory and Praxis

DAVID GILLBORN

Introduction

This chapter addresses the relationship between critical race theory (CRT) scholarship in North America and antiracist research elsewhere, especially in the United Kingdom (U.K.). I argue that a dialogue between CRT, to date dominated by a focus on the United States, and British antiracism could prove especially fruitful for scholars on both sides of the Atlantic. In particular, there is a pressing need for critical scholars to learn from the errors of the past and adapt to the new realities of the present. The latter includes the startlingly successful cultural revolution that is sometimes referred to as "conservative modernization" (Apple, 2004; Dale, 1989), fueled and given added bile through the resurgence of racist nationalism wrapped in the flag of freedom and security in a "post-9/11" world (Rizvi, 2003). The argument is made through a detailed consideration of antiracist work in Britain, but many of the wider lessons might usefully be considered elsewhere. At a time when policy borrowing is reaching new heights (Whitty et al., 1998), both the specifics of educational reform and the dilemmas facing educational researchers with a commitment to social justice are remarkably similar in many different nation-states. Notably, many scholars internationally share a common experience of increasingly market-driven education reforms in which key words like "standards" and "accountability" are having a markedly regressive impact regardless of the official tenor of the governing political party: Howard's Australia, Blair's Britain and Bush's America, for example, have all witnessed the emergence of a complex and multifaceted rightist "hegemonic bloc" (Apple, 1998a) that has come to define educational commonsense in a particular way:

> We are told to "free" our schools by placing them into the competitive market, restore "our" traditional common culture and stress discipline

241

and character, return God to our classrooms as a guide to all our conduct inside and outside the school, and tighten central control through more rigorous and tough-minded standards and tests. This is all supposed to be done at the same time. It is all supposed to guarantee an education that benefits everyone. Well, maybe not. (Apple, 2001, p. 5)

This chapter has three main sections. First, I reflect on the role of theory in British antiracism; second, I examine the consequences of the present situation; and finally, I outline CRT and consider its promise for critical antiracist scholarship and praxis internationally.

Theory and Antiracism

Many people imagine Britain to be a relatively homogeneous place where ethnic diversity only arose following World War II, but this is to neglect Britain's central role in the trans-Atlantic slave trade. Indeed, it has been shown that not only were people of color a familiar sight in the London of the 1600s, but systematic attempts to deport them were also under way (File and Power, 1981, pp. 6–7). The postwar period saw a rapid increase in migration into the British mainland from former colonies in the Caribbean and the Indian subcontinent. A succession of immigration laws have restricted new migration into the UK, but, as a result of its younger age profile, the minority ethnic population continues to grow as a proportion of the total. Children identifying as of minority ethnic heritage accounted for around 17 percent of the school-age population in 2004 (DfES 2005, p. 3). Most minority groups do not achieve as highly in education as their white counterparts, in particular, children identifying as Black Caribbean, Black African, and/or Black British are *less* likely to achieve high grade qualifications at the end of their schooling but *more* likely to be expelled from school (Gillborn and Mirza, 2000). Attempts to address race inequity in Britain have followed a rapidly changing path, and "antiracism" has become established as a major concern for some activists and educators (Gillborn, 2000).

"Antiracism" is a familiar term in many educational systems but has a wide variety of specific meanings (see Carrim and Soudien, 1999). In Britain, antiracism arose as much from a critique of liberal multiculturalism as it did from an analysis of the racist nature of the state. Academics, notably in places like Birmingham University's now disbanded Centre for Contemporary Cultural Studies (CCCS, 1982), played a vital role, but so did committed teachers and activists struggling to effect change in a wide variety of ways (Brah and Minhas, 1985; Bourne, 1980; Brandt, 1986; Chevannes and Reeves, 1987; Coard, 1971; Cole, 1986; Dhondy, 1974; Gill and Levidow, 1987; Gilroy, 1987, 1988; Lawrence, 1982; Mullard, 1984; Nixon, 1985; Sarup, 1986; Tomlinson, 1984). Antiracism established its credentials by exposing the deeply conservative nature of approaches that struck liberatory postures but accepted the status quo and frequently encoded deficit perspectives of black children, their parents and communities. Among many especially notable examples, perhaps the most influential were Hazel Carby's corrective to colorblind white middle-class feminism (Carby, 1982) and Chris Mullard's analysis of the assimilation-ist basis of multicultural education (Mullard, 1982). In education, this trend was perhaps at its strongest and most sustained in the work of Barry Troyna.

Initially Troyna had been, in his own words, "seduced by the ideology of multicultural education" (1993, p. vii), but he emerged as one of the most steadfast critics of multiculturalism and the most prominent advocate of anti-racist education throughout a career cut tragically short by illness (Troyna 1984, 1987, 1988, 1991, 1992, 1993). Troyna refused to compromise his antira-cist commitments, even when faced with the dual challenges of the postmod-ern turn in social science and the practical challenges of the so-called Burnage Inquiry, which in the late 1980s and early 1990s seemed to many commenta-tors to require a new but unspecified approach that abandoned antiracism (Macdonald et al., 1989; Troyna and Carrington, 1990; Troyna and Hatcher, 1992).[1] The Burnage Inquiry has been dealt with at length elsewhere[2]; suffice it to say that a group of highly respected antiracists delivered a damning report on the state of race relations in a Manchester school (Burnage High) where a young Asian boy, Ahmed Iqbal Ullah, had been stabbed to death by a white peer. At the time, the Burnage Inquiry was misread by many commentators as signaling the end of antiracism. This owed a great deal to a concerted press campaign that grossly distorted the report's findings (see Macdonald et al., 1989, pp. xvii–xxv). In fact, the report now stands as a landmark publication: a brave attempt to move beyond simple binary oppositions and push antiracists to confront the complexity of life in school, where issues of social class, sexism and ableism interact in an unpredictable and sometimes deadly combination of oppressions.

Sivanandan, one of the single most important writers on race and racism in Britain, made a simple but vital observation writing in the midst of the Burnage controversy. He noted that the biased and caricatured attacks in the media served to "still the voices of those, like myself, who tried to say that there was no body of thought called anti-racism, no orthodoxy or dogma, no manual of strategy and tactics, no demonology. What there was in our society was racism, in every walk of life, and it had to be combated—in every conceiv-able way" (Sivanandan, 1988, p. 147).

The absence of an antiracist "orthodoxy" can be a source of strength. Rac-ism takes many forms, and so antiracism must be flexible and constantly adapt. However, the absence of a dogmatic "manual" of antiracism does not require that we avoid all attempts to systematize our critical approaches and conceptual starting points. Unfortunately, in many ways, antiracism has fallen into this trap: our awareness of the multifaceted and constantly changing nature of racism may have led inadvertently to a failure properly to interrogate our conceptual history and theoretical frameworks. This does not mean that antiracism has been atheoretical: there have been several attempts to take forward antiracist analyses of education in general, and of schooling in particular, that have sought to engage explicitly with new developments in social theory (see, e.g., Bonnett, 2000; Bhavnani, 2001; Dadzie, 2000; Gillborn, 1995; Mac an Ghaill, 1999; Mirza, 1997; Rattansi, 1992). Nevertheless, none of this work has yet managed to elaborate an appropriately critical yet accessible conceptual map that can do two simple yet vitally important tasks: first, to describe what is characteristically antiracist about an "antiracist" analysis; and second, to offer a suitable starting point for further explorations in educational theory, policy and practice.

I believe that CRT offers a way of addressing both these issues. Before examining CRT in greater detail, however, it is worth considering why such an approach is necessary. After all, the lack of an elaborate theory may not necessarily be a bad thing, especially for activists and practitioners seeking to bring about change in the real world beyond the walls of the academy. I am certainly not advocating theory for its own sake. In the following section, therefore, I consider some of the reasons why antiracists need CRT (or something very like it).

The Need for a Systematic Approach to Racism in Education

Numerous problems arise from the absence of a clear conceptual map of antiracism. Here I will touch on two: first, the need to counter the use of antiracism as an empty rhetorical device in educational policy, and second, the need to strengthen the critical character of scholarship that addresses racialized inequalities in practice. These are by no means the only relevant issues, but they are among the most important and are sufficient to illustrate some of the dilemmas that could usefully be addressed through a more systematic approach to antiracist theory and practice.

Combating Policy Rhetoric: Beneath the Skin of Public Multiculturalism

Perhaps the most pressing reason for developing a more systematic approach to antiracist work concerns the problem of antiracism's being reduced to a meaningless slogan bereft of all critical content. Until 1999 antiracism was widely portrayed in Britain as a dangerous and extreme political ideology— usually associated with the "loony left" of socialist local administrations who took seriously issues like race and gender equity (see Gillborn, 1995; Richardson, 2002; Troyna, 1993). This situation changed, virtually overnight, with the publication of the *Stephen Lawrence Inquiry Report* (Macpherson, 1999).

Stephen Lawrence was 18 years old when, as he waited for a London bus, he was attacked and stabbed to death by a group of white youths. The police inquiry generated no arrests. Stephen's parents, Doreen and Neville, were treated more like troublemakers than grieving parents, and they became convinced that the case was being mishandled, as the death of a black young man was a not a sufficient priority for the investigating officers nor the Metropolitan Police Force as a whole. After years of campaigning, the Lawrences' demands for a public inquiry were finally met by an incoming Labour government in 1997. The *Stephen Lawrence Inquiry Report* and the consequent public debates provided the closest British parallel yet to the national furors over racism that were sparked in the United States by the Rodney King affair and the O. J. Simpson trials. The *Inquiry Report* stated categorically that "institutional racism" was a routine and pervasive factor in many of the key agencies of society, including the police, education and health service. The government, the Conservative opposition and even the Metropolitan Police were forced to accept the inquiry's findings of institutional racism, so great was the moral authority of the Lawrence family's case, and so damning was the meticulously logged evidence of police incompetence and racism. Suddenly, antiracism came in from the cold. As Sivanandan noted:

> The unrelenting struggle of the Lawrences has put institutional racism back on the agenda ... they changed the whole discourse on race relations and made the government and the media and the people of this country acknowledge that there is a deep, ingrained, systematic racism in the institutions and structures of this society. (Sivanandan 2000, p. 7)

Predictably, the charge of institutional racism was met with horror and outrage by right-wing commentators keen to defend the supposed traditional tolerance of the British people and to fight the forces of political correctness (see Gillborn, 2002 for an account of these debates). In addition to this backlash, however, a somewhat more subtle development can also be identified: antiracism has been tacitly redefined so that it can mean almost anything. *If you are against racism (and who isn't?) then you are an antiracist. Yes?* No. This approach reverts to a characteristic white assumption that racism is simple and crude and obvious. The whole thrust of the *Lawrence Inquiry*'s analysis of *institutional* racism (as being frequently unintended and hidden) has been lost amid a self-congratulatory glow of liberal righteousness. Most important of all, this tendency seems to support the illusion that something meaningful has actually changed in the way that public services operate. The language has changed, but not the reality of race inequality. Speaking at a central London conference attended by around two thousand black parents and educationists, for example, the then under-secretary of state with responsibility for "School Standards" rejoiced:

> The Race Relations Amendment Act places a new duty on all public bodies including schools and including, for that matter, the Department for Education. They will be required, not only to have a written policy on race equality, but also to assess the impact of their policies on ethnic

minority pupils, staff and parents, and to monitor levels of attainment of ethnic minority pupils. This act provided a unique opportunity for a concerted focus on raising the attainment of ethnic minority pupils. What it means in practice is that every school will need to mainstream racial equality. (Ashton 2003, p. 11)

But simply asserting our antiracist intentions means nothing if we leave unchanged the dominant systems of testing, the curriculum, teacher education, and punitive inspection regimes that penalize schools serving working class and minority communities. The Race Relations Amendment Act, referred to by Ashton above, provides a startling example. The Act arose directly from the Stephen Lawrence Inquiry and represents the government's primary response to the report's numerous recommendations. It was flagged, on the day that the *Inquiry Report* was published, when Prime Minister Blair told Parliament:

The publication of today's report on the killing of Stephen Lawrence is a very important moment in the life of our country. It is a moment to reflect, to learn and to change. It will certainly lead to new laws but, more than that, it must lead to new attitudes, to a new era in race relations, and to a new more tolerant and more inclusive Britain. (Tony Blair MP, *Hansard* 24 February, 1999, col. 380)

The amended legislation placed new duties on more than 45,000 public authorities, including every state-funded school in England, Scotland and Wales. They must (1) have a written policy on race equality; (2) monitor their activities for signs of bias (especially focusing on student attainment); and (3) actively plan to eradicate race inequity. These new duties are mandatory and require public authorities to be proactive in their pursuit of race equality. This is a major step forward and is among the most radical equalities legislation in the world. Unfortunately, early indications are that the education sector in general, and schools in particular, are lagging well behind other public authorities in their attempts to meet these new requirements.

Data gathered for the Commission for Racial Equality (CRE)[3] paint an especially discouraging picture in relation to the education sector. In a survey of more than three thousand public authorities, schools were the least likely to reply: only 20 percent of schools replied, compared with an overall rate of almost 50 percent (Schneider-Ross, 2003, p. 5). Of course, nothing substantial can be read into a return rate. For example, among countless possible explanations, it might be thought that schools were not interested in race equality, or that they were more fearful of responding to a survey sponsored by the authority that polices the relevant legislation. The most obvious explanation, in the eyes of most teachers with whom I have discussed this, is simply that school staff are too busy to fill in questionnaires. Any or all of these might have a grain of truth. Looking ahead, however, we might have assumed that since so few schools managed to respond, then at least those few that did return the questionnaire might be assumed to be among the more confident in regard to race equality. If that is the case, the detail of their responses gives even more cause for concern.

The CRE data suggest that more than half of respondents in the education sector have not identified any clear "goals" or "targets" for improvement (Schneider-Ross, 2003, p. 6). In relation to differences in attainment, which is an especially prominent area in the legislation, even fewer schools (around one in three) have set any clear goals for change (p. 11). Schools also appear skeptical about the value of any race equity work they have completed to date, in that school respondents are among the least positive of all groups when questioned about the effects of the changes that they have made: 65 percent of schools believe the work has produced positive benefits, compared with 68 percent of local government respondents, 74 percent of those in criminal justice and policing, 80 percent of Further and Higher Education, and 89 percent of Central Government (p. 8). Perhaps most worrying of all, despite the relatively poor response to the other items, educationists are the least likely to express a need for any further guidance on these issues (p. 13). Put simply, early indications are that many schools are inactive on race equality: at best they are too busy; at worst, they appear to be complacent about their duties and uninterested in further progress.

The inaction of schools would not be quite so disastrous if national policymakers had lived up to their legal duties. As Ashton noted, the Education Department faces its own set of duties under the Race Relations legislation. A mark of how far the department progressed in the five years following the Lawrence Inquiry is its "Five Year Strategy," published amid a flurry of publicity in the summer of 2004 (DfES, 2004). Running to 110 pages, the strategy sets out the government's future priorities and policies for education, yet the word "racism" does not appear once. Even the more anodyne terms "prejudice" and "discrimination" were conspicuously absent. In contrast, "business(es)" appears 36 times, and "standards" warrants 65 appearances, prompting an obvious question, "Standards for whom?"

This remarkable absence is all the more worrying because one of the key lessons of the Stephen Lawrence Inquiry was the importance of facing up to racism (in all its forms) and challenging it openly and honestly: "There must be an unequivocal acceptance of the problem of institutional racism and its nature before it can be addressed, as it needs to be, in full partnership with members of minority ethnic communities" (*Stephen Lawrence Inquiry*, p. 31). Despite the rhetoric of antiracism that now features in a kind of official or rhetorical multiculturalism in many policy pronouncements, therefore, it appears that the British education system has a long way to go before it even complies with the basics of existing race equality legislation. Antiracism has not failed—in most cases, it simply has not been tried yet. In this new context (following the Stephen Lawrence Inquiry), a radical perspective is required to cut through the superficial rhetorical changes and address the more deep-rooted state of race inequity in the education system.

The Need for a Radical, Not Reformist, Perspective

In his critical work examining the literatures on school effectiveness and school management, Martin Thrupp has attacked those he describes as "textual apologists" (Thrupp, 1999). Among these he distinguishes between the *overt apologists*, who set out explicitly to "sell" existing government policy as "best practice," and the *subtle apologists*, who make reference to inequality and wider political and economic structures but then continue the detail of their work in a largely or entirely decontextualized and uncritical way (Thrupp, 1999; Thrupp and Wilmott, 2004, pp. 228–229). Louise Morley and Naz Rassool (1999) have also noted the particular impact that school effectiveness discourse has had on the place of equity and social justice as an increasingly marginal (even irrelevant) aspect of British education. A similar argument has been made in relation to the Sociology of Education in recent years: Stephen Ball (1994, 2004), Roger Dale (1992, 2001) and Rob Moore (1996) have argued that sociologists, often in a battle to demonstrate their relevance within a new managerialist culture in the academy, have too often come to concern themselves with reforming the system, while taking for granted the essential shape and character of the system itself. Indeed, as Sara Delamont (2001) notes, British sociologists of education have often been both exclusionary (especially with regard to gender and internal colonialism) and excluded (by the mainstream of their discipline).

The tendency to adopt a perspective that is reformist, rather than radical, is already visible in work on race inequity in education. A great deal of research on race and education in Britain, for example, is concerned with mapping the scale of inequalities and attempting to generate school-level approaches that will improve the situation. This work is important but it is not sufficient, and, in isolation, it may have the unintended consequence of limiting our vision to what seems possible within the given constraints that have such a powerful determining effect on how minoritized groups experience school and ultimately achieve (or not) within the institution.

Let me be explicit here. I am not criticizing research that focuses on the scale of race inequality (this has proven to be an essential spur to even the most minimal of policy responses), nor am I criticizing work that attempts to address race equity at the school and classroom level (this is a vital tool in the struggle for greater race equity). Indeed, I have actively contributed to both strands of work, as have many colleagues—all of whom share a commitment to greater race equity in education, and some of whom are self-avowedly antiracist (Bhavnani, 2001; Blair et al., 1998; Dadzie, 2000; Gillborn, 1995;

Gillborn and Gipps, 1996; Gillborn and Mirza 2000; Haque, 2000; Modood et al., 1997; Osler, 1997; Richardson and Wood, 1999; Weekes and Wright, 1999). This is important work, but it is not the sum of critical scholarship on race and education in Britain. There is a real danger that we are being seduced (by funding priorities and demands to be "relevant") into a school-level focus that loses sight of the bigger picture (Thrupp and Wilmott, 2004, after Ozga, 1990). If we focus only on the scale of inequity and school-level approaches to address it, we lose sight of the most powerful forces operating at the societal level to sustain and extend these inequities. Essentially, we risk tinkering with the system to make its outputs slightly less awful, but leaving untouched the fundamental shape, scale and purpose of the system itself.

There is a problem, therefore, of ensuring that antiracist scholarship resists the pressure to become a reformist perspective and retains a radical, critical edge. This refers not only to the directions taken by experienced and established researchers but also, indeed especially, to the work of younger scholars. There is a pressing need to offer new researchers a clear and coherent map to help them navigate the essentials of an antiracist perspective. At present, there is a danger that each new researcher must reinvent the wheel so far as antiracism is concerned. The lack of a clear and widely understood set of antiracist perspectives means that each new contributor (scholar, activist and/or practitioner) must relearn the antecedents of any antiracist analyses that he or she wishes to develop. This is both wasteful and risky. It is wasteful because the lack of a widely recognized antiracist framework means that each new researcher must construct such a map for himself or herself. Of course, this can be rewarding and can generate new perspectives, but it may be easier for new voices to reshape and revitalize antiracism if they can be more certain of what has gone before. This can be difficult in such a diverse but relatively poorly charted field. In particular, it is becoming increasingly difficult to access many of the original sources that have shaped antiracism. The growth of information and communications technology (ICT) applications has had a major impact on how educationists identify and access previous work in their field. There is a danger that newer secondary sources (which are more easily accessed electronically) could come to take prominence over older but more detailed and contextually sensitive original sources. This is especially dangerous in the field of antiracism because of the tendency of secondary sources to oversimplify the originals. Put simply, antiracism needs a clear and accessible conceptual map in order to enable new antiracists to build on the successes, failures and frustrations of previous work.

The present situation for antiracism, therefore, is not encouraging. A range of different pressures (from the rhetoric of policy makers to the financial and lived pressures of the academy) threaten to remove antiracism's critical content and reduce it to a reformist level where it is at best a palliative to make a divisive system seem a little less exclusionary, and at worst an empty phrase to be mouthed by policy makers content that their plans can be forced unchanged on a relatively docile audience. It is in this context that I believe critical race theory offers an invaluable way ahead for antiracist scholars beyond North America and, as part of the process, CRT itself may gain from wider exposure to new territories, debates and questions.

Critical Race Theory: a View from Outside North America

Critical Race Theory embraces a movement of left scholars, most of them scholars of color, situated in law schools, whose work challenges the ways in which race and racial power are constructed and represented in American legal culture and, more generally, in American society as a whole. (Crenshaw et al., 1995, p. xiii)

CRT has its roots in U.S. legal scholarship, where it grew as a radical alternative to dominant perspectives, not only the conservative mainstream paradigmatic views but also the apparently radical tradition of critical legal studies that, in the words of Cornel West, " 'deconstructed' liberalism, yet seldom addressed the role of deep-seated racism in American life" (West, 1995, p. xi). Frustration with the silence on racism prompted CRT scholars to foreground race and to challenge not only the foci of existing analyses but also the methods and forms of argumentation that were considered legitimate (see, e.g., Bell, 1980a, 1992; Crenshaw, 1988; Delgado, 1989; Matsuda et al., 1993). In 1995 an article by Gloria Ladson-Billings and William F. Tate, in the *Teachers College Record*, set out the first steps toward taking a CRT perspective and thinking through its possible application and insights within the field of education (Ladson-Billings and Tate, 1995). Both authors have refined their views in subsequent work (e.g., Ladson-Billings 1998, 1999, 2005; Tate, 1997, 1999, 2005), and a new wave of radical scholars have begun to take the perspective forward in novel ways and in relation to different issues and a wider range of minoritized groups (e.g., Dixson and Rousseau, 2005; Parker, 1998; Taylor, 1999; Villenas et al., 1999). Despite its name, CRT is not so much a theory as a perspective. That is, CRT does not offer a finished and exclusive set of propositions that claim to explain precisely current situations and to predict what will occur under a certain set of conditions in the future. Rather, it is a set of interrelated beliefs about the significance of race/racism and how it operates in contemporary Western society, especially the United States. In fact, the vast majority of CRT in education (like CRT in law) focuses exclusively on the United States. There is no reason, however, why the underlying assumptions and insights of CRT cannot be transferred usefully to other (post-) industrial societies such as the United Kingdom, Europe and Australasia: indeed, critical race feminism has already shown how CRT can be useful in a wide range of international contexts, including nations in the global south (see Wing, 2000).

Crenshaw and colleagues state, "There is no canonical set of doctrines or methodologies to which we all subscribe" (1995, p. xiii). As with British antiracism, there is no single, unchanging statement of what CRT believes or suggests. William Tate captures well the dynamic of CRT when he describes it as "an iterative project of scholarship and social justice" (1997, p. 235). Unlike antiracism, however, a series of key elements (perspectives and insights) can be taken as largely representative of a distinctive CRT position. In addition, there is a series of more specific methodological and conceptual tools that are often used by CRT writers but whose presence in a study is neither sufficient nor necessary to identify it as part of CRT in education. This distinction between defining elements and conceptual tools is used here as a heuristic device, meant to help clarify thinking about the "shape" of CRT as an approach. I have found this approach useful in discussions about CRT with colleagues and students, but it is by no means fixed. As more writers add to the tradition and priorities alter, it is quite likely that certain features may change in status, or disappear, while new aspects might be added (see Figure 13.1). For the time being, however, this is a useful strategy that builds on a wide range of existing approaches. For the sake of clarity, therefore, in the following account I will try to present these elements and tools separately, although their use and interpretation in the literature necessarily relies on a great deal of mutual citation and application.

Defining Elements
- racism as endemic ... "normal," not aberrant nor rare: deeply ingrained legally & culturally
- crosses epistemological boundaries
- critique of civil rights laws as fundamentally limited
- critique of liberalism: claims of neutrality, objectivity, color-blindness, and meritocracy as camouflages
- call to context: challenges ahistoricism and recognizes experiential knowledge of people of color

Conceptual Tools
- story-telling and counter-stories
- interest convergence
- critical white studies

The starting point for CRT is a focus on racism, and in particular, on its central importance in society and its routine (often unrecognized) character:

> CRT begins with a number of basic insights. One is that racism is normal, not aberrant, in American society. Because racism is an ingrained feature of our landscape, it looks ordinary and natural to persons in the culture. Formal equal opportunity—rules and laws that insist on treating blacks

and whites (for example) alike—can thus remedy only the more extreme and shocking forms of injustice, the ones that do stand out. It can do little about the business-as-usual forms of racism that people of color confront every day and that account for much misery, alienation, and despair. (Delgado and Stefancic, 2000, p. xvi)

In this way, CRT argues that racism is "endemic in U.S. society, deeply ingrained legally, culturally, and even psychologically" (Tate, 1997, p. 234). It is of central importance that the term "racism" is used not only in relation to crude, obvious acts of race hatred but also in relation to the more subtle and hidden operations of power that have the *effect* of disadvantaging one or more minority ethnic groups. This is a more radical approach than many liberal multiculturalists are comfortable with. Nevertheless, it is in keeping with recent developments not only in the academy but also in British legal approaches to racism and race inequity. As I have already noted, race equality legislation in the UK was significantly amended following the Stephen Lawrence Inquiry. One of the most important aspects of the Lawrence Inquiry's approach to institutional racism is the insistence that we focus on outcomes and effects—rather than intentions:

> "Institutional Racism" consists of the collective failure of an organisation to provide an appropriate and professional service to people because of their colour, culture, or ethnic origin. It can be seen or detected in processes, attitudes and behaviour which amount to discrimination through unwitting prejudice, ignorance, thoughtlessness and racist stereotyping which disadvantage minority ethnic people. (Macpherson, 1999, p. 321)

By explicitly including "unwitting" and "thoughtless" acts, this approach moves away from endless debates about intent by insisting on a focus on the outcomes of actions and processes. The report states clearly that regardless of the type of racism involved (overt or institutional) the outcomes can be just as destructive: "In its more subtle form it [racism] is as damaging as in its overt form" (Macpherson, 1999, p. 321)

In this way, the Lawrence approach, like some longer-established definitions, presents a fundamental challenge to liberal complacency about the realities of contemporary racial politics and inequalities. As Stokely Carmichael and Charles Hamilton observed decades ago in what is widely credited as the first attempt to define the term:

> Institutional racism ... is less overt, far more subtle, less identifiable in terms of specific individuals committing the acts. But it is no less destructive of human life. [It] originates in the operation of established and respected forces in the society, and thus receives far less public

condemnation. (Carmichael and Hamilton, 1967; reprinted in Cash-more and Jennings, 2001, p. 112)

The last part of this quotation is highly significant: institutional racism "origi-nates in the operation of established and respected forces in the society." This is vital, because CRT amounts to more than a perspective on institutional rac-ism; it involves a critical perspective on the nature of U.S. politics and society. For example, among the other defining features that William Tate identifies are "CRT reinterprets civil rights law in light of its limitations, illustrating that laws to remedy racial inequality are often undermined before they can be fully implemented" (Tate, 1997, p. 234); and "CRT portrays dominant legal claims of neutrality, objectivity, color blindness, and meritocracy as camouflages for the self-interest of powerful entities of society" (p. 235).

These perspectives, of course, are not unique to those identifying with CRT. Indeed, as Tate notes, CRT borrows from numerous traditions and is frequently characterized by a readiness to cross epistemological boundaries. This theoretical eclecticism is so strong that Tate includes it as one of his key characteristics of the approach (1997, p. 234). What is most important, how-ever, is the way that these various "insights" (Delgado and Stefancic 2000, p. xvi) are brought together in a new and challenging way. These perspectives, of course, raise deeply troubling questions. Indeed, CRT is frequently misinter-preted as taking a dismissive stance on the advances achieved by the U.S. civil rights movement at enormous human cost. This criticism, however, misreads CRT. As Kimberlé Crenshaw and her colleagues argue:

Our opposition to traditional civil rights discourse is neither a criticism of the civil rights movement nor an attempt to diminish its significance … we draw much of our inspiration and sense of direction from that courageous, brilliantly conceived, spiritually inspired, and ultimately transformative mass action. (Crenshaw et al., 1995, p. xiv)

CRT's critique of liberalism springs from its understanding of racism (as wide-ranging, often hidden and commonplace) and its frustration with the inability of traditional legal discourse to address anything except the most obvious and crude versions of racism. As already noted, CRT's principal con-cern is with "the business-as-usual forms of racism" that are "normal" and ingrained in the fabric of society, not with the few exceptional cases of obvious discrimination "that do stand out" (Delgado and Stefancic, 2000, p. xvi). CRT not only criticizes the inability of traditional legal discourse to deal with such complex and comprehensive racism; it goes further by viewing legal discourse as one of the prime means by which such a critical perspective is denied legiti-macy and the status quo is defended:

Racial justice was embraced in the American mainstream in terms that excluded radical or fundamental challenges to status quo institutional practices in American society by treating the exercise of racial power as rare and aberrational rather than as systemic and ingrained. ... [This perspective] conceived racism as an intentional, albeit irrational, deviation by a conscious wrongdoer from otherwise neutral, rational, and just ways of distributing jobs, power, prestige, and wealth. ... liberal race reform thus served to legitimize the basic myths of American meritocracy. (Crenshaw et al., 1995, p. xiv)

CRT's criticisms of meritocracy, and related notions such as objectivity and colorblindness, are not a rejection of them in principle but a criticism of their raced effects in practice. It is simply and demonstrably the case that these notions, despite their apparent concern for equity and justice, operate as a mechanism by which particular groups are excluded from the mainstream (be it in relation to legal redress, employment or educational opportunities). For example, arguments about the methods of social research are constantly rehearsed in the academy, and not only in relation to antiracist scholarship, where deeply conservative and regressive perspectives frequently masquerade as a concern for "objectivity," "neutrality" and "standards of evidence."[4]

William Tate concludes his review of the defining elements of CRT by noting that the approach "challenges ahistoricism and insists on a contextual/historical examination of the law and a recognition of the experiential knowledge of people of color" (Tate, 1997, p. 235). This relates to what Richard Delgado terms the "call to context": an insistence on the importance of context and the detail of the lived experience of minoritized peoples as a defense against the colorblind and sanitized analyses generated via universalistic discourses. The concern with the perspectives and experiences of minoritized groups arises from several different perspectives and offers numerous ways ahead. In relation to the legal roots of CRT, the call to context is essential to understand the full background to any major dispute or issue (Delgado and Stefancic, 2000). Even something as seemingly simple and obvious as a speeding violation might be rethought if the contextual information revealed that the speeding vehicle was an ambulance. Sociologically, of course, ethnographic and other forms of qualitative research take for granted the need to understand the viewpoints and experiences of multiple actors as an essential step in making sense of the social world—not because of any sentimental attachment to the underdog position (as Howard Becker, 1967, is often wrongly assumed to have argued), but as a recognition that people in different social locations have different perspectives and understandings:

Every analysis of a hierarchical situation must contain explicitly or implicitly some proposition, some empirical proposition about how the subordinates view things ... they, after all, know more about certain things than the people above them ... I systematically question as a routine matter whether the people who run any organization know anything about it. I don't say they don't, I just say it's a question … it's not that you do that for political motives you do it for scientific ones. But it has political consequence and the political consequence is almost invariably in the direction of anti-establishment. (Becker, 1980, pp. 15–17)[5]

Antiracism (in Britain and elsewhere) also has a long tradition of emphasizing the need to build on and respect the viewpoints and experiences of minoritized groups (see Brandt, 1986). This approach not only adds essential data and perspective; it can also offer a fundamental challenge to the commonsense assumptions through which so much racism operates and the mechanisms by which it is legitimized. Several scholars have written, for example, of the heated and sometimes emotional exchanges that occur when the silence about white racism is challenged in university classrooms (see Dlamini, 2002; Leonardo, 2002; Rich and Cargile, 2004). The exchanges by no means guarantee an equitable outcome, but they can dramatically highlight the ways in which notions of "validity" and "objectivity" operate in racialized ways. They also draw attention to the human scale of issues that are too often reduced to an apparently technical level in academic discussion. In a recent class, for example, I was exploring institutional racism and criticisms of whiteness with a large and diverse group of adult learners, most of them experienced schoolteachers. After a long exchange with a white teacher who vehemently disagreed with my interpretation of some particularly damning statistics on race inequity, a black woman intervened to draw attention to the consequences of her white peer's apparently technical argument:

> I'm really sick and tired of sitting in class and listening to people tell me that it's not about race. My children get it. I get it every day—at school, here, in the supermarket, everywhere. How dare you sit there and tell me that I'm wrong and that *you* don't believe the statistics. Don't you believe *me*?

The class became a brief but significant episode where the "diet of disparagement" that is routinely served to people of color in higher education (Foster, 2005) was dramatically refused.

CRT: Some Conceptual and Methodological Tools

It is highly significant that CRT scholars have been unwilling to identify a set of unchanging theoretical tenets and would rather talk of "basic insights" (Delgado and Stefancic, 2000) or "defining elements" (Tate, 1997). This reflects CRT's recognition of the changing and complex character of race/racism and its opposition in contemporary society. Nevertheless, as CRT grows, so the range and sophistication of its conceptual toolbox become a little clearer. In particular, concepts that have in the past been seen as definitively "CRT" in nature can now be viewed as tools rather than defining tenets. These are lines of analysis that often appear centrally in CRT treatments but whose presence does not necessarily signify a conscious appeal to CRT.

Storytelling and Counterstorytelling

A particularly striking aspect of some CRT is the use of storytelling and counterstorytelling. Here myths, assumptions and received wisdom can be questioned by shifting the grounds of debate or presenting analyses in ways that turn dominant assumptions on their head. Of course, (auto)biography and the use of narrative have long characterized many minoritized cultures. At their best, CRT approaches appropriate such forms and use them to build a powerful challenge to "mainstream" assumptions (see Delgado, 1995; Ladson-Billings and Tate, 1995; Ladson-Billings, 1998; Tate, 1997; Williams, 1987).

One of the best-known and most influential examples is Derrick Bell's "Chronicle of the Space Traders," which posits serious questions about how the United States would respond, as a nation, to a situation in which substantial benefits accrue to the white majority, but at the cost of even the most basic rights for African Americans (Bell 1990, 1992). Even as Bell relays his fictional account, wherein the entire African American population is sacrificed to alien Space Traders offering wealth, health and safety for non-blacks, there is clear sense that similar deals have already be done in history and will likely be done again in the future. Bell's story, first told in the 1990s, has already proven prophetic in terms of the U.S. Patriot Act of 2001 and other costs to civil liberties enacted in the name of national defense.[6] British antiracists experienced a parallel situation following the bombings in London in July 2005: the response of the media, politicians and security forces exemplified the conditional status of people of color, whose presence, feelings and basic human rights were readily sacrificed in the panic to respond (Gillborn, 2005b).

Interest Convergence

Derrick Bell is generally credited with coining the concept of "interest convergence" in a paper in the *Harvard Law Review* (Bell 1980b). This notion proposes that "white elites will tolerate or encourage racial advances for blacks only when such advances also promote white self-interest" (Delgado and Stefancic, 2000, p. xvii). It has been especially important, for example, in understanding the history of affirmative action in the United States—an approach that superficially privileges black interests but whose principal beneficiaries have been white women, in terms of numbers benefiting from affirmative action hiring policies (Ladson-Billings, 1998, p. 12). Similarly, it has been argued that the *Brown v. Board of Education* decision on the desegregation of U.S. public schools owed a great deal to Cold War politics and the need to protect the U.S. image overseas (Bell, 1980b; Dudziak, 2000). More recently, a Supreme Court decision on affirmative action is widely thought to have been swayed by representations that linked the policy to national security – arguing that without black officers (promoted preferentially), the U.S. armed forces could become unmanageable.[7]

Critical White Studies

A poor rural Mississippi "white" man was asked by a New Orleans newspaper reporter, "What is white?" After musing for a little while, the man responded, "Well, I don't know a lot about that. But, I'll tell you one thing … it's not black!'" (Hare 2002, 7–8)

As Rosa Hernandez Sheets (2000, 2003) has argued, focusing on white people (their sense of self, their interests and concerns) has become such a fashionable pastime within parts of the U.S. academy that there is a danger of whiteness studies colonizing and further deradicalizing multicultural education. However, the field is extremely wide. If the guilt-ridden white introspection that Sheets fears is at one end of the spectrum, at the other pole lie Marxist analyses that firmly identify whiteness as one more "strategy for securing to some an advantage in a competitive society" (Ignatiev, 1997, p. 1).

Whiteness studies is a growing area but, in relation to CRT, it is the nature of the questions and analyses that is important. It is insufficient merely to state a concern with how whiteness is organized and understood. As Philip Howard has argued, for example, some "ostensibly antiracist" work on whiteness has allowed a concern with diversity within whiteness to erase more critical questions, ultimately leading to the highly conservative and somewhat nonsensical idea that white subjects labeled with the epithet "white trash" "might be compared to a 'racial minority' position vis-à-vis whiteness" (Newitz and Wray, 1997, p. 5, quoted by Howard, 2004, p. 71). As Howard notes, "the whiteness of white trash is still privileged" (2004, p. 70).

What matters for whiteness studies within CRT is the deeply critical and radical nature of the questioning. In some hands, whiteness studies can become just another exercise of whiteness itself, as Michael Apple has warned:

Having Whites focus on whiteness can have contradictory effects, ones of which we need to be well aware. It can enable people to acknowledge differential power and the raced nature of everyone … It can just as easily run the risk of lapsing into the possessive individualism that is so powerful in this society. That is, such a process can serve the chilling function of simply saying "but enough about you, let me tell you about me." (Apple, 1998b, p. xi)

The past two decades or so have seen a significant increase in the amount of critical scholarship on the nature of whiteness—that is, work deconstructing the taken-for-granted myths and assumptions that circulate about what it means to be, and not be, a "white" person (see Bush, 2004; Delgado and Stefancic, 1997; Fine et al., 1997; Gillborn, 2005a; Leonardo, 2002, 2004).

Critical scholarship on whiteness is not an assault on white people per se: it is an assault on the socially constructed and constantly reinforced power of white identifications and interests (see Ladson-Billings and Tate, 1995, pp. 58–60). So-called white people (Bonnett 1997, p. 189) do not necessarily reinforce whiteness any more than heterosexual people are *necessarily* homophobic, or men are *necessarily* sexist. However, these analogies are useful because they highlight the forces that re-create and extend the kinds of unthinking assumptions and actions that mean that most heterosexuals *are* homophobic and most men *are* sexist. It is possible for white people to take a real and active role in deconstructing whiteness, but such "race traitors" are relatively uncommon. It is, of course, also possible for people who do not identify as "white" nevertheless actively to reinforce and defend whiteness.

Conclusion

Although Critical Race scholarship differs in object, argument, accent and emphasis, it is nevertheless unified by two common interests. The first is to understand how a regime of white supremacy and its subordination of people of color have been created and maintained in America. ... The second is a desire not merely to understand the vexed bond between law and racial power but to *change* it. (Crenshaw et al., 1995, p. xiii)

The language and achievements of CRT are not widely recognized outside North America. Nevertheless, there is a great deal to be gained by a dynamic understanding of how antiracists and critical race theorists have approached certain key issues and dilemmas. Both schools share a concern not merely to document but to change: they are engaged in *praxis*. Building upon this common commitment, in this chapter I have argued for a conscious and reflexive engagement between antiracism and CRT.

This is a field where perspectives can quickly become confused and misunderstood. So let me end by stating, as clearly as possible, the key points that I have been trying to make. First, it may be useful to clarify what I am not saying. I am not arguing for an abandonment of antiracism. Following the Burnage inquiry and the media's manipulation of the tragedy, many writers were quick to write off antiracism in the 1990s. The gains made following the Stephen Lawrence Inquiry demonstrate that real and important changes are possible. However, antiracism must remain a critical perspective concerned with a radical analysis of power and its operation through racialized processes of exclusion and oppression.

Second, I am not seeking to establish an antiracist rule book or blueprint. Racism is complex, contradictory and fast-changing: it follows that antiracism must be equally dynamic. What works in one place at one time may not work at another place or another time (Gillborn, 1995, 2000). But we are not faced with an all-or-nothing choice. In seeking to promote a wider understanding of critical race theory beyond North America, I am not suggesting that CRT is in any sense a complete and unproblematic approach. CRT is a relatively new and developing perspective. Even the modest set of theoretical starting points outlined here would almost certainly be challenged by some within the field. Nevertheless, this level of complexity is no excuse for the continued absence of CRT from the vast majority of work on race and education outside the United States.

In this chapter, therefore, I have set out the case for a greater awareness of CRT and for its adoption within a revitalized critical antiracism. In this way CRT offers a coherent and challenging set of important sensitizing insights and conceptual tools. These provide a starting point for critical antiracist analyses that can avoid some of the dangers inherent in the current situation—where antiracism risks being reduced to the level of the worst kind of vapid "multi-culturalism": a slogan bereft of all critical content, ritually cited but leaving untouched the deep-rooted processes of racist oppression and exclusion that currently shape the education systems in many nation-states. Perhaps most significantly, CRT offers a challenge to educational studies more generally, and to the sociology of education in particular, to cease the ritualistic citation of "race" as just another point of departure on a list of exclusions to be mentioned and then bracketed away. CRT insists that racism be placed at the center of analyses and that scholarly work be engaged in the process of rejecting and deconstructing the current patterns of racist exclusion and oppression.

In turn, CRT also stands to gain from its wider adoption beyond North America. Leading CRT writers are well aware of the dangers faced by an approach that has a radical heritage but could, at any time, find itself assimilated into an uncritical stock of orthodox terms and grand narratives cited for effect but robbed of their true character (see Delgado and Stefancic, 2001; Ladson-Billings, 1998; Tate, 1999). If CRT genuinely speaks to fundamental processes of racist oppression that extend beyond the confines of a single nation-state, as I believe it does, then the approach will be strengthened and enriched by the ever-growing diversity of experience and critique offered by dialogue with fellow 'crits' globally. As CRT develops, however, a key warning must be held close by all of us. Put simply, we must ensure that we remain critical, not only of powerholders but also of our own assumptions and our vested interests. There are no easy solutions to the dilemmas we face, but an awareness of the pitfalls is a good starting point:

> We must first recognize and acknowledge (at least to ourselves) that our actions are not likely to lead to transcendent change and may indeed, despite our best efforts, be of more help to the system we despise than to the victims of that system whom we are trying to help. Then, and only then, can that realization and the dedication based on it lead to policy

positions and campaigns that are less likely to worsen conditions for those we are trying to help and more likely to remind the powers that be that out there are persons like us who are not only not on their side but determined to stand in their way. (Bell, 1992, pp. 198–199)

Notes

1. One of the most important contemporary discussions of these challenges was Ali Rattansi's (1992) contribution to a new Open University Course ED356 'Race', Education and Society . See also Nazir Carrim's (1995) discussion of how these issues have developed.
2. See Gillborn (1995).
3. The Commission for Racial Equality is a publicly funded body with responsibility for advising on race equality issues and policing the enforcement of relevant legislation.
4. See, for example, the debate about antiracist research in the UK. Foster et al. (1996), Hammersley (1995, 2000) and Tooley with Darby (1998) are leading examples of the "standards" approach; see Blair (2004), Connolly (1998) and Gillborn (1995) for critical commentaries and responses.
5. This is an extract from an interview with Howard Becker conducted by J. C. Verhoeven for his study of symbolic interaction (Verhoeven, 1989). I am extremely grateful to Professor Verhoeven for so generously sharing his data with me.
6. Uniting and Strengthening America by Providing Appropriate Tools Required to Intercept and Obstruct Terrorism (USA PATRIOT ACT) Act of 2001. Public Law 107-56-Oct. 26 2001. A full transcript of the legislation may be downloaded from the American Civil Liberties Union at http://www.aclu.org/SafeandFree/SafeandFree.cfm?ID=12251&c=207 (last accessed 21 February 2005).
7. This is one of the factors identified in the brief by the University of Michigan, defending its admissions policies. The support of then U.S. Secretary of State, the Republican former general Colin Powell, was also seen as a key factor in contemporary news coverage (CNN. com, 2003). For further background on the Michigan case, see Ethridge 2003).

References

Apple, M. W. (1998a). Education and New Hegemonic Blocs: Doing Policy the 'Right' Way. *International Studies in Sociology of Education* 8(2): 181–202.
Apple, M. W. (1998b). Foreword. In J. L. Kincheloe, S. R. Steinberg, N. M. Rodriguez and R. E. Chennault (eds.), *White Reign: Deploying Whiteness in America* (ix–xiii). New York: St. Martin's.
Apple, M. W. (2001). *Educating the "Right" Way: Markets, Standards, God and Inequality.* New York: RoutledgeFalmer.
Apple, M. W. (2004). *Ideology and Curriculum.*3rd ed. New York: RoutledgeFalmer.
Ashton, C. (2002). Untitled contribution to Greater London Authority.
Ashton, C. (2003). *Towards a Vision of Excellence: London Schools and the Black Child: 2002 Conference Report.* London: Greater London Authority.
Ball, S. J. (1994). *Education Reform: A Critical and Post-Structural Approach.* Buckingham: Open University Press.
Ball, S. J. (2004) The Sociology of Education: A Disputational Account. In S. J. Ball (ed.), *The RoutledgeFalmer Reader in Sociology of Education*, 1–12. London: RoutledgeFalmer.
Becker, H. S. (1967). Whose Side Are We On? *Social Problems* 14: 239–247.
Becker, H.S. (1980). Interview with Jeff Verhoeven, quoted in Verhoeven, J.C. (1989) *Methodological and Metascientific Problems in Symbolic Interactionism.* Leuven, Belgium: Katholieke Universiteit Leuven.
Bell, D. (1980a). *Race, Racism and American Law.* Boston: Little Brown.
Bell, D. (1980b). *Brown v. Board of Education* and the Interest Convergence Dilemma. *Harvard Law Review* 93: 518–533.
Bell, D. (1990). After We're Gone: Prudent Speculations on America in a Post-Racial Epoch. *St. Louis Law Journal,* reprinted in R. Delgado and J. Stefancic (eds.) (2000), *Critical Race Theory: The Cutting Edge,* 2–8. 2nd ed. Philadelphia: Temple University Press.
Bell, D. (1992). *Faces at the Bottom of the Well: The Permanence of Racism.* New York: Basic Books.

Bhavnani, R. (2001). *Rethinking Interventions to Combat Racism*. Stoke-on-Trent: Commission for Racial Equality with Trentham Books.
Blair, M. (2004). The Myth of Neutrality in Educational Research. In G. Ladson-Billings and D. Gillborn (eds.), *The RoutledgeFalmer Reader in Multicultural Education* (243–251). London: RoutledgeFalmer.
Blair, M. and Bourne, J.; with Coffin, C.; Creese, A.; and Kenner, C. (1998). *Making the Difference: Teaching and Learning Strategies in Successful Multi-Ethnic Schools*. London: Department for Education and Employment.
Bonnett, A. (1997). Constructions of Whiteness in European and American Anti-Racism. In P. Werbner and T. Mohood (eds.), *Debating Cultural Hybridity*. London: Zed Books, 173–192.
Bonnett, A. (2000). *Anti-Racism*. London: Routledge.
Bourne, J. (1980). Cheerleaders and Ombudsmen: The Sociology of Race Relations in Britain, *Race and Class* 21: 331–352.
Brah, A. and Minhas, R. (1985). Structural Racism or Cultural Difference: Schooling for Asian Girls. In G. Weiner (ed.), *Just a Bunch of Girls: Feminist Approaches to Schooling* (14–25). Milton Keynes: Open University Press.
Brandt, G. L. (1986). *The Realization of Anti-Racist Teaching*. Lewes: Falmer.
Bush, M. E. L. (2004). Race, Ethnicity, and Whiteness. *Sage Race Relations Abstracts* 29(3–4): 5–48.
Carby, H. (1982). 'White Women Listen! Black Feminism and the Boundaries of Sisterhood.' In CCCS (compilers), *The Empire Strikes Back: Race and Racism in 70s Britain* (212–235). London: Hutchinson.
Carmichael, S. and Hamilton, C. V. (1967). *Black Power: The Politics of Liberation in America*. New York: Random House. Excerpts reprinted in E. Cashmore and J. Jennings (eds.) (2001), *Racism: Essential Readings*. London, Sage.
Carrim, N. (1995). From 'Race' to Ethnicity: Shifts in the Educational Discourses of South Africa and Britain in the 1990s. *Compare* 25(1): 17–33.
Carrim, N. and Soudien, C. (1999). Critical Antiracism in South Africa. In S. May (ed.), *Critical Multiculturalism: Rethinking Multicultural and Antiracist Education* (153–171). London: Falmer.
Centre for Contemporary Cultural Studies (1982). *The Empire Strikes Back*. London: Hutchinson.
Chevannes, M. and Reeves, F. (1987). The Black Voluntary School Movement: Definition, Context and Prospects. In B. Troyna (ed.), *Racial Inequality in Education* (147–169). London: Tavistock.
CNN.com (2003). Powell Defends Affirmative Action in College Admissions, at http://www.cnn.com/2003/ALLPOLITICS/01/19/powell.race. Accessed 1 February 2005.
Coard, B. (1971). *How the West Indian Child Is Made Educationally Sub-Normal in the British School System*. London: New Beacon.
Cole, M. (1986). Teaching and Learning about Racism: A Critique of Multicultural Education in Britain. In S. Modgil, G. K. Verma, K. Mallick and C. Modgil (eds.), *Multicultural Education: The Interminable Debate* (123–147). Lewes: Falmer.
Connolly, P. (1998). "Dancing to the Wrong Tune": Ethnography, Generalization and Research on Racism in Schools. In P. Connolly and B. Troyna (eds.), *Researching Racism in Education: Politics, Theory and Practice* (122–139). Buckingham: Open University Press.
Crenshaw, K. (1988). Race, Reform, Retrenchment: Transformation and Legitimation in Anti-Discrimination Law. *Harvard Law Review* 101: 1331–1387.
Crenshaw, K.; Gotanda, N.; Peller, G.; and Thomas, K. (eds.) (1995). *Critical Race Theory: The Key Writings That Formed the Movement*. New York: New Press.
Dadzie, S. (2000). *Toolkit for Tackling Racism in Schools*. Stoke-on-Trent: Trentham.
Dale, R. (1989). *The State and Education Policy*. Buckingham: Open University Press.
Dale, R. (1992). Recovering from a Pyrrhic Victory? Quality, Relevance and Impact in the Sociology of Education. In M. Arnot and L. Barton (eds.), *Voicing Concerns: Sociological Perspectives on Educational Reforms* (207–210). Wallingford: Triangle.
Dale, R. (2001). Shaping the Sociology of Education over Half-a-Century. In J. Demaine (ed.), *Sociology of Education Today* (5–29). New York: Palgrave.
Delamont, S. (2001). Reflections on Social Exclusion. *International Studies in Sociology of Education* 11(1): 25–40.

Delgado, R. (1989). Storytelling for Oppositionists and Others: A Plea for Narrative. *Michigan Law Review* 87: 2411–2441.

Delgado, R. (1995). *The Rodrigo Chronicles: Conversations about America and Race*. New York: New York University Press.

Delgado, R., and Stefancic, J. (eds.) (1997). *Critical White Studies: Looking behind the Mirror*. Philadelphia: Temple University Press.

Delgado, R., and Stefancic, J. (2000). Introduction. In R. Delgado and J. Stefancic (eds.), *Critical Race Theory: The Cutting Edge* (xv–xix). 2nd ed. Philadelphia: Temple University Press.

Department for Education and Skills (2004). *Five Year Strategy for Children and Learners: Putting People at the Heart of Public Services*. London: Department for Education and Skills.

Department for Education and Skills (2005). *Ethnicity and Education: The Evidence on Minority Ethnic Pupils*. Research Topic Paper RTP01-05. London: DfES.

Dhondy, F. (1974). The Black Explosion in British Schools. *Race Today*, February, pp. 44–47.

Dixson, A. D. and Rousseau, C. K. (eds.) (2005). Special issue on Critical Race Theory in Education. *Race, Ethnicity and Education* 8(1).

Dlamini, S. N. (2002). From the Other Side of the Desk: Notes on Teaching about Race When Racialised. *Race, Ethnicity and Education* 5(1): 51–66.

Dudziak, M. L. (2000). Desegregation as a Cold War Imperative. In R. Delgado and J. Stefancic (eds.), *Critical Race Theory*, 106–117. Philadelphia: Temple University Press.

Ethridge, R. W. (2003). *AAAA Michigan FAQs: Michigan's Admissions Systems Are Equitable*. At http://www.affirmativeaction.org/michigan-FAQs.html. Accessed 1 February 2005.

File, N. and Power, C. (1981). *Black Settlers in Britain 1555–1958*. London: Heinemann.

Fine, M.; Weis, L.; Powell, L. C.; and Mun Wong, L. (eds.) (1997). *Off White: Readings on Race, Power, and Society*. New York: Routledge.

Foster, K. M. (2005) Diet of Disparagement: The Racial Experiences of Black Students in a Predominantly White University. *International Journal of Qualitative Studies in Education* 18(4): 489–505.

Foster, P.; Gomm, R.; and Hammersley, M. (1996). *Constructing Educational Inequality*. London: Falmer.

Gill, D. and Levidow, L. (eds.) (1987). *Anti-racist Science Teaching*. London: Free Association.

Gillborn, D. (1995). *Racism and Antiracism in Real Schools: Theory. Policy. Practice*. Buckingham: Open University Press.

Gillborn, D. (2000). Anti-racism: From Policy to Praxis. In G. Ladson-Billings and D. Gillborn (eds.), *The RoutledgeFalmer Reader in Multicultural Education* (35–48). New York: RoutledgeFalmer.

Gillborn, D. (2002). *Education and Institutional Racism*. London: Institute of Education, University of London.

Gillborn, D. (2005a). Education Policy as an Act of White Supremacy: Whiteness, Critical Race Theory and Education Reform. *Journal of Education Policy* 20(4): 485–505.

Gillborn, D. (2005b). *Rethinking White Supremacy: Who Counts in 'WhiteWorld'*. Ms., Education Policy Research Unit, Institute of Education, University of London.

Gillborn, D. and Gipps, C. (1996). Recent Research on the Achievements of Ethnic Minority Pupils. Report for the Office for Standards in Education, London: Her Majesty's Stationery Office.

Gillborn, D. and Mirza, H. S. (2000). *Educational Inequality: Mapping Race, Class and Gender—A Synthesis of Research Evidence*. Report #HMI 232. London: Office for Standards in Education.

Gilroy, P. (1987). *There Ain't No Black in the Union Jack*. London: Hutchinson.

Gilroy, P. (1988). *Problems in Anti-Racist Strategy*. London: Runnymede Trust.

Hammersley, M. (1995). *The Politics of Social Research*. London: Sage.

Hammersley, M. (2000). *Taking Sides in Social Research: Essays on Partisanship and Bias*. London: Routledge.

Haque, Z. (2000). The Ethnic Minority 'Underachieving' Group? Investigating the Claims of 'Underachievement' amongst Bangladeshi Pupils in British Secondary Schools, *Race, Ethnicity and Education* 3(2): 145–168.

Hare, B. R. (2002). Toward Cultural Pluralism and Economic Justice. In B. Hare (ed.), *2001 Race Odyssey: African Americans and Sociology* (3–21). New York, Syracuse University Press.

Howard, P. S. S. (2004). White Privilege: For or Against? A Discussion of Ostensibly Antiracist Discourses in Critical Whiteness Studies. *Race, Gender and Class* 11(4): 63–79.

Ignatiev, N. (1997). The Point Is Not To Interpret Whiteness But To Abolish It. Talk given at the conference "The Making and Unmaking of Whiteness," University of California, Berkeley, 11–13 April 1997. Available at www.postfun.com/racetraitor

Ladson-Billings, G. (1998). Just What Is Critical Race Theory and What's It Doing in a *Nice* Field Like Education? *International Journal of Qualitative Studies in Education* 11: 7–24.

Ladson-Billings, G. (1999). Preparing Teachers for Diverse Student Populations: A Critical Race Theory Perspective. In A. Iran-Nejad and P. D. Pearson (eds.), *Review of Research in Education*, vol. 24, 211–247. Washington, DC: American Educational Research Association.

Ladson-Billings, G. (2005). The Evolving Role of Critical Race Theory in Educational Scholarship *Race, Ethnicity and Education* 8(1): 115–119.

Ladson-Billings, G. and Tate, W. F. (1995). Toward a Critical Race Theory of Education. *Teachers College Record* 97(1): 47–68.

Lawrence, E. (1982). In the Abundance of Water the Fool Is Thirsty: Sociology and Black 'Pathology.' In CCCS, *The Empire Strikes Back* (95–142). London: Hutchinson.

Leonardo, Z. (2002). The Souls of White Folk: Critical Pedagogy, Whiteness Studies, and Globalization Discourse. *Race, Ethnicity and Education* 5(1): 29–50.

Leonardo, Z. (2004). The Color of Supremacy: Beyond the Discourse of 'White Privilege.' *Educational Philosophy and Theory* 36(2): 137–152.

Mac an Ghaill, M. (1999). *Contemporary Racisms and Ethnicities: Social and Cultural Transformations*. Buckingham: Open University Press.

Macdonald, I.; Bhavnani, R.; Khan, L.; and John, G. (1989). *Murder in the Playground: The Report of the Macdonald Inquiry into Racism and Racial Violence in Manchester Schools*. London: Longsight.

Macpherson, W. (1999). *The Stephen Lawrence Inquiry*. CM 4262-I. London: Stationery Office.

Matsuda, M. J.; Lawrence, C. R.; Delgado, R.; and Crenshaw, K. W. (eds.) (1993). *Words that Wound: Critical Race Theory, Assaultive Speech, and the First Amendment*. Boulder, CO: Westview.

Mirza, H. S. (ed.) (1997). *Black British Feminism*. London: Routledge.

Modood, T.; Berthoud, R.; Lakey, J.; Nazroo, J.; Smith, P.; Virdee, S.; and Beishon, S. (1997). *Ethnic Minorities in Britain: Diversity and Disadvantage*. London: Policy Studies Institute.

Moore, R. (1996). Back to the Future: The Problem of Change and the Possibilities of Advance in the Sociology of Education, *British Journal of Sociology of Education* 17(2): 145–162.

Morley, L. and Rassool, N. (1999). *School Effectiveness: Fracturing the Discourse*. London: Falmer.

Mullard, C. (1982). Multiracial Education in Britain: From Assimilation to Cultural Pluralism. In J. Tierney (ed.), *Race, Migration and Schooling*, 120–133. London: Holt, Rinehart and Winston.

Mullard, C. (1984). *Anti-Racist Education: The Three O's*. Cardiff: National Anti-racist Movement in Education.

Newitz, A. and Wray, M. (1997). Introduction. In M. Wray and A. Newitz (eds.), *White Trash: Race and Class in America*. New York: Routledge.

Nixon, J. (1985). *A Teacher's Guide to Multicultural Education*. Oxford: Blackwell.

Osler, A. (1997). *Exclusion from School and Racial Equality*. London: Commission for Racial Equality.

Ozga, J. (1990). Policy Research and Policy Theory. *Journal of Education Policy* 5(4): 359–362.

Parker, L. (1998). "Race Is ... Race Ain't": An Exploration of the Utility of Critical Race Theory in Qualitative Research in Education. *International Journal of Qualitative Studies in Education* 11(1): 43–55.

Rattansi, A. (1992). Changing the Subject? Racism, Culture and Education. In J. Donald and A. Rattansi (eds.), *'Race', Culture and Difference* (11–48). London: Sage.

Rich, M. D. and Cargile, A. C. (2004). Beyond the Breach: Transforming White Identities in the Classroom, *Race, Ethnicity and Education* 7(4): 351–365.

Richardson, R. (2002). *In Praise of Teachers: Identity, Equality and Education*. Stoke-on-Trent: Trentham.

Richardson, R. and Wood, A. (1999). *Inclusive Schools, Inclusive Society: Race and Identity on the Agenda*. Report produced for Race on the Agenda in partnership with Association of London Government and Save the Children. Stoke-on-Trent: Trentham.

Rizvi, F. (2003). Democracy and Education after September 11. *Globalisation, Societies and Education* 1(1): 25–40.

Roithmayr, D. (1999). Introduction to Critical Race Theory in Educational Research and Praxis. In L. Parker, D. Deyhle and S. Villenas (eds.), *Race Is ... Race Isn't: Critical Race Theory and Qualitative Studies in Education* (1–6). Boulder, CO: Westview.

Sarup, M. (1986). *The Politics of Multicultural Education*. London: Routledge and Kegan Paul.

Schneider-Ross (2003). *Towards Racial Equality: An Evaluation of the Public Duty To Promote Race Equality and Good Race Relations in England and Wales*. London: CRE.

Sheets, R. H. (2000). Advancing the Field or Taking Center Stage: The White Movement in Multicultural Education. *Educational Researcher* 29(9): 15–21.

Sheets, R. H. (2003). Competency vs. Good Intentions: Diversity Ideologies and Teacher Potential. *International Journal of Qualitative Studies in Education* 16(1): 111–120.

Sivanandan, A. (1988). Left, Right and Burnage. *New Statesman*, 27 May; reprinted in A. Sivanandan (1990), *Communities of Resistance: Writings on Black Struggles for Socialism*, 145–152. London: Verso.

Sivanandan, A. (2000). Reclaiming the Struggle – One Year On. *Multicultural Teaching* 18(2): 6–8, 20.

Tate, W. F. (1997). Critical Race Theory and Education: History, Theory, and Implications. In M. W. Apple (ed.), *Review of Research in Education, vol. 22* (195–247). Washington, DC: American Educational Research Association.

Tate, W. F. (1999). Conclusion. In L. Parker et al. (eds.), *Race Is … Race Isn't: Critical Race Theory and Qualitative Studies in Education* (251–271). Boulder, CO: Westview.

Tate, W. F. (2005). Ethics, Engineering and the Challenge of Racial Reform in Education. *Race, Ethnicity and Education* 8(1): 123–129.

Taylor, E. (1999). Critical Race Theory and Interest Convergence in the Desegregation of Higher Education. In L. Parker et al. (eds.), *Race Is... Race Isn't: Critical Race Theory and Qualitative Studies in Education* (181–204). Boulder, CO: Westview.

Thrupp, M. (1999). *Schools Making a Difference: Let's be Realistic!* Buckingham: Open University Press.

Thrupp, M. and Wilmott, R. (2004). *Education Management in Managerialist Times: Beyond the Textual Apologists*. Maidenhead: Open University Press.

Tomlinson, S. (1984). *Home and School in Multicultural Britain*. London: Batsford.

Tooley, J. with Darby, D. (1998). *Educational Research: A Critique*. London: Office for Standards in Education.

Troyna, B. (1984). Multicultural Education: Emancipation or Containment? In L. Barton and S. Walker (eds.), *Social Crisis and Educational Research*, 75–97. London: Croom Helm.

Troyna, B. (1987). A Conceptual Overview of Strategies To Combat Racial Inequality in Education. In B. Troyna (ed.), *Racial Inequality in Education* (1–10). London: Tavistock.

Troyna, B. (1988). The Career of an Antiracist Education School Policy: Some Observations on the Mismanagement of Change. In A. G. Green and S. J. Ball (eds.), *Progress and Inequality in Comprehensive Education*, 158–178. London: Routledge.

Troyna, B. (1991). Underachievers or Underrated? The Experiences of Pupils of South Asian Origin in a Secondary School. *British Educational Research Journal* 17(4): 361–376.

Troyna, B. (1992). Can You See the Join? An Historical Analysis of Multicultural and Antiracist Education Policies. In D. Gill, B. Mayor and M. Blair (eds.), *Racism and Education: Structures and Strategies*, 63–91. London: Sage.

Troyna, B. (1993). *Racism and Education*. Buckingham: Open University Press.

Troyna, B. (1998). Paradigm Regained: A Critique of 'Cultural Deficit' Theories in Contemporary Educational Research. *Comparative Education* 24(3): 273–284.

Troyna, B. and Carrington, B. (1990). *Education, Racism and Reform*. London: Routledge.

Troyna, B. and Hatcher, R. (1992). *Racism in Children's Lives: A Study of Mainly White Primary Schools*. London: Routledge.

Verhoeven, J. C. (1989). *Methodological and Metascientific Problems in Symbolic Interactionism*. Leuven: Katholieke Universiteit Leuven.

Villenas, S., Deyhle, D., and Parker, L. (1999). Critical Race Theory and Praxis: Chicano(a)/Latino(a) and Navajo Struggles for Dignity, Educational Equity, and Social Justice. In L. Parker et al. (eds.), *Race Is … Race Isn't: Critical Race Theory and Qualitative Studies in Education* (31–52). Boulder, CO: Westview.

Weekes, D. and Wright, C. (1999). *Improving Practice: A Whole School Approach to Raising the Achievement of African Caribbean Youth*. London: Runnymede Trust in association with Nottingham Trent University.

West, C. (1995). Foreword. In K. Crenshaw et al. (eds.), *Critical Race Theory: The Key Writings That Formed the Movement* (xi–xii). New York: New Press.

Whitty, G., Power, S., and Halpin, D. (1998). *Devolution and Choice in Education: The School, the State and the Market.* Buckingham: Open University Press.

Williams, P. J. (1987). Alchemical Notes: Reconstructing Ideals from Deconstructed Rights. *Harvard Civil Rights – Civil Liberties Law Review*; reprinted in R. Delgado and J. Stefancic (eds.) (2000), *Critical Race Theory: The Cutting Edge*, 80–90. Philadelphia: Temple University Press.

Wing, A. K. (ed.) (2000). *Global Critical Race Feminism: An International Reader.* New York: New York University Press.

14

Ethics, Engineering, and the Challenge of Racial Reform in Education

WILLIAM F. TATE IV

The chapters of this book are the intellectual products of the New Race Group of Legal Studies, more commonly referred to as the critical race theory (CRT) movement. Originally a theoretical movement in the field of law, CRT has expanded over the past decade to include scholars in the social sciences, humanities and education. My colleague Gloria Ladson-Billings and I co-authored a paper, "Toward a Critical Race Theory of Education," initially presented at the 1994 annual meeting of the American Educational Research Association (AERA) in New Orleans, Louisiana, and ultimately published in *Teachers College Record* (Ladson-Billings and Tate, 1995). The purpose of this chapter is to provide a brief discussion of my thinking about CRT in educational scholarship more than ten years after the presentation of that initial paper and to offer recommendations for scholars interested in building on and moving beyond this theoretical project. My remarks are framed as a global response to the chapters of this volume. As background, I review part of my academic career as it relates to CRT and education. Specifically, my purpose is to provide history relevant to the development of the initial CRT and education paper co-presented at AERA in 1994.

My doctoral studies in mathematics education were completed in 1991. I was very dissatisfied with many theoretical perspectives associated with the field. Largely drawing from psychology and mathematics, the traditional paradigmatic boundaries of mathematics education lacked the kind of explanatory power required to capture the dynamics of race and scientific attainment, broadly defined. The focus on individuals and at times on classroom settings provided important insights into student reasoning and distributive cognition. However, broader notions relating structural barriers and ideological projects to the realities of access and opportunity for various racial groups to learn scientific knowledge were emerging in the U.S. context, but not yet fully articulated as theoretical propositions. My perception at the time was that there did not appear to be a great deal of interest among researchers to create a sociology

This chapter originally appeared in *Race, Ethnicity and Education* 8(1), March 2005, pp. 121–126.

of mathematics education. Other scholars outside mathematics education were clearly dealing with the sociology of education, which at times addressed subject matter learning in mathematics and science. However, the systematic study of relationships among educational actors building on the assumption that behavior is influenced by social, political, occupational and intellectual groupings of students and parents and by the particular settings in which individuals and families find themselves was not part of the mainstream discourse in mathematics education. Nor was race a salient aspect of that research. Instead, demographic trends describing in careful detail achievement differences among racial groups were the predominant form of "race-based" scholarship.

In 1991, during my tenure as an Ann Julia Cooper Fellow at the University of Wisconsin, my soon-to-be wife shared with me an article by Kimberlé Crenshaw (1991) in the *Harvard Law Review*, entitled "Race Reform and Retrenchment: Transformation and Legitimation in Anti-discrimination Law." Crenshaw called for a critique of liberal and conservative legal discourse in the post-Reagan era. This intellectual space provided room for instrumentalism yet called for a historical analysis that focused on understanding "raced" decision making in both legal and political settings. However, Crenshaw did not view this as sufficient. There needed to be more cogent insights into the lives of African Americans and other groups typically invisible in mainstream legal thought and scholarship. The intersection of historical analysis with examinations of the lived realities of "invisible" racial and ethnic groups and the recognition of incremental gains attained by traditional civil rights methods provided a rhetorical and analytical mechanism to question assumptions of both liberals and conservatives with respect to the goals and the means of racial reform. Critical race theory presented a new paradigm using a variety of methodological tools, including storytelling, to inform understanding of racial injustice and to provide new ways of seeing the links among race, gender and class. From my perspective at the time, this movement represented the kind of intellectual space required for understanding the opportunity structures within education in the United States. There was one factor that I did not foresee—media and the role of public intellectuals.

Most academic movements are restricted to college campuses, think tanks, policy consortiums, and so on. The work of Derrick Bell, Kimberlé Crenshaw, Patricia Williams, Richard Delgado, and other members of the CRT movement has expanded beyond the ivory tower. These scholars and their writings appear in books, newsletters, listserves, web-based outlets, bibliographic tools and other digital media. The rapid expansion of digital media in conjunction with the hallmarks of CRT—storytelling methodology, legal insights, and historical analysis related to racial reform—proved a powerful combination. This media-ready combination, though complementary, was not unique to CRT. Other intellectual movements also have expanded in ways not possible before the digital age. However, it is important to understand that the rapid proliferation of writings and articles associated with CRT, including critiques of the movement, is partly a function of media access. I have found the reaction to CRT to be largely bifurcated. The negative response to CRT provides important lessons for the authors of this volume and other interested scholars. In the next section I will give an example.

Ethics, Engineering and Racial Theorizing

Critical race theory has been labeled a dangerous framework for examining matters of race. A common concern involves the intersection among race, religion and social policy. In discussing his disdain for CRT writings and other raced-based perspectives, the Reverend Jesse Lee Peterson (2003) stated:

> By preaching race hatred and the cleverly packaged ideology of social-ism, these leaders have convinced millions of blacks that white America owes them special treatment: welfare checks, affirmative action pro-grams, and even different grading systems in our nation's universities. Black educators have even created a fictional Afrocentrist history that pushes phony notions of black racial superiority in our nation's schools. Other educators have devised what they call critical race theory, which claims that there is no such thing as objective reality—that "rationality" is simply a tool of white males and is designed to oppress minorities. (Peterson, 2003, p. 2)

Unpacking the comments above is worthy of a separate article. However, the goal of this section is to illustrate that to understand race and how it operates requires an understanding of truth, morality, and in particular, ethics. I will use one of the definitions of the word "ethics" offered in the *American Diction-ary of the English Language* produced by Noah Webster in 1828: "The doctrines of morality or social manners; the science of moral philosophy, which teaches men their duty and the reasons of it." This definition of ethics is relevant in light of a recent study of how Americans view matters of morality and truth. In two national surveys administered by Barna Research (2002), one among adults and one among teenagers, people were questioned to determine if they believed whether moral truth is unchanging or depends on the situation. By nearly a 3-to-1 margin (64 vs. 22 percent), adults said truth always depends on the situation. Teenagers were more likely to say moral truths were context-dependent (83 percent) rather than unchanging (6 percent). The Barna report also demonstrated that there is a racial difference here. Among white respondents, 60 percent embraced relativism, while 26 percent advocated absolut-ism. Among nonwhite respondents, however, 74 percent embraced relativism and just 15 percent supported absolute morality. More specifically, African American and Hispanic adult respondents' belief in absolute moral truth was 10 percent and 15 percent, respectively. It is not a shock that born-again Chris-tians respondents were more likely than other individuals to report accepting moral absolutes—32 percent and 15 percent, respectively. What do these views of moral reasoning have to do with CRT? Obviously, Reverend Peterson, religious leaders operating from traditional Christian theology, or similar-thinking policy makers would charge that any academic writings that involve CRT and advocate moral relativism are at best limited and at worst dangerous (e.g., Bork, 1997; Noebel, 1991; Zacharias, 1994). I concur. Perhaps an example will illustrate my point.

On Election Day, November 2, 2004, Alabama residents cast votes to approve a constitutional amendment to erase legislation left over from the segregation era. Specifically, the amendment would have done the following:

It would have eliminated a law requiring "separate schools … for white and colored children."

It would have erased the requirement for poll taxes, which Alabama and many other southern states effectively implemented for many years to keep most blacks and poor whites from voting.

It would have eliminated language that stated, "nothing in the Constitution shall be construed as creating any rights to education or training at public expense."

Rather than embrace eliminating these symbols of Jim Crow ideology and the post-*Brown* southern resistance movement, forces in Alabama rallied to oppose Amendment 2. Opposition to the amendment argued that eliminating the last issue related to the right to be educated at public schools protected the state and its citizens from zealous judges who might at some future date seek to remedy school inequality with significant tax increases to support public education. Flono (2004) provides important insights into the opposition forces:

It was deceitful demagoguery, Alabama voters approved a law eight years ago that won't allow state courts to mandate spending without legislative approval. And just two years ago in upholding a lower court ruling on equitable school funding, the state's Supreme Court ruled that the legislature, not the courts, had the power to decide what that funding should be. The neo-Confederates and religious conservatives [including Alabama Christian Coalition (ACC)] who joined to defeat the amendment disavowed any racial motives. One chief opponent, former Alabama Judge Roy Moore, called the opposition a stand against more education spending and for protecting parochial and home-school facilities. Moore is the Alabama judge ousted for refusing to remove the Ten Commandments monument in the courthouse. … The notion of protecting parochial and home schools is telling. The constitutional phrase abdicating state responsibility to fund schools wasn't even on the books until 1956. The language was added to the constitution to thwart

desegregation efforts after the 1954 Brown v. Board of Education decision. That is when private schools surged in the South. (Flono, 2004, p.
11A)

The argument provided by the forces opposed to Amendment 2, including Judge Moore and the ACC, was built on a foundation of moral relativism.
Maintaining Jim Crow laws on the books is morally wrong in absolute terms.
Yet the parties opposing Amendment 2 claimed to prioritize a projected
economic cost over correcting a long-standing social injustice. The political opposition has at least one interesting ironic twist. The first is that Judge
Moore and the ACC have transparent links to theological positions that stand
on principles of moral absolutism, yet in the face of social policy, relativism
appears to guide their thinking and is linked to self-interest rather than the
greater good. The concept "You shall love you neighbor as yourself" (Matthew
19:19) does not appear to factor into the opposition's decision making. I submit that the question "How do I love my neighbor?"is a foundational one for
scholars interested in race, social policy and education. When this question
is applied to societal problems, I do not expect universal responses to difficult challenges. However, I firmly contend that we must begin with a set of
common understandings. One recommendation for common understanding
emerges from my background in mathematics education and the Alabama
case. In the next section, I explore one common understanding that should be
foundational for scholars using tenets of CRT and others interested in race-
related research.

Engineering and Intergenerational Challenges

In this section, like Derrick Bell (1996) and Gloria Ladson-Billings (2001), I look
to moral and spiritual texts to ground this discussion of what should be common in CRT-related scholarship in education. Many in the African American
community have used the story of Moses as a reference for freedom and liberation. Part of the story of Moses that is often ignored states, "[F]or I the Lord
your God am a jealous God, visiting the iniquity of the fathers upon the children to the third and fourth generation of those who hate Me" (Exodus 20:5).
Notice the intergenerational effect described in this theological argument. So
much of what we have learned about race, opportunity structures and educational performance in the United States carries a similar weight. For example, a
careful examination of academic attainment reveals a significant intergenerational effect. Miller (1995) argues that there are three intergenerational factors
that should inform the development of strategies to engineer positive change in
the school achievement of traditional underserved racial groups.

Generally, differences in academic achievement patterns among racial/
ethnic groups reflect the fact that the variation in family resources is greater
than the variation in school resources. Miller's analysis of achievement pat-

terns and resource allocations indicates that most high-socioeconomic status (SES) students receive several times more resources than most low-SES students receive, and much of this resource gap is a function of family resources rather than school resources. Second, a demographic group's educational attainment is an intergenerational process. From this perspective, education-related family resources are school resources that have accumulated across multiple generations. On average, investments in the current generation of African American, Hispanic, and American Indian children in the form of intergenerationally accrued education-relevant family resources are significantly less than comparable investments in white and Asian children. Finally, educational attainment is in large part a product of the quality of education-relevant opportunity structures over several generations. The pace of educational advancement depends on multiple generations of children attending good schools.

Miller's findings complement and reinforce the research conducted by Shapiro (2004), who argues:

> The enormous racial wealth gap perpetuates racial inequality in the United States. Racial inequality appears intransigent because the way families use wealth transmits advantages from generation to generation. Furthermore, the twenty-first century marks the beginning of a new racial dilemma for the United States: Family wealth and inheritances cancel gains in classrooms, workplaces, and paychecks, worsening racial inequality. (Shapiro, 2004, p. 183)

The intergenerational nature of learning and its relationship to wealth is very much a reality in the United States. This reality must be directly addressed in CRT and other race-based scholarship. In my field of study, mathematics education, the wealth factor was prominent in study conducted by the Organisation for Economic Co-operation and Development (2004) consisting in part of a survey of student achievement including mathematics that examined 15 year-olds in industrialized countries. The study found in the United States a strong relationship between student performance and economic status. This is consistent with other studies in mathematics education (Tate, 1997). My point is as Alabama and other like-minded entities run from projected economic support for education, the role of wealth and resources remains foundational to opportunity structures and intergenerational advancement in education. Today more than ever, the need to conceptualize race-based scholarship that better informs intergenerational problem solving is more vital than in 1994 when Professor Ladson-Billings and I wrote our AERA paper on CRT. This is the challenge for all who want to build on and move beyond that initial paper.

Final Remarks

CRT and other forms of race-based scholarship must carefully examine theo-retical tenets that position their moral reasoning as part of a relativistic proj-ect. In a world driven by slogans and media, some may be confusing basic notions derived from the sociology of knowledge which recognize the influ-ence of cultural heritage, worldview and societal values upon all perceptions of reality. This is not a call for moral relativism. Sound moral reasoning should not be divorced from matters of race and racism.

Derrick Bell has argued for the past two decades that racism is permanent, and its formation and implementation shift and morph in the form of differ-ent political and legal arguments and tools. New tools are needed to under-stand the asset-driven models of social inequality. I submit that the effects of intergenerational achievement and wealth are vital constructs that will assist scholars of race in fundamental problem solving and thinking related to engi-neering positive change in schools. Most certainly, understanding the role of intergenerational effects will provide insights into the question, "How can I love my neighbor?"

References

Bell, D. (1996). *Gospel Choirs: Psalms of Survival in an Alien Land Called Home.* New York: Basic Books.

Barna Research (2002). Americans Are Most Likely To Base Truth on Feelings. Ventura, CA: Author. Available at http://www.barna.org/FlexPage.aspx?Page=BarnaUpdateandBarna UpdateID=106, retrieved December 4, 2004.

Bork, R. H. (1997). *Slouching towards Gomorrah: Modern Liberalism and American Decline.* New York: Regan.

Crenshaw, K. W. (1988). Race, Reform, and Retrenchment: Transformation and Legitimation in Anti-discrimination Law. *Harvard Law Review* 101: 1331–1387.

Flono, F. (2004). On Race, the Past Is Still Not Past in Alabama. *Charlotte Observer,* 12 Novem-ber, p. 11A). Available at http://www.miami.com/mld/charlotte/news/columnists/fan-nie_flono/10160967.htm, retrieved December 4, 2004.

Ladson-Billings, G. (2001). *Crossing over to Canaan: The Journey of New Teachers in Diverse Classrooms.* San Francisco: Jossey-Bass.

Ladson-Billings, G. and Tate, W. F. (1995). Towards a Critical Race Theory of Education. *Teach-ers College Record* 97: 47–68.

Miller, L. S. (1995). *An American Imperative: Accelerating Minority Educational Advancement.* New Haven: Yale University Press.

Noebel, D. A. (1991). *Understanding the Times: The Religious Worldviews of Our Day and the Search for Truth.* Eugene, OR: Harvest House.

Organisation for Economic Co-operation and Development (2004). *Learning for Tomorrow's World: First Results from Pisa 2003.* Paris: OECD.

Peterson, J. L. (2003). *Scam: How the Black Leadership Exploits Black America.* Nashville, TN: WND Books

Shapiro, T. M. (2004). *The Hidden Cost of Being African American: How Wealth Perpetuates Inequality.* Oxford: Oxford University Press.

Tate, W. F. (1997). Race-Ethnicity, SES, Gender, and Language Proficiency Trends in Math-ematics Achievement: An Update. *Journal for Research in Mathematics Education* 28: 652–679.

Zacharias, R. (1994). *Can Man Live without God?* Nashville, TN: W Publishing Group.

Index